A JOURNEY

MADE IN THE SUMMER OF 1794,

THROUGH

HOLLAND

AND THE

WESTERN FRONTIER OF GERMANY,

WITH A

RETURN DOWN THE RHINE:

TO WHICH ARE ADDED,

OBSERVATIONS DURING A ~~TOUR~~ TO

THE LAKES

OF

LANCASHIRE, WESTMORELAND, AND CUMBERLAND.

BY ANN RADCLIFFE.

DUBLIN:

Printed by William Porter,

FOR P. WOGAN, P. BYRNE, H. COLBERT, W. PORTER,
W. JONES, J. RICE, H. FITZPATRICK,
G. FOLINGSBY.

1795.

TABLE OF CONTENTS.

A 2

TABLE OF CONTENTS.

THE

THE Author begs leave to obſerve, in explanation of the uſe made of the plural term in the following pages, that, her journey having been performed in the company of her neareſt relative and friend, the account of it has been written ſo much from their mutual obſervation, that there would be a deception in permitting the book to appear, without ſome acknowledgment, which may diſtinguiſh it from works entirely her own. The title page would, therefore, have contained the joint names of her huſband and herſelf, if this mode of appearing before the Public, beſides being thought by that relative a greater acknowledgment than was due to his ſhare of the work, had not ſeemed liable to the imputation of a deſign to attract attention by extraordinary novelty. It is, however, neceſſary to her own ſatisfaction, that ſome notice ſhould be taken of this aſſiſtance. She may therefore be permitted to intrude a few more words, as to this ſubject, by ſaying, that where the œconomical and political conditions of countries are touched upon in the following work, the remarks are leſs her own than elſewhere.

With reſpect to the book itſelf, it is, of courſe, impoſſible, and would be degrading if it were

not

not fo, to prevent juft cenfure by aoplogies, and unjuft cenfure fhe has no reafon, from her experience, to fear;—but fhe will venture to defend a practice adopted in the following pages, that has been fometimes blamed for its apparent nationality, by writers of the moft refpectable authority. The references to England, which frequently occur during the foreign part of the tour, are made becaufe it has feemed that one of the beft modes of defcribing to any clafs of readers what they may not know, is by comparing it with what they do.

May 20, 1795.

A JOURNEY,

A

JOURNEY, &c.

HELVOETSLUYS.

ABOUT twenty hours after our embarkation, at Harwich, and fix after our firſt fight of the low-ſpread and barren coaſt of *Goree*, we reached this place, which is feated on one of many in-lets, that carry the waters of the German Ocean through the ſouthern part of the province of Holland. *Goree*, rendered an iſland by theſe incroachments of the ſea, is always the firſt land expected by the feamen; or rather they look out for the lofty tower of its church, which, though feveral miles more diſtant than the ſhore, is viſible when that cannot be difcerned. The entrance of the water between the land, in a channel probably three leagues wide, foon after commences; and Helvoetſluys is then preſently feen, with the maſts of veſſels riſing above its low houſes, amidſt green embankments and paſ-tures, that there begin to reward the care of ex-cluding the ſea.

The

The names of Dutch towns are in themselves expreffive of the objects moft interefting to a people, who, for opportunities of commerce, have increafed their original and natural dangers by admitting the water in fome parts, while, for their homes and their lives, they muft prevent it from encroaching upon others. *Dam*, *Sluice*, or *Dyke*, occur in almoft all their compounded titles. The fluice, which gives this town part of its name, is alfo its harbour; affording, perhaps, an outlet to the overflowings of the country behind, but filled at the entrance to the depth of more than eighty feet by the fea, with which it communicates.

Upon the banks of this fluice, which are partly artificial, the town is built in one fhort ftreet of fmall houfes, inhabited chiefly by tradefmen and inn-keepers. The dockyard bounds the fluice; and the town, communicating with the former by gates, over which a fmall pivot bridge connects the two fides of the ftreet. Each head of the pier, or harbour, has been extended beyond the land for feveral yards, by pile work, filled with earth and large ftones, over which there is no pavement, that its condition may be conftantly known. We ftepped from the packet upon one of thefe, and, walking along the beams, that pafs between the immenfe piles, faw how clofely the *interftices* were filled, and how the earth and ftones were again compacted by a ftrong kind of bafketwork.

The arrival of a packet is the chief incident known at Helvoetfluys; and as ours entered the harbour about noon, and in fine
weather,

weather, perhaps, a fourth part of the inhabitants were collected as spectators. Their appearance did not surprise us with all the novelty, which we had expected from the first sight of a foreign people. The Dutch seamen every where retain the national dress; but the other men of Helvoetsluys differ from Englishmen in their appearance, chiefly by wearing coarser clothes, and by bringing their pipes with them into the street. Further on, several women were collected about their baskets of herbs, and their dress had some of the novelty, for which we were looking; they had hats of the size of a small chinese umbrella, and almost as gaudily lined within; close white jackets, with long flaps; short coloured petticoats, in the shape of a diving-bell; yellow slippers, without quarters at the heel; and caps, that exactly fitted the head and concealed the hair, but which were ornamented at the temples by gold filigree clasps, twirling, like vine tendrils, over the cheeks of the wearer.

Our inn was kept by English people, but the furniture was entirely Dutch. Two beds, like cribs in a ship, were let into the wainscot; and we were told, that, in all the inns on our journey, we should seldom, or never, be shewn into a room which had not a bed.

Helvoetsluys, it sufficiently appears, is a very inconsiderable place, as to its size and inhabitants. But it is not so in naval or military estimation. It is distant about ten or twelve miles from the open sea, yet is nearly secure from attack on this side, because that part of the approach, which is deep enough for large
vessels,

veffels, is commanded by batteries on fhore. It ftands in the middle of an immenfe bay, large enough to contain all the navy of Holland, and has a dock-yard and arfenal in the centre of the fortifications. When we paffed through it, fix fhips of the line and two frigates were lying in the dock-yard, and two fhips of the line and three frigates, under the command of an Admiral, in the bay.

The fortifications, we were affured upon good military authority, were in fuch repair, that not a fod was out of its place, and are ftrong enough to be defended by five thoufand men againft an hundred thoufand, for five weeks. The fea water rifes to a confiderable height in a wide ditch, which furrounds them. We omitted to copy an infcription, placed on one of the walls, which told the date of their completion; but this was probably about the year 1696, when the harbour was perfected. Though the dockyard can be only one of the dependencies upon that of Rotterdam, the largeft fhips of that jurifdiction are preferved here, on account of the convenient communication between the port and the fea.

Near this place may be obferved, what we examined with more leifure upon our return, the ingenuity, utility and vaftnefs of the embankments, oppofed by the Dutch to the fea. From Helvoetfluys eaftward, for many miles, the land is preferved from the fea only by an artificial mound of earth, againft which the water heavily and often impetuoufly ftrives for admiffion into the fheltered plains below. The fea, at high water, is fo much above the level of the ground, from which it is thus boldly feparated,

parated, that one who ftands on the land fide of
the embankment hears the water foaming, as if
over his head. Yet the mound itfelf, which has
ftood for two centuries, at leaft, without repair,
though with many renewals of the means, that
protect it, is ftill unhurt and undiminifhed, and
may yet fee generations of thofe, whom it
defends, rifing and paffing away, on one fide,
like the fluctuations of the tides, which affail
and retire from it, on the other.

It is better, however, to defcribe than to
praife. The mound, which appears to be
throughout of the fame height, as to the fea, is
fometimes more and fometimes lefs raifed above
the fields; for, where the natural level of the
land affifts in refiftance to the water, the Hol-
landers have, of courfe, availed themfelves of
it, to exert the lefs of their art and their labour.
It is, perhaps, for the moft part, thirty feet
above the adjoining land. The width at top is
enough to permit the paffage of two carriages,
and there is a fort of imperfect road along it. In
its defcent, the breadth increafes fo much, that
it is not very difficult to walk down either fide.
We could not meafure it, and may therefore be
excufed for relating how its fize may be gueffed.

On the land fide, it is faid to be ftrengthened
by ftone and timber, which we did not fee, but
which may be there, covered by earth and
grafs. Towards the fea, fomewhat above, and
confiderably below high-water mark, a ftrong
matting of flags prevents the furge from carrying away the furface of the mound; and this is
the defence which has fo long preferved it. The
matting is held to the fhore by bandages of
twifted

twisted flags, running horizontally, at the distance of three or four yards from each other, and staked to the ground by strong wooden pins. As this matting is worn by every tide, a survey of it is frequently made, and many parts appear to have been just repaired. Further in the sea, it is held down by stones; above, there are posts at every forty yards, which are numbered, that the spot may be exactly described where repairs are necessary. The impost for the maintenance of these banks amounts to nearly as much as the land-tax; and as the land could not be possessed without it, this tax has the valuable character of being occasioned by no mismanagement, and of producing no discontent.

ROTTERDAM.

FROM Helvoetsluys to this place the usual way is by the Brill and Maesland sluice, with several changes of carriages and boats; but on the days of the arrival of mails, a Rotterdam skipper, whose vessel has been left at a hamlet on the Maese, takes his party in carriages across the island of Voorn, on which Helvoetsluys stands, to his schuyt, and from thence by the Maese to Rotterdam. We paid two ducats, or about seventeen shillings, for the whole, and found this the highest price given for travelling

in

in Holland. Our carriage was a fort of fmall coach of the fafhion, exhibited in paintings of the fixteenth century, but open before, and fo ill-furnifhed with fprings, that the Dutch name, " a covered waggon," was not an improper defcription of it. A bad road led us through fome meadows of meagre grafs, and through fields in which corn was higher, though thinner, than in England. The profpect was over an entire level to the horizon, except that the fpires of diftant villages, fome fmall clufters of trees, and now and then a wind-mill, varied it. As we approached any of thefe clufters, we found ufually a neat farm-houfe fheltered within, and included, together with its garden and orchard, in a perfect green fence; the fields were elfewhere feparated from each other and from the road, neither by hedges or walls, but by deep ditches filled with water, over which are laid fmall bridges, that may be opened in the middle by a fort of trap-door, raifed and locked to a poft, to prevent the intrufion of ftrangers.

On the way we paffed now and then a waggon filled with large brafs jugs, bright as new gold. In thefe veffels, which have fhort narrow necks, covered with a wooden ftopper, milk is brought from the field throughout Holland. It is always carried to the towns in light waggons, or carts, drawn frequently by horfes as fleek and well conditioned as thofe in our beft coaches.

The hamlet at which we were to embark, was bufied in celebrating fome holiday. At the only cottage, that had a fign, we applied for refrefhment, partly for the purpofe of feeing its infide, by which we were not a little gratified. Thirty.

or

or forty peasants were seated upon benches, about a circle, in which children were dancing to the scraping of a French fiddler. The women wore their large hats, set up in the air like a spread fan, and lined with damask, or flowered linen. Children of seven years old, as well as women of seventy were in this preposterous disguise. All had necklaces, ear-rings, and ornamental clasps for the temples, of solid gold: some wore large black patches of the size of a shilling. The old woman of the house had a valuable necklace and head-dress. Among the group were many of Teniers' beauties; and over the countenances of the whole assemblage was an air of modesty, decorum, and tranquillity. The children left their dancing to see us; and we had almost lost our tide to Rotterdam, by staying to see them.

Our sail up the Maese was very delightful. The river flows here with great dignity, and is animated with vessels of all countries passing to and from Rotterdam. The huge Archangelman, the lighter American, the smart, swift Englishman, and the bulky Dutchman, exhibit a various scene of shipping, upon a noble surface of water, winding between green pastures and rich villages, spread along the low shores, where pointed roofs, trees, and masts of fishing-boats, are seen mingled in striking confusion. Small trading schuyts, as stout and as round as their masters, glided by us, with crews reposing under their deep orange sails, and frequently exchanging some salute with our captain. On our left, we passed the little town of Flaarding, celebrated for its share of the herring-fishery on our coasts; and Schiedam, a larger port, where what is called the Rotterdam Geneva is made, and

where

where feveral Englifh veffels were vifible in the
chief ftreet of the place. After a fail of two
hours we diftinguifhed Rotterdam, furrounded
by more wood than had yet appeared, and overtopped by the heavy round tower of the great
church of St. Lawrence. The flatnefs of its fituation did not allow us here to judge of its extent; but we foon perceived the grandeur of an
ample city, extending along the north fhore of
the Maefe, that, now fpreading into a noble
bay, along the margin of which Rotterdam
rifes, fweeps towards the fouth-eaft.

The part of the city firft feen, from the river,
is faid to be among the fineft in Europe for
magnificence and convenience of fituation. It
is called the *Boom Quay*, i. e. the quay with
trees, having rows of lofty elms upon the broad
terrace, that fupports many noble houfes, but
which is called a quay, becaufe fhips of confiderable burthen may moor againft it, and deliver their cargoes. The merchants accordingly,
who have refidences here, have their warehoufes
adjoining their houfes, and frequently build
them in the form of domeftic offices. The quay
is faid to be a mile in length, but appears to be
fomewhat lefs. There are houfes upon it, as
handfome as any in the fquares of London.

At the top of the *Boom Quay* is one of the
Heads, or entrances by water into the city,
through which the greater part of its numerous
canals receive their fupplies. On the approach
to it, the view further up the Maefe detains attention to the bank of this noble river. A vaft
building, erected for the Admiralty, is made,
by a bend of the Maefe, almoft to face you;
and the interval, of more than a quarter of a

B mile,

mile, is filled by a line of houses, that open directly, and without a terrace, upon the water. The fronts of these are in another street; but they all exhibit, even on this side, what is the distinction of Dutch houses and towns, a nicety and a perfectness of preservation, which give them an air of gaiety without, and present you with an idea of comfort within. What in England would be thought a symptom of extraordinary wealth, or extravagance, is here universal. The outside of every house, however old or humble, is as clean as water and paint can make it. The window-shutters are usually coloured green; and whatever wood appears, whether in cornices or worse ornaments, is so frequently cleaned, as well as painted, that it has always the gloss of newness. Grotesque ornaments are sometimes by these means rendered conspicuous; and a street acquires the air of a town in a toy shop; but in general there is not in this respect such a want of taste as can much diminish the value of their care.

Our skipper reached his birth, which is constantly in the same place, soon after passing the *Head*, and entering by a canal into one of the principal streets of the city. Between the broad terraces of this street, which are edged with thick elms, the innumerable masts of Dutch schuyts, with gay pendants and gilded tops; the hulls of larger vessels from all parts of the world; the white drawbridges, covered with passengers; the boats continually moving, without noise or apparent difficulty; all this did somewhat surprise us, who had supposed that a city so familiarly known, and yet so little mentioned as Rotterdam, could have nothing so remarkable as its wealth and trade.

In

In our way from the boat to the inn, other fine canals opened upon us on each side, and we looked at them till we had loft the man, whom we fhould have followed with our baggage. We had no fear that it would be ftolen, knowing the infrequency of robberies in Holland; and the firft perfon, of whom we could enquire our way in broken Dutch, acknowledged his country people by anfwering in very good Englifh. There are many hundreds of Britifh refidents in this place, and our language and commerce have greatly the fway here over thofe of all other foreign nations. The Dutch infcrip tions over ware-houfes and fhops have frequently Englifh tranflations underneath them. Of large veffels, there are nearly as many Englifh as Dutch in the harbour; and, if you fpeak to any Dutchman in the ftreet, it is more probable that he can anfwer in Englifh than in French. On a Sunday, the Englifh fill two churches, one of which we attended on our return. It is an oblong brick building, permitted by the States to be within the jurifdiction of the Bifhop of London, Parliament having given 2500l. towards its completion in the beginning of the prefent century. There are alfo many Proteftant Diffenters here, who are faid to have their offices of worfhip performed with the ability, fimplicity, and zeal, which are ufually to be obferved in the devotions of that clafs of Chriftians.

Rotterdam is the fecond city for fize, and perhaps the firft for beauty in the United Provinces; yet, when we walked through it the next day, and expected to find the magnificence of the approach equalled in its interior, we were compelled to withdraw a little of the

premature

premature admiration, that had begun to extend to the whole place. The ſtreet, where there is moſt trade and the greateſt paſſage, the *Hoogſtraat*, is little wider, though it is abundantly cleaner, than a London lane. The Stadthouſe is in this ſtreet, and is an old brick building, with a peaked roof, not entirely free from fantaſtic ornament. It has been built too early to have the advantages of modern elegance, and too late for the ſanction of ancient dignity. The market-place has only one wide acceſs; and the communication between the ſtreet, from the principal *Head*, and that in which the Exchange is placed, is partly through a very narrow, though a ſhort paſſage. The Exchange itſelf is a plain ſtone building, well deſigned for its purpoſe, and completed about fifty years ago. The happieſt circumſtance relating to it is, that the merchants are numerous enough to fill the colonnades on the four ſides of its interior. Commerce, which cannot now be long diſcouraged in any part of Europe, becauſe without it the intereſt of public debts cannot be paid, is the permanent defender of freedom and knowledge againſt military glory and politics.

From the Exchange there is an excellent walk to the market-place, where the well-known ſtatue of ERASMUS is raiſed. Being repreſented in his doctor's dreſs, the figure can diſplay little of the artiſt's ſkill; but the countenance has ſtrong lines, and a phyſiognomiſt would not deny them to be expreſſive of the diſcernment and ſhrewdneſs of the original.

The market-place is really a large bridge, for a canal paſſes under it; but its ſize, and the eaſineſs of aſcent from the ſides, prevent this

from

from being immediately obferved. Some of the furrounding houfes have their dates marked upon glazed tiles. They were built during the long war, that refcued the provinces from the Spanifh dominion; a time when it might be fuppofed that nothing would have been attended to, except the bufinefs of providing daily food, and the duty of refifting the enemy; but in which the Dutch enlarged and beautified their cities, prepared their country to become a medium of commerce, and began nearly all the meafures, whicff have led to their prefent extenfive profperity.

Near this place is the great church of St. LAWRENCE, which we entered, but did not find to be remarkable; except for a magnificent brafs baluftrade that croffes it at the upper end. A profufion of *achievements*, which cover the walls almoft to the top, contribute to its folemnity. In addition to the arms of the deceafed, they contain the dates of their birth and death, and are ufed inftead of infcriptions, though no names are expreffed upon them. Under the pulpit was an hour-glafs, which limits the difcourfe of the preacher: on one fide a wand, having at the end a velvet bag and a fmall bell; this is carried about, during an interval in the fervice, and every body puts fomething into it for the poor. The old beadle, who fhewed us the church, laid his hands upon us with pleafure, when he heard that we were Englifh, and Proteftants. There are three minifters to this church, with falaries of nearly two hundred pounds fterling each.

We

We went to our inn through the *Hoogftraat*, which was filled with people and carriages, but has no raifed pavement to feparate the one from the other. In all the towns which we faw, the footpath is diftinguifhed from the road only by being paved with a fort of light coloured brick. The Dutch fhops are in the fhape, which thofe of London are defcribed to have had fifty years fince, with fmall high windows, and blocks between them and the ftreet. Silverfmiths expofe their goods in fmall glafs cupboards upon the blocks, and nearly all the trades make upon them what little fhew is cuftomary. Almoft every tenth houfe difplays the infcription *Tabak te koop,* " Tobacco to be fold." This ftreet having no canal, is occupied entirely by retail traders. We bought in it the Antwerp Gazette for two doights, or one farthing; ftrawberries, large and well coloured, at a lower price than they could be had fix weeks later in England, but without flavour; and went into feveral book-fellers' fhops, expecting to have found fome-thing in Latin, or French, but could fee only Dutch books. In another ftreet a bookfeller had feveral Englifh volumes, and there are no doubt well filled fhops, but not fo numerous as that we could find any.

Over the canals, that flow through almoft every ftreet of Rotterdam, are great num-bers of large drawbridges, which contribute much to the neat and gay appearance of the city; but when thefe are raifed, the obftruc-tion to the paffage occafions crowds on each fide; and, therefore, in fome of the moft fre-quented parts, the bridges are intire and perma-nent, except for the breadth of three feet in the centre, centro, where there is a plank, which opens upon hinges almost as easy as the lid of a trunk. Through this opening the masts of the small Dutch schuyts are easily conducted, but ships can pass only where there are drawbridges. The number of the former is immense; for, throughout the provinces, every village, if it is near a canal, has several schuyts, which carry away the superfluous produce of the country, and return with the manufactures, or stores, of the towns. But neither their number, nor their neatness, is so remarkable as the ease and stillness, with which they traverse the city; and indeed ease and stillness are much the characteristics of all the efforts of Dutch industry. The noise and agitation, usual whenever many persons are employed together in other countries, are unknown here. Ships are brought to their moorings, schuyts pass each other in crowded canals, heavy burthens are raised and cargoes removed, almost without a word, that can be heard at twenty yards distance.

Another circumstance, rendering Dutch towns freer from noise than others of equal traffic, is the little use which is made of waggons and carts, even where some sort of land carriage must be employed. Heavy commodities are usually carried about the streets in sledges; and almost the greatest noise is, when the driver of one of these, after having delivered his load, meaning to render himself a prodigy of frolicsomeness, stands upon the hinder edges of his sledge, and then preventing himself from falling backward by his hold of the reins, is drawn rapidly through the admiring crowd.

We

We were long enough at Rotterdam, during three vifits, to fee how well it is provided with avenues towards the country and along the banks of the Maefe. To one of thefe the way is over the two *Heads*, or chief canals, each of which you crofs for a doight, or half a farthing, in boats that are continually pafling between the two fides. This little voyage faves a walk of about three hundred yards to the neareft bridge. The boats will hold twenty or thirty perfons, and the profit of them is very cohfiderable to the city government, which applies the money to public purpofes. Each boat is worked by one man, who pulls it over by a rope in about two minutes.

Many of the inhabitants have what they call garden-houfes upon thefe walks, and upon a femi-circular road, which pafles on the land fide of the city; but the moft wealthy have feats at greater diftances, where they can be furrounded with grounds, and make the difplay of indepen-dent refidences.

Upon the whole, Rotterdam has from its fi-tuation many conveniences and delights, and from its ftructure fome magnificence, toge-ther with a general neatnefs; but is, for the moft part, deficient in elegance, and its beau-ties have too much the air of prettineffes. The canals are indifputably fine, crowned with lofty terraces, and deep enough to carry large veffels into the centre of the city.

DELFT.

DELFT.

BETWEEN Rotterdam and this place we commenced our travelling in trechtfchuyts, which are too well known to need defcription. The fare is at the rate of about a penny per mile, and a trifle more hires the *roof*, which is a fmall feparate chamber, neareft to the ftern of the veffel, lighted by windows on each fide. In engaging this, you have an inftance of the accuracy of the Dutch in their minuteft tranfactions; a formal printed receipt, or ticket, is given for the few pence which it cofts, by a commiffary, who has no other bufinefs than to regulate the affairs of the trechtfchuyts at his gate of the city. We could never learn what proportion of the fare is paid as a tax to the State, but it is faid to be a confiderable part; and not only thefe fchuyts, but the ferries, the poft-waggons, and the pilotage throughout the United States, are made contributory to the public funds.

The punctuality of the departure and arrival of the trechtfchuyts is well known, and juftifies the Dutch method of reckoning diftances, which is by hours, and not by leagues or miles. The canals being generally full to the brim, the top of the veffel is above the level of the adjoining country, and the view over it is of courfe extenfive;

but

but the houfes and gardens, which are beft worth
feeing, are almoft always upont he banks of the
canal. We paffed feveral fuch in the way to
Delft, towards which the Rotterdam merchants
have their favourite feats; but Dutch gardens
are rather to be noticed by an Englifhman
as curiofities than luxuries. It is not only by
the known ill tafte of their ornaments, but
by the effects of climate and the foil, that
gardens are deprived of value, in a country,
where the moifture is fo difproportioned to the
heat, that the verdure, though bright, has no
fragrance, and the fruit, at its utmoft fize,
fcarcely any flavour.

A paffage of two hours brought us to Delft,
which we had expected to find a fmall and ill-
inhabited place, knowing it to be not now occupied by any confiderable trade. Our inn, we
fuppofed, muft be within a few minutes walk.
We proceeded, however, through one ftreet
for half a mile, and after fome turnings, did
not reach our inn, though we were led by
the neareft way, in lefs than twenty minutes.
During all this time we were upon the terraces
of clear canals, amongft excellent houfes, with
a fmall intermixture of fhops and fome public
buildings. The mingled admiration and weari-
nefs, which we felt here, for the firft time,
have been, however, often repeated; for if there
is a neceffity for faying what is the next diftinction of Dutch towns, after their neatnefs, their fize
muft be infifted upon. There are Dutch villages,
fcarcely marked in a map, which exceed in fize
fome of the county towns in England. *Maefland
Sluice*, a place oppofite to the Brill, is one. And
here is Delft, a place with fcarcely any other trade
than confifts in the circulation of commodities
from

from Rotterdam through some neighbouring villages; which is not the seat of any confiderable part of the national government, and is inferior, in point of fituation, to all the' furrounding towns. Delft, thus undiftinguifhed, fills a large circumference, with ftreets fo intricately thick, that we never went from our inn without lofing our way.

The *Doolen*, one of the beft inns in Holland, is a large building of the fixteenth century, raifed by the Spaniards, and firft intended to be a convent; but, having been ufed by the burghers of Delft for public purpofes, during the ftrugglcs of the Provinces againft Spain, it is now venerable as the fcene of their councils and preparations. In the fuite of large apartments, which were ufed by them, fome of the city bufinefs is ftill tranfacted, and in thefe ftrangers are never entertained. Behind, is a bowling-green, in which the burghers to this day perform their military exercifes: they were fo employed when we came in; and it was pleafing to confider, that their inferiority to their anceftors, in point of martial appearance, was the refult of the long internal peace fecured by the exertions of the latter.

Over two arches of the building is the date of its erection, 1565, the year in which the deftruction of all families, profeffing the Proteftant religion either in France or Spain, is fuppofed to be agreed upon at Bayonne between the fovereigns of the two countries, and one year preceding the firft meafures of confederate refiftance in the Low Countries, which that and other efforts of perfecution produced. One of thefe arches communicates with the rooms fo long ufed by the burghers; and our hoftefs, an intelligent wo-

man,

man, accompanied us through them. The firſt
is ornamented with three large pictures, repre-
ſenting ſeveral of the early burghers of the Commonwealth, either in arms or council. A portrait of BARNEVELDT is marked with the date
and the painter's name, " MICHAEL MIERE-
" VELD *delineavit ac perfunctorie pinxit*, 1617,"
one year before the flagitious arreſt of BARNE-
VELDT, in defiance of the conſtitution of the
provinces, by MAURICE of ORANGE. A piece, exhibiting ſome of the burghers in arms, men of an
handſome and heroic appearance, is alſo dated,
by having 1648 painted on a drum ; that, which
ſhews them in council, has a portrait of GRO-
TIUS, painted when he was ſeventeen. His
face is the ſeventh from the right hand in the
ſecond row.

Beyond this room are others containing ſeveral ſcore of ſmall cupboards, on the doors of
each of which are two or three blazonries of
arms. Here are depoſited ſome parts of the
dreſs and arms of an aſſociation of Arqueſbu-
ſiers, uſual in all the Dutch towns; the members of which ſociety aſſemble annually in October, to ſhoot at a target placed in a pavilion
of the old convent garden. The markſman
takes his aim from the fartheſt room; and between him and the mark are two walls, per-
forated two feet and a half in length, and eight
inches in breadth, to permit the paſſage of the
ſhot. A man ſtands in the pavilion, to tell
where the ball has ſtruck; and every markſman, before he ſhoots, rings a bell, to warn this
perſon out of the way. He that firſt hits a white
ſpot in the target, has his liquor, for the enſuing
year, free of exciſe duty; but, to render this
more

more difficult, a ftork is fufpended by the legs from a ftring, which, paffing down the whole length of the target, is kept in continual motion by the agitation of the bird. It did not appear whether the ftork has any other fhare in this ancient ceremony, which is reprefented in prints of confiderable date. It is held near the ground, out of the way of the fhot, and is certainly not intended to be hurt, for the Dutch have no tafte for cruelty in their amufements. The ftork, it is alfo known, is efteemed by them a fort of tutelary bird; as it once was in Rome, where Asellus Sempronius Rufus, who firft had them ferved at an entertainment, is faid to have loft the Prætorfhip for his facrilegious gluttony. In thefe trivial enquiries we paffed our firft evening at Delft.

Early the next morning, a battalion of regular troops was reviewed upon a fmall plain within the walls of the town. The uniform is blue and red, in which the Dutch officers have not quite the fmart appearance of ours. One of thefe, who gave the word to a company, was a boy, certainly not more than fifteen, whofe fhrill voice was ludicroufly heard between the earneft fhouts of the others. The firing was very exact, which is all that we can tell of the qualities of a review.

Delft was a place of early importance in the United Provinces, being one of the fix original cities that fent deputies to the States of the province; a privilege, which, at the inftance of their glorious William the Firft of Orange, was afterwards properly extended to twelve others, including Rotterdam and the Brill.
Yet

Yet it is little celebrated for military events, being unfortified, and having probably always obeyed the fortune of the neighbouring places. The circumstance which gives it a melancholy place in history, is the murder of the wise and beneficent Prince who founded the republic. His palace, a plain brick building, is still in good repair, where strangers are always shewn the staircase on which he fell, and the holes made in the wall by the shot that killed him. The old man, who keeps the house, told the story with as much agitation and interest as if it had happened yesterday. " The prince and princess came out of that chamber—here stood the prince, here stood the murderer; when the prince stepped here to speak to him about the passport, the villain fired, and the prince fell all along here and died. Yes, so it was—there are the holes the balls made." Over one of these, which is large enough to admit two fingers, is this inscription :

" *Hier onder staen de Teykenen der Kooglen daar meede Prins Willem van Orange is doorschootten op 10 July, A.* 1584."

To this detestable action the assassin acknowledged himself to have been instigated by the proclamation of Philip the Second, offering a reward for its perpetration. The princess, who had the wretchedness to witness it, had lost her father and her former husband in the massacre of St. Bartholomew in France, which, though contrived by Catherine and [Charles the Ninth of that country, is believed to have been the consequence of their interview at Bayonne, with Isabella, the wife of the same Philip.

The

The melancholy excited on this fpot is continued by paffing from it to the tomb of WIL
LIAM, in the great church, called the *Nieuwe
Kerk.* There the gloomy pageantry of the
black efcutcheons, above a choir, filent,
empty and vaft, and the withering remains of
colours, won by hands long fince gone to their
decay, prolong the confideration of the tranfientnefs of human worth and happinefs, which
can fo eafily be deftroyed by the command, or
the hand of human villainy.

This tomb is thought to be not exceeded by
any piece of fepulchral grandeur in Europe.
Standing alone, in a wide choir, it is much more
confpicuous and ftriking than a monumental fabric raifed againft a wall, at the fame time that
its fides are fo varied as to prefent each a new
fpectacle. It was begun in 1609, by order of
the States General, and completed in 1621;
the artift, HENDRIK DE KEYZER, receiving
28,000 florins as its price, and 2000 more as a
prefent. The length is 20 feet, the breadth 15,
and height 27. A bronze ftatue of the prince,
fitting in full armour, with his fword, fcarf, and
commander's ftaff, renders one fide the chief;
on the other is his effigy in white marble, lying
at full length; and at his feet, in the fame marble, the figure of the dog, which is faid to have
refufed food from the moment of his mafter's
death. Round the tomb, twenty-two columns
of veined or black Italian marble, of the Doric order, and, with bafés and capitals of white marble,
fupport a roof or canopy, ornamented with many
emblems, and with the *achievements* of the prince

At the corners, are the ftatues of Religion,
Liberty, Juftice, and Fortitude, of which the
firft

firſt reſts upon a piece of black marble, on which is inſcribed in golden letters the name of CHRIST; and the ſecond holds a cap, with the inſcription *Aurea Libertas.* On the four ſides of the canopy are the devices of the prince, with the inſcriptions JEHOVAH,—*Je maintiendrai Pièté et Juſtice.—Te vindice, tuta libertas.*—And, *Sævis tranquillus in undis.*

There are many other ornaments, which give dignity or elegance to the ſtructure, but cannot be deſcribed without tediouſneſs. The well-known Epitaph is certainly worth tranſcribing:

D. O. M. et eternæ memoriæ Gulielmi Naſſoviæ, ſupremi Auranſionenſium Principis, Patr. patriæ, qui Belgii fortunis ſuas poſthabuit et ſuorum; validiſſimos exercitus ære plurimum privato bis conſcripſit, bis induxit; ordinum auſpiciis Hiſpaniæ tyrannidem propulit; veræ religionis cultum, avitas patriæ leges revocavit, reſtituit; ipſam denique libertatem tantum non aſſertam, Mauritio principi, paternæ virtutis hæredi filio, ſtabiliendam reliquit. Herois vere pii, prudentis, invicti, quem Philip. II. Hiſp. R. Europæ timor, timuit; non domuit, non terruit; ſed empto percuſſore fraude nefanda ſuſtulit; Fædcrat. Belgii provinc. perenni memor. monum. fec.

" To GOD the beſt and higheſt, and to the eternal memory of William of Naſſau, Sovereign Prince of Orange, the father of his country, whoſe welfare he preferred to that of himſelf and his family; who, chiefly at his own expençe, twice levied and introduced a powerful army; under the ſanction of the States repelled the tyranny of Spain; recovered and reſtored the ſervice of true religion

religion and the ancient laws of the country; and finally left the liberty, which he had himself afferted, to be eftablifhed by his fon, Prince Maurice, the heir of his father's virtues. The Confederated Belgic Provinces have erected this monument, in perpetual memory of this truly pious, prudent and unconquered Hero, whom Philip II. King of Spain, the dread of Europe, dreaded; never overcame, never terrified; but, with wicked treachery, carried off by means of an hired affaffin."

The tomb of GROTIUS is in the fame church, which is a ftately building of brick and ftone, but has nothing of the " dim religious light," that fooths the mind in Gothic ftructures. Upon the fteeple are many fmall bells, the chimes rung upon which are particularly efteemed, both for tone and tune.

On the oppofite fide of a very large market-place is the town-houfe, an old building, but fo frefh and fo fantaftic with paint, as to have fome refemblance to a Chinefe temple. The body is coloured with a light, or yellowifh brown, and is two ftories high to the roof, in which there are two tier of peaked windows, each under its ornament of gilded wood, carved into an awkward refemblance of fhells. Upon the front is infcribed, " *Delphenfium Curia Reparata*," and immediately over the door " *Reparata* 1761."

The *Oude Kerk*, or Old Church, is in another part of the town, and is not remarkable, except for the tombs of LEUWENHOEK, PETER HEINE and VAN TROMP. That of LEUWENHOEK has a fhort infcription, in Latin almoft as bad as that of a verfe epitaph upon

C GROTIUS

GROTIUS in the other church. He was born, it appears, in October 1632, and died in August 1723. The tombs of HEINE and VAN TROMP are very handsome. There are the effigies of both in white marble, and one of the victories gained by the latter is reprefented in *alto relievo*. On account of the tombs, both churches are open, during certain hours in the day; and a beadle, or, perhaps, an almfman, is placed in each, who prefents a padlocked box, into which money may be put for the poor.

In this town is the chief arfenal of the province of Holland, except that the magazine of powder is at the diftance of about a mile from it, near the canal to Rotterdam. In 1787, when the diffentions between the STATES GENERAL and the PRINCE of ORANGE were at their height, a provincial free corps feized this arfenal, and held it for the States till the return of the PRINCE of ORANGE to the Hague, a few weeks afterwards.

Having feen what was pointed out to our notice at Delft, and learned that its extenfivenefs was owing to the refidence of a great number of retired merchants from Rotterdam, we left it in a *trechtfchuyt* for the Hague, having little other notion of it in our minds, than that it is very dull and very rich, and of a fize, for which there is no recompence to a ftranger, except in confidering, that its dullnefs is the reft of thofe, who have once been bufy, and that its riches are at leaft not employed in aggravating the miferies of poverty by oftentation,

THE

THE HAGUE.

A VOYAGE of an hour and a half brought us here over a canal well bordered by country houses and gardens, all of which, as in other parts of Holland, have some inscription upon their gates, to say that they are pleasant, or are intended for pleasure. *Fine Sight, Pleasant Rest, High Delight*, or some similar inscription, is to be seen over the door of every country house, in gold letters. On our way, we looked for Ryswick, where the treaty of 1697 was signed, and saw the village, but not the palace, which, being of freestone, is mentioned as a sort of curiosity in the country. It is this palace, which is said to contain proofs of an extraordinary dispute upon questions of ceremony. The Ambassadors, sent to prepare the treaty, are related to have contended so long, concerning their rights of precedence, that the only mode of reconciling them was to make separate entrances, and to allow the mediating minister alone admission by the principal gate.

From the *trechtschuyt* we had a long walk to our inn, an handsome house, standing almost in the midst of palaces, and looking over a noble sheet of water, called the *Vyver*, which extends behind the *Court*, for its whole length, flowing nearly to the level of the lower windows.

C 2   The

The *Court* itfelf, a large brick building, irregular, but light and pleafant, was entirely within our view, on the left; on the right, a row of magnificent houfes, feparated from the *Vyver* by a large mall; and, in front, beyond the *Vyver*, a broad place, bordered by feveral public buildings. In this Court all the fuperior colleges of government have their chambers, and the PRINCE of ORANGE his fuite of apartments. The foffé, which furrounds it, three drawbridges and as many gates are the only fortifications of the Hague, which has been feveral times threatened with the entrance of an enemy, but has not been taken fince 1595, when the magiftrates of the then infant republic, and all the fuperior inhabitants, retired to *Delft*, leaving the ftreets to be over-run with grafs, and the place to become a defert under the eyes of its oppreffors. During the invafion of LOUIS the FOURTEENTH, it efcaped the ravages of the DUKE of LUXEMBOURG's column, by the fudden diffolution of the ice, on which he had placed 9000 foot and 2000 cavalry. Yet the advice of WILLIAM the THIRD, who probably thought money better expended in ftrengthening the frontier than the interior of the country, counteracted a plan of fortification which was then propofed, for the third or fourth time.

The Court confifts of two fquares; in the inner of which are the apartments of the STADT-HOLDER, and none but himfelf and his family can enter this in carriages, or on horfeback. On the northern fide, in the firft floor, are the apartments of the STATES GENERAL, which we faw. The principal one is fpacious, as a room, but has not the air of a hall of debate.

Twenty-

Twenty-fix chairs for the Deputies are placed on two fides of a long table: the Prefident, whofe chair is in the centre, has on his right hand, firft, a deputy of his own province, then three Deputies of Friefland, and two of Groningen; on his left, fix Deputies of Holland; oppofite to him, neareft to the head of the table, fix Deputies of Guelderland, then three of Zealand, then two of Utrecht, and two of Overyffel. The STADT-HOLDER, who has a place, but not a vote, has a raifed chair at the upper end of the table; The Secretary is feated oppofite to him, and is allowed to wear his hat, like the deputies, during their deliberations, but muft ftand uncovered, behind the Prefident, when he reads letters, or other papers. The number of Deputies is known to be indefinite; about fifty are generally returned; and thofe, who are prefent from each province, more than the number allowed at the table, place themfelves below it. The walls of this room are covered with tapeftry, not reprefenting hiftorical events, but rural fcenery; the backs and feats of the chairs are of green velvet; and all the furniture, though ftately and in the beft condition, is without the leaft approach to fhew. Thefe apartments, and the whole of this fide of the Court, were the refidence of CHARLES the FIFTH, when he vifited the Hague, and of the EARL of LEICESTER, when he commanded the troops lent to the Republic by ELIZABETH.

The government of the United Provinces is too well known to permit a detailed defcription here, but fome notice may reafonably be expected of it.

The chief depofitaries of the fovereignty are not the States General, but the Provincial States, of whose Deputies the former body is compofed, and without whofe confent they never vote upon important meafures. In the States General each Province has one vote; which, with the reafons for it, may be delivered by an unlimited number of Deputies; and the firft Deputy of each province prefides in the States by rotation for a week. In queftions relative to peace or war, alliances, taxes, coinages, and to the privileges of provinces, no meafures can be taken but by unanimous confent; upon other occafions, a majority is fufficient. No perfons holding military offices can be Deputies to the States General, which appoints and receives all ambaffadors, declares war, makes peace, and names the Greffier, or Secretary of State, and all Staff Officers.

The Provincial States are varioufly compofed, and the interior government of the provinces varioufly formed. In the province of Holland, which contains the moft profperous part of the Republic, there are eighteen Deputies to the Provincial States, for as many towns, and one for the nobility. The Grand Penfionary prefides in this affembly, and is always one of the Deputies from it to the Sates General.

The Council of Deputies is compofed of ten members: nine from the towns, and one from the nobility. This Council, in which the Grand Penfionary alfo prefides, regulates the finances of the province, and takes cognizance of the diftribution of troops within it.

The Council, called the Council of State, is compofed, like the States General, of Deputies returned from the provinces, and appears to be to that body, in a great meafure,
what

what the Council of Deputies is to the Provincial States; having the direction of the army and the finances.

As provincial affairs are directed by the Provincial States, so the affairs of each town are governed by its own Senate, which also returns the members, if the town is entitled to send one, to the States of the Province, and directs the vote, which that member shall give. The Burgomasters in each town are the magistrates charged with the police and the finances, and are usually elected annually by the old Council, that is, by those who have been Burgomasters, or *Echevins*. These latter officers have the administration of civil and criminal affairs, and are, in some places, appointed by the Stadtholder from a double number nominated to him; in others, are accepted from the recommendation of the Stadtholder. The Bailiffs preside in the Council of Burgomasters and Echevins; and in their name prosecutions are instituted.

Of the Deputies to the States General, some are for life, and some for one or more years.

Such is the nicely complicated frame of this government, in which the Senates of the Towns elect the Provincial States, and the Provincial States the States General; the latter body being incapable of deciding in certain cases, except with unanimity and with the express consent of their constituents, the Provincial States; who again cannot give that consent, except with unanimity and with the consent of their constituents, the Senates.

The

The Stadtholder, it is seen, has not directly, and in consequence of that office, any share of the legiflative power; but, being a Noble of four provinces, he, of courfe, participates in that part of the fovereignty, which the Nobility enjoy when they fend Deputies to the Provincial States. Of Zealand he is the only Noble, all the other titled families having been deftroyed in the original conteft with Spain; and there are no renewals or creations of titles in the United Provinces. In Guelderland, Holland, and Utrecht, he is Prefident of the Nobles. He is Commander of all the Forces of the Republic by fea and land; and the Council of State, of which he is a member, is, in military affairs, almoft entirely under his direction; he names all fubaltern officers, and recommends thofe for higher appointments to the States General. In Guelderland, Utrecht, and Overyffel, which are called *Provinces aux Reglemens*, becaufe, having fubmitted to Louis the Fourteenth, in 1672, they were not re-admitted to the Union, but with fome facrifice of their privileges, he appoints to offices, without the nomination of the cities; he is Governor General of the Eaft and Weft Indian Companies, and names all the Directors from a treble number of candidates offered by the Proprietors. His name prefides in all the courts of law; and his heart, it may be hoped, dictates in the noble right of pardoning.

This is the effential form of a government, which, for two centuries, has protected as great a fhare of civil and religious liberty, as has been enjoyed in any other part of Europe, refifting equally the chances of diffolution, contained

tained within itself; and the less dangerous
schemes for its destruction, dictated by the jealousy of arbitrary interests without.

Its intricacy and delicacy are easily seen;
yet, of the objections made to it on this account, more are founded on some maxims,
assumed to be universal, than upon the separate considerations due to the condition of a
separate people. How much the means of political happiness depend, for their effect, upon the civil characters of those for whom they
are designed, has been very little seen, or in-
sisted upon. It has been unnoticed, because
such enquiries have not the brilliancy, or the
facility, of general speculations, nor can command equal attention, nor equally reward systems with those parts of their importance, that
consist in the immensity of the sphere, to
which they pretend. To extend their arms is
the flagitious ambition of warriors; to enlarge
their systems is the ambition of writers, especially of political writers. A juster effort
of understanding would aim at rendering the
application of principles more exact, rather
than more extensive, and would produce enquiries into the circumstances of national character and condition, that should regulate that
application. A more modest estimate of human means of doing good would shew the
gradations, through which all human advances
must be made. A more severe integrity of
views would stipulate, that the means should
be as honest as the end, and would strive to
ascertain, from the moral and intellectual character of a people, the degree of political
happiness, of which they are capable; a pro-
cess, without which projected advances become

come obftru&ions; and the philofopher begins his experiment, for the amelioration of
fociety, as prematurely as the fculptor would
polifh his ftatue before he had delineated the
features.

Whether the conftitution of the United
Provinces is exa&ly as good an one as the
people are capable of enjoying, can be determined only after a much longer and abler enquiry than we could make; but it feemed proper to obferve, that, in judging this queftion,
it is not enough to difcover better forms of
government, without finding alfo fome reafon
to believe, that the intelle&ual and moral
condition of the people would fecure the exiftence of thofe better forms. In the mean
time, they, who make the enquiry, may be
affured, that under the prefent * government,
there is a confiderable degree of political liberty, though political happinefs is not permitted by the prefent circumftances of Europe;
that the general adoption of the Stadtholder's
meafures by the States has been unduly mentioned to fhew an immoderate influence, for
that, in point of fa&, his meafures are often
reje&ed; that this reje&ion produces no public agitation, nor can thofe, who differ from
him in opinion, be fuccefsfully reprefented as
enemies to their country; that there are very
few offices which enable private perfons to become rich, at the expence of the public, fo as
to have a different intereft from them; that the
fober induftry and plain manners of the people
prevent them from looking to political condu&
of any fort as a means of improving their for-

* June 1794.

tunes;

tunes; that, for thefe reafons, the intricate connections between the parts of their government
are lefs inconvenient than may be fuppofed,
fince good meafures will not be obftructed, or
bad ones fupported, for corrupt purpofes, though
mifconceptions may fometimes produce nearly
the fame effect; that converfation is perfectly
free; and that the habit of watching the ftrength
of parties, for the purpofe of joining the ftrongeft and perfecuting the weakeft, does not occupy
the minds of any numerous claffes amongft them.

We faw no other apartments than thofe of the
States General, the PRINCE of ORANGE being
then in his own. The Princefs was at a feat in
Guelderland, with her daughter-in-law, the wife
of the Hereditary Prince, who had been indif-
pofed fince the furprife of the Dutch troops at
Menin, on the 12th of September, 1793, in
which affair her hufband was engaged. When
the officer, who brought the firft accounts,
which were not written, to the Hague, had related that the younger prince was wounded, the
Hereditary Princefs enquired, with great eagernefs, concerning his brother. The officer indif-
creetly replied, that he knew nothing of him;
which the Princefs fuppofed to imply, that he
was dead; and fhe has fince been fomewhat an
invalid.

Though the falaries enjoyed by the Prince of
Orange, in confequence of his offices, are by
no means confiderable, he is enabled, by his pa-
trimonial eftates, to maintain fome modeft fplendour. The Court is compofed of a grand mafter,
a marfhal, a grand equerry, ten chamberlains,
five ladies of honour, and fix gentlemen of the
chamber. Ten young men, with the title of
Pages, are educated at the expence of the Prince;

in

in a houfe adjoining his *manege*. As Captain-General, he is allowed eight adjutants, and, as Admiral, three.

We could not learn the amount of the income enjoyed by the PRINCE of ORANGE, which muſt, indeed, be very variable, ariſing chiefly from his own eſtates. The greater part of theſe are in the province of Zealand, where ſeventeen villages and part of the town of Breda are his property. The fortifications of ſeveral places there are ſaid to have been chiefly erected at the expence of the Orange family. His farms in that neighbourhood ſuffered greatly in the campaign of 1792, and this part of his income has ſince been much diminiſhed. The management of his revenues, derived from poſſeſſions in Germany, affords employment to four or five perſons, at an Office, ſeparate from his ordinary Treaſury; and he had eſtates in the Low Countries. All this is but the wreck of a fortune, honourably diminiſhed by William the Firſt of Orange, in the conteſt with Spain; the remembrance of whom may, perhaps, involuntarily influence one's opinion of his ſucceſſors.

During May, the weſtern gate of the palace is ornamented, according to ancient cuſtom, with garlands for each perſon of the Orange family. Chaplets, with the initials of each, in flowers, are placed under large coronets, upon green flag-ſtaffs. We paſſed by when they were taking theſe down, and perceived that all the ornaments could ſcarcely have coſt five ſhillings. So humble are the Dutch notions of pageantry.

Among the offices included within the walls of the court is a printing-houſe, in which the
STATES

STATES GENERAL and the States of Holland employ only perfons fworn to fecrecy as to the papers committed to them. It may feem ftrange to require fecrecy from thofe, whofe art is chiefly ufeful in conferring publicity; but the truth is, that many papers are printed here, which are never communicated to the public, the States employing the prefs for the fake of its cheapnefs, and confidering that any of their members, who would fhew a printed paper, would do the fame with a written one.

In a large fquare, near the court, is the cabinet of natural hiftory, of which we have not the knowledge neceffary for giving a defcription. It is arranged in fmall rooms, which are opened, at twelve o'clock, to thofe who have applied the day before. One article, faid to be very rare, and certainly very beautiful, was an animal of the Deer fpecies, about fourteen inches high, exquifitely fhaped and marked, and believed to be at its full growth. It was brought from the coaft of Africa.

The Stadtholder's library was accidentally fhut, owing to the illnefs of the librarian; the picture gallery was open, but of paintings we have refolved to exempt our readers from any mention. The former is faid to contain eight thoufand volumes, and fourteen thoufand prints in portfolios. Among the illuminated MSS. in vellum is one, ufed by the fanguinary Catherine De Medicis and her children; and another, which belonged to Ifabella of Caftille, the grandmother of Charles the Fifth. What muft be oddly placed in a library is a fuit of armour of Francis the Firft, which was once in the cabinet of Chriftina of Sweden. Though this collection is
the

the private property of the Prince, the librarian is permitted to lend books to perfons, known to him and likely to ufe them advantageoufly for fcience.

We paffed a long morning in walking through the ftreets of this place, which contain probably more magnificent houfes than can be found in the fame fpace in any city of Northern Europe. The Grand *Voorhout* is rather, indeed, two feries of palaces than a ftreet. Between two broad carriage-ways, which pafs immediately along the fides, are feveral alleys of tall lime trees, canopying walks, firft laid out by Charles the Fifth, in 1536, and ordered to be carefully preferved, the *placard* being ftill extant, which directs the punifhment of offenders againft them. It would be tedious to mention the many fplendid buildings in this and the neighbouring ftreets. Among the moft confpicuous is the prefent refidence of the Britifh Ambaffadors, built by HUGUETAN, the celebrated banker of LOUIS the FOURTEENTH, and that of the Ruffian Minifter, which was erected by the Penfionary BARNEVELDT. But the building, which was intended to exceed all others at the Hague, is the Hotel of the Prince of NASSAU WEILBOURG; who, having married the fifter of the Prince of ORANGE, bought, at an immenfe expence, eight good houfes, facing the *Voorhout*, in order to erect upon their fcite a magnificent palace. What has been already built of this is extremely fine, in the crefcent form; but a German, arriving to the expenditure of a Dutch fortune, probably did not eftimate it by Dutch prices. It was begun eighteen years fince, and, for the laft twelve, has not proceeded.

Superb

Superb public buildings occur at almoſt every ſtep through the Hague. At one end of the terrace, on which we were lodged, is the *Doelen*, a ſpacious manſion, opening partly upon the *Tournois Veld*, or Place of Tournaments. The burgeſſes here keep their colours, and, what is remarkable, ſtill preſerve the *inſignia* of the *Toiſon d'Or*, given to them by CHARLES the FIFTH. Our WILLIAM the THIRD being admitted, at ten years of age, to the right of a burgeſs here, was inveſted with this order by the Burgomaſter. At the other end of the terrace is the palace, built for Prince MAURICE of NASSAU, upon his return from the government of Brazil, by KAMPFEN, Lord of Rambroek, architect of the Stadthouſe at Amſterdam. The interior of this building was deſtroyed by fire, in the commencement of the preſent century; but, the ſtately walls of ſtone and brick being uninjured, the rooms were reſtored by the proprietors, aſſiſted by a lottery. It is an inſtance of the abundance of buildings here, that this palace is now chiefly uſed as a place of meeting, for the œconomical branch of the ſociety of Haerlem, and for a ſociety, inſtituted here, for the encouragement of Dutch poetry.

The number of public buildings is much increaſed by the houſes, which the eighteen towns provide for their Deputies, ſent to the States of the Province. Theſe are called the *Logements* of the ſeveral towns; and there has been a great deal of emulation, as to their magnificence. Amſterdam and Rotterdam have the fineſt.

The churches are not remarkable for antiquity or grandeur. A congregation of Engliſh Proteſtants have their worſhip performed, in
the

the manner of the Diffenters, in a fmall chapel near the *Vyver*, where we had the fatisfaction to hear their venerable paftor, the Rev. Dr. M'CLEAN.

The refidence of a Court at the Hague renders the appearance of the inhabitants lefs national and charafteriftic than elfewhere. There are few perfons in the ftreets, who, without their orange cockades, might not be miftaken for Englifh; but ribbons of this colour are almoft univerfal, which fome wear in their hats, and fome upon a button-hole of the coat. The pooreft perfons, and there are more poor here than elfewhere, find fomething orange-coloured to fhew. Children have it placed upon their caps; fo that the practice is carried to an extent as ridiculous, as the prohibition was in 1785, when the magif-trates ordered, that *nothing orange-coloured fhould be worn, or fhewn, not even fruits, or flowers, and that carrots fhould not be expofed to fale with the ends outwards.*

The diftinctions between political claffes are very ftrongly marked and preferved in Holland. We were informed, that there are fome villages, in which the wearing of a cockade, and others, in which the want of one, would expofe a paf-fenger, efpecially a native, to infults. In the cities, where thofe of both parties muft tranfact bufinefs together, the diftinction is not much obferved. In Amfterdam, the friends of the Stadtholder do not wear cockades. For the moft part, the feamen, farmers and labouring claffes in the towns are attached to the Orange family, whofe opponents are chiefly compofed of the opulent merchants and tradefmen.

A hiftory,

A hiftory, or even a defcription of the two parties, if we were enabled to give it, would occupy too much fpace here; but it may be fhortly mentioned, that the original, or chief caufe of the diffenfion was, as might be expected, entirely of a commercial nature. The Englifh intereft had an unanimous popularity in Holland, about the year 1750. In the war of 1756, the French having fuftained a great lofs of fhipping, employed Dutch veffels to bring the produce of their American iflands to Europe, and thus eftablifhed a confiderable connection with the merchants of Amfterdam and Rotterdam. The Court of Verfailles took care, that the ftream of French wealth, which they faw fetting into the United Provinces, fhould carry with it fome French politics; while the wealth itfelf effected more than all their contrivance, and gradually produced a kindnefs for France, efpecially in the province of Holland, through which it chiefly circulated. The Englifh Minifters took all Dutch fhips, having French property on board; and the popularity of England was for a time deftroyed. Several maritime towns, probably with fome inftigation from France, demanded a war againft England. The friends of the Stadtholder prevented this; and from that time the Prince began to fhare whatever unpopularity the meafures of the Englifh Minifters, or the induftry of the Englifh traders, could excite in a rival and a commercial country.

The capture of the French Weft India iflands foon after removed the caufe of the difpute; but the effects of it furvived in the jealoufy of the great cities towards the Stadtholder, and

were

were much aggravated by the losses of their merchants, at the commencement of hostilities between England and the United Provinces, in 1780. The Dutch fleet being then unprepared to fail, and every thing, which could float, having been sent out of the harbours of Yorkshire and Lincolnshire to intercept their trading ships, the fortunes of many of the most opulent houses in Holland were severely shook, and all their members became the enemies of the Stadtholder.

If to these circumstances it is added, that the province of Holland, which pays fifty-eight parts of every hundred, levied by taxes, has an ambition for acquiring greater influence in the general government, than is bestowed by its single vote, we have probably all the original causes of the party distinctions in Holland, though others may have been incorporated with others, during a long series of events and many violent struggles of the passions.

The Stadtholder, who has had the misfortune to attract so much attention by his difficulties, is said to be a man of plain manners and sound understanding, neither capable of political intrigue, nor inclined to it. His office requires, especially during a war, a great deal of substantial, personal labour, to which he devotes himself earnestly and continually, but which he has not the vigour to bear, without an evident oppression of spirits. We saw him at a parade of the Guards, and it is not necessary to be told of his labours to perceive how much he is affected by them. It is scarcely possible to conceive a countenance more expressive of a mind, always urged, always

pressed

preffed upon, and not often receiving the relief of complete confidence in its efforts. His
person is fhort and extremely corpulent; his air
in converfation modeft and mild. This attendance upon the parade is his chief exercife, or relaxation at the Hague, where he frequently paffes
ten of the hours between five in a morning and
nine at night in his cabinet. He comes, accompanied by one or two officers, and his prefence
produces no crowd. When we had viewed the
parade and returned home, we faw him walking
under our windows towards the *Voorhout*, accompanied by an officer, but not followed by a
fingle perfon.

Converfation does not turn fo much upon the
family of the Stadtholder, as that we could acquire any diftinct opinions of the other parts of
it. Of his humanity and temper, there was fuf-
fieient proof, in 1787, when he returned to the
Hague, and was mafter of the perfons of thofe,
who had lately banifhed him. Indeed, the conduct of both parties, with refpect to the perfonal
fafety of their advcrfaries, was honourable to the
character of the nation. The States of Holland,
during the prevalence of their authority, did not
pretend, according to the injuftice of fimilar cafes,
to any right of deftroying the friends of the
Stadtholder, who were in their hands; the Stadtholder, when he returned, and when the public deteftation of his adverfaries was at an height,
which would have permitted any meafures againft
them, demanded no other retribution, than that
feventeen, named in a lift, fhould be declared incapable of holding offices under the Republic.

One of the beft excurfions from the Hague is

made

made to the *Maifon du Bois*, a fmall palace of the Prince of ORANGE, in a wood, which commences almoft at the northern gate of the town. This wood is called a park, but it is open to the public roads from Leyden, Haerlem and Amfterdam, which pafs through its noble alleys of oak and beech. It is remarkable for having fo much attracted the regard of Philip the Second, that, in the campaign of 1574, he ordered his officers not to deftroy it; and is probably the only thing, not deftined for himfelf, of which this ample deftroyer of human kind and of his own family ever directed the prefervation. Louis the FOURTEENTH, probably having heard the praifes of this care, left the mall of Utrecht to be a monument of fimilar tendernefs, during an unprovoked invafion, which coft ten thoufand lives.

The apartments of the *Maifon du Bois* are very varioufly furnifhed. The beft are fitted up with a light grey fattin, imboffed with Chinefe birds and plants, in filk and feathers of the moft beautiful tints; the window curtains, fcreens and coverings of the fophas and chairs are the fame, and the frames of the latter are alfo of Chinefe workmanfhip. Nothing more delicate and tafteful can be conceived; but, that you may not be quite diftracted with admiration, the carpets are fuch as an Englifh merchant would fcarcely receive into a parlour. The furniture of the ftate bed-chamber is valuable, and has once been fplendid; a light baluftrade of curious Japan work, about three feet high, runs acrofs the room, and divides that part, in which the bed ftands, from the remainder. The Princefs's drawing

ing-room, in which card parties are sometimes
held, is well embellished with paintings, and may
be called a superb apartment; but here again
there is an instance of the incompletenefs, said to
be obfervable in the furniture of all rooms, out of
England. Of four card tables two are odd ones,
and literally would be defpifed in a broker's fhop
in London. The great glory of the houfe is the
Salle d'Orange, an oblong faloon of noble height,
with pannels, painted by nine celebrated painters
of the Flemifh and Dutch fchools, among whom
VAN TULDEN, a pupil of RUBENS, has obferved
his manner fo much in a workfhop of Vulcan and
in a figure of Venus forming a trophy, that they
have been ufually attributed to his mafter. The
fubjects on the pannels and ceiling are all allegorical, and complimentary, for the moft part, to
the Princes of the Houfe of Orange, efpecially to
FREDERIC HENRY, the fon of the firft WILLIAM
and the grandfon of the Admiral COLIGNY. It
was at the expence of his widow, that the
houfe was built and the faloon thus ornamented.

Almoft all the rooms are decorated with family portraits, of which fome have juft been contributed by the pencil of the Hereditary Princefs.
A large piece reprefents herfelf, taking a likenefs of the Princefs her mother-in-law, and includes what is faid to be an admirable portrait of
her hufband. On the fix doors of the grand
cabinet are fix whole lengths of ladies of the
Houfe of Orange, exhibited in allegorical characters. The doors being covered by the
paintings, when that, by which you have entered, is fhut, you cannot tell the way back
again. A portrait of LOUISA DE COLIGNY,
the

the widow of William the Firſt, is enriched with a painter's pun; ſhe is preſented by *Hope* with a branch of an *orange* tree, containing only *one* orange; from which the ſpectator is to learn, that her *ſon* was her *only hope*.

The moſt delightful outlet from the Hague is towards Schevening, a village on the ſea-ſhore, nearly two miles diſtant, the road to which has been often and properly celebrated as a noble monument of taſteful grandeur. Commencing at the canal, which ſurrounds the Hague, it proceeds to the village through a viſta ſo exactly ſtraight, that the ſteeple of Schevening, the central object at the end of it, is viſible, at the firſt entrance. Four rows of lofty elms are planted along the road, of which the two central lines form this perfect and moſt pic9tureſque viſta; the others ſhelter paths on each ſide of it, for foot paſſengers.

The village itſelf, containing two or three hundred houſes of fiſhermen and peaſants, would be a ſpectacle, for its neatneſs, any where but in Holland. There is no ſquare, or ſtreet of the moſt magnificent houſes in London, that can equal it for an univerſal appearance of freſhneſs. It is poſitively bright with cleanlineſs; though its only ſtreet opens upon the ſea, and is the reſort of hundreds of fiſhermen. We paſſed a moſt delightful day at a little inn upon the beach, ſometimes looking into the hiſtory of the village, which is very antient; then enquiring into its preſent condition; and then enjoying the proſpect of the ocean, boundleſs to our view, on one ſide, and appearing to be but feebly reſtrained by a long tract of low white coaſt on the other.

The

The fea beats furioufly upon the beach here, which has no doubt been much raifed by art for the defence of the village. There is at leaft no other way of accounting for its fecurity, fince 1574, between which year and the latter end of the preceding century, it fuftained fix inundations. The firft, in 1470, demolifhed a church; the laft wafhed away an hundred and twenty houfes; notwithftanding which, the inhabitants built again upon their ftormy fhore; and their induftry, that, at length, protected them from the fea, enabled them to endure alfo the more inveterate ravages of the Spaniards. On this beach lie occafionally great numbers of herring buffes, too ftoutly built to be injured by touching it. We fufpect our information to have been exaggerated; but we heard on the fpot, that no lefs than one hundred and five belong to this village of little more than two hundred houfes, or are managed by agents in it. About forty were fet on float by the tide in the afternoon, and, being hauled by means of anchors beyond a very heavy furf, were out of fight, before we left the place.

It was amufing to fee the perfevering, effectual, but not very active exertions of the feamen in this bufinefs, which could not often be more difficult than it then was, when a ftrong wind blew directly upon the fhore. We here firft perceived, what we had many other opportunities of obferving, that, notwithftanding the general admiration of Dutch induftry, it is of a nature which would fcarcely acquire that name in England. A Dutchman of the labouring clafs is, indeed, feldom feen unemployed; but we never obferved one man working hard, according to the Englifh notion of the

the term. Perseverance, carefulnefs, and fteadi-
nefs are theirs, beyond any rivalfhip; the vehe-
mence, force, activity and impatience of an Englifh failor, or workman, are unknown to them.
You will never fee a Dutchman enduring the fatigue, or enjoying the reft, of a London porter.
Heavy burthens, indeed, they do not carry. At
Amfterdam, where carriages are even fomewhat
obnoxious, a cafk, holding four or five gallons of
liquor, is removed by a horfe and a fledge.

On our way from Schevening, where a dinner
cofts more than at an hotel in the Hague, we
turned a little to the right to fee Portland Gardens,
once the favourite refort of William and Mary;
and faid to be laid out in the Englifh tafte. They
are now a bad fpecimen even of Dutch gardens.
The fituation is unufually low, having on one
hand the raifed bank of the Schevening road,
and, on another, the fand hills of the coaft. Between thefe, the moifture of the fea air is held for
a long time, and finally drawn down upon the
earth. The artificial ornaments are ftained and
decaying; and the grafs and weeds of the neglected plots are capable only of a putrid green.
Over walks of a black mould you are led to the
orangery, where there is more decay, and may
look through the windows of the green-houfe, to
perceive how every thing is declining there. Some
pavilions, provided with water fpouts, are then to
be feen; and, if you have the patience to wait the
conclufion of an operation, intended to furprife
you, you may count how many of the pipes refufe
to perform their office.

Nearer to the Hague, we were ftopped to pay
a toll of a few doights; a circumftance which
was attended with this proof of civility. Having
passed

paſſed in the morning, without the demand, we enquired why it ſhould be made now. The gatherer replied, that he had ſeen us paſs, but, knowing that we muſt return by the ſame way, had avoided giving more trouble than was neceſſary. This tax is paid for the ſupport of the bank, or digue, over which the road paſſes; a work, begun on the 1ſt of May 1664, and finiſhed on the 5th of December 1665, by the aſſiſtance of a loan granted for the enterpriſe. The breadth of the road is thirty-two yards.

The next day, after ſeeing the relief of the Stadtholder's *garde du corps*, the privates of which wear feathered hats, with uniforms of ſcarlet and gold, we left the Hague, with much admiration of its pleaſantneſs and quiet grandeur, and took the *roof* of the trechtſchuyt for Leyden.

LEYDEN.

_____

LEYDEN.

_____

THREE hours pleafant floating along a canal, adorned with frequent country houfes, gardens, fummer-houfes and fquare balconies, or rather platforms, projecting over the water, within an hand's breadth of its level, brought us to this city, which was efteemed the fecond in Holland, before Rotterdam gained its prefent extent. Leyden is, however, fo large, that a traveller is likely to have a walk of half a league to his inn; and thofe who arrive, as we did, at the time of the fair, may find the proceffion not very pleafant. We increafed our difficulties by turning away from the dirt and incivility of what was called the beft inn, and did not afterwards find a better, though fuch, it feems, might have been had.

Having, at length, become contented with the worft, we went towards the fair, of which we had as yet feen only the crowd. The booths, being difpofed under trees and a long the borders of canals, made the whole appearance differ from that of an Englifh fair, though not quite fo much as we had expected. The ftock of the fhop-keepers makes a greater diftinction. There were feveral booths filled with filverfmiths' and jewellers' wares, to the amount of, probably, fome thoufand pounds each. Large French clocks in *or moulu* and

and porcelain were among their stores. . All the trades displayed the most valuable articles, that could be asked for in similar shops in large cities. We had the pleasure to see great quantities of English goods, and there were English names over three, or four of the booths.

The Dutch dresses were now become so familiar to us, that the crowd seemed as remarkable for the number of other persons in it, as for the abundance of peasants in their holiday finery, which, it is pleasant to know, displays the ornamental relics of several generations, fashion having very little influence in Holland. The fair occupied about a fourth part of the town, which we soon left to see the remainder. Two streets, parallel to each other, run through its whole length, and include the few public halls of an University, which would scarcely be known to exist, if it had no more conspicuous objects than its buildings. The Dutch universities contain no endowed foundations; so that the professors, who have their salaries from the States, live in private houses, and the students in lodgings. The academical dress is worn only in the schools, and by the professors. The library, to which Joseph Scaliger was a benefactor, is open only once in a week, and then for no more than two hours. It is the constant policy of the Dutch government, to make strangers leave as much money as possible behind them; and Leyden was once so greatly the resort of foreigners, that it was thought important not to let them read for nothing what they must otherwise be obliged to buy. The University is, of course, declining much, under this commercial wisdom of the magistrates.

There

These are students, however, of many nations and religions, no oaths being imposed, except upon the professors. Physic and botany especially are said to be cultivated here with much success; and there is a garden, to which not only individuals, but the East India Company, industriously contribute foreign plants. The salaries of the professors, who receive, besides, fees from the students, are nearly two hundred pounds a-year. The government of the University is in the rector, who is chosen out of three persons returned by the Senate to the States; the Senate consists of the professors; and, on extraordinary occasions, the Senate and Rector are directed by Curators, who are the agents for the States.

The chief street in the town is of the crescent form, so that, with more public buildings, it would be a miniature resemblance of High-street, Oxford. The town-house is built with many spires, and with almost Chinese lightness. We did not see the interior of this, or, indeed, of any other public buildings; for, in the morning, when curiosity was to be indulged, our fastidiousness as to the inns returned, and induced us to take a passage for Haerlem. The MSS. of the Dutch version of the Bible, which are known to be deposited here, could not have been shewn, being opened only once in three years, when the Deputies of the Synod and States attend; but we might have seen, in the town-house, some curious testimonies of the hardships and perseverance of the inhabitants, during the celebrated blockade of five months, in 1574, in consideration of which the University was founded.

After

After viewing some well-filled bookfellers' fhops, and one wide ftreet of magnificent houfes, we again made half the circuit of this extenfive city, in the way to the treehtfchuyt for

---

HAERLEM.

THE canal between Leyden and this place is nearly the pleafanteft of the great number, which connect all the towns of the province with each other, and render them to the traveller a feries of fpectacles, almoft as eafily vifited as the amufements of one large metropolis. Though this is faid to be one of the loweft parts of Holland, the country does not appear to have fuffered more than the reft by water. The many country feats, which border the canals, are alfo proofs that it is thought to be well fecured; yet this is the diftrict, which has been proved, by indifputable obfervations, to be lower than the neighbouring fea, even in the profoundeft calm. During the voyage, which was of four hours, we paffed under feveral bridges, and faw numbers of fmaller canals, croffing the country in various directions; but the paffage of a trechtfchuyt is not delayed for an inftant by a bridge, the towrope being loofened from the boat, on one fide, and immediately caught again, on the other, if it fhould not be delivered by fome perfon, purpofely ftationed on the arch. It is not often that a canal makes any bend in its courfe; when it does fo, there are fmall, high pofts at the point, round

round which the tow-rope is drawn; and, that
the cord may not be deftroyed by the friction,
the pofts fupport perpendicular rollers, which are
turned by its motion. Such pofts and rollers
might be advantageoufly brought into ufe in
England. On moft of the canals are half-way
villages, where paffengers may ftop, about five
minutes, for refrefhment; but they will be left
behind, without any ceremony, if they exceed
the limited time, which the boatman employs in
exchanging letters for fuch of the neighbouring
country houfes as have not packet boxes placed
on the banks.

Haerlem, like Leyden, is fortified by brick
walls, but both feem to be without the folid
earthen works, that conftitute the ftrength of
modern fortreffes. A few pieces of cannon are
planted near the gate, in order to command the
bridge of a wide *foffé*; and the gate-houfe itfelf
is a ftout building, deep enough to render the
paffage underneath fomewhat dark. There is
otherwife very little appearance of the ftrength,
that refifted the Duke of Alva, for twelve months,
and exafperated his defire of vengeance fo far,
that the murder of the inhabitants, who at laft
furrendered to his promifes of protection, could
alone appeafe it.

A narrow ftreet leads from the gate to the market-place, where two pieces of cannon are planted
before the guard-houfe; the firft precaution againft
internal commotion, which we had feen in the
country. Haerlem had a great fhare in the difputes of 1787, and is faid to adhere more fully
than any other city to the Anti-Stadtholderian politics of that period.

The

The market-place is very fpacious, and furrounds the great church, perhaps the largeft facred building in the province of Holland. The lofty oak roof is marked with dates of the early part of the fixteenth century. The organ, fometimes faid to be the beft in Europe, is of unufual fize, but has more power of found than fweetnefs. The pipes are filvered, and the body carefully painted; for organs are the only objects in Dutch churches, which are permitted to be fhewy. They are now building, in the great church at Rotterdam, a rival to this inftrument, and need not defpair of furpaffing it.

A great part of the congregation fit upon chairs in the large aifle, which does not feem to be thought a much inferior place to the other parts. During an evening fervice, at which we were prefent, this was nearly filled; and while every perfon took a feparate feat, women carried *chauffepieds*, or little wooden boxes, with pans of burning peat in them, to the ladies. This was on the 4th of June. The men enter the church with their hats on, and fome wear them, during the whole fervice, with the moft difgufting and arrogant hardihood.

We paffed a night at Haerlem, which is fcarcely worth fo long a ftay, though one ftreet, formed upon the banks of a canal, confifts of houfes more uniformly grand, than any out of the Hague, and furprifes you with its extenfive magnificence at a place, where there is little other appearance of wealth and none of fplendour. But the quietnefs of the Great in Holland is daily aftonifhing to a ftranger, who fometimes paffes through rows of palaces, without meeting a carriage, or a fervant.

The

The inhabitants of thofe palaces have, however, not lefs earneft views, than they who are more agitated; the difference between them is, that the views of the former are only fuch as their fituation enables them to gratify, without the agitation of the latter. They can fit ftill and wait for the conclufion of every year, at which they are to be richer, or rather are to have much more money, than in the preceding one. They know, that, every day the filent progrefs of intereft adds fo much to their principal; and they are content to watch the courfe of time, for it is time alone that varies their wealth, the fingle object of their attention. There can be no motive, but its truth, for repeating the trite opinion of the influence of avarice in Holland: we expected, perhaps, with fome vanity, to have found an opportunity for contradicting it; but are able only to add another teftimony of its truth. The infatuation of loving money not as a means, but as an end, is paramount in the mind of almoft every Dutchman, whatever may be his other difpofitions and qualities; the addiction to it is fervent, inveterate, invincible, and univerfal from youth to the feebleft old age.

Haerlem has little trade, its communication with the fea being through Amfterdam, which latter place has always been able to obftruct the reafonable fcheme of cutting a canal through the four miles of land, that feparate the former from the ocean. Its manufactures of filk and thread are much lefs profperous than formerly. Yet there are no fymptoms of decay, or poverty, and the environs are well covered with gardens efpecially on the banks of the *Sparen*, of which one branch flows through the town and the other paffes

under

under the walls. Some charitable inftitutions, for the inftruction and employment of children, fhould be mentioned alfo, to affuage the general cenfure of a too great fondnefs for money.

The houfe of LAURANCE COSTER, who is oppofed to FAUST, GOTTENBURGH and SCHEFFER, for the honour of having invented the art of printing, is near the great church, and is ftill inhabited by a bookfeller. An infcription, not worth copying, afferts him to be the inventor. The houfe, which is fmall and ftands in a row with others, muft have received its prefent brick front in fome time fubfequent to that of COSTER.

AMSTERDAM.

THE voyage between Haerlem and this place is lefs pleafant, with refpect to the country, than many of the other trips, but more gratifying to curiofity. For great part of the way, the canal paffes between the lake, called *Haerlemer Maer*, and a large branch of the *Zuyder Zee*, called the River Y. In one place, the neck of land, which feparates thefe two waters, is fo thin, that a canal cannot be drawn through it; and, near this, there is a village, where paffengers leave their firft boat, another waiting for them at the renewal of the canal, within a quarter of a mile. Here, as upon other occafions of the fame fort, nearly as much is paid for the carriage of two or three trunks between the boats, as for the whole voyage; and there is

E   an

an *Ordonnatie* to authorize the price; for the Magiftrates have confidered, that thofe, who have much baggage, are probably foreigners, and may be thus made to fupport many of the natives. The Dutch themfelves put their linen into a velvet bag, called a *Ryfack*, and for this accordingly no charge is made.

The *Half Wegen Sluice* is the name of this feparation between two vaft waters, both of which have gained confiderably upon their fhores, and, if united, would be irrefiftible. At the narroweft part, it confifts of pile-work and mafonry, to the thicknefs of probably forty feet. On this fpot the fpectator has, on his left hand, the Y, which, though called a river, is an immenfe inundation of the Zuyder Zee, and would probably carry a fmall veffel, without interruption, into the German ocean. On the other hand, is the Haerlem lake, about twelve miles long and nine broad, on which, during the fiege of Haerlem, the Dutch and Spaniards maintained fleets, and fought battles. Extending as far as Leyden, there is a paffage upon it from that city to Amfterdam, much fhorter than by the canal, but held to be dangerous. Before the year 1657, there was, however, no other way, and it was probably the lofs of the Prince of Bohemia and the danger of his dethroned father upon the lake, that inftigated the making of the canal.

This fluice is one of feveral valuable pofts, by which Amfterdam may be defended againft a powerful army, and was an important ftation, during the approach of the Duke of BRUNSWICK in 1787, when this city was the laft, which furrendered. All the roads being formed upon dikes, or embankbankments, may be defended by batteries, which can be attacked only by narrow columns and in front. The Half Wegen Sluice, was, however, eafily taken by the Duke of BRUNSWICK; his opponents having neglected to place gun-boats on the Haerlem lake, over which he carried eight hundred men in thirty boats, and furprifed the Dutch before day-break, on the morning of the firft of October. This was one of his real affaults, but there were all together eleven made on that day, and, on the next, the city propofed to furrender.

Beyond the fluice, the canal paffes feveral breaches, made by inundations of the Y, and not capable of being drained, or repaired. In thefe places the canal is feparated from the inundations either by piles, or floating planks. None of the breaches were made within the memory of the prefent generation, yet the boatmen have learned to fpeak of them with horror.

There is nothing magnificent, or grand, in the approach to Amfterdam, or the profpect of the city. The fails of above an hundred windmills, moving on all fides, feem more confpicuous than the public buildings of this celebrated capital.

The trechtfchuyt having ftopped on the outfide of the gate, we waited for one of the public coaches, which are always to be had by fending to a livery ftable, but do not ftand in the ftreet for fares. It coft half-a-crown for a drive of about two miles into the city; the regulated price is a guilder, or twenty-pence. Our direction was

to the *Doelen*; but the driver chofe to take us to
another inn, in the fame ftreet, which we did not
difcover to be otherwife called, till we had become
fatisfied with it.

Nearly all the chief thorough-fares of Amfterdam are narrow, but the carriages are neither fo
numerous as in other places of the fame fize, nor
fuffered to be driven with the fame fpeed; fo that,
though there is no raifed pavement, foot paffengers are as fafe as elfewhere. There are broad
terraces to the ftreets over the two chief canals,
but thefe are fometimes encumbered by workfhops, placed immediately over the water, between which and the houfes the owners maintain an intercourfe of packages and planks, with
very little care about the freedom of the paffage.
This, indeed, may be conftantly obferved of the
Dutch: they will never, either in their focieties,
or their bufinefs, employ their time, for a moment, in gratifying the little malice, or fhewing
the little envy, or affuming the little triumphs,
which fill fo much of life with unneceffary miferies; but they will feldom ftep one inch out of
their way, or furrender one moment of their
time, to fave thofe, whom they do not know,
from any inconvenience. A Dutchman, throwing cheefes into his warehoufe, or drawing iron
along the pathway, will not ftop, while a lady,
or an infirm perfon paffes, unlefs he perceives
fomebody inclined to protect them; a warehoufe-
man trundling a cafk, or a woman in the favourite occupation of throwing water upon her
windows, will leave it entirely to the paffengers to take care of their limbs, or their
clothes.

The

The canals themselves, which are the ornaments of other Dutch cities, are, for the moft part, the nuifances of Amfterdam. Many of them are entirely ftagnant, and, though deep, are fo laden with filth, that, on a hot day, the feculence feems peftilential. Our windows opened upon two, but the fcent very foon made us willing to relinquifh the profpect. The bottoms are fo muddy, that a boat-hook, drawn up, perhaps, through twelve feet of water, leaves a circle of flime at the top, which is not loft for many minutes. It is not unufual to fee boats, laden with this mud, paffing during mid-day, under the windows of the moft opulent traders; and the fetid cargoes never difturb the intenfe ftudies of the counting-houfes within.

After this diftafte of the ftreets and canals of Amfterdam, it was a fort of duty to fee, what is the glory of the city, the interior of the Stadthoufe; but we loft this fpectacle, by a negligence of that fevere punctuality, in which the Dutch might be ufefully imitated throughout the world. Our friends had obtained for us a ticket of admiffion at ten; we called upon them about half an hour afterwards; but, as the ride from their houfe would have required ten minutes more, the time of this ticket was thought to be elapfed. We would not accept one, which was offered to be obtained for another day, being unwilling to render it poffible, that thofe, who were loading us with the fincereft civilities, fhould witnefs another apparent inftance of inattention.

The Stadthoufe, as to its exterior, is a plain ftone building, attracting attention chiefly from its

length,

length, folidity and height. The front is an hundred and eight paces long. It has no large gate, but feveral fmall ones, and few ftatues, that would be obferved, except one of Atlas on the top. The tales, as to the expence of the building, are inexhauftible. The foundation alone, which is entirely of piles, is faid to have coft a million of guilders, or nearly ninety thoufand pounds, and the whole edifice treble that fum. Its contents, the ftock of the celebrated Bank, are eftimated at various amounts, of which we will not repeat the loweft.

The Exchange is an humble building, and not convenient of accefs. The Poft Office is well fituated, upon a broad terrace, near the Stadt-houfe, and feems to be properly laid out for its ufe.

None of the churches are confpicuous for their ftructure; but the regulation, with refpect to their minifters, fhould be more known. Two are affigned to each, and all throughout the city have equal and refpectable falaries.

At a diftance rom the Exchange are fome magnificent ftreets, raifed on the banks of canals, nearly equalling thofe of the Hague for the grandeur of houfes, and much exceeding in length the beft of Leyden and Haerlem. Thefe are the ftreets, which muft give a ftranger an opinion of the wealth of the city, while the Port, and that alone, can difplay the extenfivenefs of its commerce. The fhops and the preparations for traffic in the interior have a mean appearance to thofe, who try them by the ftandard of London conveniences and elegance.

The

The beſt method of ſeeing the Port is to paſs
down it in a boat to ſome of the many towns,
that ſkirt the Zuyder Zee. One convenience,
eaſy to be had every where, is immediately viſible from the quays. Small platforms of planks
ſupported by piles projeċt from the ſhore between
the veſſels, which are diſpoſed with their heads
towards the ſides of theſe little bridges; the furtheſt has thus a communication with the quay,
and, if the cargo is not of very heavy articles,
may be unladen at the ſame time with the others.
The port is ſo wide, that, though both ſides are
thronged with ſhipping, the channel in the middle is, at leaſt, as broad as the Thames at London
Bridge; but the harbour does not extend to more
than half the length of the *Pool* at London, and
ſeems to contain about half the number of veſſels.
The form of the port is, however, much more
advantageous for a diſplay of ſhipping, which
may be here ſeen nearly at one glance in a fine
bay of the *Zuyder*.

After a ſail of about an hour, we landed at
Saardam, a village celebrated for the Dock-yards,
which ſupply Amſterdam with nearly all its fleets.
A ſhort channel carries veſſels of the greateſt burthen from Saardam to the Zuyder Zee, which
the founders of the place took care not to approach too nearly: and the terrace at the end of
this channel is prepared for the reception of cannon, that muſt eaſily defend it from any attack
by ſea. Though the neighbourhood of a dock-
yard might be ſuppoſed a ſufficient antidote to
cleanlineſs, the neatneſs of this little town renders it a ſpeċtacle even to the Dutch themſelves.
The ſtreets are ſo carefully ſwept, that a piece of
orange

orange peel would be noticed upon the pavement, and the houses are washed and painted to the highest polish of nicety. Those, who are here in a morning, or at night, may probably see how many dirty operations are endured for the sake of this exceffive cleanliness.

We were shewn nearly round the place, and, of courfe, to the cottage, in which the indefatigable Peter the Firft of Ruffia refided, when he was a workman in the dockyard. It is a tenement of two rooms, standing in a part of the village, fo very mean, that the alleys near it are not cleaner, than thofe of other places. An old woman lives in the cottage, and fubfifts chiefly by fhewing it to vifitors, amongft whom have been the prefent Grand Duke and Duchefs of Ruffia; for the Court of Peterfburgh acknowledge it to have been the refidence of Peter, and have ftruck a medal in commemoration of fo truly honourable a palace. The old woman has received one of thefe medals from the prefent Emprefs, together with a grant of a fmall annuity to encourage her care of the cottage.

We paffed an agreeable afternoon, at an inn on the terrace, from whence pleafure veffels and paffage boats were continually departing for Amfterdam, and had a fmart fail, on our return, during a cloudy and fomewhat a ftormy funfet. The approach to Amfterdam, on this fide, is as grand as that from Haerlem is mean, half the circuit of the city, and all its fpires, being vifible at once over the crowded harbour. The great church of Haerlem is alfo feen at a fmall diftance, on the right.

4

The

The Amſtel, a wide river, which flows through
the city into the harbour, fills nearly all the canals, and is itſelf capable of receiving ſhips of
conſiderable burthen: one of the bridges over it,
and a terrace beyond, are among the few plea-
ſant walks enjoyed by the inhabitants. The Admiralty, an immenſe building, in the interior of
which is the dock-yard, ſtands on this terrace, or
quay; and the Eaſt India Company have their
magazine here, inſtead of the interior of the city,
where it would be benevolence to let its perfume
counteract the noxiouſneſs of the canals.

The government of Amſterdam is ſaid to collect by taxes, rents and dues of various ſorts,
more than an Engliſh million and a half annually;
and, though a great part of this ſum is afterwards
paid to the uſe of the whole Republic, the power
of collecting and diſtributing it muſt give conſiderable conſequence to the magiſtrates. The Senate, which has this power, conſiſts of thirty-ſix
members, who retain their ſeats during life, and
were formerly choſen by the whole body of
burghers; but, about two centuries ago, this privilege was ſurrendered to the Senate itſelf, who
have ever ſince filled up the vacancies in their
number by a majority of their own voices. The
Echevins, who form the court of juſtice, are here
choſen by the burghers out of a double number, nominated by the Senate: in the other cities, the Stadtholder, and not the burghers, makes
this choice.

It is obvious, that when the City Senates,
which return the Provincial ſtates, and, through
them, the States General, were themſelves elected
by

by the burghers, the legiflature of the United
Provinces had a charaĉter entirely reprefentative;
and, at prefent, a refpeĉt for public opinion is
faid to have confiderable influence in direĉting the
choice of the Senates.

The province of Holland, of which this city is
the moft important part, is fuppofed to contain
800,000 perfons, who pay taxes to the amount of
twenty-four millions of guilders, or two millions
fterling, forming an average of two pounds ten
fhillings per perfon. In eftimating the real taxation of a people, it is, however, neceffary to
confider the proportion of their confumption to
their imports; for the duties, advanced upon im-
ported articles, are not ultimately and finally paid
till thefe are confumed. The frugal habits of
the Dutch permit them to retain but a fmall part
of the expenfive commodities, which they colleĉt;
and the foreigners, to whom they are refold, pay,
therefore, a large fhare of the taxation, which
would be fo enormous, if it was confined to the
inhabitants. Among the taxes, really paid by
themfelves, are the following;—a land-tax of
about four fhillings and nine pence per acre; a
fale-tax of eight per cent. upon horfes, one and
a quarter per cent. upon other moveables, and
two and an half per cent. upon land and buildings; a tax upon inheritances out of the direĉt
line, varying from two and an half to eleven per
cent.; two per cent. upon every man's income;
an excife of three pounds per hogfhead upon
wine, and a charge of two per cent. upon all public offices. The latter tax is not quite fo popular here as in other countries, becaufe many of
thefe offices are aĉtually purchafed, the holders
being

being compelled to buy stock to a certain amount, and to destroy the obligations. The excise upon coffee, tea and salt is paid annually by each family, according to the number of their servants.

The inhabitants of Amsterdam, and some other cities, pay also a tax, in proportion to their property, for the maintenance of companies of city-guards, which are under the orders of their own magistrates. In Amsterdam, indeed, taxation is somewhat higher than in other places. Sir William Temple was assured, that no less than thirty duties might be reckoned to have been paid there, before a certain dish could be placed upon a table at a tavern.

The exact sums, paid by the several provinces towards every hundred thousand guilders, raised for the general use, have been often printed. The share of Holland is 58,309 guilders and a fraction; that of Overyssell, which is the smallest, 3571 guilders and a fraction.

Of five colleges of Admiralty, established within the United Provinces, three are in Holland, and contribute of course to point out the pre-eminence of that province. It is remarkable, that neither of these supply their ships with provisions: They allow the captains to deduct about four-pence halfpenny per day from the pay of each sailor for that purpose; a regulation, which is never made injurious to the seamen by any improper parsimony, and is sometimes useful to the public; in a country where pressing is not permitted. A captain, who has acquired a character for generosity amongst the sailors, can muster a crew in a few days, which, without such a temptation, could not be raised in as many weeks.

We

We cannot fpeak with exactnefs of the prices of provifions in this province, but they are generally faid to be as high as in England. The charges at inns are the fame as on the roads within an hundred miles of London, or, perhaps, fomething more. Port wine is not fo common as a wine which they call Claret, but which is compounded of a ftrong red wine from Valencia, mixed with fome from Bourdeaux. The general price for this is twenty pence Englifh a bottle; three and four pence is the price for a much better fort. About half-a-crown per day is charged for each apartment; and *logement* is always the firft article in a bill.

Private families buy good claret at the rate of about eighteen pence per bottle, and chocolate for two fhillings per pound. Beef is fold for much lefs than in England, but is fo poor that the Dutch ufe it chiefly for foup, and falt even that which they roaft. Good white fugar is eighteen pence per pound. Bread is dearer than in England; and there is a fort, called milk-bread, of uncommon whitenefs, which cofts nearly twice as much as our ordinary loaves. Herbs and fruits are much lower priced, and worfe in flavour; but their colour and fize are not inferior. Fifh is cheaper than in our maritime counties, thofe excepted which are at a great diftance from the metropolis. Coffee is very cheap, and is more ufed than tea. No kind of meat is fo good as in England; but veal is not much inferior, and is often dreffed as plainly and as well as with us. The innkeepers have a notion of mutton and lamb chops; but then it is *à la Maintenon;* and the

rank

rank oil of the paper is not a very delightful fauce. Butter is ufually brought to table *clarified*, that is, purpofely melted into an *oil*; and it is difficult to make them underftand that it may be otherwife.

The Dutch have much more refpeft for Englifh than for other travellers; but there is a jealoufy, with refpeft to our commerce, which is avowed by thofe, who have been tutored to calm difcuffion, and may be perceived in the converfation of others, whenever the ftate of the two countries is noticed. This jealoufy is greater in the maritime than in the other provinces, and in Amfterdam than in fome of the other cities. Rotterdam has fo much direft intercourfe with England, as to feel, in fome degree, a fhare in its interefts.

Some of our excurfions round Amfterdam were made in a curious vehicle; the body of a coach placed upon a fledge, and drawn by one horfe. The driver walks by the fide, with the reins in one hand, and in the other a wetted rope, which he fometimes throws under the fledge to prevent it from taking fire, and to fill up the little gaps in the pavement. The appearance of thefe things was fo whimfical, that curiofity tempted us to embark in one; and, finding them laughed at by none but ourfelves, the convenience of being upon a level with the fhops, and with the faces that feemed to contain the hiftory of the fhops, induced us to ufe them again. There are great numbers of them, being encouraged by the magiftrates, in preference to wheel carriages, and, as is faid, in tendernefs to the piled foundations of the city, the only one in Holland in which they are ufed.

The

The price is eight pence for any distance within the city, and eight pence an hour for attendance.

Near Amsterdam is the small village of Ouderkirk, a place of some importance in the short campaign of 1787, being accessible by four roads, all of which were then fortified. It consists chiefly of the country houses of Amsterdam merchants, at one of which we passed a pleasant day. Having been but slightly defended, after the loss of the posts of *Half Wegen* and *Amstelreen*, it was not much injured by the Prussians; but there are many traces of balls thrown into it. The ride to it from Amsterdam is upon the chearful banks of the Amstel, which is bordered, for more than five miles, with gardens of better verdure and richer groves than had hitherto appeared. The village was spread with booths for a fair, though it was Sunday; and we were somewhat surprised to observe, that a people in general so gravely decorous as the Dutch, should not pay a stricter deference to the Sabbath. We here took leave of some friends, whose frank manners and obliging dispositions are remembered with much more delight than any other circumstances, relative to Amsterdam.

UTRECHT.

UTRECHT.

THE paffage from Amfterdam hither is of eight hours; and, notwithftanding the pleafantnefs of trechtfchuyt conveyance, feemed fomewhat tedious, after the habit of paffing from city to city in half that time. The canal is, however, juftly preferred to others, on account of the richnefs of its furrounding fcenery; and it is pleafing to obferve how gradually the country improves, as the diftance from the province of Holland and from the fea increafes. Towards Utrecht, the gardens rife from the banks of the canal, inftead of fpreading below its level, and the grounds maintain avenues and plantations of lofty trees. Vegetation is ftronger and more copious; fhrubs rife to a greater height; meadows difplay a livelier green; and the latticework of the bowery avenues, which occur fo frequently, ceafes to be more confpicuous than the foliage.

It was Whitfuntide, and the banks of the canal were gay with holiday people, riding in waggons and carts; the latter frequently carrying a woman wearing a painted hat as large as an umbrella, and a man with one in whimfical contraft clipped nearly clofe to the crown. The lady fometimes refrefhed herfelf with a fan, and the gentleman, meanwhile, with a pipe of tobacco. Every village we paffed
refounded

refounded with hoarfe mufic and the clatter
of wooden fhoes : among thefe the prettieft was
Nieuverfluys, bordering each fide of the canal,
with a white draw-bridge picturefquely fhadowed
with high trees, and green banks floping to the
water's brim. Pleafure-boats and trechtfchuyts
lined the fhores ; and the windows of every houfe
were thronged with broad faces. On the little
terraces below were groups of fmokers, and of
girls in the neat trim Dutch drefs, with the fair
complexion and air of decorous modefty, by which
their country women are diftinguifhed.

About half-way from Amfterdam ftands a fmall
modern fortification ; and it is an inftance of
Dutch carefulnefs, that grafs had juft been mowed
even from the parapets of the batteries, and was
made up in heaps within the works. Not far from
it is an ancient caftle of one tower, left in the
ftate to which it was reduced during the conteft
with the Spaniards.

Near Utrecht, the ground has improved fo
much, that nothing but its evennefs diftinguifhes
it from other countries ; and, at fome diftance
eaftward, the hills of Guelderland rife to deftroy
this laft difference. The entrance into the city is
between high terraces, from which fteps defcend
to the canal ; but the ftreet is not wide enough to
have its appearance improved by this fort of approach. Warehoufes, formed under the terraces,
fhew alfo that the latter have been raifed more for
convenience than fplendour.

The fteeple of the great church, formerly a cathedral, excites, in the mean time, an expectation
of dignity in the interior, where fome confiderable

ble ſtreets and another canal complete the air of an
opulent city. It is not immediately ſeen, that a
great part of the body of this cathedral has been
deſtroyed, and that the canals, being ſubject to
tides, have dirty walls during the ebb. The
ſplendour, which might be expected in the capital
of a province much inhabited by nobility, does
not appear; nor is there, perhaps, any ſtreet equal
to the beſt of Leyden and Haerlem; yet, in general beauty, the city is ſuperior to either of
theſe.

We arrived juſt before nine, at which hour a
bell rings to denote the ſhutting of the larger
gates; for the rules of a walled town are obſerved here, though the fortifications could be of little other uſe than to prevent a ſurpriſe by horſe.
The *Chateau d'Anvers*, at which we lodged, is an
excellent inn, with a landlord, who tells, that he
has walked ſixty years in his own paſſage, and that
he had the honour of entertaining the Marquis of
Granby thirteen times, during the war of 1756.
Though the Dutch inns are generally unobjection-
able, there is an air of Engliſh completeneſs about
this which the others do not reach.

Utrecht is an univerſity, but with as little appearance of ſuch an inſtitution as Leyden. The
ſtudents have no academical dreſs; and their halls,
which are uſed only for lectures and exerciſes, are
formed in the cloiſters of the ancient cathedral.
The chief ſign of their reſidence in the place is,
that the houſeholders, who have lodgings to let,
write upon a board, as is done at Leyden, *Cubi-
cula locanda.* We were ſhewn round the town by
a member of the univerſity, who carefully avoided the halls; and we did not preſs to ſee them.

F   There

There are still some traces remaining of the Bishopric, which was once so powerful, as to excite the jealousy, or rather, perhaps, to tempt the avarice of Charles the Fifth, who seized upon many of its possessions. The use made of the remainder by the States General, is scarcely more justifiable; for the prebends still subsist, and are disposed of by sale to lay canons, who send delegates to the Provincial States, as if they had ecclesiastical characters.

The substantial remains of the Cathedral are one aisle, in which divine service is performed, and a lofty, magnificent Gothic tower, that stands apart from it. The ascent of this tower is one of the tasks prescribed to strangers, and, laborious as it is, the view from the summit sufficiently rewards them. A stone staircase, steep, narrow, and winding, after passing several grated doors, leads into a floor, which you hope is at the top, but which is little more than half way up. Here the family of the belfryman fill several decently furnished apartments, and shew the great bell, with several others, the noise of which, it might be supposed, no human ears could bear, as they must, at the distance of only three, or four yards. After resting a few minutes in a room, the windows of which command, perhaps, a more extensive land view than any other inhabited apartment in Europe, you begin the second ascent by a staircase still narrower and steeper, and, when you seem to be so weary as to be incapable of another step, half the horizon suddenly bursts upon the view, and all your meditated complaints are overborne by expressions of admiration.

Towards the west, the prospect, after including the

4

the rich plain of gardens near Utrecht, extends over the province of Holland, interfected with water, fpeckled with towns, and finally bounded by the fea, the mifts of which hide the low fhores from the fight. To the northward, the Zuyder Zee fpreads its hazinefs over Amfterdam and Naerden; but from thence to the eaft, the fpires of Amersfoort, Rhenen, Arnheim, Nimeguen and many intermediate towns, are feen amongft the woods and hills, that gradually rife towards Germany. Southward, the more mountainous diftrict of Cleves and then the level parts of Guelderland and Holland, with the windings of the Waal and the Leck, in which the Rhine lofes itfelf, complete a circle of probably more than fixty miles diameter, that ftrains the fight from this tremendous fteeple. The almoft perpendicular view into the ftreets of Utrecht affords afterwards fome relief to the eye, but increafes any notions of danger, you may have had from obferving, that the openwork Gothic parapet, which alone prevents you from falling with dizzinefs, has fuffered fomething in the general decay of the church.

While we were at the top, the bells ftruck; and, between the giddinefs communicated by the eye, and the ftunning efect of a found that feemed to fhake the fteeple, we were compelled to conclude fooner than had been intended this comprehenfive and farewell profpect of Holland.

The Mall, which is efteemed the chief ornament of Utrecht, is, perhaps, the only avenue of the fort in Europe, ftill fit to be ufed for the game that gives its name to them all. The feveral rows of noble trees include, at the fides,

roads

roads and walks; but the centre is laid out for the game of *Mall*, and, though not often used, is in perfect prefervation. It is divided so as to admit of two parties of players at once, and the fide-boards fufficiently reftrain fpectators. The Mall in St. James's Park was kept in the fame ftate, till 1752, when the prefent great walk was formed over the part, which was feparated by fimilar fide-boards. The length of that at Utrecht is nearly three quarters of a mile. The luxuriance and loftinefs of the trees preferve a perfpective much fuperior to that of St. James's, but in the latter the whole breadth of the walks is greater, and the view is more extenfive, as well as more ornamented.

This city, being a fort of capital to the neighbouring nobility, is called the politeft in the United Provinces, and certainly abounds, more than the others, with the profeffions and trades, which are fubfervient to fplendour. One practice, obferved in fome degree, in all the cities, is moft frequent here; that of bows paid to all parties, in which there are ladies, by every gentleman who paffes. There are, however, no plays, or other public amufements; and the feftivities, or ceremonies, by which other nations commemorate the happier events in their hiftory, are as unufual here as in the other parts of the United Provinces, where there are more occafions to celebrate and fewer celebrations than in moft European countries. Mufic is very little cultivated in any of the cities, and plays are to be feen only at Amfterdam and the Hague, where German and Dutch pieces are acted upon alternate nights. At Amfterdam, a French Opera-houfe has been fhut up,

and,

and, at the Hague, a *Comédie*, and the actors ordered to leave the country.

The ramparts of the city, which are high and command extenfive profpects, are rather emblems of the peacefulnefs, which it has long enjoyed, than figns of any effectual refiftance, prepared for an enemy. They are in many places regularly planted with trees, which muft be old enough to have been fpared, together with the Mall, by Louis the Fourteenth; in others, pleafure houfes, inftead of batteries, have been raifed upon them. A few pieces of old cannon are planted for the purpofe of faluting the Prince of ORANGE, when he paffes the city.

Trechtfchuyts go no further eaftward than this place, fo that we hired a voiturier's carriage, a fort of curricle with a driver's box in front, for the journey to Nimeguen. The price for thirty-eight, or thirty-nine miles, was fomething more than a guinea and a half; the horfes were worth probably fixty pounds upon the fpot, and were as able as they were fhowy, or they could not have drawn us through the deep fands, that cover one-third of the road.

We were now fpeedily quitting almoft every thing, that is generally characteriftic of Dutch land. The paftures were intermixed with fields of profperous corn; the beft houfes were furrounded by high woods, and the grounds were feparated by hedges, inftead of water, where any fort of partition was ufed. Windmills were feldom feen, and thofe only for corn. But thefe improvements in the appearance of the country

were

were accompanied by many fymptoms of a diminifhed profperity among the people. In eight-
and-thirty miles there was not one confiderable
town; a fpace, which, in the province of Holland, would probably have included three opulent cities, feveral extenfive villages, and ranges
of manfions, erected by merchants and manufacturers.

Wyk de Duerftede, the firft town in the road, is
diftinguifhable at fome diftance, by the fhattered
tower of its church, a monument of the defolation, fpread by the Spaniards. The inhabitants,
probably intending, that it fhould remain as a
leffon to pofterity, have not attempted to reftore
it, further than to place fome ftones over the part
filled by the clock. The body of the church and
the remainder of the tower are not deficient of
Gothic dignity. The town itfelf confifts of one,
or two wide ftreets, not well filled either with inhabitants, or houfes.

The road here turns to the eaftward and is
led along the right bank of the Leck, one of the
branches of the Rhine, upon a raifed mound, or
dique, fometimes twenty, or thirty feet, above
the river on the one fide, and the plains, on the
other. Small pofts, each numbered, are placed
along this road, at unequal diftances, for no other
ufe, which we could difcover, than to enable the
furveyors to report exactly where the mound may
want repairs. The carriage way is formed of a
deep fand, which we were very glad to leave, by
croffing the river at a ferry; though this road had
given us a fine view of its courfe and of fome
ftately veffels, preffing againft the ftream, on their
voyage to Germany.

On

On the other fide, the road went further from the river, though we continued to fkirt it occafionally as far as a fmall ferry-houfe, oppofite to Rhenen, at which we dined, while the horfes refted under a fhed, built over the road, as weigh houfes are at our turnpikes. Rhenen is a walled town, built upon an afcent from the water, and appears to have two, or three neat ftreets.

Having dined in a room, where a table, large enough for twenty perfons, was placed, on one fide, and a line of four, or five beds, covered by one long curtain, was formed againft the wainfcot, on the other, the voiturier clamoured, that the gates of Nimeguen would be fhut before we could get to them, and we foon began to crofs the country between the Leck and the Waal, another branch of the Rhine, which, in Guelderland, divides itfelf into fo many channels, that none can be allowed the pre-eminence of retaining its name. Soon after reaching the right bank of the Waal, the road affords a view of the diftant towers of Nimeguen, which appear there to be very important, ftanding upon a brow, that feems to front the whole ftream of the river. In the way we paffed feveral noble eftates, with manfions, built in the caftellated form, which James the Firft introduced into England, inftead of the more fortified refidences; and there was a fufficient grandeur of woods and avenues, to fhew, that there might be parks, if the owners had the tafte to form them. Between the avenues, the gilded ornaments of the roof, and the peaked coverings, placed, in fummer, over the chimneys, glittered to the fight, and fhewed the fantaftic ftyle of the architecture, fo exactly copied in Flemifh landfcapes of the fixteenth and feventeenth centuries.

As

As the sun declined and we drew near Nimeguen, the various colouring of a scene more rich than extensive rendered its effect highly interesting. The wide Waal on our left, reflecting the evening blush, and a vessel whose full sails caught a yellow gleam from the west; the ramparts and pointed roofs of Nimeguen rising over each other, just tinted by the vapour that ascended from the bay below; the faint and fainter blue of two ridges of hills in Germany retiring in the distance, with the mellow green of nearer woods and meadows, formed a combination of hues surprisingly gay and beautiful. But Nimeguen lost much of its dignity on a nearer approach; for many of the Towers, which the treachery of fancy had painted at distance, changed into forms less picturesque; and its situation, which a bold sweep of the Waal had represented to be on a rising peninsula crowning the flood, was found to be only on a steep beside it. The ramparts, however, the high old tower of the citadel, the Belvidere, with the southern gate of the town beneath, composed part of an interesting picture on the opposite margin of the river. But there was very little time to observe it: the driver saw the flying bridge, making its last voyage, for the night, towards our shore, and likely to return in about twenty minutes; he, therefore, drove furiously along the high bank of the river, and, turning the angle of the two roads with a velocity, which would have done honour to a Brentford postillion, entered that adjoining the first half of the bridge, and shewed the directors of the other half, that we were to be part of their cargo.

This

This bridge, which is partly laid over boats and partly over two barges, that float from the boats to the shore, is so divided, because the stream is occasionally too rapid to permit an entire range of boats between the two banks. It is thus, for one half, a bridge of boats, and, for the other, a flying bridge; which last part is capable of containing several carriages, and joins to the other so exactly as not to occasion the least interruption. It is also railed for the safety of foot passengers, of whom there are commonly twenty, or thirty. The price for a carriage is something about twenty-pence, which the toll-men carefully collect as soon as the demi-bridge has begun its voyage.

NIMEGUEN

NIMEGUEN

HAS, towards the water, little other fortification than an ancient brick wall, and a gate. Though it is a garrifon town, and certainly no trifling object, we were not detained at the gate by troublefome ceremonies. The commander, affecting no unneceffary carefulnefs, is fatisfied with a copy of the report, which the innkeepers, in all the towns, fend to the Magiftrates, of the names and conditions of their guefts. A printed paper is ufually brought up, after fupper, in which you are afked to write your name, addition, refidence, how long you intend to ftay, and to whom you are known in the province. We did not fhew a paffport in Holland.

The town has an abrupt but fhort elevation from the river, which you afcend by a narrow but clean ftreet, opening into a fpacious market-place. The great church and the guard-houfe are on one fide of this; from the other, a ftreet runs to the eaftern gate of the town, formed in the old wall, beyond which commence the modern and ftrong fortifications, that defend it, on the land fide. At the eaftern extremity of the place, a fmall mall leads to the houfe, in which the Prince of Orange refided, during the troubles of 1786; and, beyond it, on a fudden promontory towards the river, ftands a profpect houfe, called

the

the Belvidere, which, from its eaftern and
fouthern windows, commands a long view into
Germany, and to the north looks over Guelderland. From this place all the fortifications, which
are very extenfive, are plainly feen, and a military
perfon might eftimate their ftrength. There are
feveral forts and outwoks, and, though the ditch
is pallifadoed inftead of filled, the place muft be
capable of a confiderable defence, unlefs the befieging army fhould be mafters of the river and the
oppofite bank. There was formerly a fortrefs
upon this bank, which was often won and loft,
during the fieges of Nimeguen, but no remains
of it are vifible now.

The town is claffic ground to thofe, who vene-
rate the efforts, by which the provinces were refcued from the dominion of the Spaniards. It
was firft attempted by SENGIUS, a Commander in
the Earl of LEICESTER's army, who propofed to
enter it, at night, from the river, through a
houfe, which was to be opened to him; but his
troops by miftake entered another, where a large
company was collected, on occafion of a wedding,
and, being thus difcovered to the garrifon, great
numbers of thofe, already landed upon the beach,
were put to the fword, or drowned in the confufion of the retreat. An attempt by Prince Maurice to furprife it was defeated by the failure of a
petard, applied to one of the gates; but it was
foon after taken by a regular fiege, carried on
chiefly from the other fide of the river. This and
the neighbouring fortrefs of Grave were among
the places, firft taken by Louis the Fourteenth,
during his invafion, having been left without fufficient garrifons.

The

'The citadel, a remnant of the antient fortifications, is near the eaftern gate; which appears to
be thought ftronger than the others, for, on this
fide, alfo is the arfenal.

Nimeguen has been compared to Nottingham,
which it refembles more in fituation than in ftructure, though many of the ftreets are fteep, and
the windows of one range of houfes fometimes
overlook the chimnies of another; the views alfo,
as from fome parts of Nottingham, are over a
green and extenfive level, rifing into diftant hills;
and here the comparifon ends. The houfes are
built entirely in the Dutch fafhion, with many
coloured, painted fronts, terminating in peaked
roofs; but fome decline of neatnefs may be obferved by thofe who arrive here from the province
of Holland. The market-place, though gay and
large, cannot be compared with that of Nottingham, in extent, nor is the town more than half
the fize of the latter, though it is faid to contain
nearly fifty thoufand inhabitants. From almoft
every part of it you have, however, a glimpfe of
the furrounding landfcape, which is more extenfive than that feen from Nottingham, and is
adorned by the fweeps of a river of much greater
dignity than the Trent.

We left Nimeguen, in the afternoon, with a
Voiturier, whofe price, according to the *ordonnatie*, was higher than if we had fet out half an hour
fooner, upon the fuppofition that he could not
return that night. The road lies through part
of the fortifications, concerning which there can,
of courfe, be no fecrecy. It then enters an extenfive plain, and runs almoft parallel to a range
of

of heights, at the extremity of which Nimeguen
ſtands, and preſents an appearance of ſtill greater
ſtrength and importance than when ſeen from the
weſtward.

After a few miles, this road leaves the territories of the United Provinces, and enters the Pruſſian duchy of Cleves, at a ſpot where a mill is in
one country, and the miller's houſe in the other.
An inſtance of difference between the conditions
of the people in the two countries was obſervable
even at this paſſage of their boundary. Our poſtillion bought, at the miller's, a loaf of black
bread, ſuch as is not made in the Dutch provinces, and carried it away for the food of his
horſes, which were thus initiated into ſome of the
bleſſings of the German peaſantry. After another quarter of a mile you have more proofs that
you have entered the country of the King of
Pruſſia. From almoſt every cluſter of huts barefooted children run out to beg, and ten or a dozen
ſtand at every gate, nearly throwing themſelves
under the wheels to catch your money, which,
every now and then, the bigger ſeize from the
leſs.

Yet the land is not ill-cultivated. The diſtinction between the culture of land in free and arbitrary countries, was, indeed, never very apparent
to us, who ſhould have been ready enough to perceive it. The great landholders know what
ſhould be done, and the peaſantry are directed to
do it. The latter are, perhaps, ſupplied with
ſtock, and the grounds produce as much as elſewhere,

where, though you may read, in the looks and manners of the people, that very little of its productions is for them.

Approaching nearer to Cleves, we travelled on a ridge of heights, and were once more cheared with the " pomp of groves." Between the branches were delightful catches of extensive landscapes, varied with hills clothed to their summits with wood, where frequently the distant spires of a town peeped out most picturesquely. The open vales between were chiefly spread with corn; and such a prospect of undulating ground, and of hills tufted with the grandeur of forests, was inexpressibly chearing to eyes fatigued by the long view of level countries.

At a few miles from Cleves the road enters the Park and a close avenue of noble plane trees, when these prospects are, for a while, excluded. The first opening is where, on one hand, a second avenue commences, and, on the other, a sort of broad bay in the woods, which were planted by Prince Maurice, includes an handsome house, now converted into an inn, which, owing to the pleasantness of the situation, and its vicinity to a mineral spring, is much frequented in summer. A statue of General Martin Schenck, of dark bronze, in complete armour, and with the beaver down, is raised upon a lofty Ionic column, in the centre of the avenue, before the house. Resting upon a lance, the figure seems to look down upon the passenger, and to watch over the scene, with the sternness of an ancient knight. It appears to be formed with remarkable skill, and has an air more striking and grand than can be readily described.

The

The *orangerie* of the palace is still preserved, together with a femicircular pavilion, in a recefs of the woods, through which an avenue of two miles leads you to

CLEVES.

THIS place, which, being the capital of a duchy, is entitled a City, confifts of fome irregular ftreets, built upon the brow of a fteep hill. It is walled, but cannot be mentioned as fortified, having no folid works. The houfes are chiefly built of ftone, and there is a little of Dutch cleanlinefs; but the marks of decay are ftrongly impreffed upon them, and on the ancient walls. What little trade there is, exifts in retailing goods fent from Holland. The Dutch language and coins are in circulation here, almoft as much as the German.

The eftablifhed religion of the town is Proteftant; but here is an almoft univerfal toleration, and the Catholics have feveral churches and monafteries. Cleves has fuffered a various fate in the fport of ward uring many centuries, but has now little to diftinguifh it except the beauty of its profpects, which extend into Guelderland and the province of Holland, over a country enriched with woody hills and vallies of corn and pafturage.

Being

Being convinced, in two or three hours, that there was nothing to require a longer ftay, we fet out for Xanten, a town in the fame duchy, diftant about eighteen miles. For nearly the whole of this length the road lay through a broad avenue, which frequently entered a foreft of oak, fir, elm, and majeftic plane-trees, and emerged from it only to wind along its fkirts. The views then opened over a country, diverfified with gentle hills, and ornamented by numberlefs fpires upon the heights, every fmall town having feveral convents. The caftle of Eltenberg, on the fummit of a wooded mountain, was vifible during the whole of this ftage and part of the next day's journey. Yet the fewnefs, or the poverty, of the inhabitants appeared from our meeting only one chaife, and two or three fmall carts, for eighteen miles of the only high-road in the country.

It was a fine evening in June, and the rich lights, thrown among the foreft glades, with the folitary calmnefs of the fcene, and the ferenenefs of the air, filled with fcents from the woods, were circumftances which perfuaded to fuch tranquil rapture as Collins muft have felt when he had the happinefs to adrefs to Evening—

For when thy folding ftar, arifing, fhews
His paly circlet, at his warning lamp,
The fragrant hours and elves
Who flept in buds the day:
And many a nymph, who wreaths her brows with fedge,
And fheds the fresh'ning dew, and, lovelier ftill,
The penfive pleafures fweet
Prepare thy fhadowy car.

A fmall

A fmall half-way village, a ftately convent, with its gardens, called Marienbaum, founded in the 15th century by Maria, Duchefs of Cleves, and a few mud cottages of the woodcutters, were the only buildings on the road: the foot paffengers were two Pruffian foldiers. It was moon-light, and we became impatient to reach Xanten, long before our driver could fay, in a mixture of German and Dutch, that we were near it. At length from the woods, that had concealed the town, a few lights appeared over the walls, and diffipated fome gloomy fancies about a night to be paffed in a foreft.

G XANTEN.

XANTEN.

THIS is a fmall town, near the Rhine, without much appearance of profperity, but neater
than moſt of the others around it. Several narrow ſtreets open into a wide and pleafant market-
place, in the centre of which an old but flouriſh-
ing elm has its branches carefully extended by a
circular railing, to form an arbour over benches.
A cathedral, that proves the town to have been
once more confiderable, is on the north fide of
this place; a fine building, which, ſhewn by the
moon of a fummer midnight, when only the bell
of the adjoining convent calling the monks to
prayers, and the waving of the aged tree, were to
be heard, prefented a fcene before the windows of
our inn, that fully recompenfed for its want of accommodation.

There were alfo humbler reafons towards contentment; for the people of the houfe were extremely defirous to afford it; and the landlord
was an orator in French, of which and his addrefs he was pleafantly vain. He received us
with an air of humour, mingled with his com-
plaifance, and hoped, that, " as *Monfieur* was *Anglois*, he ſhould furprife him with his *vin extraor-
dinaire*, all the Rheniſh wine being adulterated
by the Dutch, before they lent it to England.
His houfe could not be fine, becaufe he had little money; but he had an excellent cook, otherwife it could not be expected that the prebenda-
ries

ries of the cathedral would dine at it, every day, and become, as they were, *vraiment, Monsieur, gros comme vous me voyez!*"

There are in this small town several monasteries and one convent of noble canonesses, of which last the members are few and the revenues very great. The interior of the cathedral is nearly as grand as the outside; and mass is performed in it with more solemnity than in many, which have larger institutions.

We left Xanten, the next morning, in high spirits, expecting to reach Cologne, which was little more than fifty miles distant, before night, though the landlord and the postmaster hinted, that we should go no further than Neuss. This was our first use of the German post, the slowness of which, though it has been so often described, we had not estimated. The day was intensely hot, and the road, unsheltered by trees, lay over deep sands, that reflected the rays. The refreshing forests of yesterday we now severely regretted, and watched impatiently to catch a freer air from the summit of every hill on the way. The postillion would permit his horses to do little more than walk, and every step threw up heaps of dust into the chaise. It had been so often said by travellers, that money has as little effect in such cases as intreaties, or threats, that we supposed this slowness irremediable, which was really intended only to produce an offer of what we would willingly have given.

RHEINBERG.

IN something more than three hours, we reached Rheinberg, diftant about nine miles; a place often mentioned in the military hiftory of the fixteenth and feventeenth centuries, and which we had fuppofed would at leaft gratify us by the fhew of magnificent ruins, together with fome remains of its former importance. It is a wretched place of one dirty ftreet, and three or four hundred mean houfes, furrounded by a decayed wall that never was grand, and half filled by inhabitants whofe indolence, while it is probably more to be pitied than blamed, accounts for the fullennefs and wretchednefs of their appearance. Not one fymptom of labour, or comfort, was to be perceived in the whole town. The men feemed, for the moft part, to be ftanding at their doors, in unbuckled fhoes and woollen caps. What few women we faw were brown, without the appearance of health, which their leannefs and dirtinefs prevented. Some fmall fhops of huckfters' wares were the only figns of trade.

The inn, that feemed to be the beft, was fuch as might be expected in a remote village, in a erofs road in England. The landlord was ftanding before the door in his cap, and remained there fome time after we had found the way into a fitting room, and from thence, for want of attendance, into a kitchen; where two women, without ftockings, were watching over fome fort

of

of cookery in earthen jugs. We were fupplied, at length, with bread, butter and four wine, and did not fuffer ourfelves to confider this as any fpecimen of German towns, becaufe Rheinberg was not a ftation of the poft; a delufion, the fpirit of which continued through feveral weeks, for we were always finding reafons to believe, that the wretchednefs of prefent places and perfons was produced by fome circumftances, which would not operate in other diftricts.

This is the condition of a town, which, in the fixteenth and feventeenth centuries, was thought important enough to be five times attacked by large armies. FARNESE, the Spanifh commander, was diverted from his attempt upon it, by the neceffity of relieving Zutphen, then befieged by the Earl of Leicefter: in 1589, the Marquis of Varambon invefted it, for the Spaniards, by order of the Prince of Parma; but it was relieved by our Colonel Vere, who, after a long battle, completely defeated the Spanifh army. In 1599, when it was attacked by Mendoza, a magazine caught fire. The governor, his family, and a part of the garrifon were buried in the ruins of a tower, and the explofion funk feveral veffels in the Rhine; after which, the remainder of the garrifon furrendered the place. The Prince of Orange retook it in 1633. Four years afterwards, the Spaniards attempted to furprife it in the night; but the Deputy Governor and others, who perceived that the garrifon could not be immediately collected, paffed the walls, and, pretending to be deferters, mingled with the enemy, whom they perfuaded to delay the attack for a few minutes. The troops within were in the mean time prepared for their defence, and fucceeded in it; but the Governor,

with

with two officers and fifteen foldiers who had accompanied him, being difcovered, were killed. All thefe contefts were for a place not belonging to either party, being in the electorate of Cologne, but which was valuable to both, for its neighbourhood to their frontiers.

Beyond Rheinberg, our profpects were extenfive, but not fo woody, or fo rich as thofe of the day before, and few villages enlivened the landfcape. Open corn lands, intermixed with fields of turnips, fpread to a confiderable diftance, on both fides; on the eaft, the high ridges of the Weftphalian mountains fhut up the fcene. The Rhine, which frequently fwept near the road, fhewed a broad furface, though fhrunk within its fandy fhores by the drynefs of the feafon. Not a fingle veffel animated its current, which was here tame and fmooth, though often interrupted by fands, that rofe above its level.

HOOG-

HOOGSTRASS.

THE next town was Hoogſtraſs, a poſt ſta-
tion, fifteen miles from Xanten, of which we
ſaw little more than the inn, the other part
of this ſmall place being out of the road. A
large houſe, which might have been eaſily made
convenient, and was really not without plenty,
confirmed our notion, that, at the poſt ſtages,
there would always be ſome accommodation.
We dined here, and were well attended. The
landlord, a young man who had ſerved in the
army of the country, and appeared by his dreſs
to have gained ſome promotion, was very in-
duſtrious in the houſe, during this interval of
his other employments.

The next ſtage was of eighteen miles, which
make a German poſt and an half; and, during
this ſpace, we paſſed by only one town, Ordin-
gen, or Urdingen, the greateſt part of which
ſpread between the road and the Rhine.

Towards evening, the country became more
woody, and the ſlender ſpires of convents frequently appeared, ſheltered in their groves and
ſurrounded by corn lands of their own domain.
One of theſe, nearer to the road, was a noble
manſion, and, with its courts, offices and gardens, ſpread over a conſiderable ſpace. A ſum-
mer-houſe,

mer-houfe, built over the garden wall, had no windows towards the road, but there were feveral fmall apertures, which looked upon it and beyond to a large tract of inclofed wood, the property of the convent.

NEUSS.

SOON after fun-fet, we came to Neufs, which, as it is a poft town, and was mentioned as far off as Xanten, we had been fure would afford a comfortable lodging, whether there were any veftiges, or not, of its ancient and modern hiftory. The view of it, at fome little diftance, did not altogether contradict this notion, for it ftands upon a gentle afcent, and the fpires of feveral convents might juftly give ideas of a confiderable town to thofe, who had not learned how flightly fuch fymptoms are to be attended to in Germany.

On each fide of the gate, cannon balls of various fizes remain in the walls. Within, you enter immediately into a clofe ftreet of high, but dirty ftone houfes, from which you expect to efcape prefently, fuppofing it to be only fome wretched quarter, appropriated to difeafe and misfortune. You fee no paffengers, but, at the door of every houfe, an haggard group of men and women ftare upon you with looks of hungry rage, rather than curiofity, and their

gaunt

gaunt figures excite, at firſt, more fear than pity. Continuing to look for the better quarter, and to paſs between houſes, that ſeem to have been left after a ſiege and never entered ſince, the other gate of the town at length appears, which you would rather paſs at midnight than ſtop at any place yet perceived. Within a ſmall diſtance of the gate, there is, however, a houſe with a wider front, and windows of unſhattered glaſs and walls not quite as black as the others, which is known to be the inn only becauſe the driver ſtops there, for, according to the etiquette of ſullenneſs in Germany, the people of the houſe make no ſhew of receiving you.

If it had not already appeared, that there was no other inn, you might learn it from the manners of the two hoſteſſes and their ſervants. Some ſort of accommodation is, however, to be had ; and thoſe, who have been longer from the civilities and aſſiduities of ſimilar places in England, may, by more ſubmiſſion and more patience, obtain it ſooner than we did. By theſe means they may reduce all their difficulties into one, that of determining whether the windows ſhall be open or ſhut ; whether they will endure the cloſeneſs of the rooms, or will admit air, loaded with the feculence of putrid kennels, that ſtagnate along the whole town.

This is the *Noveſium* of Tacitus, the entrance of the thirteenth legion into which he relates, at a time when the Rhine, *incognita illi cælo ſiccitate*, became *vix navium patiens*, and which VOCULA was ſoon after compelled to ſurrender by the treachery of other leaders and the corruption of his army, whom he addreſſed, juſt before

his

his murder, in the fine fpeech, beginning, " *Nunquam apud vos verba feci, aut pro vobis folicitior, aut pro me fecurior;* a paffage fo near to the *cunctifque timentem, fecurumque fui,* by which Lucan defcribes Cato, that it muft be fuppofed to have been infpired by it.

This place ftood a fiege, for twelve months, againft 60,000 men, commanded by Charles the Bold, Duke of Burgundy, and fucceeded in its refiftance. But, in 1586, when it held out for Gebhert de Truschkes, an elector of Cologne, expelled by his Chapter, for having married, it was the fcene of a dreadful calamity. Farnese, the Spanifh. General, who had juft taken Venlo, marched againft it with an army, enraged at having loft the plunder of that place by a capitulation. When the inhabitants of Neufs were upon the point of furrendering it, upon fimilar terms, the army, refolving not to lofe another prey of blood and gold, rufhed to the affault, fet fire to the place, and murdered all the inhabitants, except a few women and children, who took refuge in two churches, which alone were faved from the flames.

When the firft fhock of the furprife, indignation and pity, excited by the mention of fuch events, is overcome, we are, of courfe, anxious to afcertain whether the perpetrators of them were previoufly diftinguifhed by a voluntary entrance into fituations, that could be fuppofed to mark their characters. This was the army of Philip the Second. The foldiers were probably, for the moft part, forced into the fervice. The officers, of whom only two are related to have oppofed the maffacre, could not have been fo.

What

What was then the previous diſtinction of the officers of Philip the Second? But it is not proper to enter into a diſcuſſion here of the nature of their employment.

Neuſs was rebuilt, on the ſame ſpot; the ſituation being convenient for an intercourſe with the eaſtern ſhore of the Rhine, eſpecially with Duſſeldorff, to which it is nearly oppoſite. The ancient walls were partly reſtored by the French, in 1602. One of the churches, ſpared by the Spaniards, was founded by a daughter of CHARLEMAGNE, in the ninth century, and is now attached to the Chapter of Noble Ladies of St. Quirin; beſides which there are a Chapter of Canons, and five or ſix convents in the place.

COLOGNE.

FROM Neuſs hither we paſſed through a deep, ſandy road, that ſometimes wound near the Rhine, the ſhores of which were yet low and the water tame and ſhallow. There were no veſſels upon it, to give one ideas either of the commerce, or the population of its banks.

The country, for the greater part of twenty miles, was a flat of corn lands; but, within a ſhort diſtance of Cologne, a gentle riſe affords a view of the whole city, whoſe numerous towers and

and fteeples had before appeared, and of the extenfive plains, that fpread round it. In the fouthern perfpective of thefe, at the diftance of about eight leagues, rife the fantaftic forms of what are called the Seven Mountains; weftward, are the cultivated hills, that extend towards Flanders; and, eaftward, over the Rhine, the diftant mountains, that run through feveral countries of interior Germany. Over the wild and gigantic features of the Seven Mountains dark thunder mifts foon fpread an awful obfcurity, and heightened the expectation, which this glimpfe of them had awakened, concerning the fcenery we were approaching.

The appearance of Cologne, at the diftance of one, or two miles, is not inferior to the conception, which a traveller may have already formed of one of the capitals of Germany, fhould his mind have obeyed that almoft univerfal illufion of fancy, which dreffes up the images of places unfeen, as foon as much expectation, or attention is directed towards them. The air above is crowded with the towers and fpires of churches and convents, among which the cathedral, with its huge, unfinifhed mafs, has a ftriking appearance. The walls are alfo high enough to be obferved, and their whole inclofure feems, at a diftance, to be thickly filled with buildings.

We fhould have known ourfelves to be in the neighbourhood of fome place larger than ufual, from the fight of two, or three carriages, at once, on the road; nearly the firft we had feen in Germany. There is befides fome fhew of labour in the adjoining villages; but the fallow countenances

ces and miserable air of the people prove, that it is not a labour beneficial to them. The houses are only the desolated homes of these villagers; for there is not one that can be supposed to belong to any prosperous inhabitant of the city, or to afford the coveted stillness, in which the active find an occasional reward, and the idle a perpetual misery.

A bridge over a dry fossé leads to the northern gate, on each side of which a small modern battery defends the ancient walls. The city is not fortified, according to any present sense of the term, but is surrounded by these walls and by a ditch, of which the latter, near the northern gate, serves as a sort of kitchen garden to the inhabtants.

Before passing the inner gate, a soldier demanded our names, and we shewed our passport, for the first time; but, as the inquisitor did not understand French, in which language passports from England are written, it was handed to his comrades, who formed a circle about our chaise, and began, with leaden looks, to spell over the paper. Some talked, in the mean time, of examining the baggage; and the money, which we gave to prevent this, being in various pieces and in Prussian coin, which is not perfectly understood here, the whole party turned from the passport, counting and estimating the money in the hand of their collector, as openly as if it had been a legal tribute. When this was done and they had heard, with surprise, that we had not determined where to lodge, being inclined to take the pleasantest inn, we wrote our names in the corporal's dirty book, and were allowed to drive, under a dark tower, into the city.

Instantly,

Inſtantly, the narrow ſtreet, gloomy houſes, ſtagnant kennels and wretchedly looking people reminded us of the horrors of Neuſs. The lower windows of theſe priſon-like houſes are ſo ſtrongly barricadoed, that we had ſuppoſed the firſt two, or three, to be really parts of a gaol; but it ſoon appeared, that this profuſion of heavy iron work was intended to exclude, not to confine, robbers. A ſucceſſion of narrow ſtreets, in which the largeſt houſes were not leſs diſguſting than the others for the filthineſs of their windows, door-ways and maſſy walls, continued through half the city. In one of theſe ſtreets, or lanes, the poſtillion ſtopped at the door of an inn, which he ſaid was the beſt; but the ſuffocating air of the ſtreet rendered it unneceſſary to enquire, whether, contrary to appearances, there could be any accommodation within, and, as we had read of many ſquares, or market-places, he was deſired to ſtop at an inn, ſituated in one of theſe. Thus we came to the Hotel de Prague, a large ſtraggling building, ſaid to be not worſe than the others, for wanting half its furniture, and probably ſuperior to them, by having a landlord of better than German civility.

Having counted from our windows the ſpires of ten, or twelve churches, or convents, we were at leiſure to walk farther into the city, and to look for the ſpacious ſquares, neat ſtreets, noble pub-lic buildings and handſome houſes, which there could be no doubt muſt be found in an Imperial and Electoral city, ſeated on the Rhine, at a point where the chief roads from Holland and Flanders join thoſe of Germany, treated by all writers as a conſiderable place, and evidently by its ſituation
capable

capable of becoming a fort of *emporium* for the three countries. The fpot, into which our inn opened, through a parallelogram of confiderable extent, bordered by lime trees, we paffed quickly through, perceiving, that the houfes on all its fides were mean buildings, and therefore fuch as could not deferve the attention in the Imperial and Electoral city of Cologne. There are ftreets from each angle of this place, and we purfued them all in their turn, narrow, winding and dirty as they are, peftilent with kennels, gloomy from the height and blacknefs of the houfes, unadorned by any public buildings, except the churches, that were grand, or by one private dwelling, that appeared to be clean, with little fhew of traffic and lefs of paffengers, either bufy, or gay, till we faw them ending in other ftreets ftill worfe, or concluded by the gates of the city. One of them, indeed, led through a market-place, in which the air is free from the feculence of the ftreets, but which is inferior to the other opening in fpace, and not better furrounded by buildings.

" Thefe diminutive obfervations feem to take away fomething from the dignity of wriking, and therefore are never communicated, but with hefitation, and a little fear of abafement and contempt *." And it is not only becaufe they take away fomething from the dignity of writing, that fuch obfervations are with-held. To be thought capable of commanding more pleafures and preventing more inconveniences than others is a too general paffport to refpect; and, in the ordinary affairs of life, for one, that will fhew fomewhat

* Dr. Samuel Johnfon.

lefs

lefs profperity than he has, in order to try who will really refpect him, thoufands exert themfelves to affume an appearance of more, which they might know can procure only the mockery of efteem for themfelves, and the reality of it for their fuppofed conditions. Authors are not always free from a willingnefs to receive the fallacious fort of refpect, that attaches to accidental circum-ftances, for the real fort, of which it would be more reafonable to be proud. A man, relating part of the hiftory of his life, which is always ne-ceffarily done by a writer of travels, does not choofe to fhew that his courfe could lie through any fcenes deficient of delights; or that, if it did, he was not enough elevated by his friends, impor-tance, fortune, fame, or bufinefs, to be incapable of obferving them minutely. The curiofities of cabinets and of courts are, therefore, exactly de-fcribed, and as much of every occurrence as does not fhew the relater moving in any of the plainer walks of life; but the difference between the ftock of phyfical comforts in different countries, the character of conditions, if the phrafe may be ufed, fuch as it appears in the ordinary circumftances of refidence, drefs, food, cleanlinefs, opportunities of relaxation; in fhort, the information, which all may gain, is fometimes left to be gained by all, not from the book, but from travel. A wri-ter, iffuing into the world, makes up what he miftakes for his beft appearance, and is continu-ally telling his happinefs, or fhewing his good-humour, as people in a promenade always fmile, and always look round to obferve whether they are feen fmiling. The politeft falutation of the Chinefe, when they meet, is, " Sir, profperity is painted on your countenance;" or, " your whole air announces your felicity;" and the wri-

ters

ters of travels, especially since the censure thrown upon SMOLLET, seem to provide, that their prosperity shall be painted on their volumes, and all their observations announce their felicity.

Cologne, though it bears the name of the Electorate, by which it is surrounded, is an imperial city; and the Elector, as to temporal affairs, has very little jurisdiction within it. The government has an affectation of being formed upon the model of Republican Rome; a form certainly not worthy of imitation, but which is as much disgraced by this burlesque of it, as ancient statues are by the gilding and the wigs, with which they are said to be sometimes arrayed by modern hands. There is a senate of forty-nine persons, who, being returned at different times of the year, are partly nominated by the remaining members, and partly chosen by twenty-two tribes of burgesses, or rather by so many companies of traders. Of six burgomasters, two are in office every third year, and, when these appear in public, they are preceded by LICTORS, bearing *fasces*, surmounted by their *own arms!* Each of the tribes, or companies, has a President, and the twenty-two Presidents form a Council, which is authorised to enquire into the conduct of the Senate: but the humbleness of the burgesses in their individual condition has virtually abolished all this scheme of a political constitution. Without some of the intelligence and personal independence, which are but little consistent with the general poverty and indolence of German traders, nothing but the forms of any constitution can be preserved, long after the virtual destruction of it has been meditated by those in a better con-

H   dition.

dition. The greater part of thefe companies of traders having, in fact, no trade which can place them much above the rank of menial fervants to their rich cuftomers, the defign, that their Council fhall check the Senate, and the Senate direct the Burgomafters, has now, of courfe, little effect. And this, or a ftill humbler condition, is that of feveral cities in Germany, called free and independent, in which the neighbouring fovereigns have fcarcely lefs authority, though with fomething more of circumftance, than in their own dominions.

The conftitution of Cologne permits, indeed, fome direct interference of the Elector; for the Tribunal of Appeal, which is the fupreme court of law, is nominated by him: he has otherwife no direct power within the city; and being forbidden to refide there more than three days fucceffively, he does not even retain a palace, but is contented with a fuite of apartments, referved for his ufe at an inn. That this exclufion is no punifhment, thofe, who have ever paffed two days at Cologne, will admit; and it can tend very little to leffen his influence, for the greateft part of his perfonal expenditure muft reach the merchants of the place; and the officers of feveral of his territorial jurifdictions make part of the inhabitants. His refidences, with which he is remarkably well provided, are at Bonn; at Bruhl, a palace between Cologne and that place; at Poppelfdorff, which is beyond it; at Herzogs Freud, an hunting feat; and in Munfter, of which he is the Bifhop.

The duties of cuftoms and excife are impofed by the magiftrates of the city, and thefe

enable

enable them to pay their contributions to the
Germanic fund; for, though such cities are formally independent of the neighbouring princes
and nobility, they are not so of the general
laws or expences of the empire, in the Diet of
which they have some small share, forty-nine
cities being allowed to send two representatives,
and thus to have two votes out of an hundred and thirty-six. These duties, of both
sorts, are very high at Cologne; and the first
form a considerable part of the interruptions,
which all the States upon the Rhine give to
the commerce of that river. Here also commodities, intended to be carried beyond the
city by water, must be re-shipped; for, in order to provide cargoes for the boatmen of the
place, vessels from the lower parts of the Rhine
are not allowed to ascend beyond Cologne, and
those from the higher parts cannot descend it
farther. They may, indeed, reload with other
cargoes for their return; and, as they constantly do so, the Cologne boatmen are not
much benefited by the regulation; but the
transfer of the goods employs some hands,
subjects them better to the inspection of the
customhouse officers, and makes it necessary
for the merchants of places, on both sides,
trading which each other, to have intermediate
correspondents here. Yet, notwithstanding all
this aggression upon the freedom of trade,
Cologne is less considerable as a port, than
some Dutch towns, never mentioned in a book,
and is inferior, perhaps, to half the minor sea-
ports in England. We could not find more than
thirty vessels of burthen against the quay, all
mean and ill-built, except the Dutch, which are
very large, and, being constructed purposely for

a tedious

a tedious navigation, contain apartments upon the deck for the family of the skipper, well furnished, and so commodious as to have four or five sashed windows on each side, generally gay with flower-pots. Little flower-gardens, too, sometimes formed upon the roof of the cabin, increase the domestic comforts of the skipper; and the neatness of his vessel can, perhaps, be equalled only by that of a Dutch house. In a time of perfect peace, there is no doubt more traffic; but, from what we saw of the general means and occasions of commerce in Germany, we cannot suppose it to be much reduced by war. Wealthy and commercial countries may be injured immensely by making war either for Germany or against it; by too much friendship or too much enmity; but Germany itself cannot be proportionately injured with them, except when it is the scene of actual violence. Englishmen, who feel, as they always must, the love of their own country much increased by the view of others, should be induced, at every step, to wish, that there may be as little political intercourse as possible, either of friendship or enmity, between the blessings of their Island and the wretchedness of the Continent.

Our inn had formerly been a convent, and was in a part of the town where such societies are more numerous than elsewhere. At five o'clock, on the Sunday after our arrival, the bells of churches and convents began to sound on all sides, and there was scarcely any entire intermission of them till evening. The places of public amusement, chiefly a sort of tea-gardens, were then set open, and, in many streets, the sound of music and dancing was heard almost as plainly as that of the bells had been before; a disgust-
ing

ing excefs of licentioufnefs, which appeared in other inftances, for we heard, at the fame time, the voices of a choir on one fide of the ftreet, and the noife of a billiard table on the other. Near the inn, this contraft was more obfervable. While the ftrains of revelry arofe from an adjoining garden, into which our windows opened, a paufe in the mufic allowed us to catch fome notes of the vefper fervice, performing in a convent of the order of Clariffe, only three or four doors beyond. Of the fevere rules of this fociety we had been told in the morning. The members take a vow, not only to renounce the world, but their deareft friends, and are never after permitted to fee even their fathers or mothers, though they may fometimes converfe with the latter from behind a curtain. And, left fome lingering remains of filial affection fhould tempt an unhappy nun to lift the veil of feparation between herfelf and her mother, fhe is not allowed to fpeak even with her, but in the prefence of the abbefs. Accounts of fuch horrible perverfions of human reafon make the blood thrill and the teeth chatter. Their fathers they can never fpeak to, for no man is fuffered to be in any part of the convent ufed by the fifterhood, nor, indeed, is admitted beyond the gate, except when there is a neceffity for repairs, when all the votaries of the order are previoufly fecluded. It is not eafily that a cautious mind becomes convinced of the exiftence of fuch fevere orders; when it does, aftonifhment at the artificial miferies, which the ingenuity of human beings forms for themfelves by feclufion, is as boundlefs as at the other miferies, with which the moft trivial vanity and envy fo frequently pollute the intercourfes of focial life. The poor nuns, thus nearly entombed during

ing their lives, are, after death, tied upon a board, in the clothes they die in, and, with only their veils thrown over the face, are buried in the garden of the convent.

During this day, Trinity Sunday, proceſſions were paſſing on all ſides, moſt of them attended by ſome ſort of martial muſic. Many of the pariſhes, of which there are nineteen, paraded with their officers; and the burgeſſes, who are diſtributed into eight corps, under a ſuppoſition that they could and would defend the city, if it was attacked, preſented their captains at the churches. The hoſt accompanied all theſe proceſſions. A party of the city guards followed, and forty or fifty perſons out of uniform, the repreſentatives probably of the burgeſſes, who are about ſix thouſand, ſucceeded. Beſides the guards, there was only one man in uniform, who, in the burleſque dreſs of a drum-major, entertained the populace by a kind of extravagant marching dance, in the middle of the proceſſion. Our companion would not tell us that this was the captain.

The cathedral, though unfiniſhed, is conſpicuous, amongſt a great number of churches, for the dignity of ſome detached features, that ſhew part of the vaſt deſign formed for the whole. It was begun, in 1248, by the Elector Conrad, who is related, in an hexameter inſcription over a gate, to have laid the firſt ſtone himſelf. In 1320, the choir was finiſhed, and the workmen continued to be employed upon the other parts in 1499, when of two towers, deſtined to be 580 feet above the roof, one had riſen 21 feet, and the other 150 feet, according to the meaſurement mentioned in a printed deſcription. We did not learn at what
period

period the defign of completing the edifice was abandoned; but the original founder lived to fee all the treafures expended, which he had collected for the purpofe. In its prefent ftate, the inequality of its vaft towers renders it a ftriking object at a confiderable diftance; and, from the large un-filled area around it, the magnificence of its Go-thic architecture, efpecially of fome parts, which have not been joined to the reft, and appear to be the ruined remains, rather than the commence-ment of a work, is viewed with awful delight.

In the interior of the cathedral, a fine choir leads to an altar of black marble, raifed above feveral fteps, which, being free from the incon-gruous ornaments ufual in Romifh churches, is left to imprefs the mind by its majeftic plainnefs. The tall painted windows above, of which there are fix, are fuperior in richnefs of colouring and defign to any we ever faw; beyond even thofe in the Chapter-houfe at York, and moft refembling the very fine ones in the cathedral of Canterbury. The nave is deformed by a low wooden roof, which appears to have been intended only as a temporary covering, and fhould certainly be fuc-ceeded by one of equal dignity to the vaft co-lumns placed for its fupport, whether the other parts of the original defign can ever be completed or not.

By fome accident we did not fee the tomb of the three kings of Jerufalem, whofe bodies are af-firmed to have been brought here from Milan in 1162, when the latter city was deftroyed by the Emperor Frederic Barbaroffa. Their boafted treafures of golden crowns and diamonds pafs, of courfe, without our eftimation.

A defcription

A defcription of the churches in Cologne, fet out with good antiquarian minutenefs, would fill volumes. The whole number of churches, chapters and chapels, which laft are by far the moft numerous, is not lefs than eighty, and none are without an hiftory of two or three centuries. They are all opened on Sundays; and we can believe, that the city may contain, as is afferted, 40,000 fouls, for nearly all that we faw were well attended. In one, indeed, the congregation confifted only of two or three females, kneeling at a great diftance from the altar, with an appearance of the utmoft intentnefs upon the fervice, and abftraction from the noife of the proceffions, that could be eafily heard within. They were entirely covered with a loofe black drapery; whether for penance, or not, we did not hear. In the cathedral, a figure in the fame attitude was rendered more interefting by her fituation beneath the broken arches and fhattered fret-work of a painted window, through which the rays of the fun fcarcely penetrated to break the fhade fhe had chofen.

Several of the chapels are not much larger than an ordinary apartment, but they are higher, that the nuns of fome adjoining convent may have a gallery, where, veiled from obfervation by a lawn curtain, their voices often mingle fweetly with the choir. There are thirty-nine convents of women and nineteen of men, which are fuppofed to contain about fifteen hundred perfons. The chapters, of which fome are noble and extremely opulent, fupport nearly four hundred more; and there are faid to be, upon the whole, between two and three thoufand perfons, under religious denominations,

minations, in Cologne. Walls of convents and their gardens appear in every ſtreet, but do not attract notice, unleſs, as frequently happens, their bell ſounds while you are paſſing. Some of their female inhabitants may be ſeen in various parts of the city, for there is an order, the members of which are employed, by rotation, in teaching children and attending the ſick. Thoſe of the noble chapters are little more confined than if they were with their own families, being permitted to viſit their friends, to appear at balls and promenades, to wear what dreſſes they pleaſe, except when they chaunt in the choir, and to quit the chapter, if the offer of an acceptable marriage induces their families to authoriſe it; but their own admiſſion into the chapter proves them to be noble by ſixteen quarterings, or four generations, and the offer muſt be from a perſon of equal rank, or their deſcendants could not be received into ſimilar chapters; an important circumſtance in the affairs of the German nobleſſe.

Some of theſe ladies we ſaw in the church of their convent. Their habits were remarkably graceful; robes of lawn and black ſilk flowed from the ſhoulder, whence a quilled ruff, ſomewhat reſembling that of Queen Elizabeth's time, ſpread round the neck. The hair was in curls, without powder, and in the Engliſh faſhion. Their voices were peculiarly ſweet, and they ſung the reſponſes with a kind of plaintive tenderneſs, that was extremely intereſting.

The Jeſuits' church is one of the grandeſt in Cologne, and has the greateſt diſplay of paintings over its numerous altars, as well as of marble pillars. The churches of the chapters are, for the moſt part, very large, and endowed with the
richeſt

richeft ornaments, which are, however, not fhewn to the public, except upon days of fête. We do not remember to have feen that of the chapter of St. Urfula, where heads and other relics are faid to be handed to you from fhelves, like books in a library; nor that of the convent of Jacobins, where fome MSS. and other effects of Albert the Great, bifhop of Ratifbon, are among the treafures of the monks.

Oppofite to the Jefuits' church was an hofpital for wounded foldiers, feveral of whom were walking in the court yard before it, half-cloathed in dirty woollen, through which the bare arms of many appeared. Sicknefs and neglect had fubdued all the fymptoms of a foldier; and it was impoffible to diftinguifh the wounded French from the others, though we were affured that feveral of that nation were in the crowd. The windows of the hofpital were filled with figures ftill more wretched. There was a large affemblage of fpectators, who looked as if they were aftonifhed to fee, that war is compounded of fomething elfe, befides the glories, of which it is fo eafy to be informed.

The foldiery of Cologne are under the command of the magiftrates, and are employed only within the gates of the city. The whole body does not exceed an hundred and fifty, whom we faw reviewed by their colonel, in the place before the Hotel de Prague. The uniform is red, faced with white. The men wear whifkers, and affect an air of ferocity, but appear to be moftly invalids, who have grown old in their guard-houfes.

Proteftants, though protected in their perfons, are not allowed the exercife of their religion within in the walls of the city, but have a chapel in a village on the other fide of the Rhine. As fome of the chief merchants, and thofe who are moft ufeful to the inhabitants, are of the reformed church, they ventured lately to requeft that they might have a place of worfhip within the city; but they received the common anfwer, which oppofes all fort of improvement, religious or civil, that, though the privilege in itfelf might be juftly required, it could not be granted, becaufe they would then think of afking fomething more.

The government of Cologne in ecclefiaftical affairs is with the Elector, as archbifhop, and the Chapter as his council. In civil matters, though the city conftitution is of little effect, the real power is not fo conftantly with him as might be fuppofed; thofe, who have influence, being fometimes out of his intereft. Converfation, as we were told, was fcarcely lefs free than in Holland, where there is juftly no oppofition to any opinion, however improper, or abfurd, except from the reafon of thofe, who hear it. On that account, and becaufe of its eafy intercourfe with Bruffels and Spa, this city is fomewhat the refort of ftrangers, by whom fuch converfation is, perhaps, chiefly carried on; but thofe muft come from very wretched countries, who can find pleafure in a refidence at Cologne.

Amongft the public buildings muft be reckoned the Theatre, of which we did not fee the infide, there being no performance, during our ftay, except on Sunday. This, it feems, may be opened, without offence to the Magiftrates, though a proteftant church may not. It ftands in a row of fmall houfes, from which it is diftinguifhed only
by

by a painted front, once tawdry and now dirty, with the infcription, " *Mufis Gratiifque decentibus.*" The Town-houfe is an awkward and irregular ftone building. The arfenal, which is in one of the narroweft ftreets, we fhould have paffed, without notice, if it had not been pointed out to us. As a building, it is nothing more than fuch as might be formed out of four or five of the plaineft houfes laid into one. Its contents are faid to be chiefly antient arms, of various fafhions and fizes, not very proper for modern ufe.

BONN.

AFTER a ftay of nearly three tedious days, we left Cologne for Bonn, paffing through an avenue of limes, which extends from one place to the other, without interruption, except where there is a fmall half way village. The diftance is not lefs than eighteen miles, and the diverfified culture of the plains, through which it paffes, is unufually grateful to the eye, after the dirty buildings of Cologne and the long uniformity of corn lands in the approach to it. Vines cover a great part of thefe plains, and are here firft feen in Germany, except, indeed, within the walls of Cologne itfelf, which contain many large inclofures, converted from gardens and orchards into well fheltered vineyards. The vines reminded us of Englifh hop plants, being fet, like them, in rows, and led round poles to various heights, though all lefs than that of hops. Corn, fruit or herbs were frequently growing between the rows, whofe light green foliage mingled beautifully with yellow wheat and larger patches of garden plantations, that fpread,

without

without any inclofures, to the fweeping Rhine, on the left. Beyond, appeared the blue ridges of Weftphalian mountains. On the right, the plains extend to a chain of lower and lefs diftant hills, whofe fkirts are covered with vines and fummits darkened with thick woods.

The Elector's palace of Bruhl is on the right hand of the road, at no great diftance, but we were not told, till afterwards, of the magnificent architecture and furniture, which ought to have attracted our curiofity.

On a green and circular hill, near the Rhine, ftands the Benedictine abbey of Siegbourg, one of the firft picturefque objects of the rich approach to Bonn ; and, further on, the caftle-like towers of a convent of noble ladies ; both focieties cele-brated for their wealth and the pleafantnefs of their fituations, which command extenfive prof-pects over the country, on each fide of the river. As we drew near Bonn, we frequently caught, be-tween the trees of the avenue, imperfect, but awakening glimpfes of the pointed mountains be-yond ; contrafted with the folemn grandeur of which was the beauty of a round woody hill, ap-parently feparated from them only by the Rhine and crowned with the fpire of a comely convent. Bonn, with tall flender fteeples and the trees of its ramparts, thus backed by fublime mountains, looks well, as you approach it from Cologne, though neither its noble palace, nor the Rhine, which wafhes its walls, are feen from hence,

We were afked our names at the gate, but had no trouble about paffports, or baggage. A long and narrow ftreet leads from thence to the market place,

place, not difgufting you either with the gloom, or the dirt of Cologne, though mean houfes are abundantly intermixed with the others, and the beft are far from admirable. The *phyfiognomy of the place*, if one may ufe the expreffion, is wholefome, though humble. By the recommendation of a Dutch merchant, we went to an inn in another ftreet, branching from the market place, and found it-the cleaneft, fince we had left Holland.

Bonn may be called the political capital of the country, the Elector's Court being held only there; and, what would not be expected, this has importance enough to command the refidence of an agent from almoft every Power in Europe. The prefent Elector being the uncle of the Emperor, this attention is, perhaps, partly paid, with the view, that it may be felt at the Court of Vienna. Even Ruffia is not unreprefented in this miniature State.

The Elector's palace is, in point of grandeur, much better fitted to be the fcene of diplomatic ceremonies, than thofe of many greater Sovereigns; and it is fitted alfo for better than diplomatic purpofes, being placed before fome of the moft ftriking of nature's features, of which it is nearly as worthy an ornament as art can make. It is feated on the weftern bank of the Rhine, the general courfe of which it fronts, though it forms a confiderable angle with the part immediately neareft. The firft emotion, on perceiving it, being that of admiration, at its vaftnefs, the wonder is, of courfe, equal, with which you difcover, that it is only part of a greater defign. It confifts of a centre and an eaftern wing, which are completed, and of a weftern wing, of which not half is yet raifed. The extent from eaft to weft is fo great, that, if we

had

had enquired the meafurement, we fhould have been but little affifted in giving an idea of the fpectacle, exhibited by fo immenfe a building.

It is of ftone, of an architecture, perhaps, not adequate to the grandeur of its extent, but which fills no part with unfuitable, or inelegant ornaments. Along the whole garden front, which is the chief, a broad terrace fupports a promenade and an orangery of noble trees, occafionally refrefhed by fountains, that, ornamented with ftatues, rife from marble bafons. An arcade through the centre of the palace leads to this terrace, from whence the profpect is ftrikingly beautiful and fublime. The eye paffes over the green lawn of the garden and a tract of level country to the groupe, called the Seven Mountains, broken, rocky and abrupt towards their fummits, yet fweeping finely near their bafes, and uniting with the plains by long and gradual defcents, that fpread round many miles. The neareft is about a league and a half off. We faw them under the cloudlefs fky of June, invefted with the miftinefs of heat, which, foftening their rocky points, and half veiling their receffes, left much for the imagination to fupply, and gave them an aërial appearance, a faint tint of filvery grey, that was inexpreffibly interefting. The Rhine, that winds at their feet, was concealed from us by the garden groves, but from the upper windows of the palace it is feen in all its majefty.

On the right from this terrace, the fmaller palace of Poppelfdorff terminates a long avenue of limes and chefnut trees, that communicates with both buildings, and above are the hill and the convent, *Sancta Crucis,* the latter looking out from

among

among firs and fhrubby fteeps. From thence the weftern horizon is bounded by a range of hills, cloathed to their fummits with wood. The plain, that extends between thefe and the Rhine, is cultivated with vines and corn, and the middle diftance is marked by a pyramidal mountain, darkened by wood and crowned with the tower and walls of a ruined caftle.

The gardens of the palace are formally laid out in ftraight walks and alleys of cut trees; but the fpacious lawn between thefe gives fine effect to the perfpective of the diftant mountains; and the bowery walks, while they afford refrefhing fhelter from a fummer fun, allow partial views of the palace and the romantic landfcape.

It was the Elector Jofeph Clement, the fame who repaired the city, left in a ruinous ftate by the fiege of 1703, under the Duke of Marlborough, that built this magnificent refidence. There are in it many fuits of ftate rooms and every fort of apartment ufual in the manfions of Sovereigns; faloons of audience and ceremony, a library, a cabinet of natural hiftory and a theatre. Though thefe are readily opened to ftrangers, we are to confefs, that we did not fee them, being prevented by the attentions of thofe, whofe civilities gave them a right to command us, while their fituations enabled them to point out the beft occupation of our time. The hall of the grand mafter of the Teutonic order, ornamented with portraits of all the grand mafters, we are, however, forry to have neglected even for the delights of Poppelfdorff, which we were prefently fhewn.

Leaving the palace, we paffed through the garden, on the right, to a fine avenue of turf, nearly
a mile

a mile long, bordered by alleys of tall trees, and
fo wide, that the late Elector had defigned to form
a canal in the middle of it, for an opportunity
of paffing between his palaces, by land, or water,
as he might wifh. The palace of Poppelfdorff terminates the perfpective of this avenue. It is
a fmall building, furrounded by its gardens, in
a tafte not very good, and remarkable chiefly for
the pleafantnefs of its fituation. An arcade, en-
compaffing a court in the interior, communicates
with all the apartments on the ground floor, which
is the principal, and with the gardens, on the
eaftern fide of the chateau. The entrance is
through a fmall hall, decorated with the enfigns
of hunting, and round nearly the whole arcade
ftags' heads are placed, at equal diftances. Thefe
have remained here, fince the reign of Clement
Auguftus, the founder of the palace, who died
in 1761; and they exhibit fome part of the hiftory
of his life; for, under each, is an infcription,
relating the events and date of the hunt, by which
he killed it. There are twenty-three fuch ornaments.

The greateft part of the furniture had been removed, during the approach of the French, in
1792; and the Archduchefs Maria Chriftina, to
whom the Elector, her brother, had lent the
chateau, was now very far from fumptuoufly accommodated. On this account, fhe paffed much
of her time at Goodefberg, a fmall watering
place in the neighbourhood. After her retreat
from Bruffels, in confequence of the advances of
the French in the fame year, fhe had accompanied her hufband, the Duke of Saxe Tefchen,
into Saxony; but, fince his appointment to the
command of th Emperor's army of the Upper

I   Rhine,

Rhine, her refidence had been eftablifhed in the dominions of her brother.

We were fhewn through her apartments, which fhe had left for Goodefberg, a few hours before. On the table of her fitting room lay the fragments of a painted crofs, compofed of fmall pieces, like our diffected maps, the putting of which together exercifes ingenuity, and paffes, perhaps, for a fort of piety. The attendant faid, that it ferved to pafs the time ; but it cannot be fuppofed, that rank and fortune have fo little power to beftow happinefs, as that their poffeffors fhould have recourfe to fuch means of lightening the hours of life.

On another table, was fpread a map of all the countries, then included in the Theatre of War, and on it a box, filled with fmall pieces of various coloured wax, intended to mark the pofitions of the different armies. Thefe were of many fhades, for the Archduchefs, who is faid to be converfant with military affairs and to have defcended to the firing of bombs at the fiege of Lifle, was able to diftinguifh the feveral corps of the allied armies, that were acting feparately from each other. The pofitions were marked up to the lateft accounts then public. The courfe of her thoughts was vifible from this chart, and they were interefting to curiofity, being thofe of the fifter of the late unfortunate Queen of France.

The walls of an adjoining cabinet were ornamented with drawings from the antique by the Archduchefs, difpofed upon a light ground and ferving inftead of tapeftry.

The

The chapel is a rotunda, rifing into a dome, and, though fmall, is fplendid with painting and gilding. In the centre are four altars, formed on the four fides of a fquare pedeftal, that fupports a figure of our Saviour; but the beauty of this defign is marred by the vanity of placing near each altar the ftatue of a founder of the Teutonic order. The furniture of the Elector's gallery is of crimfon velvet and gold.

On another fide of the chateau, we were fhewn an apartment entirely covered with grotto work, and called the hall of fhells; a curious inftance of patient induftry, having been completed by one man, during a labour of many years. Its fituation in the middle of an inhabited manfion is unfuitable to the character of a grotto; but its coolnefs muft render it a very convenient retreat, and the likeneffes of animals, as well as the other forms, into which the fhells are thrown, though not very elegant, are fanciful enough, efpecially as the ornaments of fountains, which play into feveral parts of the room.

Leaving the palace by the bridge of a moat, that nearly furrounds it, we paffed through the pleafant village of Poppelfdorff, and afcended the hill SANCTÆ CRUCIS, called fo from the convent of the fame name, which occupies its fummit. The road wound between thick woods, but we foon left it for a path, that led more immediately to the fummit, among fhrubs and plantations of larch and fir, and which opened into eafy avenues of turf, that fometimes allowed momentary views of other woody points and of the plains around.

I 2   The

The turf was uncommonly fragrant and fine, abounding with plants, which made us regret the want of a Botanist's knowledge and pleasures. During the afcent, the peaked tops of the mountains of the Rhine, fo often admired below, began to appear above a ridge of dark woods, very near us, in a contraft of hues, which was exquifitely fine. It was now near evening; the miftinefs of heat was gone from the furface of thefe mountains, and they had affumed a blue tint fo peculiar and clear, that they appeared upon the fky, like fupernatural tranfparencies.

We had heard, at Bonn, of the Capauchins' courtefy, and had no hefitation to knock at their gate, after taking fome reft in the portico of the church, from whence we looked down another fide of the mountain, over the long plains between Bonn and Cologne. Having waited fome time at the gate, during which many fteps fled along the paffage, and the head of a monk appeared peeping through a window above, a fervant admitted us into a parlour, adjoining the refectory, which appeared to have been juft left. This was the firft convent we had entered, and we could not help expecting to fee more than others had defcribed; an involuntary habit, from which few are free, and which need not be imputed to vanity, fo long as the love of furprife fhall be fo vifible in human purfuits. When the lay-brother had quitted us, to inform the fuperior of our requeft, not a footftep, or a voice approached, for near a quarter of an hour, and the place feemed as if uninhabited. Our curiofity had no indulgence within the room, which was of the utmoft plainnefs, and that plainnefs

nefs free from any thing, that the moft tractable
imagination could fuppofe peculiar to a convent.
At length, a monk appeared, who received us
with infinite good humour, and with the eafe
which muft have been acquired in more general
fociety. His fhaven head and black garments
formed a whimfical contraft to the character of
his perfon and countenance, which bore no fymptoms of forrow, or penance, and were, indeed,
animated by an air of cheerfulnefs and intelligence, that would have become the happieft inhabitant of the gayeft city.

Through fome filent paffages, in which he did
not fhew us a cell and we did not perceive
another monk, we paffed to the church, where
the favour of feveral Electors has affifted the difplay of paintings, marble, fculpture, gold and
filver, mingled and arranged with magnificent
effect. Among thefe was the marble ftatue,
brought from England, at a great expence, and
here called a reprefentation of St. Anne, who is
faid to have found the Crofs. Our conductor
feemed to be a man of good underftanding and
defirous of being thought fo ; a difpofition, which
gave an awkwardnefs to his manner, when, in no-
ticing a relic, he was obliged to touch upon fome
unproved and unimportant tradition, peculiar to
his church and not effential to the leaft article of
our faith. His fenfe of decorum as a member
of the convent feemed then to be ftruggling
with his vanity, as a man.

But there are relics here, pretending to a connection with fome parts of chriftian hiftory, which

it

it is shocking to see introduced to consideration by any means so trivial and so liable to ridicule. It is, indeed, wonderful, that the absurd exhibitions, made in Romish churches, should so often be minutely described, and dwelt upon in terms of ludicrous exultation by those, who do not intend that most malignant of offences against human nature, the endeavour to excite a wretched vanity by sarcasm and jest, and to employ it in eradicating the comforts of religion. To such writers, the probable mischief of uniting with the mention of the most important divine doctrines the most ridiculous of human impositions ought to be apparent; and, as the risk is unnecessary in a Protestant country, why is it encountered? That persons otherwise inclined should adopt these topics is not suprising; the easiest pretences to wit are found to be made by means of familiar allusions to sacred subjects, because their necessary incongruity accomplishes the greatest part of what, in other cases, must be done by wit itself; there will, therefore, never be an end of such allusions, till it is generally seen, that they are the resources and symptoms of mean understandings, urged by the feverish desire of an eminence, to which they feel themselves inadequate.

From the chapel we ascended to a tower of the convent, whence all the scattered scenes, of whose beauty, or sublimity, we had caught partial glimpses between the woods below, were collected into one vast landscape, and exhibited almost to a single glance. The point, on which the convent stands, commands the whole horizon. To the north, spread the wide plains, before seen, covered with corn, then just embrowned, and

and with vines and gardens, whofe alternate colours formed a gay checker work with villages, convents and caftles. The grandeur of this level was unbroken by any inclofures, that could feem to diminifh its vaftnefs. The range of woody heights, that bound it on the weft, extend to the fouthward, many leagues beyond the hill *Sanctæ Crucis;* but the uniform and unbroken ridges of diftant mountains, on the eaft, ceafe before the Seven Mountains rife above the Rhine in all their awful majefty. The bafes of the latter were yet concealed by the woody ridge near the convent, which gives fuch enchanting effect to their aërial points. The fky above them was clear and glowing, unftained by the lighteft vapour; and thefe mountains ftill appeared upon it, like unfubftantial vifions. On the two higheft pinnacles we could juft diftinguifh the ruins of caftles, and, on a lower precipice, a building, which our reverend guide pointed out as a convent, dedicated to St. Bernard, giving us new occafion to admire the fine tafte of the monks in their choice of fituations.

Oppofite to the Seven Mountains, the plains of Goodefberg are fcreened by the chain of hills already mentioned, which begin in the neighbourhood of Cologne, and whofe woods, fpreading into France, there affume the name of the Foreft of Ardennes. Within the recesses of thefe woods the Elector has a hunting-feat, almoft every window of which opens upon a different alley, and not a ftag can acrofs thefe without being feen from the chateau. It is melancholy to confider, that the moft frequent motives of man's retirement among the beautiful recefses receffes of nature, are only thofe of deftroying the innocent animals that inhabit her fhades. Strange! that her lovely fcenes cannot foften his heart to milder pleafures, or elevate his fancy to nobler purfuits, and that he muft ftill feek his amufement in fcattering death among the harmlefs and the happy.

As we afterwards walked in the garden of the convent, the greater part of which was planted with vines, the monk further exhibited his good humour and liberality. He enquired concerning the events of the war, of which he appeared to know the lateft; fpoke of his friends in Cologne and other places; drew a ludicrous picture of the effect which would be produced by the appearance of a capuchin in London, and laughed immoderately at it. "There," faid he, "it would be fuppofed, that fome harlequin was walking in a capuchin's drefs to attract fpectators for a pantomime; here nobody will follow him, left he fhould lead them to church. Every nation has its way, and laughs at the ways of others. Confidering the effects, which differences fometimes have, there are few things more innocent than that fort of laughter."

The garden was ftored with fruits and the vegetable luxuries of the table, but was laid out with no attention to beauty, its inimitable profpects having, as the good monk faid, rendered the fociety carelefs of lefs advantanges. After exchanging our thanks for his civilities againft his thanks for the vifit, we defcended to Poppelfdorff by a fteep road, bordered with firs and fragrant fhrubs, which frequntly opened to corn lands and vineyards, where peafants were bufied in dreffing the vines.

About

About a mile from Bonn is a garden, or rather nurſery, to which they have given the name of *Vauxhall.* It is much more rural than that of London, being planted with thick and lofty groves, which, in this climate, are gratefully refreſhing, during the ſummer-day, but are very pernicious in the evening, when the vapour, ariſing from the ground, cannot eſcape through the thick foliage. The garden is lighted up only on great feſtivals, or when the Elector or his courtiers give a ball in a large room built for the purpoſe. On ſome days, half the inhabitants of Bonn are to be ſeen in this garden, mingling in the promenade with the Elector and his nobility; but there were few viſitors when we ſaw it. Count GIMNICH, the commander, who had ſurrendered Mentz to the French, was the only perſon pointed out to us.

The road from hence to Bonn was laid out and planted with poplars at the expence of the Elector, who has a taſte for works of public advantage and ornament. His Grand-maſterſhip of the Teutonic Order renders his Court more frequented than thoſe of the other eccleſiaſtical Princes, the poſſeſſions of that Order being ſtill conſiderable enough to ſupport many younger brothers of noble families. Having paſſed his youth in the army, or at the courts of Vienna or Bruſſels, he is alſo environed by friends, made before the vacancy of an eccleſiaſtical electorate induced him to change his profeſſion; and the union of his three incomes, as Biſhop of Munſter, Grand Maſter and Elector, enables him to ſpend ſomething more than two hundred thouſand pounds annually. His experience and revenues are, in

many

many refpects, very ufefully employed. To the
nobility he affords an example of fo much perfonal dignity, as to be able to reject many oftentatious cuftoms, and to remove fome of the ce-
remonial barriers, which men do not conftantly
place between themfelves and their fellow-beings,
except from fome confcioufnefs of perfonal weak-
nefs. All fovereigns, who have had any fenfe
of their individual liberty and power, have fhewn
a readinefs to remove fuch barriers; but not
many have been able to effect fo much as the Elector of Cologne againft the chamberlains, pages,
and other footmanry of their courts, who are always upon the *alerte* to defend the falfe magnificence that makes their offices feem neceflary.
He now enjoys many of the bleffings, ufual only
in private ftations; among others, that of converfing with great numbers of perfons, not forced into his fociety by their rank, and of difpenfing with much of that attendance, which
would render his menial fevants part of his company.

His fecretary, Mr. Floret, whom we had the
pleafure to fee, gave us fome accounts of the induftry and carefulnefs of his private life, which
he judicioufly thought were better than any other
panegyrics upon his mafter. His attention to
the relief, employment and education of the poor,
to the ftate of manufactures and the encouragement of talents, appears to be continual;
and his country would foon have elapfed from
the general wretchednefs of Germany, if the
exertions of three campaigns had not deftroyed
what thirty years of care and improvement cannot
reftore.

His

His refidence at Bonn occafions expenditure enough to keep the people bufy, but he has not been able to divert to it any part of the commerce, which, though it is of fo little ufe at Cologne, is here fpoken of with fome envy, and feems to bo eftimated above its amount. The town, which is much neater than the others in the electorate, and fo pleafantly fituated, that its name has been fuppofed to be formed from the Latin fynonym for good, is ornamented by few public buildings, except the palace. What is called the Univerfity is a fmall brick building, ufed more as a fchool than a college, except that the mafters are called profeffors. The principal church of four, which are within the walls, is a large building, diftinguifhed by feveral fpires, but not remarkable for its antiquity or beauty.

Many of the German powers retain fome fhew of a reprefentative government, as to affairs of finances, and have States, by which taxes are voted. Thofe of the electorate of Cologne confift of four colleges, reprefenting the clergy, nobility, knights and cities; the votes are given by colleges, fo that the inhabitants of the cities, if they elect their reprefentatives fairly, have one vote in four. Thefe States affemble at Bonn.

One of the privileges, which it is furprifing that the prefent Elector fhould retain, is that of grinding corn for the confumption of the whole town. His mill, like thofe of all the towns on the Rhine, is a floating one, moored in the river, which turns its wheel. Bread is bad at Bonn; but this oppreffive privilege is not entirely anfwerable for it, there being little better throughout the whole country. It generally appears in rolls, with glazed crufts, half hollow; the crumb not brown, but a fort of dirty white.

There

There are few cities in Germany without walls, which, when the dreadful science of war was less advanced than at present, frequently protected them against large armies. These are now so useless, that such cannon as are employed against batteries could probably not be fired from them without shaking their foundations. The fortifications of Bonn are of this sort; and, though they were doubtless better, when the Duke of Marlborough arrived before them, it is wonderful that they should have sustained a regular siege, during which great part of the town was demolished. The electorate of Cologne is, so ill prepared indeed, for war, that it has not one town, which could resist ten thousand men for three days.

The inhabitants of Bonn, whenever they regret the loss of their fortifications, should be reminded of the three sieges, which, in the course of thirty years, nearly destroyed their city. Of these the first was in 1673, when the Elector had received a French garrison into it; but the resistance did not then continue many days. It was in this siege that the Prince of Orange, afterwards our honoured William the Third, had one of his few military successes. In 1689, the French who had lately defended it, returned to attack it; and, before they could subdue the strong garrison left in it by the Elector of Brandenburg, the palace and several public buildings were destroyed. The third siege was commanded by the Duke of Marlborough, and continued from the 24th of April to the 16th of May, the French being then the defenders, and the celebrated Cohorn one of the assailants. It was not till fifteen years afterwards, that all the houses, demolished in this siege,

　　　　　　　　　　　　　　　could

could be reftored by the efforts of the Elector Jofeph.

The prefent Elector maintains, in time of peace, about eight hundred foldiers, which is the number of his contingent to the army of the Empire: in the prefent war he has fupplied fomewhat more than this allotment; and, when we were at Bonn, two thoufand recruits were in training. His troops wear the general uniform of the Empire, blue faced with red, which many of the Germanic fovereigns give only to their contingent troops, while thofe of their feparate eftablifhments are diftinguifhed by other colours. The Auftrian regiments are chiefly in white, faced with light blue, grey, or red; but the artillery are dreffed, with very little fhew, in a cloak fpeckled with light brown.

Bonn was one of the very few places in Germany, which we left with regret. It is endeared to the votaries of landfcape by its fituation in the midft of fruitful plains, in the prefence of ftupendous mountains, and on the bank of a river, that, in fummer, is impelled by the diffolved fnows of Switzerland, and, in winter, rolls with the accumulation of a thoufand torrents from the rocks on its fhores. It contained many inhabitants, who had the independence to aim at a juft tafte in morals and letters, in fpite of the ill examples with which fuch countries fupply them; and, having the vices of the form of government, eftablifhed in it, corrected by the moderation and immediate attention of the governor, it might be confidered as a happy region in the midft of ignorance, injuftice and mifery, and remembered like the green

fpot,

spot, that, in an Arabian defert, cheers the fenfes and fuftains the hopes of the weary traveller.

GOODESBERG.

THE ride from Bonn to this delightful village is only one league over a narrow plain, covered with corn and vineyards. On our right was the range of hills, before feen from the mountain SANCTÆ CRUCIS, fweeping into frequent receffes, and ftarting forward into promontories, with inequalities, which gave exquifite richnefs to the foreft, that mantled from their bafes to their utmoft fummits. Many a lurking village, with its flender grey fteeple, peeped from among the woody fkirts of thefe hills. On our left, the tremendous mountains, that bind the eaftern fhore of the Rhine, gradually loft their aërial complexion, as we approached them, and difplayed new features and new enchantments; an ever-varying illufion, to which the tranfient circumftance of thunder clouds contributed. The fun-beams, ftreaming among thefe clouds, threw partial gleams upon the precipices, and, followed by dark fhadows, gave furprifing and inimitable effect to the natural colouring of the mountains, whofe pointed tops we now difcerned to be covered with dark heath, extended down their rocky fides, and mingled with the reddifh and light yellow tints of other vegetation and the foil. It was delightful to watch the fhadows fweeping over thefe fteeps, now involving them in deep obfcurity, and then leaving
them

them to the fun's rays, which brought out all their hues into vivid contraft.

Near Goodefberg, a fmall mountain, infulated, abrupt and pyramidal, rifes from the plain, which it feems to terminate, and conceals the village, that lies along its fouthern fkirt. This mountain, covered with vineyards and thick dwarf wood to its fummit, where one high tower and fome fhattered walls appear, is a very interefting object.

At the entrance of the village, the road was obftructed by a great number of fmall carts, filled with foldiers apparently wounded. The line of their proceffion had been broken by fome carriages, haftening with company to the ridotto at Goodefberg, and was not eafily reftored. Mifery and feftivity could fcarcely be brought into clofer contraft. We thought of Johnfon's " many-coloured-life," and of his picture, in the preface to Shakefpeare, of cotemporary wretchednefs and joy, when " the reveller is haftening to his wine, and the mourner is burying his friend." This was a proceffion of wounded French prifoners, chiefly boys, whofe appearance had, indeed, led us to fufpect their nation, before we faw the ftamp of the *fafces*, and the words " *Republique Françoife*" upon the buttons of fome, whom our driver had nearly overfet. The few, that could raife themfelves above the floor of their carts, fhewed countenances yellow, or livid with ficknefs. They did not talk to their guards, nor did the latter fhew any figns of exultation over them.

In a plain, beyond the village, a row of large houfes, built upon one plan, and almoft refembling a palace, form the little watering place of Goodefberg,

Goodefberg, which has been founded partly at the expence of the Elector, and partly by individuals under his patronage. One of the houfes was occupied by the Archduchefs, his fifter, and is often ufed by the Elector, who is extremely folicitous for the profperity of the place. A large building at the end contains the public rooms, and is fitted up as an hotel.

The fituation of this houfe is beautiful beyond any hope or power of defcription; for defcription, though it may tell that there are mountains and rocks, cannot paint the grandeur, or the elegance of outline, cannot give the effect of precipices, or draw the minute features, that reward the actual obferver by continual changes of colour, and by varying their forms at every new choice of his pofition. Delightful Goodefberg! the fublime and beautiful of landfcape, the charms of mufic, and the pleafures of gay and elegant fociety, were thine! The immediate unhappinefs of war has now fallen upon thee; but, though the graces may have fled thee, thy terrible majefty remains, beyond the fphere of human contention.

The plain, that contains the village and the Spa, is about five miles in length and of half that breadth. It is covered by uninclofed corn and nearly furrounded by a vaft amphitheatre of mountains. In front of the inn, at the diftance of half a league, extend, along the oppofite fhore of the Rhine, the Seven Mountains, fo long feen and admired, which here affume a new attitude. The three talleft points are now neareft to the eye, and the lower mountains are feen either in the perfpective between them, or finking, with lefs

abrupt

abrupt declivities, into the plains, on the north.
The whole mass exhibits a grandeur of outline,
such as the pencil only can describe; but fancy
may paint the stupendous precipices of rock, that
rise over the Rhine, the rich tuftings of wood,
that emboss the cliffs or lurk within the recesses,
the spiry summits and the ruined castles, faintly
discerned, that crown them. Yet the appearance
of these mountains, though more grand, from
Goodesberg, is less sublime than from Bonn; for
the nearness, which increases their grandeur, di-
minishes their sublimity by removing the obscurity that had veiled them. To the south of this
plain, the long perspective is crossed by further
ranges of mountains; which open to glimpses of
others still beyond; an endless succession of summits, that lead on the imagination to unknown
vallies and regions of solitary obscurity.

Amidst so many attractions of nature, art
cannot do much. The little, which it attempts,
at Goodesberg, is the disposition of some walks
from the houses to a spring, which is said to resemble that at Spa; and through the woods
above it. Twice a week there are some musi-
cal performances and a ball given by the Elector, who frequently appears, and with the ease
and plainness of a private gentleman. At these
entertainments the company, visiting the spring,
are joined by neighbouring families, so as to be
in number sixty, or a hundred. The balls,
agreeably to the earliness of German hours, begin at six; and that, which we meant to see,
was nearly concluded before our arrival. The
company then retired to a public game, at which
large sums of gold were risked, and a severe

K · anxiety

anxiety defied the influence of Mozart's music, that continued to be played by an excellent orcheſtra. The dreſſes of the company were in the Engliſh taſte, and, as we were glad to believe, chiefly of Engliſh manufacture: the wearing of countenances by play appears to be alſo according to our manners, and the German ladies, with features ſcarcely leſs elegant, have complexions, perhaps, finer than are general in England.

- Meditating cenſures againſt the Elector's policy, or careleſſneſs, in this reſpect, we took advantage of the laſt gleams of evening, to aſcend the ſlender and ſpiry mountain, which bears the name of the village, and appears ready to precipitate the ruins of its ancient caſtle upon it. A ſteep road, winding among vineyards and dwarf wood, enters, at the ſummit of the mountain, the broken walls, which ſurround the ancient citadel of the caſtle; an almoſt ſolid building, that has exiſted for more than five centuries. From the area of theſe ruins we ſaw the ſun ſet over the whole line of plains, that extend to the weſtward of Cologne, whoſe ſpires were diſtinctly viſible. Bonn, and the hill SANCTÆ CRUCIS, appeared at a league's diſtance, and the windings of the Rhine gleamed here and there amidſt the rich ſcene, like diſtant lakes. It was a ſtill and beautiful evening, in which no ſhade remained of the thunder clouds, that paſſed in the day. To the weſt, under the glow of ſun-ſet, the landſcape melted into the horizon in tints ſo ſoft, ſo clear, ſo delicately roſeate as Claude only could have painted. Viewed, as we then ſaw it, beyond

yond a deep and dark arch of the ruin, its effect was enchanting ; it was to the eye, what the fineſt ſtrains of Paiſiello are to the heart, or the poetry of Collins is to the fancy—all tender, ſweet, elegant and glowing.

From the other ſide of the hill the character of the view is entirely different, and, inſtead of a long proſpect over an open and level country, the little plain of Goodeſberg appears repoſing amidſt wild and awful mountains. Theſe were now melancholy and ſilent ; the laſt rays were fading from their many points, and the obſcurity of twilight began to ſpread over them. We ſeemed to have found the ſpot, for which Collins wiſhed :

> " Now let me rove ſome wild and heathy ſcene,
> Or find ſome ruin 'midſt its dreary dells,
> Whoſe walls more awful nod
> By thy religious gleams."
>
> ODE TO EVENING.

And this is a place almoſt as renowned in the hiſtory of the country, as it is worthy to exerciſe the powers of poetry and painting. The ſame Erneſt, in the cauſe of whoſe ſovereignty the maſſacre of Neuſs was perpetrated, beſieged here the ſame Gerard de Truſches, the Elector, who had embraced the Proteſtant religion, and for whom Neuſs held out. The caſtle of Goodeſberg was impregnable, except by famine, but was very liable to that from its inſulated ſituation, and the eaſe, with which the whole baſe

of

of the mountain could be furrounded. Gerard's defence was rendered the more obstinate by his belief, that nothing lefs than his life, and that of a beautiful woman, the marrying of whom had conftituted one of the offences againft his Chapter, would appeafe his ferocious enemies. He was perfonally beloved by his garrifon, and they adhered to him with the affection of friends, as well as with the enthufiafm of foldiers. When, therefore, they perceived, that their furrender could not be much longer protracted, they refolved to employ their remaining time and ftrength in enabling him to feparate his fortunes from theirs. They laboured inceffantly in forming a fubterraneous paffage, which fhould open beyond the befiegers' lines; and, though their diftrefs became extreme before this was completed, they made no overtures for a furrender, till Gerard and his wife had efcaped by it. The fugitives arrived fafely in Holland, and the vengeance of their adverfaries was never gratified further than by hearing, many years after, that they died poor.

The fortrefs, rendered interefting by thefe traits of fidelity and misfortune, is not fo far decayed, but that its remains exhibit much of its original form. It covered the whole fummit of the hill, and was valuable as a refidence, as well as a fortification. What feem to have been the walls of the great hall, in which probably the horn of two quarts was often emptied to welcome the gueft, or reward the foldier, are ftill perfect enough to preferve the arches of its capacious windows, and the door-ways, that admitted its feftive trains. The vaft ftrength of the citadel has been unfubdued by war, or time. Though

the

the battlements, that crown it, are broken, and
of a gallery, that once encircled it half way from
the ground, the corbells alone remain, the folid
walls of the building itfelf are unimpaired. At
the narrow door-way, by which only it could be
entered, we measured their thicknefs, and found
it to be more than ten feet, nearly half the diameter of its area. There has never been a fixed
ftaircafe, though thefe walls would fo well have
contained one; and the hole is ftill perfect in the
floor above, through which the garrifon afcended
and drew up their ladder after them. Behind
the loop-holes, the wall has been hollowed, and
would permit a foldier, half bent, to ftand within them and ufe his bow. It was twilight without and night within the edifice; which fancy
might have eafily filled with the ftern and filent
forms of warriors, waiting for their prey, with
the patience of fafety and fure fuperiority.

We wandered long among thefe veftiges of
ancient ftory, rendered ftill more interefting by
the fhadowy hour and the vefper bell of a chapel
on a cliff below. The village, to which this belongs, ftraggles half way up the mountain, and
there are feveral little fhrines above it, which
the cottagers, on feftivals, decorate with flowers.
The Prieft is the fchoolmafter of the parifh, and
almoft all the children, within feveral miles of
the hill, walk to it, every day, to prayers and
leffons. Whether it is from this care of their
minds, or that they are under the authority of
milder landlords than elfewhere, the manners of
the inhabitants in this plain differ much from
thofe, ufual in Germany. Inftead of an inveterate fullennefs, approaching frequently to malignity,

nity, they shew a civility and gentleness in their intercourse with strangers, which leave the enjoyments derived from inanimate nature, unalloyed by the remembrances of human deformity, that mingle with them in other districts. Even the children's begging is in a manner, which shews a different character. They here kifs their little hands, and filently hold them out to you, almost as much in falute, as in entreaty; in many parts of Germany their manner is fo offenfive, not only for its intrufion, but as a fymptom of their difpofition, that nothing but the remembrance of the oppreffion, that produces it, can prevent you from denying the little they are compelled to require.

The mufic had not ceafed, when we returned to the inn; and the mellownefs of French horns, mingled with the tendernefs of hautboys, gave a kind of enchantment to the fcenery, which we continued to watch from our windows. The oppofite mountains of the Rhine were gradually vanifhing in twilight and then as gradually reappearing, as the rifing moon threw her light upon their broken furfaces. The perfpective in the eaft received a filvery foftnefs, which made its heights appear like fhadowy illufions, while the nearer mountains were diftinguifhed by their colouring, as much as by their forms. The broad Rhine, at their feet, rolled a ftream of light for their boundary, on this fide. But the firft exquifite tint of beauty foon began to fade; the mountains became mifty underneath the moon, and, as fhe afcended, thefe mifts thickened, till they veiled the landfcape from our view.

The

The fpring, which is fuppofed to have fome medicinal qualities, is about a quarter of a mile from the rooms, in a woody valley, in which the Elector has laid out feveral roads and walks. It rifes in a ftone bafon, to which the company, if they wifh to drink it on the fpot, defcend by an handfome flight of fteps. We were not told its qualities, but there is a ferrugineous tint upon all the ftones, which it touches. The tafte is flightly unpleafant.

The three fuperior points of the Seven Mountains, which contribute fo much to the diftinction of Goodefberg, are called Drakenfels, Wolkenbourg and Lowenbourg, and have each been crowned by its caftle, of which two are ftill vifible in ruins. There is a ftory faintly recorded, concerning them. Three brothers, refolving to found three diftinguifhed families, took the method, which was anciently in ufe for fuch a purpofe, that of eftablifhing themfelves in fortreffes, from whence they could iffue out, and take what they wanted from their induftrious neighbours. The pinnacles of Drakenfels, Wolkenbourg and Lowenbourg, which, with all affiftance, cannot be afcended now, without the utmoft fatigue, were inacceffible, when guarded by the caftles, built by the three brothers. Their depredations, which they called fucceffes in war, enriched their families; and placed them amongft the moft diftinguifhed in the empire.

They had a fifter, named Adelaide, famed to have been very beautiful; and, their parents being dead, the care of her had defcended to them. Roland, a young knight, whofe caftle was on the
oppofite

oppofite bank of the Rhine, became her fuitor, and gained her affections. Whether the brothers had expected, by her means, to form a more fplendid alliance, or that they remembered the ancient enmity between their family and that of Roland, they fecretly refolved to deny the hand of Adelaide, but did not choofe to provoke him by a direct refufal. They ftipulated, that he fhould ferve, a certain number of years, in the war of Paleftine, and, on his return, fhould be permitted to renew his fuit.

Roland took a reluctant farewell of Adelaide, and went to the war, where he was foon diftinguifhed for an impetuous career. Adelaide remained in the caftle of Drakenfels, waiting, in folitary fidelity, for his return. But the brothers had determined, that he fhould not return for her. They clothed one of their dependents in the difguife of a pilgrim, and introduced him into the caftle, where he related, that he was arrived from the holy wars, and had been defired by Roland in his lateft moments to affure Adelaide of his having loved her till death.

The unhappy Adelaide believed the tale, and, from that time, devoted herfelf to the memory of Roland and to the nourifhment of her forrow. She rejected all the fuitors, introduced by her brothers, and accepted no fociety, but that of fome neighbouring nuns. At length, the gloom of a cloifter became fo neceffary to the melancholy of her imagination, that fhe refolved to found a convent and take the veil; a defign, which her brothers affifted, with the view of placing her effecpally beyond the reach of her lover. She chofe

an

an ifland in the Rhine between her brother's caftle and the feat of Roland, both of which fhe
could fee from the windows of her convent; and
here fhe paffed fome years in the placid performance of her new duties.

At length, Roland returned, and they both
difcovered the cruel device, by which they had
been feparated for ever. Adelaide remained in
her convent, and foon after died; but Roland,
emulating the fidelity of her retirement, built, at
the extreme point of his domains towards the
Rhine, a fmall caftle, that overlooked the ifland,
where he wafted his days in melancholy regret,
and in watching over the walls, that fhrouded his
Adelaide.

This is the ftory, on which the wild and vivid
imagination of Ariofto is faid to have founded his
Orlando.

THE VALLEY OF ANDERNACH.

AFTER fpending part of two days at Goodefberg, we fet out, in a fultry afternoon, for the
town of Andernach, diftant about five and twenty
Englifh miles. The road wound among corn-
lands towards the Rhine, and approached almoft
as near to the Seven Mountains, as the river
would permit. Oppofite to the laft, and nearly
the talleft of thefe, called Drakenfels, the open
plain terminates, and the narrower valley begins.
This

This mountain towers, the majestic sentinel of the river over which it aspires, in vast masses of rock, varied with rich tuftings of dwarf-wood, and bearing on its narrow peak the remains of a castle, whose walls seem to rise in a line with the perpendicular precipice, on which they stand, and, when viewed from the opposite bank, appear little more than a rugged cabin. The eye aches in attempting to scale this rock; but the sublimity of its height and the grandeur of its intermingled cliffs and woods gratify the warmest wish of fancy.

The road led us along the western bank of the Rhine among vineyards, and corn, and thick trees, that allowed only transient catches of the water between their branches; but the gigantic form of Drakenfels was always seen, its superior features, perhaps, appearing more wild, from the partial concealment of its base, and assuming new attitudes as we passed away from it. Lowenberg, whose upper region only had been seen from Goodesberg, soon unfolded itself from behind Drakenfels, and displayed all its pomp of wood, sweeping from the spreading base in one uninterrupted line of grandeur to the spiry top, on which one high tower of the castle appears enthroned among the forests. This is the loftiest of the Seven Mountains; and its dark sides, where no rock is visible, form a fine contrast with the broken cliffs of Drakenfels. A multitude of spiry summits appeared beyond Lowenberg, seen and lost again, as the nearer rocks of the shore opened to the distance, or re-united. About a mile further, lies the pleasant island, on which Adelaide raised her convent. As it was well endowed, it has been rebuilt, and is now a large and handsome fome quadrangle of white ftone, furrounded with trees, and corn, and vineyards, and ftill allotted to the fociety, which fhe eftablifhed.   An abrupt, but not lofty rock, on the weftern fhore of the Rhine, called Roland's Eck, or Roland's Corner, is the fite of her lover's caftle, of which one arch, picturefquely fhadowed with wood, is all that remains of this monument to faithful love. The road winds beneath it, and nearly overhangs the narrow channel, that feparates Adelaide's ifland from the fhore. Concerning this rock there is an ancient rhyme in the country, amounting to fomething like the following :

Was not Roland, the knight, a ftrange filly wight,
For the love of a nun, to live on this height ?

After paffing the ifland, the valley contracts, and the river is foon fhut up between fruitful and abrupt hills, which rife immediately over it, on one fide, and a feries of rocky heights on the other.   In the fmall fpace, left between thefe heights and the Rhine, the road is formed.   For the greater part of the way, it has been hollowed in the folid rock, which afcends almoft perpendicularly above it, on one hand, and finks as abruptly below it, to the river, on the other; a work worthy of Roman perfeverance and defign, and well known to be a monument of both. It was made during the reign of Marcus Aurelius and Lucius Verus; and as the infcription, whofe antiquity has not been doubted, dates its completion in the year 162, it muft have been finifhed in one year, or little more, Marcus Aurélius having been raifed to the purple in 161.
The

The Elector Palatine having repaired this road, which the Electors of Cologne had neglected, in 1768, has caufed his name to be joined with thofe of the Roman Emperors, in the following infcription upon an obelifk:

VIAM

SUB M.

AURELIO

ET L. VERO

I. M. P. P.

ANNO CHR.

CLXII

MUNITAM

CAROLUS

THEODORUS

ELECTOR PAL.

DUX BAV. JUL. CL. M.

REFECIT

ET AMPLIAVIT

AN. M.DCCLXVIII

CURANTE JO. LUD. COMITE
DE GOLDSTEIN

PRO PRINCIPE.

We did not fufficiently obferve the commencement and conclufion of this road, to be certain of its exact length; but it is probably about twelve miles. The rock above is, for the moft part, naked to the fummit, where it is thinly covered with earth; but fometimes it flopes fo much

as

as to permit patches of foil on its fide, and thefe are carefully planted with vines. This fhore of the Rhine may be faid to be bounded, for many miles, by an immenfe wall of rock, through which the openings into the country behind are few; and thefe breaks fhew only deep glens, feen and loft again fo quickly, that a woody mountain, or a caftle, or a convent, were the only objects we could afcertain.

This rock lies in oblique *ftrata*, and refembles marble in its brown and reddifh tints, marked with veins of deeper red; but we are unable to mention it under its proper and feientific denomination. The colouring of the cliffs is beautiful, when mingled with the verdure of fhrubs, that fometimes hang in rich drapery from their points, and with the moffes, and creeping vegetables of bright crimfon, yellow, and purple, that embofs their fractured fides.

The road, which the Elector mentions himfelf to have widened, is now and then very narrow, and approaches near enough to the river, over which it has no parapet, to make a traveller anxious for the fobriety and fkill of his poftillion. It is fometimes elevated forty feet above the level of the Rhine, and feldom lefs than thirty; an elevation from whence the water and its fcenery are viewed to great advantage; but to the variety and grandeur of thefe fhores, and the ever-changing form of the river, defcription cannot do juftice.

Sometimes, as we approached a rocky point, we feemed going to plunge into the expanfe of water beyond; when, turning the fharp angle of the promontory, the road fwept along an ample bay,

where

where the rocks, receding, formed an amphitheatre, covered with *ilex* and dwarf-wood, round a narrow, but cultivated level ſtripe : then, winding the furtheſt angle of this creſcent, under huge cliffs, we ſaw the river beyond, ſhut in by the folding baſes of more diſtant promontories, aſſume the form of a lake, amidſt wild and romantic landſcapes. Having doubled one of theſe capes, the proſpect opened in long perſpective, and the green waters of the Rhine appeared in all their majeſty, flowing rapidly between ranges of marbled rocks, and a ſucceſſion of woody ſteeps, and overlooked by a multitude of ſpiry ſummits, which diſtance had ſweetly coloured with the blue and purple tints of air.

The retroſpect of the river, too, was often enchanting, and the Seven Mountains long maintained their dignity in the ſcene, ſuperior to many intervening heights ; the dark ſummit of Lowenburg, in particular, appeared, for ſeveral leagues, overlooking the whole valley of the Rhine.

The eaſtern margin of the river ſometimes exhibited as extenſive a range of ſteep rocks as the weſtern, and frequently the fitneſs of the ſalient angles on one ſide, to the recipient ones on the other, ſeemed to juſtify the ſpeculation, that they had been divided by an earthquake, which let the river in between them. The general ſtate of the eaſtern bank, though ſteep, is that of the thickeſt cultivation. The rock frequently peeps, in rugged projections, through the thin ſoil, which is ſcattered over its declivity, and every where appears at top ; but the ſides are covered with vines ſo abundantly, that the labour of cultivating them, and of expreſſing the wine, ſupports a village at
                                                            leaſt

leaſt at every half mile. The green rows are led up the ſteeps to an height, which cannot be aſcended without the help of ſteps cut in the rock : the ſoil itſelf is there ſupported by walls of looſe ſtones, or it would fall either by its own weight, or with the firſt preſſure of rain ; and ſometimes even this ſcanty mould appears to have been placed there by art, being in ſuch ſmall patches, that, perhaps, only twenty vines can be planted in each. But ſuch exceſſive labour has been neceſſary only towards the ſummits, for, lower down the ſoil is ſufficiently deep to ſupport the moſt luxuriant vegetation.

It might be ſuppoſed from ſo much produce and exertion, that this bank of the Rhine is the reſidence of an opulent, or at leaſt, a well-conditioned peaſantry; and that the villages, of which ſeven or eight are frequently in ſight at once, are as ſuperior to the neighbouring towns by the ſtate of their inhabitants, as they are by their picturefque ſituation. On the contrary, the inhabitants of the wine country are ſaid to be amongſt the pooreſt in Germany. The value of every hill is exactly watched by the landlords, ſo that the tenants are very ſeldom benefited by any improvement of its produce. If the rent is paid in money, it leaves only ſo much in the hands of the farmer as will enable him to live, and pay his workmen ; while the attention of a great number of ſtewards is ſuppoſed to ſupply what might be expected from his attention, had he a common intereſt with his landlord in the welfare of the eſtate. But the rent is frequently paid in kind, amounting to a ſettled proportion of the produce ; and this proportion is ſo fixed, that, though the farmer

farmer is immoderately diftreffed by a bad vintage, the beft will not afford him any means of approaching to independence. In other countries it might be afked, " But, though we can fuppofe the ingenuity of the landlord to be greater than that of the tenant, at the commencement of a bargain, how happens it, that, fince the refult muft be felt, the tenant will remain under his burthens, or can be fucceeded by any other, on fuch terms?" Here, however, thefe queftions are not applicable; they prefume a choice of fituations, which the country does not afford. The feverity of the agricultural fyftem continues itfelf by continuing the poverty, upon which it acts; and thofe, who would efcape from it find few manufactures and little trade to employ them, had they the capital and the education neceffary for either. The choice of fuch perfons is between the being a mafter of day-labourers for their landlord, or a labourer under other mafters.

Many of thefe eftates belong immediately to Princes, or Chapters, whofe ftewards fuperintend the cultivation, and are themfelves inftead of the farmers, fo that all other perfons employed in fuch vineyards are ordinary fervants. By one or other of thefe means it happens, that the bounteoufnefs of nature to the country is very little felt by the body of the inhabitants. The payment of rents in kind is ufual, whereever the vineyards are moft celebrated; and, at fuch places, there is this fure proof of the wretchednefs of the inhabitants, that, in a month after the wine is made, you cannot obtain one bottle of the true produce, except by favour of the proprietors, or their ftewards.

How

How much is the delight of looking upon plenteoufnefs leffened by the belief, that it fupplies the means of excefs to a few, but denies thofe of competence to many!

Between this pafs of cultivated fteeps on one fide of the river, and of romantic rocks on the other, the road continues for feveral miles. Being thus commanded on both fides, it muft be one of the moft difficult paffages in Europe to an enemy, if refolutely defended. The Rhine, pent between thefe impenetrable boundaries, is confiderably narrower here than in other parts of the valley, and fo rapid, that a loaded veffel can feldom be drawn fafter than at the rate of fix Englifh miles a day, againft the ftream. The paffage down the river from Mentz to Cologne may be eafily performed in two days; that from Cologne to Mentz requires a fortnight.

The view along this pafs, though bounded, is various and changeful. Villages, vineyards and rocks alternately ornament the borders of the river, and every fifty yards enable the eye to double fome maffy projection that concealed the fruitful bay behind. An object at the end of the pafs is prefented fingly to the fight as through an inverted telefcope. The furface of the water, or the whole ftillnefs of the fcene, was very feldom interrupted by the paffing of a boat; carriages were ftill fewer; and, indeed, throughout Germany, you will not meet more than one in twenty miles. Travelling is confidered by the natives, who know the fatigue of going in carriages nearly without fprings, and ftopping at inns where there is little of either accommodation or civility, as productive of no pleafure; and they have feldom

I.   curiofity

curiofity or bufinefs enough to recompenfe for its inconveniencies.

We paffed through two or three fmall towns, whofe ruined gates and walls told of their antiquity, and that they had once been held of fome confequence in the defence of the valley. Their prefent defolation formed a melancholy contraft with the cheerful cultivation around them. Thefe, however, with every village in our way, were decorated with green boughs, planted before the door of each cottage, for it was a day of feftival. The little chapels at the road-fide, and the image, which, every now and then, appeared under a fpreading tree, were adorned with wreaths of frefh flowers; and though one might fmile at the emblems of fuperftition, it was impoffible not to reverence the fentiment of pious affection, which had adjufted thefe fimple ornaments.

About half-way to Andernach, the weftern rocks fuddenly recede from the river, and, rifing to greater height, form a grand fweep round a plain cultivated with orchards, garden-fields, corn and vineyards. The valley here fpreads to a breadth of nearly a mile and an half, and exhibits grandeur, beauty and barren fublimity, united in a fingular manner. The abrupt fteeps, that rife over this plain, are entirely covered with wood, except that here and there the ravage of a winter torrent appeared, which could fometimes be traced from the very fummit of the acclivity to the bafe. Near the centre, this noble amphitheatre opens to a glen, that fhews only wooded mountains, point above point, in long perfpective; fuch fylvan pomp we had feldom feen!
But

But though the tuftings of the nearer woods were beautifully luxuriant, there seemed to be few timber trees amongst them. The opposite shore exhibited only a range of rocks, variegated like marble, of which purple was the predominating tint, and uniformly disposed in vast, oblique strata. But even here, little green patches of vines peeped among the cliffs, and were led up crevices where it seemed as if no human foot could rest. Along the base of this tremendous wall, and on the points above, villages, with each its tall, grey steeple, were thickly strewn, thus mingling in striking contrast the cheerfulness of populous inhabitation with the horrors of untamed nature. A few monasteries, resembling castles in their extent, and known from such only by their spires, were distinguishable ; and, in the widening perspective of the Rhine, an old castle itself, now and then, appeared on the summit of a mountain somewhat remote from the shore ; an object rendered sweetly picturesque, as the sun's rays lighted up its towers and fortified terraces, while the shrubby steeps below were in shade.

We saw this landscape under the happiest circumstances of season and weather ; the woods and plants were in their midsummer bloom, and the mellow light of evening heightened the richness of their hues, and gave exquisite effect to one half of the amphitheatre we were passing, while the other half was in shadow. The air was scented by bean-blossoms, and by lime-trees then in flower, that bordered the road. If this plain had mingled pasture with its groves, it would have been truly Arcadian ; but neither here, nor through the whole of this delightful valley, did we see a

L 2   single

fingle pafture or meadow, except now and then
in an ifland on the Rhine; deficiencies which
are here fupplied, to the lover of landfcape, by
the verdure of the woods and vines. In other
parts of Germany they are more to be regretted, where, frequently, only corn and rock
colour the land.

Fatigued at length by fuch prodigality of
beauty, we were glad to be fhrouded awhile from
the view of it, among clofe boughs, and to fee
only the wide rivulets, with their ruftic bridges
of faggots and earth, that, defcending from among
the mountains, frequently croffed our way; or
the fimple peafant-girl, leading her cows to feed
on the narrow ftripe of grafs that margined the
road. The little bells, that jingled at their necks,
would not fuffer them to ftray beyond her hearing.
If we had not long fince difmiffed our furprife at
the fcarcity and bad quality of cheefe and butter
in Germany, we fhould have done fo now, on
perceiving this fcanty method of pafturing the
cattle, which future obfervation convinced us was
the frequent practice.

About fun-fet we reached the little village of
Namedy, feated near the foot of a rock, round
which the Rhine makes a fudden fweep, and con-
tracted by the bold precipices of Hammerftein
on the oppofite fhore, its green current paffes
with aftonifhing rapidity and founding ftrength.
Thefe circumftances of fcenery, with the tall mafts
of veffels lying below the fhrubby bank, on which
the village ftands, and feeming to heighten by comparifon the ftupendous rocks, that rofe around
them; the moving figures of boatmen and horfes
employed

employed in towing a barge againſt the ſtream, in the bay beyond; and a group of peaſants on the high quay, in the fore ground, watching their progreſs; the ancient caſtle of Hammerſtein over-looking the whole—theſe were a combination of images, that formed one of the moſt intereſting pictures we had ſeen.

The valley again expanding, the walls and tur-rets of Andernach, with its Roman tower riſing independently at the foot of a mountain, and the ruins of its caſtle above, appeared athwart the perſpective of the river, terminating the paſs; for there the rocky boundary opened to plains and remote mountains. The light vapour, that roſe from the water, and was tinged by the ſetting rays, ſpread a purple haze over the town and the cliffs, which, at this diſtance appeared to impend over it; colouring extremely beautiful, contraſted as it was by the clearer and deeper tints of rocks, wood and water nearer to the eye.

As we approached Andernach, its ſituation ſeemed to be perpetually changing, with the winding bank. Now it appeared ſeated on a low peninſula, that nearly croſſed the Rhine, overhung by romantic rocks; but this viſion va-niſhed as we advanced, and we perceived the town lying along a curving ſhore, near the foot of the cliffs, which were finely fringed with wood, and at the entrance of extenſive plains. Its towers ſeen afar, would be ſigns of a conſiderable place, to thoſe who had not before been wearied of ſuch ſymptoms by the towers of Neuſs, and other German towns. From a wooded precipice

over

over the river we had foon after a fine retrofpective glimpfe of the valley, its fantaftic fhores,
and long mountainous diftance, over which evening had drawn her fweeteft colouring. As we
purfued the pafs, the heights on either hand gradually foftened ; the country beyond fhewed remote mountains lefs wild and afpiring than thofe
we had left, and the blooming tint, which had
invefted the diftance, deepened to a dufky purple,
and then vanifhed in the gloom of twilight. The
progreffive influence of the hour upon the landfcape was interefting ; and the fhade of evening,
under which we entered Andernach, harmonized
with the defolation and filence of its old walls and
the broken ground around them. We paffed a
drawbridge and a ruinous gateway, and were
fufficiently fatigued to be fomewhat anxious as to
our accommodation. The Englifh habit of confidering, towards the end of the day's journey,
that you are not far from the cheerful reception,
the ready attendance, and the conveniences of a
fubftantial inn, will foon be loft in Germany.
There, inftead of being in good fpirits, during
the laft ftage, from fuch a profpect, you have to
confider, whether you fhall find a room, not ab-
folutely difgufting, or a houfe with any eatable
provifion, or a landlady, who will give it you, before the delay and the fatigue of an hundred re-
quefts have rendered you almoft incapable of receiving it. When your carriage ftops at the inn,
you will perhaps perceive, inftead of the alacrity
of an Englifh waiter, or the civility of an Englifh
landlord, a huge figure, wrapt in a great coat,
with a red worfted cap on his head, and a pipe
in his mouth, ftalking before the door. This is
the landlord. He makes no alteration in his

pace

pace on perceiving you, or, if he ftops, it is to
eye you with curiofity; he feldom fpeaks, never
bows, or affifts you to alight; and perhaps ftands
furrounded by a troop of flovenly girls, his
daughters, whom the found of wheels has
brought to the door, and who, as they lean in-
dolently againft it, gaze at you with rude curiofity and furprife.

The drivers in Germany are all bribed by the
innkeepers, and, either by affecting to mifunder-
ftand you, or otherwife, will conftantly ftop at the
door, where they are beft paid. That this money comes out of your pocket the next morning
is not the grievance; the evil is, that the worft
inns give them the moft, and a traveller, unlefs
he exactly remembers his directions, is liable to
be lodged in all the vileft rooms of a country,
where the beft hotels have no lodging fo clean
and no larder fo wholefomely filled as thofe of
every half-way houfe between London and Canterbury. When you are within the inn, the landlord, who is eager to keep, though not to accommodate you, will affirm, that his is the inn
you afk for, or that the other fign is not in the
place; and, as you foon learn to believe any
thing of the wretchednefs of the country, you are
unwilling to give up one lodging, left you fhould
not find another.

Our driver, after paffing a defolate, half filled
place, into which the gate of Andernach opened,
entered a narrow paffage, which afterwards appeared to be one of the chief ftreets of the place.
Here he found a miferable inn, and declared that
there was no other; but, as we had feen one of
a much better appearance, we were at length
brought

brought to that, and, though with some delay, were not ill accommodated, for the night.

Andernach is an ancient town, and it is believed, that a tower, which stands alone, at one end of the walls, was built by Drusus, of whom there are many traces in walls and castles, intended to defend the colonies, on this side of the Rhine, against the Germans, on the other. The fortifications can now be of little other use than to authorise the toll, which travellers pay, for entering a walled town; a tax, on account of which many of the walls are supported, though it is pretended, that the tax is to support the walls. By their means also, the Elector of Cologne collects here the last of four payments, which he demands for the privilege of passing the Rhine from Urdingen to Andernach; and this is the most Southern frontier town of his dominions on the western side of the Rhine, which soon after join those of the Elector of Treves. Their length from hence to Rheinberg is not less than ninety miles; the breadth probably never more than twenty.

There is some trade, at Andernach, in tiles, timber, and mill-stones, but the heaps of these commodities upon the beach are the only visible symptoms of the traffick; for you will not see one person in the place moving as if he had business to attract him, or one shop of a better appearance, than an English huckster's, or one man in the dress of a creditable trader, or one house, which can be supposed to belong to persons in easy circumstances. The port contains, perhaps, half a dozen vessels, clinker built, in shape

shape between a barge and a sloop; on the quay,
you may see two or three fellows, harnessing half
a dozen horses to a tow line, while twenty more
watch their lingering manœuvres, and this may
probably be the morning's business of the town.
Those, who are concerned in it, say that they are
engaged in *commerce.*

This, or something like it, is the condition, as
to trade, of all the towns we saw in Germany,
one or two excepted. They are so far from having well filled, or spacious repositories, that you
can scarcely tell at what houses there are any, till
you are led within the door; you may then wait
long after you are heard, or seen, before the
owner, if he has any other engagement, thinks
it necessary to approach you : if he has what you
ask for, which he probably has not, unless it is
something very ordinary, he tells the price and
takes it, with as much sullenness, as if you were
forcing the goods from him : if he has not, and
can shew you only something very different, he
then considers your enquiry as an intrusion, and
appears to think himself injured by having had
the trouble to answer you. What seems unac-
countable in the manners of a German trader,
is, that, though he is so careless in attending
you, he looks as much distressed, as vexed, if
you do not leave some money with him ; but he
probably knows, that you can be supplied no
where else in the town, and, therefore, will not
deny himself the indulgence of his temper. Even
when you are satisfied, his manner is so ill, that
he appears to consider you his dependent, by
wanting something which he can refuse. After
perceiving, that this is nearly general, the pain

of

of making continual difcoveries of idlenefs and malignity becomes fo much greater than the inconvenience of wanting any thing fhort of necefraries, that you decline going into fhops, and wait for fome eafier opportunity of fupplying whatever you may lofe upon the road.

COBLENTZ.

IT is one poft from Andernach hither, over a road, as good as any in England. Beyond the dominions of the Elector of Cologne, the face of the country, on this fide of the Rhine, entirely changes its character. The rocks ceafe, at Andernach, and a rich plain commences, along which the road is led, at a greater diftance from the Rhine, through corn lands and uninclofed orchards. About a mile from Andernach, on the other fide of the river, the white town of Neuwiedt, the capital of a fmall Proteftant principality, is feen; and the general report, that it is one of the moft commercial places, on the Rhine, appeared to be true from the chearful neatnefs of the principal ftreet, which faces towards the water. There were alfo about twenty fmall veffels, lying before it, and the quay feemed to be wide enough to ferve as a fpacious terrace to the houfes. The Prince's palace, an extenfive ftone building, with a lofty orangery along the fhore, is at the end of this ftreet, which, as well as the greateft part of the town, was built, or improved under the aufpices of his father; a wife prince, diftinguifhed by having negotiated, in 1735, a

peace

peace between the Empire and France, when the continuance of the war had feemed to be inevitable. The fame benevolence led him to a voluntary furrender of many oppreffive privileges over his fubjeḍs, as well as to the moſt careful protection of commerce and manufaḍures. Accordingly, the town of Neuwiedt has been continually increaſing in profperity and fize, for the laſt fifty years, and the inhabitants of the whole principality are faïd to be as much more qualified in their charaḍers as they are happier in their conditions than thoſe of the neighbouring ſtates. But then there is the *wretchednefs* of a deficiency of game in the country, for the late Prince was guilty of fuch an innovation as to mitigate the feverity of the laws refpeḍing it.

The foreſt hills, that rife behind Neuwiedt and over the rocky margin of the river, extend themfelves towards the more rugged mountains of Wetteravia, which are feen, a ſhapeleſs multitude, in the eaſt.

The river is foon after loſt to the view between high, fedgy banks; but, near Coblentz, the broad bay, which it makes in conjunḍion with the Mofelle, is feen expanding between the walls of the city and the huge pyramidal precipice, on which ſtands the fortreſs of Ehrenbreitſtein, or rather which is itſelf formed into that fortreſs. The Mofelle is here a noble river, by which the ſtreams of a thouſand hills, covered with vines, pour themfelves into the Rhine. The antient ſtone bridge over it leads to the northern gate of Coblentz, and the entrance into the city is ornamented by feveral large chateau-like manfions,

fions, erected to command a view of the two rivers. A narrow ftreet of high, but antient houfes
then commences, and runs through the place.
Thofe, which branch from it extend, on each
fide, towards the walls, immediately within which
there are others, that nearly follow their courfe
and encompafs the city. Being built between two
rivers, its form is triangular, and only one fide
is entirely open to the land; a fituation fo convenient both for the purpofes of commerce and
war, that it could not be overlooked by the Romans, and was not much neglected by the mo-
derns, till the induftry of maritime countries and
the complicated conftitution of the Empire reduced Germany in the fcale of nations. This was
accordingly the ftation of the firft legion, and the
union of the two rivers gave it a name; *Conflu-
entia.* At the commencement of the modern di-
vifion of nations, the fucceffors of Charlemagne
frequently refided here, for the convenience of an
intercourfe between the other parts of the Empire
and France; but, in the eleventh century, the
whole territory of Treves regained the diftinction,
as a feparate country, which the Romans had
given it, by calling the inhabitants *Treveri.*

Coblentz is a city of many fpires, and has eftablifhments of chapters and monafteries, which
make the great pride of German capitals, and
are fometimes the chief objects, that could diftinguifh them from the neglected villages of other
countries. The ftreets are not all narrow, but
few of them are ftraight; and the fame pavement
ferves for the horfes of the Elector and the feet of
his fubjects. The port, or beach, has the appearance of fomething more bufinefs than that of Andernach,

dernach, being the refort of paffage-veffels between Mentz and Cologne; but the broad quay, which has been raifed above it, is chiefly ufeful as a promenade to the vifitors of a clofe and gloomy town. Beyond the terrace ftands the Elector's palace, an elegant and fpacious ftone edifice, built to the height of three ftories, and inclofing a court, which is large enough to be light as well as magnificent. The front towards the Rhine is fimple, yet grand, the few ornaments being fo well proportioned to its fize, as neither to debafe it by minutenefs, nor encumber it by vaftnefs. An entablature, difplaying fome allegorical figures in bas relief, is fupported by fix Doric columns, which contribute much to the majeftic fimplicity of the edifice. The palace was built, about ten years fince, by the reigning Elector, who mentions, in an infcription, his attention to the architectural art; and a fountain, between the building and the town, is infcribed with a few words, which feem to acknowledge his fubjects as beings of the fame fpecies with himfelf; CLEMENS WINCESLAUS VICINIS SUIS.

But the moft ftriking parts of the view from this quay are the rock and fortrefs of Ehrenbreitftein, that prefent themfelves immediately before it, on the other fide of the river; notwithftanding the breadth of which they appear to rife almoft perpendicularly over Coblentz. At the bafe of the rock ftands a large building, formerly the palace of the Electors, who chofe to refide under the immediate protection of the fortrefs, rather than in the midft of their capital. Adjoining it is the village of Ehrenbreitftein, between which and

Coblentz

Coblentz a flying bridge is continually paffing, and, with its train of fubordinate boats, forms a very picturefque object from the quay. The fortrefs itfelf confifts of feveral tier of low walls, built wherever there was a projection in the rock capable of fupporting them, or wherever the rock could be hewn fo as to afford room for cannon and foldiers. The ftone, taken out of the mafs, ferved for the formation of the walls, which, in fome places, can fcarcely be diftinguifhed from the living rock. Above thefe tier, which are divided into feveral fmall parts, according to the conveniences afforded by the cliff, is built the caftle, or citadel, covering its fummit, and furrounded by walls more regularly continued, as well as higher. Small towers, fomewhat in the antient form, defend the caftle, which would be of little value, except for its height, and for the gradations of batteries between it and the river. Thus protected, it feems impregnable on that fide, and is faid to be not much weaker on the other; fo that the garrifon, if they fhould be willing to fire upon Coblentz, might make it impoffible for an enemy to remain within it, under the cover of very high entrenchments. This is the real defence of the city, for its walls would prefently fall before heavy artillery; and this, it is believed, might be preferved as long as the garrifon could be fupplied with ftores.

We croffed the river from the quay to the fortrefs, by means of the very fimple invention, a flying bridge. That, by which part of the paffage of the Waal is made at Nimeguen, has been already mentioned; this is upon the fame principle, but on a much larger fcale. After the

barges,

barges, upon which the platform is laid, are clear of the bank, the whole paſſage is effected with no other labour. than that of the rudder. A ſtrong cable, which is faſtened to an anchor at each ſide of the river, is ſupported acroſs it by a ſeries of ſmall boats; the bridge has two low maſts, one on each barge, and theſe are connected at the top by a beam, over which the cable is paſſed, being confined ſo as that it cannot ſlip beyond them. When the bridge is launched, the rapidity of the current forces it down the Rhine as far as the cable will permit: having reached that point, the force, received from the current, gives it the only direction of which it is capable, that acroſs the river, with the cable which holds it. The ſteerſman manages two rudders, by which he aſſiſts in giving it this direction. The voyage requires nine or ten minutes, and the bridge is continally paſſing. The toll, which, for a foot paſſenger, is ſomething leſs than a penny, is paid, for the benefit of the Elector, at an office, on the bank; and a ſentinel always accompanies the bridge, to ſupport his government, during the voyage.

The old palace of Ehrenbreitſtein, deſerted becauſe of its dampneſs, and from the fear of its being overwhelmed by the rock, that ſometimes ſcatters its fragments upon it, is now uſed as a barrack and hoſpital for ſoldiers. It is a large building, even more pleaſantly ſituated than the new one, being oppoſite to the entrance of the Moſelle into the Rhine; and its ſtructure, which has been once magnificent, denotes ſcarcely any other decay, than all buildings will ſhew, after a few years neglect. The rock has allowed little

room

room for a garden, but there are some ridiculous ornaments upon a very narrow strip of ground, which was probably intended for one.

'The entrance into the fortress, on this side, is by a road, cut in the solid rock, under four gateways. It is so steep, that we were compelled to decline the honour of admission, but ascended it far enough to judge of the view, commanded from the summit, and to be behind the batteries, of which some were mounted with large brass cannon. Coblentz lies beneath it, as open to inspection as a model upon a table. The sweeps of the Rhine and the meanders of the Moselle, the one binding the plain, the other intersecting it, lead the eye towards distant hills, that encircle the capacious level. The quay of the city, with the palace and the moving bridge, form an interesting picture immediately below, and we were unwilling to leave the rock for the dull and close streets of Coblentz. On our return, the extreme nakedness of the new palace, which is not sheltered by trees, on any side, withdrew our attention from the motley group of passengers, mingled with hay carts and other carriages, on the flying bridge.

The long residence of the emigrant princes and noblesse of France in this city is to be accounted for not by its general accommodations, or gaieties, of which it is nearly as deficient as the others of Germany; but first by the great hospitality of the Elector towards them, and then by the convenience of its situation for receiving intelligence from France, and for communicating with other countries. The Elector held frequent levies for the French nobility, and continued for them

part

part of the fplendour which they had enjoyed in their own country. The readinefs for lending money upon property, or employments in France, was alfo fo great, that thofe, who had not brought cafh with them, were immediately fupplied, and thofe, who had, were encouraged to continue their ufual expences. We know it from fome of the beft poffible authority, that, at the commencement of the march towards Longwy, money, at four per cent. was even preffed upon many, and that large fums were refufed.

Here, and in the neighbourhood, between fixty and feventy fquadrons of cavalry, confifting chiefly of thofe who had formerly enjoyed military, or other rank, were formed; each perfon being mounted and equipped chiefly at his own expence. We heard feveral anecdotes of the confidence, entertained in this army, of a fpeedy arrival in Paris; but, as the perfons, to whom they relate, are now under the preffure of misfortune, there would be as little pleafure, as propriety in repeating them.

At Cöblentz, we quitted, for a time, the left bank of the Rhine, in order to take the watering place of Selters, in our way to Mentz. Having croffed the river and afcended a fteep road, near the fortrefs, we had fine glimpfes of its walls, baftions and out-towers, and the heathy knolls, around them, with catches of diftant country. The way continued to lie through the dominions of the Elector of Treves, which are here fo diftinguifhed for their wretchednefs as to be named the *Siberia of Germany!* It is paved and called a *chauffée;* but thofe, who have not experienced its

M ruggednefs,

ruggednefs, can have no idea of it, except by fuppof-
·ing the pavement of a ftreet torn up by a plough,
and then fuffered'to fix itfelf, as it had fallen.   Always fteep, either in afcent, or defcent, it si not
only the roughnefs, that prevents your exceeding
the ufual poft-pace of three Englifh miles an hour.
Sometimes it runs along edges of mouñtains, that
might almoft be called precipices, and commands
fhort views of other mountains and of vallies entirely covered with thick, but not lofty forefts;
fometimes it buries itfelf in the depths of fuch forefts and glens; fometimes the turrets of an old
chateau peep above thefe, but rather confirm than
contradict the notion of their defolatenefs, having
been evidently built for the purpofes of the chace;
and fometimes a mud village furprifes you with a
few inhabitants, emblems of the mifery and favagenefs of the country.

Thefe are the mountains of Wetteravia, the
boundaries of many a former and far-feen profpect,
then picturefque, fublime, or graceful, but now
defolate, fhaggy, and almoft hideous; as in life,
that, which is fo grand as to charm at a diftance,
is often found to be forlorn, difguftful and comfort-
lefs by thofe, who approach it.

MONTABAUR

MONTABAUR.

SIX hours after leaving Coblentz, we reached Montabaur, the firft poft-town on the road, and diftant about eighteen miles. An ancient chateau, not ftrong enough to be a caftle, nor light enough to be a good houfe, commands the town, and is probably the refidence of the lord. The walls and gates fhew the antiquity of Montabaur, but the ruggednefs of its fite fhould feem to prove, that there was no other place in the neighbourhood, on which a town could be built. Though it is fituated in a valley, as to the nearer mountains, it is conftructed chiefly on two fides of a narrow rock, the abrupt fummit of which is in the centre of this very little place.

The appearance of Montabaur is adequate in gloominefs to that of feveral before feen; but it would be endlefs to repeat, as often as they fhould be true, the defcriptions of the fqualidnefs and decay, that characterife German towns; nor fhould we have noticed thefe fo often, if the negligence of others, in this refpect, had not left us to form deceitful expectations, fuitable to the fuppofed importance of feveral very confpicuous, but really very wretched cities.

LIMBOURG.

LIMBOURG.

OVER a fucceffion of foreft mountains, fimilar to thofe juft paffed, we came, in the afternoon, to Limbourg, another poft town, or, perhaps, city, and another collection of houfes, like tombs, or forfaken hofpitals. At an inn, called the Three Kings, we faw firft the fullennefs and then the ferocious malignity of a German landlord and his wife, exemplified much more fully than had before occurred. When we afterwards expreffed our furprife, that the magiftrates fhould permit perfons of fuch conduct to keep an inn, efpecially where there was only one, we learned, that this fellow was himfelf the chief magiftrate, or burgomafter of the place; and his authority appeared in the fearfulnefs of his neighbours to afford any fort of refrefhment to thofe, who had left his inn. One of the elector's minifters, with whom we had the pleafure to be acquainted, informed us, that he knew this man, and that he muft have been intoxicated, for that, though civil when fober, he was madly turbulent and abufive, if otherwife. It appeared, therefore, that a perfon was permitted to be a magiftrate, who, to the knowledge of government, was expofed by his fituation to be intoxicated, and was outrageous, whenever he was fo. So little is the order of fociety eftimated here, when it is not connected with the order of politics.

Near

Near Limbourg, the foreft fcenery, which had fhut up the view, during the day, difappeared, and the country loft, at leaft, an uniformity of favagenefs. The hills continue, but they are partly cultivated. At a fmall diftance from the town, a fteep afcent leads to a plain, on which a battle was fought, during the fhort ftay of the French in this diftrict, in the campaign of 1792.

Four thoufand French were advancing towards Limbourg; a fmall Pruffian corps drew up to oppofe them, and the engagement, though fhort, was vivid, for the Pruffians did not perceive the fuperiority of the French in numbers, till the latter began to fpread upon the plain, for the purpofe of furrounding them. Being then compelled to retreat, they left feveral of the Elector's towns open to contribution, from which five-and-twenty thoufand florins were demanded, but the remonftrances of the magiftrates reduced this fum to 8000 florins, or about 700*l.* The French then entered Limbourg, and extended themfelves over the neighbouring country. At Weilbourg, the refidence of a Prince of the Houfe of Naffau, they required 300,000 florins, or 25,000*l.* which the Prince neither had, nor could collect, in two days, through his whole country. All his plate, horfes, coaches, arms, and fix pieces of cannon, were brought together, for the purpofe of removal; but afterwards two individuals were accepted as hoftages, inftead of the Prince himfelf, who had been at firft demanded. The action near Limbourg took place on the 9th of November, and, before the conclufion of the month, the French had fallen back to Franckfort, upon the re-approach of the Pruffian and Auftrian troops.

SELTERS.

SELTERS.

WE had a curiofity to fee this place, which, under the name of Seltzer, is fo celebrated throughout Europe, for its medicinal water. Though it is rather in the high road to Franckfort than to Mentz, there feemed no probability of inconvenience in making this fhort departure from our route, when it was to be joined again from a place of fuch public accefs as Selters appeared likely to be found.

About feven miles from Limbourg, a defcent commences, at the bottom of which ftands this village. What a reproof to the expectations of comfort, or convenience in Germany! Selters, a fpot, to which a valetudinarian might be directed, with the profpect of his finding not only abundant accommodation, but many luxuries, Selters is literally and pofitively nothing more than an affemblage of miferable cottages, with one inn and two houfes for officers of the Elector, ftuck in a dirty pafs, which more refembles a ditch than a road. The village may be faid to be near half a mile long, becaufe the huts, being moftly feparated from each other, continue as far; and this length would increafe its inconvenience to invalids, if fuch fhould ever ftay there longer than to fee it, for there is nothing like a fwept path-way, and the road, in which they muft walk, is probably always deeply covered with mud, being fo when we were there in the beginning

ginning of July. There was then, however, not one stranger, beside ourselves, in the place, and we found, that very rarely any aggravate the miseries of sickness by a stay at Selters.

The only lodgings to be had are at the inn, and fortunately for travellers this is not such as might be expected from the appearance of the village. Finding there the novelty of an obliging host and hostess, we were very well contented to have reached it, at night, though we were to stay there also the next day, being Sunday. The rooms are as good as those in the inns of German cities, and three, which are called Court Chambers, having been used by the Elector and lately by the King of Prussia, are better. These are as open as the others to strangers.

The spring is at the foot of one of several hills, which immediately surround the village, and is separated from the road by a small court yard. An oaken covering, at the height of ten or twelve feet, prevents rain from falling into the wooden bason, in which the stream rises; and two or three of the Elector's guards watch over it, that no confiderable quantity may be taken, without payment of the duty, which forms a large part of his income. Many thousands of stone bottles are piled round this court, and, for the reputation of the spring, care is taken to fill them as immediately as possible, before their removal for exportation.

The policy of keeping this income intire is said to be a motive for neglecting the condition of the village. A duty could not well be demanded of those, who should drink at the spring, but is easily
collected

collected before the water is bottled for removal; it is, therefore, not wifhed, that there fhould be many vifitors, at Selters. We did not hear this reafon upon the fpot, but it is difficult otherwife to account for a negligence, which prevents the inhabitants of the neighbouring country from being enriched at the expence of wanderers from others.

Nor is it only a duty, but the whole profit of the traffick, till the water leaves the place, which rewards the care of the Elector. His office for the fale of it is eftablifhed here, and his agents alone tranfmit it into foreign countries. The bufinefs is fufficient to employ feveral clerks, and the number of bottles annually filled is fo immenfe, that, having omitted to write it down, we will not venture to mention it from memory. The water is brought to table conftantly and at an eafy price in all the towns near the Rhine. Mixed with Rhenifh wine and fugar it forms a delightful, but not always a fafe beverage, in hot weather. The acid of the wine, expelling the fixed air of other ingredients, occafions an effervefcence, like that of Champagne, but the liquor has not a fourth part of the obnoxious ftrength of the latter. The danger of drinking it is, that the acid may be too powerful for fome conftitutions.

After being furprifed by the defolatenefs of the village, we were not lefs fo to find amongft its few inhabitants one, whofe manners and information, fo far from bearing the character of the drearinefs around him, were worthy of the beft fociety in the moft intelligent cities. This was the Commiffary and Privy Counfellor of the Elector for the diftrict, who, having heard, that there were fome
Englifh

English visitors at the well, very frankly introduced himself to us by his civilities, and favoured us with his company in the afternoon. He had been in England, with many valuable introductions, and had formed from the talents and accomplishments of a distinguished Marquis an high opinion of the national character; a circumstance, which probably united with his natural disposition, in inducing him to emulate towards us the general politeness of that truly honourable person.

When we enquired how the journey of the next day was to be performed, it appeared, that no other carriage could be hired in the place than a sort of one-horse chair, which would take us to the next post town, from whence we might proceed with the usual chaises. The driver walked at the side of this uncouth carriage, which had shafts and wheels strong enough for a waggon; and, either by the mistake or intention of his master in directing him, we were led, not to the post town, for a chaise, if it could be had, but entirely through a forest country to Mentz, by roads made only for the woodcutters, and, as it afterwards proved, known to few others, except to our ingenious voiturier. We did not pass a town, or village, at which it was possible to change the carriage, and had, therefore, no other alternative, when the mistake was discovered, than to return to Salters, or to proceed to Mentz, in this inconvenient and ludicrous vehicle. We chose to proceed, and had some reward for fatigue, by passing nearly an whole day under the shade of deep and delightful forests, little tamed by the hand of man, and appearing to acknowledge only " the season's difference."

Between

Between Selters and thefe forefts, the country is well cultivated, and frequently laid out in garden-fields, in which there was the firft appearance of cheerful labour we had feen in Germany. After paffing a fmall town, on the fummit of a hill to the left, ftill furrounded by its antient fortifications, we entered a large plain, fkirted, on one fide, by villages; another town, at the end of which, was almoft the laft fign of an inhabited country, that appeared for feveral hours. The foreft then commenced, and, with the exception of one hamlet, enveloped near the middle, we faw nothing but lofty oaks, elms and chefnuts, till we emerged from it in the afternoon, and came to a town of the Landgrave of Heffe Darmftadt. Roebucks are faid to be numerous, and wild boars not very fcarce, in this foreft; but we faw none either here, or in thofe near Limbourg, which are much inferior to this in beauty. Upon the whole, it was a fcene of perfect novelty; without which it now feems that we fhould have wanted many ideas of fylvan life and much of the delight, excited by Shakefpeare's exquifite defcription of it.

The country afterwards open towards

MENTZ,

MENTZ,

WHICH ſtands in a ſpacious plain, on the oppoſite edge of the Rhine, and is viſible, at a conſiderable diſtance, with its maſſy towers and numerous ſpires. Within two or three miles of the city, the ſymptoms of ruin, occaſioned by the ſiege in 1793, began to appear. A village, on the left, had ſcarcely one houſe entire; and the tower of the church was a mere wreck, blackened by flames, and with large chaſms, that admitted the light. The road did not paſs nearer to it than two miles, but the broken walls and roofs were diſtinguiſhable even at that diſtance, and ſometimes a part, which had been repaired, contraſted its colour with the black and ſmoky hues of the remainder. This was the village of Koſtheim, ſo often contended for in the courſe of the ſiege, being on the oppoſite bank of the Rhine to the city, and capable of obſtructing the intercourſe with it by water.

The country on the eaſtern ſide of the river was otherwiſe but little damaged, if we except the deſtruction of numerous orchards; for the allies were not ſtrong enough to beſiege the city on all ſides at once, and contented themſelves with occupying ſome poſts in this quarter, capable of holding the garriſon of Caſſel in awe.

This Caſſel is a ſmall village exactly oppoſite to Mentz, and communicating with it by a bridge of boats.

boats. It was unfortified before the invasion of the French; but these had no sooner entered the city, than they perceived the importance of such a place, and prepared themselves to render it a regular fortress. In about two months they completely surrounded it with earthen works and outworks, ditched and pallisadoed. Some of the nearest orchards were cut down to be used in these fortifications. The fruit trees still remain with their branches upwards from the ditch, and serve instead of *chevaux de frise*.

The village of Hockheim, which is also on this side of the Rhine, is further to the left than Kostheim, and remains uninjured, at the top of the round and easy hill, the vines of which are so much celebrated for their flavour, as to give a name to great quantities of wine, produced in other districts. After the siege, the merchants of the neighbourhood enhanced the price of their stocks by reporting, that all the vineyards had been destroyed; but the truth is, that Hockheim was not much contended for, and that little damage was done even to the crops then in bloom. The village is advantageously situated about the confluence of the Rhine and the Maine, and, if it had been nearer the city, would probably have been so important, as to have been contested, till it was destroyed.

This is the home ground of the scene, which spreads before the traveller, who approaches Mentz from the eastern shore of the Rhine. Furthest to the left is Hockheim, then the devastated village of Kostheim, then the fortifications of Caffel, which, with the river, are between him and the city. Beyond, the horizon is bounded

on

on all fides by gradual hills, diftant and apparently fruitful; but thofe to the north are preeminent, with gentle flopes at their feet, coloured fweetly by corn, dark wood and gleams of reddifh earth.

The works of Caffel render the approach to the city very tedious, for they have been fo contrived as that the road nearly follows them, in all their angles, for the purpofe of being commanded by many points at once. The village was now garrifoned by Pruffians, of whom, fome were lying under the fheds of their guard-houfe near the bridge, and others were riding over it, with juft fpeed enough to give one an idea of military earneftnefs. Their horfes fhook the floor of the bridge of boats, which here croffes the Rhine, at its breadth of nearly eight hundred feet, and difturbed the promenade, for which it is ufually frequented in an evening. We followed them, admiring the expanfe, and rapidity of the river more than the appearance of the city, where gloominefs is too much mingled with grandeur; till, at the end of the bridge, we were ftopped at another guard-houfe, to anfwer the ufual enquiries. A foldier accompanied us thence to a large fquare filled with cannon and mortars, where the captain of the guard examined our paffport. We were then very glad to pafs the evening at an inn without further refearches; but there were fome fymptoms of the late condition of the city to attract attention in the way.

The Elector's palace, which forms one fide of this fquare, having been converted into an hofpital by the French, is ftill ufed as fuch, or as a barrack, by the Pruffians; and the windows were

crowded

crowded with the figures of half-dressed soldiers. Many of the cannon in the square remained with the fractures, made by the balls of the besiegers. This place communicates with a broad street, in which were many buildings, filled with soldiers, and an handsome house, that, having belonged to one of the Clubbists, was destroyed immediately after the expulsion of the French. The walls still remain bare and open. Some greater ruins, occasioned by fire, during the siege, were visible at a distance, and, upon the whole, we had interest enough excited, as to the immediate history of the place, to take little notice of the narrow and difficult passages, through which we wound for half an hour, after leaving the principal street.

The next morning, the friends, to whom we had letters, began to conduct us through the melancholy curiosities, left in the city by the siege. These are chiefly in the southern quarter, against which the direct attack of the allies was made, and their approaches most advanced. Some entire streets have been destroyed here, and were still in ruins. A magnificent church, attached to a convent of Franciscan monks, is among the most lamentable spectacles; what was the roof now lies in heaps over the pavement; not a vestige of furniture, or decoration, has escaped the flames, and there are chasms in the walls larger than the noble windows, that once illuminated them. This church and convent were set on fire by a bomb; and of the sick soldiers, who were lodged in the latter, it is feared that but few were removed before the destruction of the building. We next saw the remains of a palace, built by the present Provost of the Chapter of Nobles;

an

an inftitution, which is fo rich, that their Superior had a more elegant refidence than the Elector. It was of ftone, and the principal front was
in the Corinthian order, fix columns of which
fupported a fpacious open gallery, ornamented
with ftatues, for its whole length. The wings
formed two fides of a fquare, which feparated the
palace from the ftreet. A profufion of the richeft
furniture and a valauble collection of paintings
filled the interior. Of the whole edifice little
now remains but the fhattered walls of the centre,
which have been fo fcorched as to lofe all appearance of having belonged to a fplendid ftructure.
It was burnt the night before the fire of the
Francifcan church, and two nights after the
French had removed their head quarters and their
municipality from it. On the day before the removal, a bomb had fallen upon the French General Blou, deftroying him on the fpot, and mor-
tally wounding an officer, with whom he was converfing. The ruins are now fo accumulated over
the court-yard, that we could not difcern it to
have ever had that appendage of a diftinguifhed
refidence.

But the church of Notre Dame was the moft
confpicuous of many ruined objects. The fteeple
of this had been one of the grandeft ornaments
of the city; a fhower of bombs fet fire to it; and,
while it was thus rendered an eafy mark for the
befiegers, their cannon played upon and beat a
great part of it to the ground. By its fall the roof
of the church was fhattered, but the body did not
otherwife fuffer any material injury. Wooden
galleries have been raifed round the remainder of
the fteeple, not for the purpofe of repairing, but
for

for that of entirely removing it; and, to save the trouble of letting down the stones on the outside, a wooden pipe, or channel has been made, through which they are lowered into the church. The appearance of this steeple, which was once very large and lofty, is rendered striking by these preparations for its total destruction.

The whole church is built of a stone, dug from the neighbouring hills, the colour of which is so delicate a pink, that it might be supposed to be given by art. The Elector's palace and several other public buildings in the city are formed of this stone.

Passing through the gates on this side of Mentz, we came to a slope near the river, and beyond the glacis of the place, which was then partly covered with huge masses of stone scattered among the roots of broken trees and shrubs, that had begun again to shoot their verdure over the amputated trunks. This was the site of a palace of the Elector, called, both from the beauty of its situation, and the splendour of its structure, La Favorita. The apartments of the palace and the terraces of the garden commanded extensive views of the Rhine and the surrounding country ascending from its banks; and the gardens themselves were so beautifully disposed as to be thought worthy of the name of English. They were ornamented with pavilions, which had each its distinct prospect, and with one music room in the thickest part of the shrubbery. Of the building nothing is now visible but some disjointed stones; and of the garden, only the broken trunks of trees. The palace was burned and the gardens levelled by the French, that they might not afford shelter to the Prussians, during the siege.

From

From this spot we were shewn the positions of the allied forces, the course of their approaches and the chief outworks of the city. Hockheim, Koftheim, and Caffel lay before us, on the other side of the river; a gentle rise, on this side, at the distance of nearly a mile, was the first station of the allies, part of whose force was covered behind it; their last batteries were within two hundred and fifty paces of the city. The ground had been since levelled, and was now covered with standing corn, but the track of the trenches was, in some places, visible. On the other hand, the forts, in which the strength of the whole so much consists, were completely repaired, and had no appearance of having been so lately attacked. They are five in number, and, being raised at a considerable distance from the walls of the city, no near approaches can be made, till some of them are either taken, or destroyed; for they are laid to be regular and strong fortifications, capable of containing numerous garrisons, and communicating with the city itself by passages, cut in the ground, through which they may be constantly reinforced.

Only one of these five forts, that nearest to the river, was destroyed in the late siege, which would have been much more tedious, but for the want of provisions and medicines, that began to be felt in the garrison. The walls of the city were almost uninjured, so that it has not been thought necessary to repair them in the few places, where balls may be perceived to have struck. The bombardment was the chief annoyance of the garrison, who were not sheltered in caserns, and whose magazines, both of ammunition and provision, were frequently destroyed by

N   it.

it. Their numbers were alfo greatly reduced by fallies and by engagements, on the other fide of the Rhine, in defence of Caffel, or in attack of part of an ifland, called the Bleiau.

We walked round the city upon what is termed the *glacis*, that is upon the flope, which afcends from the plain towards the top of the ditch, and which is the furtheft of the defenfive works, being very gradually raifed, that thofe, who are upon it, may be expofed at every ftep, to the fire from the walls. The forts, which are formed of folid earthen works, covered with turf, would fcarcely attract the notice of an unmilitary eye, if the channelled paffages to them did not iffue from this flope, and if the fentinels, ftalking upon the parapets, did not feem of a gigantic fize, by having their whole figures raifed againft the light.

Mentz was at this time the depôt of ftores for the Pruffian army on the Rhine, and there were perfons employed upon the *glacis*, in counting heaps of cannon balls, which had been delivered from fome neighbouring foundery. On the bank of the river, others were throwing waggon-loads of hay into large barges, on which it was piled to fuch an height, that fmall paffages were cut through it for the rowers to work in. There were nine or ten barges fo filled; and in thefe labours more activity was apparent than in any other tranfactions we faw at Mentz.

Having paffed round the city, between the walls and the forts, which protect them, to the north, weft and fouth, we came, at this latter fide, to fome other fignals of a theatre of war. Here had

3   been

been a noble alley of at leaft a mile and a half long, formed of poplars as large and high as elms, and furrounded, on each fide, by plantations, in-terfected by fmall and irregular walks. Being led along the banks of the Rhine, this alley, with its adjoining groves, afforded a moft delight-ful promenade, and was claffed amongft the beft ornaments, given to the river, in its whole courfe. This alfo was deftroyed upon the approach of the befiegers, that it might not afford them fhelter. The trunks of the fturdy trees, cut at the height of one or two feet from the ground, fhew, by their folidity and the abundance of their vigorous fhoots, how long they might have flourifhed, but for this difafter.

An Englifhman, walking amidft the enfigns of fuch artificial and premature defolation, cannot help confidering the natural fecurity of his coun-try, and rejoicing, that, even if the ftrong and plain policy of neglecting all foreign confequence, and avoiding all foreign interefts, except the commercial ones, which may be maintained by a navy, fhould for ever be rejected, ftill his home cannot be invaded; and, though the expence of wars fhould make poverty general, the immedi-ate horrors of them cannot enter the cities, or the cottages of an ifland.

Great part of our time at Mentz was occupied by enquiries concerning the fiege, which was not fo much a topic as we had expected to find it. We probably heard, however, all that was to be told, and had a German pamphlet re-commended, containing the hiftory of the place from the firft invafion of the French to their de-

N 2   parture.

parture. The authenticity of this was affured to us; and it is partly from it, partly from the accounts given by our friends, that the following fhort narrative has been extracted.

OF MENTZ IN 1792 AND 1793.

THE entrance of a French army into Worms, in the beginning of October 1792, had excited a confiderable alarm in Mentz, before the inhabitants of the latter city received the accounts, which were not long wanting, of exprefs and avowed preparations for a march towards them. Great numbers of French emigrants had been drawn to the city by the meeting of the Emperor and the King of Pruffia there, a few months before; many had arrived fince the diffolution of their army in Champagne; and, during the approach of the Republican troops to Spires and Worms, families were continually paffing through the city, joining thofe, who began to take their flight from it. The narrow ftreets were filled with carriages, and the diftrefsful hafte of the travellers ferved to deprefs the fpirits of the inhabitants, who faw how little their city was thought capable of defence. On the 15th of October, Baron d'Albini, a counfellor of the Court, called the Burgeffes together, and admonifhed them to make preparations for their fecurity; he alfo enquired, whether they thought it prudent, that the Elector fhould remain in the city with them? and, it being readily anfwered, that

that they did not, the Elector set out for Wurtzburg, a town about 100 miles distant, and was
followed by the members of the government. At
the same time, a considerable emigration of the
other inhabitants took place.

The approach of the French had been so little
foreseen, till within the few last weeks, that the
garrison did not amount to a tenth part of the
war complement. The inhabitants, however,
having happily had little experience of sieges,
did not know what this complement should be, and,
after the first alarm, began to think the deficiency
might be easily remedied. The Electoral troops,
having sent some useless detachments to Spires,
amounted to only 968 men, to whom an hundred
were added, obtained from Nassau, Oranien,
Weilburg, Bieberich and Fuld by the Elector's
demands of assistance from his neighbours. Two
hundred and seven Austrian hussars of Esterhazy
had also arrived, on the 13th, and all the inhabitants of the Rheingau, a populous district, bordering upon the Rhine, were summoned to the
assistance of the capital. The antient society of
Archers of the city laid down their bows for
musquets; the Academicians formed themselves
into a corps, and were placed, together with the
Archers, at several outposts. The traders, though
exempt from personal service, and unwilling to
surrender that privilege, resolved to pay double
watch-money for substitutes. It began to be
thought, that the threatened progress of the
French had been untruly reported; that the
siege could not be commenced at that late season
of the year; and lastly, that some promised
reinforcements of Austrian troops could not be
far off.

But,

' But, on the 19th of October, the French, in four columns, began to furround the place. They wore, at firft, white cockades, expecting to be miftaken for the army of M. de Condé; they were, however, known, and fired upon. Though fome days had been paffed in preparation, it was now found, that there was little readinefs for defence. The beft artillerymen had been loft at Spires; there were, at firft, no horfes to draw the cannon, fo that oxen were ufed for that purpofe ; the neareft balls to the batteries of twenty-four pound cannon were caft for twelve-pounders; and many of the mufquet cartridges could not be fired. In a few hours, however, feveral of the artifans applied themfelves to the making of cartridges ; horfes were fupplied by the fervants of the Court and the Nobility, and all hands were, in fome way or other, employed. It was then reported, that a corps of Auftrian troops was in the neighbourhood, and, on the 19th, 1800 men entered the city. Thefe were recruits without ammunition, and, for the moft part, without arms, being on their march to join the army of the Emperor. They were then under the command of two, or three fubalterns; but fome other Imperial officers came in from the neighbourhood, and arms were obtained from the Elector's arfenal. After this reinforcement there were probably about four thoufand men in arms in the city.

With this force, it is allowed, that a much longer defence than was made might have been expected ; and, unlefs there was fome failure of the commander's attention, the treachery of an engineer, to whom the furrender is imputed, could certainly not

not have been so effectual. EIKENMAYER, this engineer, had, it seems, made known to the French the commander's preparations for defence; intelligence, which, if the preparations had been greater, could have been but little serviceable to the assailants. His chief assistance was afforded to them by much more conspicuous means; for, as the inhabitants went frequently to a building called St. Stephen's Tower, to observe the progress of the besiegers, he assured them, that the army, which really amounted only to eleven thousand men, consisted of forty thousand; that they had with them two-and-twenty waggons, laden with scaling ladders, and that the city would presently be taken by storm. The same representations of the besiegers' force were also made by him to the Council of War; and these, it is said, determined them to the surrender, before the French had raised a battery against the works.

Many of the citizens, however, were surprised and enraged at this resolution; and the captain of the Austrian reinforcements expressed his displeasure, at the Council House, where he declared, that he would continue to defend the place, even without permission. In the mean time, the capitulation was signed, and he was induced to submit to it by the solicitations even of the citizens, by whom it was blamed, and by their representations, that, in the present agitated temper of the inhabitants, all attempts at defence must be useless.

Baron d'ALBINI carried news of the surrender to the Elector, at Wurtzburg, and, about five o'clock, on the 21st of October, two French officers came to the Council House, followed by two companies of grenadiers. On the 22d, eight
thousand

thoufand French entered the city, the other three
thoufand having marched, the preceding day, to
Franckfort; the inhabitants, aftonifhed to find
themfelves taken by fo fmall a force, now faw,
to their ftill greater furprife, that their conquerors
had fcarcely any heavy cannon. This day was paffed
in affigning quarters to the troops, and, on the
next Cuftine, the commander of the French,
called the members of the City Council together,
to whom, in a fhort fpeech, he promifed the protection of perfons and properties, inviting them,
at the fame time, to promote the fraternization of
the inhabitants with the French nation. Profeffor BOHMER, who had accepted the office of his
Secretary, tranflated this addrefs into German,
and it was circulated through the city.

It is remarkable, that the French had no fooner
taken poffeffion of this fudden prize, than they
began to forefee the probability of being reduced
to defenfive meafures and to prepare for them.
They immediately collected contributions of
forage and corn from the neighbouring villages;
the ftreets were rendered almoft impaffable by the
loads brought in; and, as the magazines were
foon filled, great quantities were wafted by being
expofed to the rain in gardens, and trodden under
the feet of horfes in the ftreets. The garrifon
was foon increafed to 20,000 men, of whom fometimes three hundred fometimes five hundred were
lodged in each convent. The French foldiery
having committed fome exceffes, Cuftine reprov-
ed their licentioufnefs, and began to habituate
them to difcipline by ordering a retirement to
their quarters, at certain hours, by beat of
drum.

The

The inhabitants soon began to suspect the contrivance and the persons, that had produced the surrender; for Eikenmayer lived in intimacy with Custine; Professor Metternich, of the Academy of Mentz, mounted the French cockade; and the Elector's physician, having left the city, upon a promise of assisting some peasants, whom he asserted to be seized with an infectious fever, had carried on a correspondence with the French, as had PATOKI, a merchant, born at Colmar, who had lately received the right of citizenship.

The palaces of the Elector and the Provost were now ransacked; and, though it had been published as a rule, that the property of private individuals should not be touched, the houses of the nobility were treated, as if they had belonged to the Prince. The profligacy and pride of Custine became every day more conspicuous, and were oppressive upon the garrison, as well as the inhabitants, though in a less degree. Johannesberg, a village upon the Rhine, at the distance of a few miles, is celebrated for its wines, which sell for three times the price of those of Hockheim. Custine sent a part of the garrison solely to bring him the wines from the cellars of the Prince of Fuld, who has a palace there; but a compromise being proposed, the negociation was protracted so long, that a Prussian corps, for which the Prince had sent, carried Johannesberg, before the terms were concluded. The Prince saved his money, and lost only eighteen barrels of wine, of which part was sent to Paris, and the rest supplied the entertainments given by Custine.

Those of the Germans, who attached themselves to Custine, supplied him with information of the state of the whole country. His Secretary,

-cretary, Profeſſor Bohmer, had begun the inſtitution of a Club ſo early as the 22d of October;
but this ſociety is thought to have become inconvenient, and they ſoon after began to prepare for
a National Convention in Mentz.

In the mean time, Caſſel was ſurveyed, and the
fortifications, for which Eikenmayer is ſaid to
have furniſhed the deſign, were commenced. The
neighbouring peaſants were ſummoned to work at
theſe, at the price of fifteen French ſous, or about
ſeven pence halfpenny a day; and intrenchments
were thrown round Koſtheim.

On the 17th of December, Cuſtine publiſhed a
proclamation, in which he ſtated, that, whereas
ſome perſons had ſuppoſed the King of Pruſſia to
have ſo little reſpect for his character as to have
invited him to a ſurrender, none ſhould preſume,
on pain of death, to ſpeak of ſuch a meaſure, in
future. This proclamation gave the inhabitants
of Mentz information, that the Pruſſians were approaching. Some German troops had, indeed,
begun by degrees to occupy the ground about
Coblentz, but in a condition, which did not pro-
miſe active meaſures, being weakened by a long
march and by ſickneſs; the Heſſians poſted themſelves between Hanau and Franckfort; and the
Pruſſians advanced ſo near to the latter city, that
the ſcattered parties of the French retired to, and
at length loſt it.

About this time, an Electoral Profeſſor of Phi-
loſophy and a Canon of Mentz, named Dorſel,
who had left his poſts, in the preceding year, to
be naturalized, at Straſbourg, returned with a
deſign for an union of Spires, Worms and Mentz
into one territory, under the protection of the
French.

French. He procured the fubftitution of a Municipality for the City Council. He obtained
confiderable influence in the city; and, on the
1ft of January 1793, when the three commiffi-
oners of the Convention, Reubell, Merlin and
Hauffman entered Mentz, and were received by
Cuftine with military honours, they fhewed more
attention to the Profeffor than to the General.

The Pruffian head quarters had been eftablifhed
within a fhort diftance of Mentz; but, during
all December, there had been only affairs of advanced pofts, fo that fome tranquillity prevailed
in the city. On the 6th of January, Hockheim
was affailed by fix thoufand Pruffians; the French,
however, had been informed of the preparations
for attack, and had time to retire to Koftheim
and Caffel, leaving 112 prifoners and twelve
pieces of cannon. Some French, who had concealed themfelves in the church tower, were
thrown headlong from it, for having fhouted, or
thrown ftones at the King of Pruffia, as he paffed.

After this, another month paffed, without
hoftile attempts on either fide. The Pruffian
troops were refrefhed by reft; the French paffed
the fame time, partly in balls, to which all the ladies of Mentz were invited, and partly in preparations for defence. On the 17th of January, a
fmall tree of liberty, which had been planted in
November, was removed, and a fir, feventy feet
high, placed in its ftead, with much ceremony.
All the inhabitants were preffingly invited, upon this
occafion; Meffrs. Reubell, Merlin, Hauffman and
Cuftine attended; the Mayor, Municipality, and
the

the members of the Clubs followed; the enſigns of the former government were burned; Cuſtine called upon the muſic of the garriſon for French airs, which occupied the reſt of the day; and the evening concluded with entertainments and dancing. Soon after, the Commiſſioners left the city, and proceeded on a journey to the Moſelle.

On the 16th of February, Cuſtine publiſhed a proclamation, and two new commiſſioners, who had juſt arrived, iſſued another, founded upon a decree of the French Convention, relative to the union of other countries with France. The Council Houſe was full from morning till night; the aſſembled traders declared their adherence to the Germanic ſyſtem; and the new commiſſioners ſeemed inclined to liſten to their remonſtrances. But, when the three former Commiſſioners returned, they treated the Deputies of the trades with great haughtineſs, and refuſed them permiſſion to ſend agents to Paris. A ſecond deputation, on the 22d of February, was no better received, and they were informed, that the 24th was the day for the commencement of the new form. The traders are deſcribed to have been much affected, at the return of their Deputies. On the 23d of February, early in the morning, the author of a remonſtrance, which had been preſented, was arreſted and carried into baniſhment, being accompanied by guards to the advanced poſts of the Pruſſians, at Hockheim.

The inhabitants now began to leave the city by paſſports, which were, however, not eaſily procured, or uſed. A proclamation by the Municipality divided Mentz into ſections, and directed the manner, in which each ſection ſhould elect a repreſentative,

representative, on the 24th. On that day, the
streets were unusually silent, all the former burgesses having resolved to remain in their houses,
except one, and only 266 persons met to take the
new oath and to make the new elections. On the
25th, another proclamation came out, and feveral banishments succeeded; but the burgesses
still adhered to their resolution. The Municipality, on the 1st of March, again invited them
to take the new oaths, and gave notice of an order of the Commissioners to the Mayor, to pub-
lish a list of the sworn and unsworn, on the
Monday or Tuesday following. Notwithstanding
this, the number of sworn did not equal 350.

Some of the neighbouring villages, which were
visited by the French Commissioners, accepted
their terms; the greater part refused them.

At Worms, where clubs, similar to those at
Mentz, had been formed, 1051 persons took
the oaths. The inhabitants of Bingen refused
them.

In the mean time, some expeditions were made
into the Palatinate, and corn, to the amount of
sixty thousand florins, was taken away, before the
reiterated remonstrances of the Palatine Resident
at Mentz, upon the subject of his master's neu-
trality, could restrain them. In the first days of
February, the French had also entered Deux
Ponts, where the Duke relied so much upon his
having supplied only his contingent to the trea-
sure of the Empire, that he had not left his palace, though he knew of their approaches to his
country. On the 9th, at eleven at night, the
Duke

Duke and Duchefs fled, with the utmoſt precipita-
tion, to Manheim, having left the palace only one
hour before the French entered it.   Great quantities of forage were fwept away from this
country, and brought to Mentz, which the allies
now approached fo nearly, that the garrifon haſtily
completed the fortifications of Caffel, and filled
the magazines with ſtores, left the communication fhould be cut off by the deſtruction of the
bridge.

On the 15th of February, they had begun to
deſtroy the palace of *La Favorita*, and to erect a
battery upon its ruins.   Though the carriage of
provifions now occupied fo much of their attention, a great number of large and fmall cannon
were brought from Landau ; frefh troops arrived,
and General Wimpfen, who had defended Thion-
ville againſt the King of Pruffia, was declared
the firſt in command.   By banifhments and emigration, the number of perfons in the city was
reduced fifteen thoufand.

The new National Affembly met in Mentz, on
the 10th of March, that city having chofen fix
deputies, Spires two, Worms two, and fome
other places one each.   On the 17th, they had
their firſt fitting, and, on the 18th, declared all
the country between Landau and Bingen, which
places were then the limits of the French poſts
near the Rhine, united in one independent ſtate.
On the 19th, was agitated the great queſtion relative to the connections of this ſtate, and it was
not till the 21ſt, that they declared their incor-
poration with the French.   Three deputies, FORS-
TER, PATOKI and LUCKS were appointed, the
next day, to carry this refolution to Paris ; and
                                             feveral

several decrees, relative to the interior administration of this state, were passed, in consequence
of which many persons were conducted over the
bridge into banishment, on the 30th.

Accounts now arrived, that the siege would
shortly commence, and orders were issued, relative to the prevention of fires, to the collection
of stores of provisions by each family, and to several other domestic particulars. All the inhabitants, those especially in the neighbourhood of the
granaries, were directed to preserve large quantities of water; and the proprietors of gardens
within the city were ordered to plant them with
herbs. Officers were sent round to examine these
gardens. Already each family had been admonished to provide subsistence for seven months;
and the richer class were now directed to furnish
a loan to the burgesses, that the latter might be
enabled to provide for the poor. In consequence
of this order, 38,646 florins 10 creitzers, or
about 3200l. were collected, and expended for
provisions. The gardens and walks round the
city were now dismantled of their trees, of which
those in the *Rheinallee*, before mentioned, were
an hundred years old. All the summer-houses
and villas, within cannot-shot of the city, were
destroyed.

On the 8th of March, the French garrison in
the fortress of Konigstein, which the Prussians
had blockaded for some months, surrendered.
In this month also other advances were made towards Mentz. The Prussian General Schonfield
brought 12,000 men into the neighbourhood of
Hockheim, near which the Saxons were posted;
the

the King of Pruffia, his fon and the Duke of
Brunfwick, who had paffed part of the winter at
Franckfort, left it on the 23d of March; a bridge
was laid, at St. Goar, over which numerous bodies of Pruffian troops paffed the Rhine; the
French fell back towards Bingen, and the Pruffians occupied a hill, not far from it. On the
28th, they were clofer preffed, and left all the
villages in the neighbourhood of Bingen, from
which place they were driven the next day, by a
bombardment.

At the fame time, a fimilar retreat towards
Mentz alfo took place from the fouthward. At
Worms, during the abandonment, great quantities of hay and ftraw were burned, and the burgeffes kept watch, all night, dreading the conflagration of the whole city by the flames, rifing from
the magazines. Immenfe maffes of hay and ftraw
were alfo burned at Frankenthal, where there had
been a garrifon, during the whole winter; but
the corn was carried away. At Spires, early on
the 31ft of March, the burgeffes and troops were
employed in throwing the hay and ftraw from the
magazines into the ditch; but it appeared that
even this mode would not be expeditious enough;
and fire was at length fet to the whole ftore at
once.

In the retreat from Oppenheim, though the
French were under confiderable difficulties, they
were upon the point of obtaining what they would
have thought an abundant reward for them. It
was on the 30th of March, that their cavalry and
flying artillery took the road by Alfheim. As
this was a place capable of making fome defence;
                                                  and

and there were Pruffian troops vifible at the
gates, they began the attack by planting cannon,
and directing a vigorous fire upon it. The King
of Pruffia, who was at dinner in the town, and
had not an hundred men with him, received
his firft intelligence of their approach from this
fire. He immediately rode out, on the oppofite
fide, and, fending fome huffars to the fpot, the
French did not continue the conteft, but made
their retreat by another road. If they had
known how few troops were in the town, they
would, of courfe, have entered it without commencing this fire; and the Pruffian officers agree,
that, if they had done fo, there would have been
little chance of faving their monarch. Had they
been aware alfo, that his Pruffian Majefty was
there, they might have reduced this flight chance
to an impoffibility; for they were fufficiently numerous to have furrounded the town, and had
approached fo quietly, that they were not known
to be near it. The Pruffians had no cannon,
and the French were otherwife greatly fuperior;
though, having no other purpofe for entering
the town, than to continue their retreat, they
did not wait to conteft it, but retired by another road. That a circumftance, which would
have had fuch an effect upon the affairs of Europe, fhould have depended upon fo flight a
chance as this, we could not have believed, if
the ftory had not been confirmed to us by ample
authority.

The garrifon of Mentz was increafed by thefe
retreats to 23,000 men; General Kalkreuth, who
commanded the blockade from Laubenheim to
Budenheim, a diftance of twelve miles, had only

16,000 men. General Schonfield, with his corps of obfervation, was at Hockheim. The befiegers, however, prefently amounted to 30,000 men. It is remarkable, that, though the French retreated from feveral quarters, at once, and in many fmall columns, not one of thefe was effectually interrupted by the Pruffian commander.

Upon intelligence of thefe advances, the Elector of Mentz paid a vifit to the King of Pruffia, at his head quarters, and left his minifter, the Baron d'ALBINI, to attend to the affairs of the recovered places.

In the beginning of April, the blockade was more clofely preffed, and the preparations for the fiege ferioufly commenced. General d'OYRE was made commander in the city, with a Council of fixteen perfons, to affift him in reftoring the means of its defence. A perfon was placed at the top of an high building, called Stephen's Tower, with glaffes, which enabled him to overlook the country for nine miles round. He had a fecretary with him, that his view might never be unneceffarily diverted, and was obliged to make a daily report of his obfervations. The beating of drums and ringing of bells were forbidden throughout the whole city, that the befiegers might not know in what quarters the corps de garde were placed, or what churches were left without the military. All profpect houfes and trees within the walls, which could ferve as marks to the fire without, were ordered to be demolifhed. Many days were paffed in bringing further ftores of provifions into the city; after which

which an account of the stock was taken, and there were found to be

24,090 sacks of wheat.
1,465 of other corn.
996 of mixed grain.

Of which 26,551 sacks, it was stated, that 23,070 sacks of meal could be made. To this was to be added in sifted meal of wheat 109 sacks, of other corn 45 sacks, of mixed grain 10,076 sacks; making in all 33,300 sacks of meal.—— There were besides

43,960 rations of biscuit.
7,275 pounds of rice.
13,045 of dried herbs.

Of forage there were

10,820 quintals of hay.
54,270 of straw.
1,518 sacks of oats.
2,503 of barley.

The Council estimated, that the garrison had corn enough for nine months, rice for seven, and herbs for six. There were fifteen hundred horses, and it was reckoned, that the straw was enough for ten months, the oats for four-and-twenty days, and the barley for eighty days. The garrison was numbered, and found to consist of 22,653 persons; of whom to each soldier was allotted, for the future, 24 ounces of bread, per day, in lieu of 28, and 4 ounces of fresh meat, or 3 ounces of salt, in lieu of 8 ounces of fresh. The allowance of the sick in

O 2 the

the hofpitals was changed from twelve to eight ounces.

During thefe preparations for a long fiege, the diminution of the number of inhabitants, by means of the clubs, was purfued. On the 8th of April, all perfons, not ufeful to the army, were ordered to leave the city, unlefs they would take the new oath; at the fame time, it was faid, that on account of the fore-feen want of money, the foldiers, employed on the works, would be no longer paid, but the other workmen would continue to receive their falaries.

The garrifon made their firft fortie, on the night of the 10th and 11th, proceeding towards the Rhine. Koftheim was immediately taken, and the attack upon the Heffians fucceeded, at firft, but a reinforcement compelled the French to retire. About this time, the Commiffioner Reubell went to Oppenheim, where he delivered a propofal for peace to the King of Pruffia.

The village of Weiffenau was contended for, on the 15th, 16th, and 17th, and finally deftroyed, the French foldiers, who remained upon the fpot, fubfcribing 460 livres for the inhabitants.

On the 18th, nearly the whole of a French convoy of 90 waggons was taken by the Pruffi-ans. On the 20th, the Imperialifts erected a fmall fort on a point of land, near the Main, and the French, on the other hand, perfected a battery, at Koftheim, with which they fet on fire fome ftables.

2   The

The price of provisions was already so much increased in the city, that salt butter cost 48 creitzers, or 16d. per pound.

In the night of the 28th and 29th, the French landed in three vessels, and destroyed a battery, erected near the Main. On the 1st of May, at one in the morning, they attacked the Prussians, at Hockheim, and set the village of Kostheim on fire. The Prussians repulsed them with loss, but they remained in Kostheim, notwithstanding the fire, which continued for three days; they were then expelled by the Prussians, but soon returned with reinforcements, and a sanguinary contest commenced, at the end of which they continued to be masters of the village. A numerous garrison was placed in it, which, on the 8th, was again attacked by the Prussians, but without effect. Thus the greatest part of May was spent in contests for villages and posts, in which the French were generally the assailants. In the night of the 30th, they beat up, in three columns, the Prussian head quarters, at Marienborn. Having marched barefooted and with such exact information, that they passed all the batteries unperceived, they entered the village itself, without resistance, and, it is supposed, would have surprised the commander, if they had not fired at his windows, beat their drums, and begun to shout *Vive la nation!* Three balls, which entered the apartment of General KALKREUTH, admonished him to quit it, and a sentinel stepped up just in time to shoot a French soldier, who had seized him. Prince Louis Ferdinand of Prussia immediately arrived with some troops, and the French began to retire, leaving
thirty

thirty prifoners and twenty killed of 6000, engaged in the enterprife. The lofs of the Pruffians was confiderable; amongft the reft Captain Vofs, a relative of Mademoifelle Vofs, well known in the Court of Pruffia.

On the 4th of June, the allowance to the garrifon was ordered to be two pounds of bread and one bottle of wine for each foldier, per day.

In the night of the 6th and 7th, the cannonade was very fierce, on both fides; in Mentz a powder magazine was fired by a bomb, and blew up with a dreadful explofion.

The fcarcenefs of provifions increafed, fo that a pound of frefh butter coft fix fhillings. Horfeflefh began to be confumed in many families.

On the night of the 9th and 10th of June, the garrifon made four forties, which ended in confiderable lofs, on both fides, and in the retirement of the French into the city. On the 10th, they attacked, at eight in the morning, a poft near Gonfenheim, retreating without lofs, after killing an officer and feveral men. This was their firft fally in open day light.

General Meufnier, who had been wounded near Caffel, on the 7th, died on the 13th, and was buried the next day, within the new fortifications, all the officers of the garrifon, with the members of the convention and clubs, attending.

Some fire fhips were now completed, which a Dutch engineer had conducted from Holland, to be employed by the befiegers in burning the bridge

of

of boats over the Rhine. It was thought, however, that their explosion would damage the city unnecessarily, and they were rejected. In the night of the 15th, one of these floated down the river, whether by accident, or by the connivance of the inventor, is not known; the inhabitants were in the utmost terror, but it struck against the quay, and, being immediately boarded, did no damage.

The trenches were opened, in the night of the 16th and 17th, but, the workmen having been ill conducted, were not covered in, at day-light, and were compelled to retire, leaving their implements behind them. Two nights afterwards, the work was renewed in good order and without loss, the King of Pruffia, his sons and the Duke of Brunfwick surveying them from a neighbouring height. The firft balls fell in a ftreet near one of the gates, and all that part of the town was prefently deferted.

The 24th was a diftrefsful day for the inhabitants. Four days before, the King of Pruffia had fent a general paffport for fuch as chofe to come out, and 1500 perfons, chiefly women and children, had accepted his offer. A fhort time after the gate had been opened, difmay was fpread through the whole city by an account, that the Pruffians would fuffer no more to pafs and the French none to return. The bridge was covered with thefe unhappy fugitives, who had no food, or fhelter, and who thought themfelves within reach of the Hockheim batteries, that played furioufly upon the city. Two children loft their fenfes through fright. At length, the French foldiers

diers took compaffion upon them; they carried feveral perfons into the city under their cloaks, and, the next day, their remonftrances againft the inhumanity of the German clubbifts, who had fhut the gates againft this defencelefs crowd, obliged them to permit the return of the whole number.

For feveral fucceeding nights, the garrifon made forties, with various effect, interrupting, but not preventing the completion of the parallel.

At funfet, on the 27th, the befiegers began a dreadful cannonade and bombardment. On this night, the fteeple of the church of Notre Dame caught fire; and during the alarm, excited by an immenfe volume of flame, arifing in the midft of the city, the Auftrians completely carried the French pofts, near Weiffenau. The next night was equally terrible to the inhabitants; the flames caught feveral parts of the city, amongft others the cathedral; fome of the magazines took fire, and eleven hundred facks of corn were burned. The church, formerly belonging to the Jefuits, was much injured. The French, intending to retaliate their laft furprife upon the Auftrians, made a fruitlefs attack upon the Weiffenau redoubt.

On the 29th of June, at mid-day, the French were driven from a point of land, near the Main, called the Bleiau. In this affair, a veffel, with 78 Pruffians on board, drove from her anchor, owing to the unfkilfulnefs of the crew, and during a fire, by which eight men were killed, made towards the city. The Pruffians were taken prifoners, and exchanged the next day. At night, the

the bombardment was renewed; the *Domprobftei*, or palace of the Provoft, was burned and feveral of the neighbouring refidences; in other parts of the city, fome houfes were reduced to afhes.

The next night, the church of the Francifcans and feveral other public buildings were deftroyed. A dreadful fire, on the night of the 2d and 4th of June, confumed the chapel of St. Alban. Families in the fouthern part of the city now conftantly paffed the night in their cellars; in the day-time, they ventured into their ufual apartments; for the batteries of the befiegers were by far the moft terrible, at night, when the whole city was a fufficient mark for them, though their works could fcarcely be difcerned by the garrifon. In the day-time, the exactnefs of the French gunners frequently did great injury to the batteries, which, at night, were repaired and ufed with equal effect againft the city.

St. Alban's fort was now demolifhed, fo that the befieged withdrew their cannon from it. Elizabeth fort was alfo much damaged. A ftrong work, which the French had raifed, in prolongation of the *glacis*, divided the opinions of the Pruffian engineers. Some thought it fhould be preferved, when taken, becaufe it would command part of the town; others that it fhould be demolifhed. The latter opinion prevailed, and, in the night of the 5th and 6th, General Manstein was ordered to make the attack with three battalions. He perfectly fucceeded, as to the neareft part of the work, but the other, on account of its folid foundation, could not be entirely deftroyed. In the mean time, two battalions were fent, under cover of the darknefs, to

attack

attack the Zahlbach fort, a part of which they carried by ſtorm; but the reinforcements, immediately ſupplied by the garriſon, obliged them to retire. Two Pruſſian officers were killed; one wounded, and another, with one-and-thirty men, taken. The Pruſſians loſt in all 183 men; the French had twelve killed and forty-ſeven wounded.

On the 6th of July, the French repaired the damaged fort, the diſtance of it from the Pruſſians preventing the latter from hindering them.

At night, General Kleiſt carried the fort, at Zahlbach, by a ſecond attack, and demoliſhed it; at the ſame time, ſome batteries of the ſecond parallel were perfected. The French could not ſupport the loſs of this fort; on the 7th, they attacked the ſcite; carried it, after a ſevere conteſt; and rebuilt it. At night, they were driven back again and the fort entirely deſtroyed. In the ſame night they were driven from Koſtheim, after a furious battle, by the Pruſſian General Schonfield. During this engagement, the rapid ſucceſſion of flaſhes and exploſion of bombs ſeemed to fill the air with flames. A Pruſſian detachment having been poſted on the road to Caſſel, in order to prevent the garriſon of that place from ſending ſuccour to Koſtheim, this road was ſo ſtrongly bombarded by the French, that ſeven bombs were frequently ſeen in the air at once. The loſs was great, on both ſides, in this engagement, after which the Council in the city reſolved, to make no more attempts upon Koſtheim, on account of the diſtance.

The

The following night, the fire was lefs than ufual, but a few bombs and grenades fell in the city,
where the inhabitants had now learned to extin-
guifh fuch as grounded, before their *fufees* were
confumed. They alfo formed themfelves into parties for the ready fuppreffion of fires. The next
morning, the garrifon 'faw the works of the befiegers brought to within two hundred and fifty
paces of the walls.

About this time, the ficklinefs of the garrifon
became apparent, and General d'Oyré informed
the Council, that, on account of this and of the
fatiguing fervice of the works, he feared the defence could not be much longer continued. He lamented, that the troops of the line were fo few,
and the others fo inexperienced.

For feveral nights, the works of the befiegers
were eagerly pufhed, but ftill they were not fo
forward, as had been expected. Some of the befieging corps began to be fickly; the King of Pruffia
having refolved to employ no more labourers, it
was reckoned, that the foldiers, for eight-and-forty
hours of work, had only eighteen of reft. On the
other hand, they were affured, that the garrifon
muft be equally fatigued, fince, in fuch an extenfive fortification, none could be left long unemployed.

The French had been, for fome time, bufied
in forming what is called a Fleche at the head of
one of their forts, and this was thought neceffary
to be deftroyed. It was attacked in the night of
the 12th and 13th by the Auftrians ; but fo much
time was paffed in their operations, that the
French fell upon them, in great force, about two
in the morning, and beat them away, with lofs.
The Auftrians were as little employed as poffible
in fervices of this fort.

On

On the 13th of July, another battery was storm-
ed by the Pruffians; but, as the officer, unlike
the Auftrians, advanced with too little caution,
his party was much hurt by fome pieces of concealed cannon, and the enterprife failed.

The night of the 13th and 14th was paffed in
much agitation by the garrifon and inhabitants.
Several of the public buildings were fet fire to
and burned by grenades. The works of the befiegers were now greatly advanced. The garrifon
made five forties in this night, and were repulfed
in all, lofing an hundred men, while the befiegers
loft eight killed and one-and-thirty wounded.

On the 14th of July, a ceffation of arms took
place from feven o'clock in the morning till one.
In the city, the French celebrated their annual
fête; the General d'Oyre and the troops took
the oath, and Merlin delivered an addrefs to
them. In the Auftrian camp, the Prince de
Conde was received with a *feu de joye*. During
this ceffation, the foldiers upon the different out-
pofts entered into converfation with each other,
and the French boafted of the difficulties they laboured under from the length of the fiege.

At night, an affair at the Fleche coft the allies,
who fucceeded in part, ninety men; the French
confeffed, that this work coft them in all three
hundred. The inhabitants of the city were again
greatly alarmed, their ftreets being covered with
a fhower of grenades. The laboratory and a part
of the Benedictine abbey were burned, and two
explofions took place at the former. The whole
city fhook with each report, and, in the nearer
parts, all the windows are broken and the doors
burft

burſt open. The remainder of the hay and ſtraw was conſumed in this fire; the whole ſtock of other forage was reduced to a ſufficiency for four days; and the ſurgeon's ſtores were much damaged.

Still the Fleche prevented the beſiegers from completing their ſecond parallel. It was, therefore, again attacked, on the night of the 16th and 17th, Prince Louis Ferdinand of Pruſſia commanding at the aſſault, in which he was one of twelve officers wounded. The Fleche was then completely carried.

The next night was very induſtriouſly ſpent by the beſiegers in forming new batteries, and thoſe of the ſecond parallel were raiſed, before there were cannon enough at hand to place upon them. The French took advantage of this, and brought a part of theirs to bear, ſo as to enfilade the parallel, with great effect; the Pruſſians almoſt immediately loſing an officer and forty men.

In the city, the ſick had now increaſed ſo much, that ſix hundred men were brought from Caſſel, on the 17th, to reinforce the garriſon. On the 18th, the commandant informed the Council, that there was a want of fodder and ſuch a loſs of horſes, by deſertion, that there were not cavalry enough left for ſervice. The ſoldiers, who knew the deficiency of medicines and other means of relief for the wounded, were unwilling to be led to ſorties. Though corn had not failed, flour, it appeared, ſoon would, for ſome of the mills had been rendered unſerviceable, for the preſent, by ſhot, and others were deſerted by the millers.

At

At night, after an unfuccefsful attempt upon the Fleche, it was refolved, that the garrifon, which had hitherto fcarcely fuffered a night to pafs, without making fome forties, fhould, for the future, adhere folely to defenfive meafures. Some engineers propofed to abandon the whole line of forts, and others, that two of the largeft fhould be blown up. The General and Council, at length, confeffed, that they could not continue the defence, and affured the inhabitants, who had declared themfelves in their favour, that a longer delay of the furrender would produce a more fevere difpofition of the befiegers towards them, without increafing the chance of efcaping it.

A negotiation, relative to the furrender, was now begun by D'Oyre, in a letter, which partly replied to one from the Pruffian commander Kalkreuth, upon the fubject of the departure of aged perfons and children from the city. Their correfpondence continued till the 20th, and feveral letters were exchanged, chiefly upon the queftion of the removal, or detention of the inhabitants, who had attached themfelves to the French; it was then broken off, upon a difagreement, as to this and fome other points. The firing, on both fides, had in the mean time continued, and the befiegers carried on the trenches, though thefe were now fuch an eafy mark for the garrifon, that they loft an officer and five-and-twenty men, in the night of the 19th and 20th. The next night, the Dominicans' church in the city took fire, and fix French foldiers were buried under its ruins.

Upon a renewal of the intercourfe, the fire flackened, on the 21ft; but, on fome delays in the

the negociation, was threatened to be recommenced. At length, the conditions, of the surrender were settled, and the negotiation, signed on the 22d of July, by the two Generals Kalkreuth and D'Oyré; the former having rendered the capitulation somewhat easier than was expected for the garrison, because the Duke of Brunswick had only nineteen thousand men to cover the siege, and Custine had forty thousand, which were near enough to attack him. General KALKREUTH's orders are supposed to have been to obtain possession of the place, upon any terms, that would give it him quickly.

At this time, the garrison, which, at the commencement of the siege, had consisted of 22,653 men, was reduced to 17,038, having had 1959 killed, 3334 wounded, or rendered unserviceable by sickness, and having lost 322 by desertion.

The loss of the besiegers is stated at about 3000 men.

The consumption of ammunition, on the part of the French, was found to have been

681,850 pounds of powder,
106,152 cannon balls,
10,278 bombs,
6592 grenades,
44,500 pounds of iron,
300,340 musquet cartridges;

and, during the siege, 107 cannon either burst, or were rendered unserviceable by the besiegers' shot. Towards the conclusion, sixty cannon also became useless by the failure of balls of the proper calibre.

On

On the 24th and 25th, the garrifon marched out, MERLIN leading the firft column of 7500 men. The members of the Clubs, who would have gone out with the troops, were pointed out by the other inhabitants and detained; but the Elector had the magnanimity to think of no other retaliation, than their imprifonment in a tower, near the Rhine, where they have fince remained.

There was now leifure to examine the city, and it was found, that fix churches were in ruins; that feven manfions of the nobility had been burned, and that very few houfes had efcaped, without fome damage. The furrounding grounds were torn up by balls and batteries. The works of Caffel were furrendered entire to the conquerors, and are an important addition to the ftrength of Mentz, already reckoned one of the ftrongeft and largeft fortifications in Europe. Between Caffel and the ruins of Koftheim not a tree was to be feen. All the neighbouring villages were more, or lefs, injured, being contended for, as pofts, at the commencement of the fiege; and the country was fo much disfigured, that the proprietors of lands had fome difficulty to afcertain their boundaries.

MENTZ.

MENTZ.

SOMETHING has been already faid of the prefent condition of this city: upon a review it appears, that from the mention of churches, palaces, burgeffes, quays and ftreets, we might be fuppofed to reprefent it as a confiderable place, either for fplendour, or commerce, or for having its middle claffes numeroufly filled. Any fuch opinion of Mentz will be very incorrect. After two broad and fomewhat handfome ftreets, all the other paffages in the city are narrow lanes, and into thefe many of the beft houfes open, having, for the moft part, their lower windows barricadoed, like thofe of Cologne. The difadvantage, with which any buildings muft appear in fuch fituations, is increafed by the neglected condition of thefe; for a German has no notion, that the outfide of his houfe fhould be clean, even if the infide is fo. An Englifhman, who fpends a few hundred pounds in a year, has his houfe in better condition, as to neatnefs, than any German nobleman's we faw; a Dutchman, with fifty pounds a year, exceeds both.

The Elector's palace is a large turretted building of reddifh ftone, with one front towards the Rhine, which it commands in a delightful point of view; but we did not hear, that it was fo much altered, by being now ufed as a barrack, as that its appearance can formerly have been much lefs fuitable than at prefent to fuch a purpofe.

P On

On the quay there is some appearance of traffic, but not much in the city; so that the transfer of commodities from vessels of other districts to those of the Electorate may be supposed to contribute great part of the show near the river. The commerce is not sufficient to encourage the building of warehouses over the quay. The vessels are ill rigged, and the hulls are entirely covered with pitch, without paint. About thirty of these, apparently from forty to seventy tons burthen, were lying near the quay; and the war could scarcely have diminished their usual number, so many being employed in carrying stores for the armies.

The burgesses are numerous, and have some privileges, which render their political condition enviable to the other inhabitants of the Electorate. But, though these have invited manufacturers, and somewhat encouraged commerce, there is not wealth enough in the neighbouring country, to make such a consumption, as shall render many traders prosperous. In point of wealth, activity and address, the burgesses of Mentz are much below the opinion, which must be formed, while German cities are described and estimated by their importance in their own country, rather than by a comparison of their condition with that of others. A trader, it will be allowed, is at least as likely to appear to advantage in his business as in any other state. His intelligence may surely be, in some degree, judged of by those, who deal with him; and that we might know something of those of Mentz, we passed some of the little time we were left to ourselves in endeavouring to buy trifles at their shops.

The

The idleness and inadvertence we generally saw are difficult to be conceived; perhaps, the trouble, experienced in purchasing a book, may give an idea of them. We wanted the German pamphlet, from which most of the above-mentioned particulars of the siege are extracted; and, as it related to a topic so general within the place, we smiled, when our friends said they would *assist* us to procure it, during a walk. Two booksellers, to whom we applied, knew nothing of it; and one supposed, that an engraved view of the works would do quite as well. Passing another shop, a young German gentleman enquired for it of the master, who was at the door, and heard, that we might have it, upon our return, in half an hour. The door, when we came back, was shut, and no knocking could procure it to be opened; so that we were obliged to send into the dwelling-house. When the shopman came, he knew nothing of the book; but, being assured that his master had promised it, went away, and returned with a copy in sheets. We paid for this, and left it to be sewed, which was agreed to be done, in three hours. At that time, it was not finished, but might be had in another hour; and, after that hour, it was again promised, within two. Finally, it could not be had, that night, but would be ready in the morning, and, in the morning, it was still unfinished; we then went to Franckfort without it, and it was sent after us by a friend. This was the most aggravated instance we saw of a German trader's manners; but something like it may be almost every where met with.

From such symptoms and from the infrequency of wealth among the middle classes it is apparent,

that

that Mentz could not have been important, as to commerce, even if there had been no fiege, which is here mentioned as the caufe of all deficiencies, and certainly is fo of many. The deftruction of property, occafioned by it, will not be foon remedied. The nobility have almoft forfaken a place, where their palaces have been either deftroyed, or ranfacked; the Prince has no refidence there; fome of the Germans, who emigrated on account of the laft fiege, fled into France; the war-taxes, as well as the partial maintenance of the garrifon, diminifh what property remains; and all expenditure is upon a reduced footing.

The contribution of the inhabitants towards a fupport of the garrifon is made by the very' irkfome means of affording them lodging. At the beft houfes, the doors are chalked over with the names of officers, lodged in them; which the fervants dare not efface, for the foldiers muft know where to find their officers. In a family, whom we vifited, four officers and their fervants were quartered; but it muft be acknowledged, that the former, fo far from adding to this inconvenience by any negligent conduct, were conftantly and carefully polite. We, indeed, never faw Pruffian officers otherwife; and can teftify, that they are as much fuperior to thofe Auftrians in manners and intelligence, as they are ufually faid to be in military qualities.

Another obftruction, which the fiege has given to the profperity of Mentz, confifts in the abfence of many members of the Noble Chapter; an inftitution, which, however ufelefs, or injurious to the ccuntry, occafions the expenditure of confiderable

rable fums in the capital. , That of Mentz is faid
to be one of the richeft of many fimilar Chapters
in Germany. From fuch foundations the younger
fons of noble families derive fometimes very ample incomes, and are but little reftricted by their
regulations from any enjoyment of temporal fplendour. Their carriages and liveries vie with thofe
of the other attendants at Court; they are not
prohibited from wearing the ornaments of orders
of knighthood; are very little enjoined to refidence; are received in the environs of the Court
with military honours, and allowed to refide in
their feparate houfes. They may wear embroidery
of gold, and cloths of any colours, except fcarlet,
or green, which, as well as filver lace, are
thought too gay. Being thus permitted and enabled to become examples of luxury, their refidence in any city diffufes fome appearance of profperity over it.

One of the largeft buildings in Mentz is the arfenal, which fronts towards the river, and attracts
the attention of thofe, who walk upon the quay,
by having armed heads placed at the windows of
the firft floor, which feem to frown, with Roman
fternnefs, upon the paffenger. In one of the principal rooms within, a party of figures in fimilar
armour are placed at a council-board. We did
not hear who contrived them; but the heads in
the windows may be miftaken for real ones, at
the diftance of fifty yards. ..

The Elector of Mentz, who is chofen by a
Chapter of twenty-four Canons, and is ufually one
of their number, is the firft ecclefiaftical Prince
in the empire, of which he is alfo the Arch-chan-
cellor and Director of the Electoral College. In
the

the Diet, he fits on the right hand of the Emperor, affixes the feal of the Empire to its decrees, and has afterwards the cuftody of them among the archives. His revenues, in a time of peace, are nearly 200,000*l.* annually; but, during a war, they are much lefs, a third part of them arifing from tolls, impofed upon the navigation of the Rhine. The vineyards fupply another large part; and his fubjects, not interefted in them, are but little taxed, except when military preparations are to be made; the taxes are then as direct as poffible, that money may be immediately collected.

The fortifications of his chief city are as much a misfortune to his country as they are an advantage to the reft of the Empire. Being always one of the firft objects, on this fide of the Rhine, fince an enemy cannot crofs the river, while fo confiderable a fortrefs and fo large a garrifon as it may contain, might, perhaps, check their return, the Electorate has been often the fcene of a tedious warfare. From the firft raifing of the works by Louis the Fourteenth, their ftrength has never been fully tried. The furrender in 1792 was partly for the want of a proper garrifon, and partly by contrivance; even in 1793, when the defence was fo furious and long, the garrifon, it is thought, might have held out further, if their ftores had been fecured in bomb-proof buildings. A German garrifon, fupported by an army, which fhould occupy the oppofite bank of the Rhine, might be continually reinforced and fupplied, fo as to be conquered by nothing but the abfolute demolition of the walls.

The

The bridge of boats over the Rhine, which, both in peace and war, is fo important to the city, is now in a much better ſtate than the French found it, being guarded, at the eaſtern end, by the fortifications of Caſſel. Notwithſtanding its great length and the rapidity of the river, it is fo well conſtructed, as to be much leſs liable to injury, than might be fuppoſed, and would probably fuſtain batteries, which might defeat every attempt at deſtroying it by fireſhips. It is 766 feet long, and wide enough for the paſſage of two carriages at once. Various repairs, and the care of a daily ſurvey, have continued it, ſince 1661, when it was thrown over the river.

The practice of modifying the names of towns ſo as to incorporate them ſeparately with every language, is no where more remarkable than with reſpect to thoſe of Germany, where a ſtranger, unleſs he is aware of them, might find the variations very inconvenient. The German name for what we call Mentz, is *Maynz ;* the French, which is moſt uſed, *Mayence ;* and the Italian, *Magontio,* by deſcent from the Roman *Magontiacum.* The German ſynonym for Liege is *Luttich ;* for Aix la Chapelle, *Achen ;* for Bois le Duc, *Herzogenbuſch ;* and for Cologne, *Cöln,* which is pronounced *Keln.* The name, borne by every town in the nation to which it belongs, ſhould ſurely be its name, wherever it is mentioned ; for the ſame reaſon, that words, derived into one language from another, are pronounced according to the authority of their roots, becauſe the uſe of the primary term is already eſtabliſhed, and there can never be a deciſion between ſubſequent varieties, which are cotemporary among themſelves, and are each produced by the ſame arrogance of invention.

FRANCKFORT.

FRANCKFORT.

WE came hither by means of a paſſage boat, which we were told would ſhew ſomething of the German populace, but which diſplayed nothing ſo much as the unſkilfulneſs of the German ſailors. Though they make this voyage, every day, they went aground in the even ſtream of the Maine, and during the calmeſt weather; fixing the veſſel ſo faſt by their ill-directed ſtruggle to get off, that they were compelled to bring the towing horſes to the ſide and tug backward with the ſtream. There were an hundred people in the boat; but the expedient of deſiring them to remove from the part, which was aground, was never uſed. We heard, that they ſeldom make the voyage, without a ſimilar ſtoppage, not againſt any ſhifting ſand, but upon the permanent ſhelves of the river.

The diſtance is about four-and-twenty miles, but we were nine hours in reaching Franckfort, the environs of which afford ſome ſymptoms of a commercial and opulent city, the banks of the Maine being covered for nearly the laſt mile with country ſeats, ſeparated from each other by ſmall pleaſure grounds.

There are gates and walls to Franckfort, but the magiſtrates do not oppreſs travellers by a military examination at their entrance. Having ſeen the worthleſſneſs of many places, which bear oſtentatious characters either for ſplendour or trade, we

were

were furprifed to find in this as much of both as had been reported. The quays were well covered with goods and labourers; the ftreets neareft to the water are lined with fhops, and thofe in the middle of the city with the houfes of merchants, of which nearly all the fpacious, and many magnificent. Some, indeed, might be called palaces, if they had nobility for their tenants; but, though the independence, which commerce fpreads among the middle claffes, does not entirely deter the German nobility from a refidence here, the fineft houfes are the property of merchants.

In our way to the *Cigne Blanc*, which is one of the beft inns, we paffed many of fo good an appearance, that it was difficult to believe there could be better in a German city. But Franckfort, which is the pride of Germany, in this refpect, has probably a greater number of large inns than any other place of equal extent in Europe. The fairs fill thefe, twice in a year, for three weeks at each time; and the order, which is indifpenfible then, continues at other periods, to the furprife and comfort of ftrangers.

This city has been juftly defcribed by many travellers; and Dr. MOORE has treated of its inhabitants with the eafe and elegant animation of his peculiar manner. We fhall not affume the difadvantage of entering upon the fame fubject after him. The inhabitants of Franckfort are very diftinct, as to manners and information, from the other Germans; but they are fo far like to thofe of our own commercial cities, that one able account leaves fcarcely any thing new to be feen or told, concerning them.

All

All their bleffings of liberty, intelligence, and wealth are obferved with the more attention, becaufe they cannot be approached, except through countries afflicted by arbitrary power, ignorance and poverty. The exiftence of fuch a city, in fuch a fituation, is little lefs than a *phenomenon*; the caufes of which are fo various and minute as to make the effect, at firft fight, appear almoft accidental. The jealoufy of the neighbouring Princes towards each other, is the known, and certainly, the chief caufe of its exterior protection againft each; the continuance of its interior liberties is probably owing to the circumftance, which, but for that jealoufy, would expofe it to fubjection from without,—the fmallnefs of its territory. Where the departments of government muft be very few, very difficult to be rendered expenfive to the public, and very near to their infpection, the ambition of individuals can be but little tempted to contrive encroachments upon the community. So complexly are the chief caufes of its exterior and interior independence connected with each other.

As to the firft of thefe, it may, perhaps, be replied, that a fimilar jealoufy has not always been fufficient to protect fimilar cities; and Dantzick is the recent inftance of its infufficiency. But the jealoufy as to Dantzick, though fimilar, was not equal to this, and the temptation to oppofe it was confiderably greater. What would the moft capable of the neighbouring Princes gain by the feizure of Franckfort? A place of ftrength? No. A place capable of paying taxes? Yes; but taxes, which would be re-impofed upon commodities, confumed partly by his own fubjects, whofe property is his own already, and partly by thofe of his

his neighbours, to whose jealousy they would afford an additional and an unappeasable provocation. Dantzick, on the contrary, being a seaport, was, if not strong, capable of supplying strength, and might pay taxes, which should not fall entirely upon its neighbours, but upon the distant countries, that traffick with it. And even to these considerations it is unnecessary to resort, unless we can suppose, that despotism would have no effect upon commerce; a supposition which does not require to be refuted. If a severe taxation was introduced here, and, in so small a district, taxation must be severe to be productive; if such a taxation was to be introduced, and if the other advantage of conquest, that of a forcible levy of soldiers, was attempted, commerce would vanish in silence before the oppressor, and the Prince, that should seize the liberties of Franckfort, would find nothing but those liberties in his grasp.

On the other hand, what are the advantages of permitting the independence of such a city to the sovereigns, who have the power of violating it? Those of a neutral barrier are well known, but apply only to military, or political circumstances. The others are the market, which Franckfort affords, for the produce and manufactures of all the neighbouring states; its value as a banking depôt and *emporium*, in which Princes may place their money, without rendering it liable to the orders of each other, or from which they may derive loans, by negotiating solely and directly with the lenders; its incapacity for offensive measures; and its usefulness as a place of meeting to themselves, or their ministers, when political connections are to be discussed.

That

That the inhabitants do enjoy this independence without and freedom within, we believe, not becaufe they are afferted by treaties, or political forms; of which the former might not have furvived the temporary interefts, that concluded them, and the latter might be fubdued by corruption, if there were the means of it; but becaufe they were acknowledged to us by many temperate and difcerning perfons, as much aloof from faction, as they were from the affectation, or fervility, that fometimes makes men boaft themfelves free, only becaufe they have, or would be thought to have, a little fhare in oppreffing others. Many fuch perfons declared to us, that they had a fubftantial, practical freedom; and we thought a teftimony to their actual enjoyments more valuable than any formal acknowledgments of their rights. As to thefe latter fecurities, indeed, Franckfort is no better provided than other imperial cities, which have proved their inutility. It ftands in the fame lift with Cologne, but is as fuperior to it in government as in wealth.

The inhabitants having had the good fenfe to forefee, that fortifications might render them a more defirable prize to their neighbours, at the fame time that their real protection muft depend upon other means, have done little more than fuftain their antient walls, which are fufficient to defend them againft a furprife by fmall parties. They maintain no troops, except a few companies of city-guards, and make their contributions to the army of the Empire in fpecie. Thefe companies are filled chiefly with middle-aged men, whofe appearance befpeaks the plenty and peacefulnefs of the city. Their uniforms, blue and

and white, are of the cut of thofe in the prints of MARLBOROUGH's days; and their grenadiers' caps are of the fame peaked fort, with tin facings, impreffed with the city arms.

In wars with France, the fate of Franckfort has ufually depended upon that of Mentz, which is properly called the key of Germany, on the weftern frontier. In the campaign of 1792, Cuftine detached 3000 troops of the 11,000, with which he had befieged Mentz, and thefe reached Franckfort, early in the morning of the 22d of October. NEUWINGER, their commander, fent a letter to the magiftrates from Cuftine, demanding a contribution of two millions of florins, which by a negotiation at Mentz, was reduced to a million and a half, for the prefent. Notice was accordingly given in the city, that the magiftrates would receive money at four per cent. intereft, and, on the 23d, at break of day, it began to flow in to the Council-houfe from all quarters. Part was immediately given to NEUWINGER, but payment of the reft was delayed; fo that Cuftine came himfelf on the 27th, and, by throwing the hoftages into prifon, obtained, on the 31ft of October, the remainder of the firft million. For the fecond, the magiftrates gave fecurity to NEUWINGER, but it was never paid; the Convention difavowed great part of the proceedings of Cuftine, and the money was not again demanded.

The French, during the whole of their ftay, were very eager to fpread exaggerated accounts of their numbers. Troops were accordingly marched out at one gate of the city, with very little parade, that they might enter with much pomp and

and in a longer column, at the other. The inhabitants, who were not expert at military numeration, easily believed, that the first party had joined other troops, and that the whole amounted to treble their real number. After the entry of the Prussians, this contrivance was related by prisoners.

The number of troops, left in the city by Custine, on his retirement from the neighbouring posts, in the latter end of November, was 1800 men, with two pieces of cannon. On the 28th, when the Prussian Lieutenant Pellet brought a summons to surrender, Helden, the commander, having sent to Custine for reinforcements and cannon, was answered, that no men could be spared; and that, as to cannon, he might use the city artillery. Helden endeavoured to remove this from the arsenal; but the populace, encouraged by the neighbourhood of the Prussians, rose to prevent him; and there might have been a considerable tumult, if Custine had not arrived, on the 29th, and assured the magistrates, that the garrison should retire, rather than expose the place to a siege. The city then became tranquil, and remained so till the 2d of December, when the inhabitants, being in church, first knew by the noise of cannon, that the place was attacked.

General Helden would then have taken his two cannon to the gate, which was contended for, but the inhabitants, remembering Custine's promise, would permit no resistance; they cut the harness of the horses, broke the cannon wheels, and themselves opened the gates to the Prussians, or rather to the Hessians, for the advanced corps of the assailants was chiefly formed of them. About 100 fell

in

in this attack. Of the French 41 were killed;
139 wounded; and 800 taken prisoners. The
remainder of the 1800 reached Cuftine's army.
A monument, erected without the northern gate
of the city, commemorates the lofs of the 100
affailants, on the fpot, on which they fell.

Thus Franckfort, having happily but few fortifications, was loft and regained, without a fiege;
while Mentz, in a period of fix more months,
had nearly all its beft buildings deftroyed, by a
fimilar change of mafters.

We ftayed here almoft a week, which was well
occupied by vifits, but fhewed nothing in addition to what is already known of the fociety of
the place. Manners, cuftoms, the topics of converfation and even drefs, differ very flightly from
thofe of London, in fimilar ranks; the merchants
of Franckfort have more generally the advantages
of travel, than thofe of England, but they have
not that minute knowledge of modern events
and characters, which an attention to public
tranfactions renders common in our ifland.
Thofe, who have been in England, or who fpeak
Englifh, feem defirous to difcufs the ftate of par-
liamentary tranfactions and interefts, and to remedy the thinnefs of their own public topics, by
introducing ours. In fuch difcuffions one error
is very general from their want of experience.
The faculty of making a fpeech is taken for the
ftandard of intellectual power in every fort of exertion; though there is nothing better known in
countries, where public fpeakers are numerous
enough to be often obferved, than that perfons
may be educated to oratory, fo as to have a facility,

lity, elegance and force in it, diftinct from the endowments of deliberative wifdom; may be taught to fpeak in terms remote from common ufe, to combine them with an unfailing dexterity of arrangement, and to inveft thought with its portion of artificial dignity, who through the chaos of benefits and evils, which the agitation of difficult times throws up before the eye of the politician, fhall be able to fee no gleam of light, to defcribe no direct path, to difcern no difference between greater and leffer evils, nor to think one wholefome truth for a confiding and an honeft country. To eftimate the general intellectual powers of men, tutored to oratory, from their fuccefs in the practice of it, is as abfurd as to judge of corporeal ftrength from that of one arm, which may have been rendered unufually ftrong by exercife and art.

Of the fociety at Franckfort, Meffrs. Bethman, the chief bankers, feem able to collect a valuable part; and their politenefs to ftrangers induces them to do it often. A traveller, who miffes their table, lofes, both as to converfation and elegant hofpitality, a welcome proof of what freedom and commerce can do againft the mental and phyfical defolation otherwife fpread over the country.

The affiftance, which the mutual ufe of languages gives to a connection between diftant places, we were happy to fee exifting and increafing, to the advantage of England, at Franckfort. At the Meffrs. Bethmans', one day, French was nearly excluded, the majority being able to converfe with nine or ten Englifh, who were there, in their own language. Of the merchants, who have not been in England,

feveral

feyeral fpeak Englifh, without difficulty, and the rifing generation, it is faid, will be generally accomplifhed in it.

One of the luxuries of Franckfort is a *Cabinet Literaire*, which is open to ftrangers by the introduction of members. There the beft periodical publications of the Continent are received, and their titles immediately entered in a book, fo that the reading is not difturbed by converfation with the librarian. It excited our fhame to hear that fome contrivance had, for feveral months, prevented the fociety from receiving a very valuable Englifh publication.

After this, the Theatre may feem to require fome notice. It is a modern, but not an elegant building, ftanding in an area, that renders it convenient of accefs, and nearly in the middle of the city. The interior, which has been gaudily decorated, contains a pit, three rows of boxes, that furround the audience part, and a gallery over them in the centre. It is larger than the Little Theatre in the Haymarket, and in form, refembles that of Covent Garden, except that fix or feven of the central boxes, in each tier, encroach upon the oval figure by a projection over the pit. The boxes are let by the year; the price of admiffion for non-fubfcribers, is a florin, for which they may find places in the boxes, engaged by their friends, or in the pit, which is in the fame proportion of efteem as that at an Opera-houfe.

The performances are plays and operas alternately; both in German; and the mufic of the latter chiefly by German compofers. The players are very far beneath mediocrity; but the orcheftra, when we heard it, accorded with the

Q.　　fame

fame of German muficians, for fpirit and preci-
fion. In thefe qualities even the wandering parties, that play at inns, are very feldom deficient.

The ftage was well lighted, but the other parts
of the theatre were left in dufkinefs, which
fcarcely permitted us to fee the diamonds, pro-
fufely worn by feveral ladies. Six o'clock is
the hour of beginning, and the performances
conclude foon after nine.

The Cabinet Literaire and the Theatre are
the only permanent places of public amufement
at Franckfort, which is, however, in want of no
more, the inhabitants being accuftomed to pafs
much of their time in friendly parties, at their
houfes. Though wealth is, of courfe, earneftly
and univerfally fought for in a place purely
mercantile, we were affured, that the richeft
perfons, and there are fome, who have above
half a million fterling, find no more attention in
thefe parties than others. This was acknowledged and feparately boafted of by fome of
the very rich, and by thofe who were comparatively poor. We are fo far able to report it for
true, as that we could never difcern the leaft
traces of the officioufnefs, or fubferviency
that, in a corrupt and debafed ftate of fociety,
frequently point to the wealthieft individuals
in every private party.

Thefe and many other circumftances would
probably render Franckfort a place of refidence
for foreigners, if the magiftrates, either dreading
the increafe of luxury, or the interference of
ftrangers with their commerce, did not prevent
this by prohibiting them from being lodged
otherwife than at inns. It was with difficulty,
that an Englifh officer, acting as Commiffary to
fome

some of the German regiments, lately raised upon our pay, could obtain an exemption from this rule, at the request of the Hanoverian Minister.

Round the city, are several well-disposed walks, as pleasant as the flatness of the nearer country will permit; and, at intervals, along these, are country houses of the merchants, who do not choose to go beyond the city territories, for a residence. Saxenhausen, a small town, on the other side of the Maine, though incorporated with Franckfort, as to jurisdiction, and connected with it, by a bridge, is chiefly inhabited by watermen and other labourers.

We left Franckfort after a stay of six days, fortified by a German passport from M. de Swartzhoff, the Hanoverian Minister, who obligingly advised us to be prepared with one in the native language of the Austrian officers. At Mentz the ceremonies of examination were rendered much more troublesome than before, the Governor, General Kalkreuth, happening to be in the great square, who chose to make several travellers wait as if for a sort of review before him, though, after all, nothing was to be said but " Go to the Commandant, who will look at your passports." This Commandant was M. de Lucadou, a gentleman of considerate and polite manners, who, knowing our friends in Mentz, added to his confirmation of M. de Swartzhoff's passport an address to M. de Wilde, the intendant of some salt mines in Switzerland, which he recommended to us to see. These circumstances are necessary to be mentioned here, because they soon led to a disagreeable and very contradictory event in our journey.

Q 2

The

The next morning, we fet out from Mentz, and were conducted by our voiturier over a fummer road, on the left bank of the Rhine, then flowing with the melted fnows of Switzerland.

OPPENHEIM.

THIS is the firft town of the Palatinate, on arriving from the north; and it bears marks of the devaftation, inflicted upon that country, in the laft century, more flagrant than could be expected, when the length of·the intervening time, and the complete recovery of other cities from fimilar difafters, are confidered. Louis the Fourteenth's fury has converted it from a populous city into little more than a picturefque ruin. It was burned in 1668; and the walls, which remain in double, or fometimes in treble circles, are more vifible at a diftance than the ftreets, which have been thinly erected within them. Above all, is the *Landfcreon*, or crown of the country, a caftle erected on an eminence, which commands the Rhine, and dignifies the view from it, for feveral miles. The whole city, or rather ruin, ftands on a brow, over this majeftic river.

The gates do not now open directly into ftreets, but into lanes of ftone walls between vineyards and gardens, formed on the fite of houfes, never reftored fince the fire. The town itfelf has fhrunk from its ancient limits into a few ftreets in the centre. In fome of the interftices, corn grows up to the walls of the prefent houfes.

houfes. In others, the ruins of former buildings remain, which the owners have not been
tempted to remove, for the fake of cultivating
their fites. Of the cathedral, faid to have been
once the fineft on the Rhine, nearly all the walls
and the tower ftill exift; but thefe are the only
remains of grandeur in a city, which feems entirely incapable of overcoming in this century
the wretchednefs it inherits from the laft.

Had the walls been as ftrong as they are extenfive, this place might not improbably have endured a fiege in the prefent age, having been feveral times loft and regained. It was furrendered to the French, without a conteft, in the
campaign of 1792. After their retreat from
Worms, and during the fiege of Mentz, it was
occupied by the Pruffians; and, in December
1793, when the allies retired from Alface, the
Duke of Brunfwick eftablifhed his head-quarters in it, for the purpofe of covering the fortrefs. His army ovens remained near the northern gate in July 1794, when we paffed through
it. In October of the fame year it fell again into
the hands of the French.

No city on the banks of the Rhine is fo well
feated for affording a view of it as this. which,
to the north, overlooks all its windings as far as
Mentz, and, fouthward, commands them towards
Worms. The river is alfo here of a noble breadth
and force, beating fo vehemently againft the wa-
ter-mills, moored near the fide, that they feem
likely to be borne away with the current. A
city might be built on the fite of Oppenheim,
which fhould faintly rival the caftle of Goodefberg, in the richnefs, though not in the fublimity of its profpect.

From

From hence the road leads through a fertile country of corn and vines, but at a greater diſtance from the river, to Worms, five or fix miles from which it becomes broad, ſtraight, and bordered with regularly-planted trees, that form an avenue to the city. Soon after leaving Oppenheim, we had the firſt ſymptom of an approach to the immediate theatre of the war, meeting a waggon, loaded with wounded ſoldiers. On this road there was a long train of carriages, taking ſtores to ſome military *depôt*. The defacement of the Elector's arms, on poſts near the road, ſhewed alſo, that the country had been lately occupied by the French; as the delay in cutting the ripe corn did, that there was little expectation of their return.

WORMS.

THE condition of Worms is an aggravated repetition of the wretchedneſs of Oppenheim. It ſuffered ſomething in the war, which the unfortunate Elector, ſon-in-law of our James the Firſt, provoked by accepting the kingdom of Bohemia. Louis the Fourteenth came upon it next, and in 1569, burned every thing that could be conſumed. Nothing was reſtored, but on that part, which was the centre of the antient city; and the walls include, as at Oppenheim, corn and vineyards upon the ground, which was once covered with houſes, and which plainly appears to have been ſo, from the lanes that paſs between, and doors that open into the incloſures. A much larger

ſpace

fpace is fo covered, than at Openheim, for you are fome time in driving from the northern gate of the old city to the firft ftreet of the prefent one.

On the right of the road ftands the fkeleton of the Electoral palace, which the French burned in one of the late campaigns, and it is as curious as melancholy to obferve how the figns of antient and modern defolation mingle with each other. On one hand is a palace, burned by the prefent French; on the other the walls of a church, laid open by Louis the Fourteenth.

The firft and principal ftreet of the place leads through thefe mingled ruins, and through rows of dirty houfes, miferably tenanted, to the other end of the city. A few others branch from it, chiefly towards the Rhine, including fometimes the ruins, and fometimes the repaired parts of churches; of which ftreets, narrow, ill-paved and gloomy, confifts the city of Worms. The French General, that lately wrote to Paris, "We entered the fair epifcopal city of Worms," may be fuppofed to have derived his terms from a geographical dictionary, rather than from a view of his conqueft.

We were now in a place, occupied by part of the acting army of the allies, which if not immediately liable to be attacked, was to be defended by the maintenance of pofts at a very fhort diftance. Troops paffed through it daily, for the fervice of thefe pofts, the noife of every cannonade was audible, and the refult of every engagement was immediately known, for it might make an advance, or a retreat neceffary from Worms. The wounded men arrived, foon after the intelligence, to the military hofpitals of the

the Pruffians. A city fo circumftanced, feemed to differ but little from a camp; and we were aware, for a few hours, of a departure from the fecurity and order of civil life.

The inn, which was not otherwife a mean building, was nearly deftitute of furniture; fo that the owner was prepared to receive any fort of guefts, or mafters. The only provifion which we could obtain was bread, the commoneft fort of wine, and one piece of cold veal; for the city was under military jurifdiction, and no guefts were allowed to have more than one difh at their table.

In the afternoon, we faw, for the firft time, a crowd in a German city. A narrow waggon, of which nearly all but the wheels was bafketwork, had arrived from the army, with a wounded officer, who lay upon the floor, fupported by his fervant, but occafionally rofe to return the falutes of paffengers. This was the Prince of Anhalt Pleffis, who had been wounded, in the morning, when the French attacked all the neighbouring lines of the allies, and an indecifive engagement enfued, the noife of which had been diftinctly heard at Worms. He was hurt in the leg, and defcended, with much difficulty, from the waggon; but did not, for an inftant, lofe the elegance of his addrefs, and continued bowing through the paffage to his apartment. No doubt was entertained of his recovery, but there feemed to be a confiderable degree of fympathy attending this young man.

We had not time to look into the churches, or numerous monafteries, that yet remain, at Worms; the war appeared to have depopulated

the

the latter, for not a monk was to be feen. The cathedral, or church of St. Mary and St. Peter, is one of the moft antient facred buildings in Germany, having been founded at leaft as early as the commencement of the feventh century. One of the prebends was eftablifhed in 1033, another in 1058. The Dominicans, Carmelites, Capuchins and Auguftines, have each a monaftery, at Worms; as have the Ciftercians and the Auguftines a nunnery. A Proteftant'church was alfo confecrated, on the 9th of June, 1744; fomething more than two hundred years after the ineffectual conference held here of Proteftant and Catholic divines, which Charles the Fifth interrupted, when Melancthon, on one fide, and Echius, on the other, had engaged in it, ordering them to refume their arguments, in his prefence, at Ratifbon. This meeting was five years previous to the celebrated diet of Worms, at which Charles, having then eftimated the temporal ftrength of the two parties, openly fhewed his animofity to the Proteftants, as Maurice of Saxony did his intriguing ambition, by referring the queftion to the Council of Trent.

The Jews, at Worms, inhabit a feparate ftreet, and have a fynagogue, of great antiquity, their numbers having been once fuch as to endanger the peace of the city; but, in 1689, when the French turned their fynagogue into a ftable, they fled with the reft of the opulent inhabitants to Holland. Thofe of the prefent day can have very few articles of traffic, except money, the changing of which may have been frequent, on account of the neighbourhood of France.

Worms is fomewhat connected with Englifh hiftory, having been occupied by the troops
which

which James the Firft ufelefsly fent to the affiftance of the profcribed Elector Palatine, when his juft abhorrence of continental wars was once, though tardily, overcome by the entreaties of his daughter. Here too George the Second held his head quarters, from the 7th to the 20th of September, 1743; on the 14th of which month, Lord Carteret concluded, in his name, an offenfive and defenfive treaty with the Minifters of Hungary and Sardinia.

This city, like Cologne, retains fome affectation of the Roman form of government, to which it was rendered fubject by Cæfar, with the title of *Augufta Vangionum*. The STADT-MEISTER is fometimes called the CONSUL, and the SCHULTHEIS, or Mayor, the PRÆTOR. But in 1703, fome trivial tumult afforded a pretence for abolifhing its little remains of liberty, and the Elector Palatine was declared its protector. This blow completed the defolation, which the difafters of the preceding century had commenced; and a city, that was once called the market of the Palatinate, as the Palatinate was reputed the market of Germany, continues to exhibit nothing more than the ruins of its antient profperity.

Few of the prefent inhabitants can be the defcendants of thofe, who witneffed its deftruction in 1689; for we could not find, that the particulars of that event were much known, or commemorated by them, dreadful and impreffive as they muft have been. A column of Louis the Fourteenth's army had entered the city in September of the preceding year, under the command of the Marquis de Bonfleur, who foon diftreffed the inhabitants by preparations for blowing up

the

the walls with gunpowder. The mines were so numerous and large, as to threaten nothing less than the entire overwhelming of the city; but, being fired at different times, the walls of the houses were left standing, though they shook with almost every explosion. The artillery and balls had been previously carried away to Landau, or Mentz, then possessed by Louis. At length, on the 12th of May 1689, the Intendant sent the melancholy news to the magistracy, that he had received orders from his monarch to burn the whole city. Six days were allowed for the departure of the inhabitants and the removal of their property; which period was prolonged by their intreaties to nineteen. At the expiration of these, on Ascension Day, the 31st of May, the French grenadiers were employed from twelve o'clock till four, in placing combustibles about the houses and public buildings, against several of which large heaps of hay and straw were raised. The word being then given, fire was set to almost every house at once, and, in a few hours, the city was reduced to ashes; the conflagration being so general and strong as to be visible in day-light at the distance of more than thirty English miles. Such was one of the calamities of a city so unfortunately situated, that the chapter of the cathedral alone proved a loss by wars, previous to the year 1743, amounting to 1,262,749 florins.

The attention, due to so memorable a place, detained us at Worms, till the voiturier talked of being unable to reach Manheim, before the gates would be shut, and we let him drive vehemently towards

FRANCK-

FRANCKENTHAL,

ANOTHER place, deftroyed by Louis the Fourteenth, but reftored upon a plan fo uniform and convenient, that nothing but a fuller population is neceffary to confirm its title of a flourifhing city. The ftreets, which interfect each other at right angles, are wide and exactly ftraight; the houfes are handfomely built, but the poverty, or indolence of the owners fuffers them to partake of the air of neglect, which is general in German habitations; and the ftreets, though fpacious and not ill paved, had fo few paffengers, that the depopulation of the place feemed to be rendered the more obfervable by its grandeur.

Yet it would be unfair to eftimate the general profperity of Franckenthal by its prefent circumftances, even had we ftayed long enough to know them more accurately. This place had been occupied but a few weeks before by the French army, who had plundered it as well as feveral other towns of the Palatinate, after the retreat of the allies from Alface, at the latter end of 1793. The inhabitants had, for the moft part, returned to their houfes; but their commerce, which is faid to have been not contemptible, could not be fo eafily reftored. The manufactures of porcelain, cloths, filk, fpangles, vinegar and foap, of which fome were eftablifhed and all are protected by the wife liberality of the Elector, though far from being anfwerable,

either

either in their capitals, or produce, to the English ideas of similar enterprises, command some
share with England and France in supplying the
rest of Germany. One method of facilitating
the operations of trade the Elector has advantageously adopted here; that of instituting a
court upon the spot for the decision of all causes,
in which the traders are interested; and at his
expence a navigable canal has been. formed
from the town to the Rhine. Artists and merchants
have also some privileges, at Franckenthal, of which that of- being exempt from the
military press is not the least.

This press, or levy, is the method, by which
all the German Princes return their contingents
to the army of the Empire. The population of
every town and district in their dominions is
known with sufficient accuracy, and a settled number of recruits is supplied by each. When these
are wanted, notice is given, that the men of a certain age must assemble and cast lots for the service. Those, who are drawn, may find substitutes, but with this condition, that the deputy
must be at least as tall as his principal; a regulation, which makes the price of substitutes depend upon their height, and frequently renders
it impossible for the principals to avail themselves of the permission. A farmer in this neighbourhood, who was considerably above six feet
in height, could not obtain a substitute for less
than a hundred louis d'ors.

Another unpleasant condition is attached to
this exchange: if the substitute is disabled, or
deserts, another must be supplied; and if he

carries

carries his arms, or accoutrements, away, thefe muft be paid for by the perfon, who fent him.

After a ride of a few miles, we reached

OGGERSHEIM,

A SMALL town on the weft bank of the Rhine, rebuilt in uniform ftreets, like Franckenthal, having been deftroyed by the fame exertion of Louis the Fourteenth's cruelty. Here alfo the modern French had very lately been, and fome of the ruins, left near the road by Louis, appeared to have ferved them for kitchens in their excurfion.

At the eaft end of the town, towards the Rhine, ftands a chateau of the Elector, built with modern, but not very admirable tafte, and commanding the diftant river in feveral fine points of view. We could not be admitted to fee the infide, which is faid to have been fplendidly decorated; for the French had juft difmantled it of the furniture.

The road from hence to Manheim was bordered for its whole length, of at leaft two miles, by rows of poplars, of which fome ftill remain near Oggerfheim; but thofe within a mile and a half of Manheim, have been felled at one or two feet from the ground. This was done in December 1793, when the French began to advance from Landau, and were expected to befiege Manheim,

heim, their operations againſt which might have been covered, in ſome meaſure, by this noble alley.

Near the Rhine, the road is now commanded by two forts, of which one was thrown up during the approach of the French, and completed in the middle of the ſummer, with great care. Theſe contribute much to the preſent ſecurity of the city, which might otherwiſe be bombarded from the oppoſite bank of the river, even by an enemy, who ſhould not be able and ſhould not propoſe to attempt the conqueſt of the place. They are ditched and palliſadoed, but, being divided from the body of the city, by the Rhine, are, of courſe, without the communication, which renders ſuch works capable of a long defence. Round one of theſe forts, the road now winds, entering a part of the works, near the bridge, where there is a guard-houſe for the troops of the Elector.

MANHEIM.

IT was twilight when we approached Manheim; and the palace, the numerous turrets and the fortifications had their grandeur probably increaſed by the obſcurity. The bridge of boats is not ſo long as that at Mentz; but we had time enough in paſſing it to obſerve the extent of the city, on the left of which the Neckar pours itſelf into the Rhine, ſo that two ſides are entirely waſhed by their ſtreams. At the next guard-houſe, where we were detained by the
 uſual

usual enquiries, the troops were more numerous; and surely no military figures ever accorded so well with the gloomy gates and walls they guarded. The uniform of the Palatine light troops is a close jacket of motley brown, and pantaloons of the same that reach to their half-boots. They have black helmets, with crests and fronts of brass, large whiskers, and their faces, by constant exposure to the sun, are of the deepest brown that can be, without approaching to black. As they stood singly on the ramparts, or in groups at the gates, their bronze faces and Roman helmets seemed of a deeper hue, than the gloom, that partly concealed their figures.

The entrance into Manheim, from the Rhine, is by a spacious street, which leads directly into the centre of the city, and to a large square planted with limes, consisting, on one side, of public buildings, and on the other, of several noble houses, one of which is the chief inn, called the *Cour Palatine*. This is the first city in Germany, that can answer, by its appearance, the expectations of a foreigner, who has formed them from books. Its aspect is truly that of a capital, and of the residence of a Court; except that in the day-time a traveller may be somewhat surprised at the fewness of passengers and the small shew of traffic, amidst such public buildings, and in streets of such convenience and extent. The fairness, the grandeur and the stateliness which he may have seen attributed to other German cities, till he is as much disgusted as deceived by every idea derived from description, may be perceived in several parts of Manheim, and the justness of disposition in all.

Nor

Nor is the beauty of the prefent city folely owing to the deftruction of the ancient one by Louis the Fourteenth, in 1689, the year of general devaftation in the Palatinate. It was laid out in right lines, though to a lefs extent, in the beginning of the feventeenth century, when Frederic the Fifth laid the foundation of the fortifications, behind which a town was built, that adopted the antient name of Manheim, from a neighbouring one then in decay. Thefe were the fortifications and the town deftroyed by the French in 1689. The plan of both was but extended, when the prefent works were formed upon the fyftem of Cohorn, and the city by degrees reftored, with ftreets, which, interfecting each other at right angles, divide it into an hundred and feven fquare portions. The number of the inhabitants, exclufive of the garrifon, was, in 1784, 21,858.

Some of the ftreets are planted with rows of trees, and there are five or fix open places, fuitable for promenades, or markets. The cuftomhoufe, which forms a fide to one of thefe, is a noble ftone building, rather appearing to be a palace, than an office, except that under the colonnades, which furround it, are fhops for jewellery and other commodities.

The Electoral palace, which opens, on one fide, to the city, and, on the other, to the ramparts, was built by the Elector Charles-Philippe, who, in the year 1721, removed his refidence hither from Heidelberg, on account of fome difference with the magiftrates, or, as is faid, of the prevalence of religious difputes in that city.

R · He

He began to erect it in 1720; but the edifice was not completed, till the right wing was added by the present Elector, not to be used as a residence, but to contain a gallery of paintings, cabinets of antiquities and natural history, a library, treasury and *manege*. We passed a morning in viewing the apartments in the other wing, all the paintings and books having been removed from this, as well as great part of the furniture from the whole palace, in the dread of an approaching bombardment. The person, who shewed them, took care to keep the credit of each room safe, by assuring us at the door, that it was not in its usual condition. The Elector had been, for some months, at Munich, but the Duke and Duchess of Deux Ponts and their family have resided in this palace, since their retirement from Deux Ponts, in the latter end of the campaign of 1792.

The rooms are all lofty, and floored with inlaid work of oak and chesnut; the ceilings, for the most part, painted; and the walls covered with tapestry, finely wrought, both as to colour and design. Some of this came from a manufactory, established by the Elector, at Frackenthal.

The furniture, left in several of the rooms, was grand and antient, but could never have been so costly as those, who have seen the mansions of wealthy individuals in England, would expect to find in a palace. The Elector's state-bed was inclosed not only by a railing, but by a glass case to the height of the ceiling, with windows, that could be opened at pleasure, to permit a conversation with his courtiers,

courtiers, when compliments were paid literally at a levee. In the court of France, this practice continued even to very late years, and there were three diftinct privileges of entrée, denoting the time, at which perfons of different claffes were permitted to enter the chamber. In the Earl of Portland's embaffy for King William to Louis the Fourteenth, it was thought a fignal mark of honour, that he was admitted to his audience, not only in the chamber, but within the rails; and there the French Monarch ftood with the three young Princes, his grandfons, the Count de Tholoufe, the Duke d'Aumont and the Marefchal de Noailles. The Duke made his fpeech covered, after which the King entered into converfation with him, for feveral minutes.

One room, at Manheim, was called the Silver Chamber, from the quantity of folid filver, ufed about the furniture. Such articles as could be carried away entire, had been removed, but the walls were disfigured by the lofs of the ornaments torn from them, on account of their value. In feveral rooms, the furniture, that remained, was partly packed, to be carried away upon the next alarm. The contents of the wardrobe were in this ftate, and the interior of thefe now defolated apartments feemed like the fkeleton of grandeur. The beauty of the painted ceilings, however, the richnefs of the various profpects, commanded by the windows, and the great extent of the building fufficiently accounted for the reputation, which this palace has, of being the fineft in Germany.

It

It is built of ftone, which has fomewhat the reddifh hue of that ufed at Mentz, and, though feveral parts are pofitively difapproved by perfons of fkill in architecture, the whole is certainly a grand and fumptuous building.

The fituation of Manheim and the fcenery around it are viewed to great advantage from the tower of the Obfervatory, in which ftrangers are politely received by the Profeffor of Aftronomy, whofe refidence is eftablifhed in it. From this are feen the fruitful plains of the Palatinate, fpreading, on all fides, to bold mountains, of which thofe of Lorrain, that extend on the weft, lofe in diftance the variety of their colouring, and, affuming a blue tint, retain only the dignity of their form. Among thefe the vaft and round headland, called the *Tonnefberg*, which is in fight, during the greateft part of the journey from Mentz to Manheim, is pre-eminent.

But the chain, that binds the horizon on the eaft, and is known by the name of the *Bergftraffe*, or road of mountains, is near enough to difplay all their wild irregularity of fhape, the foreft glens, to which they open, and the various tints of rock and foil, of red and purple, that mingle with the corn and wood on their lower fteeps. Thefe mountains are feen in the north from their commencement near Franckfort, and this line is never interrupted from thence fouthward into Switzerland. The rivals to them, on the fouth weft, are the mountains of Alface, which extend in long perfpective, and at a dif-tance appear to unite with thofe of the Bergftraffe.

Among

Among the numerous towns and villages that throng the Palatinate, the spires of Oppenheim and Worms are distinctly visible to the north; almost beneath the eye are those of Francken- thal, and Oggersheim, and to the southward Spires shews its many towers.

In the nearer scene the Neckar, after tumbling from among the forests of the Bergstraffe, falls into the Rhine, a little below the walls of Man- heim; and the gardens of a summer chateau be- longing to the Elector occupy the angle between the two rivers.

These gardens were now surrendered by the Prince to be the camp of three thousand of his troops, detached from the garrison of the city, which, at this time, consisted of nearly ten thou- sand men. In several places, on the banks of the two rivers, batteries were thrown up, and, near the camp, a regular fort, for the purpose of commanding both; so that Manheim, by its natural and artificial means of defence, was supposed to be rendered nearly unaffailable, on two sides. On that of Heidelberg, it was not so secure; nor could the others be defended by a garrison of less than 15,000 men. It was on this account, that the Elector detained ten thousand of his troops from actual service, con- trary, as is said, to the remonstrances of the Emperor, who offered, but without success, to garrison his capital with Austrians. From the observatory, the camp and the works were easi- ly feen, and, by the help of a Dollond tele- scope, the only optical instrument remaining, the order of both was so exactly pointed out

by

by our guide, that it was not difficult to comprehend the ufes of them. Military preparations, indeed, occurred very frequently in Manheim. In the gardens of the chief Electoral palace, extending to the ramparts over the Rhine, cannon were planted, which were as regularly guarded by fentinels as in the other parts of the fortifications.

All the gates of Manheim appear to be defended by fortifications of unufual ftrength. Befides two broad ditches, there are batteries, which play directly upon the bridges, and might deftroy them in a few minutes. The gates are guarded, with the utmoft ftrictnefs, and no perfon is fuffered to enter them, after ten at night, without the exprefs permiffion of the governor. When a courier arrives, who wifhes to ufe his privilege of paffing, at all hours, he puts fome token of his office into a fmall tin box, which is kept on the outfide of the ditch, to be drawn acrofs it by a cord, that runs upon a roller on each bank. The officer of the guard carries this to the governor, and obtains the keys; but fo much time is paffed in this fort of application, that couriers, when the nights are fhort, ufually wait the opening of the gates, which is foon after day-light, in fummer, and at fix, or feven, in winter.

The abfence of the Elector, we were affured, had much altered the appearance of Manheim, where fcarcely a carriage was now to be feen, though there were traces enough of the gaiety and general fplendour of this little Court. Here are an Opera Houfe, a German Comedy,

an

an Amateur Concert, an Electoral Lottery, an
Academy of Sculpture and Design, and an
Academy of Sciences. The Opera performances
are held in a wing of the palace, and were established in 1742, but have not attained much
celebrity, being supported chiefly by performers
from the other Theatre. This last is called a
national establishment, the players being Germans, and the Theatre founded in 1779 at
the expence of the Elector. The Baron de
Dahlberg, one of his Ministers, has the super-
intendance of it. The Amateur Concert is held,
every Friday, during the winter, and is much
frequented.

The Electoral Lotteries, for there are two,
are drawn in the presence of the Minister of
Finances, and one of them is no less disadvan-
tageous for the gamesters than is usual with
such undertakings. That, which consists of
chances determined in the customary way, gives
the Elector an advantage of only five to four
over the subscribers. The other, which is
formed upon the more intricate model of that
of Genoa, entitles the subscribers to prizes,
proportioned to the number of times a certain
ticket issues from the wheel, five numbers being
drawn out of ninety, or rather five drawings
of one number each being successively made out
of ninety tickets. A ticket, which issues once
in these five drawings, wins fifteen times the value of the stake; or, that should be drawn
each of the five times, would entitle the owner
to have his original stake multiplied by sixty
thousand, and the product would be his prize.
The undertaker of this latter Lottery has the
chances immensely in his favour.

From

From the very large income, to which these Lotteries contribute a part, the present Elector has certainly made confiderable difburfements, with ufeful purpofes, if not to ufeful effects. Of his foundation are the Academy of Sciences, which was opened in 176;, for weekly fittings, and has proceeded to fome correfpondence with other Academies; the German Society, established for the eafy purpofe of purifying and the difficult one of fixing language; the Cabinet of Phyfics, or rather of experimental philofophy, celebrated for the variety and magnitude of its inftruments, among which are two burning glaffes of three feet diameter, faid to be capable of liquefying bodies, even bottles filled with water, at o feet diftance; the Obfervatory, of 108 feet high, in which all the chief inftruments were Englifh; a Botanical Garden and Directorship; an Academy of Sculpture, and a Cabinet of Engravings and Drawings, formed under the direction of M. Krahe of Duffeldorff, in 400 folio volumes.

Of all thefe eftablifhments, none of the ornaments, or materials, that were portable, now remain at Manheim. The aftronomical inftruments, the celebrated collection of ftatues, the paintings and the prints have been removed, together with the Electoral treafure of diamonds and jewels, fome to Munich and fome to other places of fecurity. But, though we miffed a fight, which even its rarity would have rendered welcome, it feems proper, after fuch frequent notice of the barrennefs of Germany, to mention what has been collected in one of its chief cities.

The.

The expectation of an attack had difmantled
other houfes, befides the Elector's, of their
furniture; for, in the Cour Palatine, a very
fpacious, and really a good inn, not a curtain
and fcarcely a fpoon was left. *A caufe de la
guerre* was, indeed, the general excufe for every
deficiency, ufed by thofe, who had civility
enough to offer one; but, in truth, the war
had not often incroached upon the ordinary
ftock of conveniencies in Germany, which was
previoufly too low to be capable of much re-
duction. The places, which the French had
actually entered, are, of courfe, to be excepted; but it may otherwife be believed, that
Germany can lofe little by a war, more than
the unfortunate labourers, whom it forces to
become foldiers. The lofs of wealth muft
come chiefly from other countries. A rich nation may give prefent treafure; a commercial
nation may give both prefent treafure and the
means of future competence.

The land near Manheim is chiefly planted
with tobacco and madder, and the landfcape is
enlivened with fmall, but neat country-houfes,
fcattered along the margin of the Necker. The
neighbourhood abounds in pleafant rides, and,
whether you wind the high banks of the majeftic Rhine, or the borders of the more tranquil Neckar, the mountains of the Bergftraffe,
tumbled upon each other in wild confufion,
generally form the magnificent back ground of
the fcene.

On returning from an excurfion of this kind
at the clofe of evening, the foldiers at the gates
are frequently heard chanting martial fongs in
parts

parts and chorus ; a fonorous mufic in fevere uni-
fon with the folemnity of the hour and the imperfect forms, that meet the eye, of fentinels
keeping watch beneath the dufky gateways,
while their brethren, repofing on the benches
without, mingle their voices in the deep chorus.
Rude and fimple as are thefe ftrains, they are
often fingularly impreffive, and touch the imagination with fomething approaching to horror,
when the circumftances of the place are remembered, and it is confidered how foon thefe
men, fent to inflict death on others, may themfelves be thrown into the unnumbered heap of
the military flain.

SCHWEZINGEN.

AN excellent road, fheltered for nine Englifh miles by rows of high poplars, conducted
us through richly cultivated plains from Manheim to Schwezingen, a fmall village, diftinguifhed by an Electoral chateau and gardens.
This was one of the pleafanteft rides we had
found in Germany, for the road, though it exhibited little of either the wild or picturefque,
frequently opened towards the mountains,
bright with a variety of colouring, and then
again was fhrouded among woods and plantations, that bordered the neighbouring fields,
and brought faintly to remembrance the ftyle
and mingled verdure of our native landfcape.

Schwezingen

Schwezingen had been very lately the Auſ-
trian head-quarters, for the army of the Upper
Rhine, and ſome ſoldiers were ſtill ſtationed
near the road to guard an immenſe magazine
of wood; but there were otherwiſe no military
ſymptoms about the place.

The chateau is an old and inelegant building,
not large enough to have been ever uſed as a
formal, reſidence. The preſent Elector has
added to it two wings, each of ſix hundred feet
long, but ſo low, that the apartments are all
on the ground floor. Somewhat of that air
of neglect, which can ſadden even the moſt
delightful ſcenes, is viſible here; ſeveral of the
windows are broken, and the theatre, muſic-
room, and ball-room, which have been laid
out in one of the wings, are abandoned to duſt
and lumber.

The gardens, however, are preſerved in better order. Before the palace, a long viſta of
lawn and wood, with numerous and ſpacious
fountains, guarded by ſtatues, diſplay ſomething of the old French manner; other parts
ſhew charming ſcenery, and deep ſylvan re-
ceſſes, where nature is again at liberty; in a
bay formed by the woods is an amphitheatre
of fragrant orange trees, placed in front of a
light ſemicircular green-houſe, and crowned
with lofty groves. Near this delicious ſpot,
extends a bending arcade of lattice-work, in-
terwoven with vines and many beautifully
flowering plants; a ſort of ſtructure, the fila-
gree lightneſs of which it is impoſſible not to
admire, againſt precept, and perhaps, when
general effect is conſidered, againſt neceſſary
taſte.

tafte. In another part, fheltered by the woods, is an edifice in the ftyle of a Turkifh mofque, with its light cloiftered courts, flender minarets, and painted entrances, infcribed with Arabic mottos, which by the German tranfiations appear to exprefs the pleafure of friendly converfation and of indolence in fummer. The gardens have this refult of a judicious arrangement, that they feem to extend much beyond their real limits, which we difcovered only by afcending one of the minarets. They are open to the public, during great part of every day, under certain rules for their prefervation, of which copies are pafted up in feveral places.

CARLSRUHE.

AT Schwezingen the fine Electoral road concludes, and we began to wind along the fkirts of a foreft on the left, having on the right an open corn country, beyond which appeared the towers of Spires and Philipfburg, of which the former was then the head-quarters of the Auftrian army, and the latter is memorable for having given birth to Melancthon in 1491. Waghaufel and Bruchfal are fmall pofting places in this route, at a village between which we had another inftance of the little attention paid to travellers in Germany. At a fmall inn, noxious with fome fumigation ufed againft bugs, we were detained a quarter of an hour, becaufe the landlord, who had gone out after our arrival,

val,

val, had not left word how much we fhould pay, and the poor old woman, who, without fhoes or ftockings, attended us, was terrified when we talked of leaving what was proper, and proceeding before his return.

About a mile beyond Bruchfal our poftillion quitted the chauffée, and entered a fummer road through the deep and extenfive foreft of Carlfruhe, preferved by the Margrave of Baden for the fhelter of game. Avenues cut through this foreft for nine or ten miles in every direction, converge at his palace and city of Carlfruhe, as at a point. Other cruelties than thofe of the chafe fometimes take place in thefe delightful fcenes, for an amphitheatre has been formed in the woods, where imitations of a Spanifh bull feaft have been exhibited; to fuch horrid means of preventing vacuity of mind has a prince had recourfe, who is otherwife diftinguifhed for the elegance of his tafte, and the fuavity of his manners!

The fcenery of this foreft is very various. Sometimes we found our way through groves of ancient pine and fir, fo thickly planted that their lower branches were withered for want of air, and it feemed as if the carriage could not proceed between them; at others we paffed under the fpreading fhade of chefnuts, oak and walnut, and croffed many a cool ftream, green with the impending foliage, on whofe fequeftered bank one almoft expected to fee the moralizing Jacques; fo exactly did the fcene accord with Shakefpeare's defcription. The woods again opening, we found ourfelves in a noble avenue, and faw the ftag gracefully bounding acrofs

acrofs it " to more profound repofe;" while
now and then a hut, formed of rude green
planks under fome old oak, feemed, by its
fmoked fides, to have often afforded a fheltered
repaft to hunting parties.

Near Carlfruhe the gardens of the Prince and
then the palace become vifible, the road winding along them, on the edge of the foreft, till
it enters the northern gate of the city, the uniformity of which has the fame date as its completion, the ground plot having been entirely
laid out between January and June 1715, on
the 17th of which month the Margrave Charles
William laid the foundation ftone.

The ftreets are accordingly fpacious, light,
and exactly ftraight; but not fo magnificent as
thofe of Manheim, and ftill lefs enlivened with
paffengers. Since the commencement of the
war, the gaieties of the Court, which afforded
fome occupation to the inhabitants, have ceafed; the nobility have left their houfes; and the
Margrave is contented with the amufements of
his library, in which Englifh literature is faid
to fill a confiderable fpace.

Carlfruhe has the advantage of not being fortified; fo that the inhabitants are not oppreffed
by a numerous garrifon, and ftrangers pafs
through it, though fo near the feat of war,
without interruption. It is lefs than Manheim
by at leaft half, and has no confiderable public
building, except the palace, from the fpacious
area before before which, all the ftreets proceed as *radii*, till their furtheft ends fill up the
figure of a femicircle. The houfes in the area,
which

which immediately front the palace, are built over a piazza interrupted only by the commencement of the ſtreets: The palace has, of courſe, an unexampled advantage in the mixture of town and rural ſcenery in its proſpects, looking on one ſide through all the ſtreets of the city, and on the other through thirty-two foreſt alleys, cut to various lengths of from ten to fifteen Engliſh miles each; few, however, of the latter proſpects are now commanded except from the upper windows, the preſent Elector having entirely changed the ſtyle of the intervening gardens, and permitted them to be laid out in the Engliſh taſte, without reſpect to the thirty-two interſections, that rendered them conformable with the foreſt.

We paſſed part of two days at Carlſruhe, and were chiefly in theſe gardens, which are of the moſt enchanting beauty and richneſs. The warmth of the climate draws up colours for the ſhrubs and plants, which we thought could not be equalled in more northern latitudes; two thouſand and ſeven hundred orange and lemon trees, loaded with fruit and bloſſoms, perfumed the air; and choice ſhrubs, marked with the Linnean diſtinctions, compoſed the thickets. The gardens, being limited only by the foreſts, appear to unite with them; and the deep verdure and luxuriance of the latter are contraſted ſweetly with the tender green of the lawns and plants, and with the variety of ſcarce and majeſtic trees, mingled with the garden groves.

The palace is a large and ſumptuous, though not an elegant edifice, built of ſtone like all
the

the reft of the city, and at the fame period. The Margrave generally refides in it, and has rendered it a valuable home, by adding greatly to the library, filling an obfervatory with excellent inftruments, and preferving the whole ftructure in a condition not ufual in Germany. The fpot, compared with the furrounding country, appeared like Milton's Eden—like Paradife opened in the wild.

Beyond Carlfruhe the road begins to approach the Rhine, which we had loft fight of near Manheim; and, though the river is never within view, the country is confidered as a military frontier, being conftantly patrolled by troops. Some of thefe were of the Prince of Condé's army of emigrants, who have no uniform, and are diftinguifhed only by the white cockade, and by a bandage of white linen, impreffed with black *fleurs de lis*, upon the right arm. They were chiefly on foot, and then wore only their fwords, without fire-arms.

Near the road, a fmall party of Auftrians were guarding a magazine, before a tent, marked, like their regimentals, with green upon white. Soon afterwards, our poftillion drew up on one fide, to permit a train of carriages to pafs; and immediately announced the *Prinz von Condé*, who was in an open landau, followed by two covered waggons for his kitchen and laundry, and by a coach with attendants.

He appeared to be between fifty and fixty; tall, not corpulent, and of an air, which might have announced the French courtier, if his rank had been unknown. A ftar was embroidered

upon

upon his military furtout, but he had no guards, though travelling within the jurifdiction allotted to him as a general officer. So little was the road frequented at this period, that his was the fecond or third carriage we had met, except military waggons, fince leaving Mentz; a diftance of more than eighty Englifh miles.

The road for the whole ftage between Carlfruhe and Raftadt, about fifteen miles, is planted, as feems cuftomary in Germany between the palaces of fovereigns, with lofty trees, of which the fhade was extremely refrefhing at this feafon; the clouds of fand, that rofe from the road, would otherwife have made the heat intolerable.

The firft houfe in Raftadt is the palace of the Margrave of Baden Baden, brother of the Mar-grave of Baden Durlach, whofe refidence is at Carlfruhe, a fmall and heavy building, that fronts the avenue, and is furrounded with ftone walls. The interior is faid to be fplendidly decorated, and a chamber is preferved in the ftate, in which Prince Eugene and Marfhal Villars left it in 1714, after concluding the peace between the Emperor and Louis the Fourteenth. The Prince of Baden, being then a general in the fervice of the Empe-ror, had not been able to efcape the vengeance of Louis, whofe troops in 1688 firft plundered, and then burnt, the palace and city, and in the war of the Succeffion they had a camp on the adjoining plain. The Prince is therefore fuppofed to have lent the palace, which he had rebuilt, with the more readinefs, that the Marfhal might fee how perfectly he could overcome his lofs. The plun-der of the city in 1688 had continued for five days, and it is mentioned in its hiftory that the

S

French

French carried away fifteen waggon loads of wine of the vintage of 1572.

Raftadt, like Carlfruhe, is built upon one plan, but is as inferior to it in beauty, as in fize. The chief ftreet is, however, uncommonly broad, fo much fo, that the upper end is ufed as a market-place, and the ftatue of the founder, Prince Louis, in the centre, is feen with all the advantages of fpace and perfpective. There is, notwithftanding, little appearance of traffic, and the inbabitants feemed to be much lefs numerous than the emi-grant corps, which was then ftationed there, the head quarters of the Prince of Condé being efta-blifhed in the city. We paffed an hour at an inn, which was nearly filled by part of this corps, and were compelled to witnefs the diftrefs and difap-pointment, excited by intelligence juft then re-ceived of the ftate of affairs in the Low Countries.

A fmall park of artillery was kept on the fouth-ern fide of Raftadt, where there is a handfome ftone bridge over the river Murg, that falls into the Rhine, at the diftance of a league from the city. Soon after, the road paffes by the groves of the *Favorita*, a fummer palace built by a Dowager Margravine. We now drew nearer to the moun-tains of the Bergftraffe, which had difappeared near Schwezingen, and had rifen again partially through the morning mifts, foon after our quitting Carlfruhe. They are here of more awful height, and abrupt fteepnefs than in the neighbourhood of Manheim, and, on their pointed brows, are frequently the ruins of caftles, placed fometimes where it feems as if no human foot could climb. The nearer we approached thefe mountains, the more we had occafion to admire the variqus tints

of

of their granites. Sometimes the precipices were of a faint pink, then of a deep red, a dull purple, or a blush approaching to lilac, and sometimes gleams of a pale yellow mingled with the low shrubs, that grew upon their sides. The day was cloudless and bright, and we were too near these heights to be deceived by the illusions of aerial colouring; the real hues of their features were as beautiful, as their magnitude was sublime. The plains, that extend along their feet to the Rhine, are richly cultivated with corn, and, beyond the river, others, which appear to be equally fruitful, spread towards the mountains of Alsace, a corresponding chain with the Bergstrasse, vast and now blue with distance.

The manners of the people from Manheim downwards, are more civilized than in the upper parts of Germany; an improvement, which may with great probability be imputed to the superior fruitfulness of the country, that amends their condition, and with it the social qualities. The farms are more numerous, the labourers less dejected, and the women, who still work barefooted in the fields, have somewhat of a ruddy brown in their complexion, instead of the sallowness, that renders the ferocious, or sullen air of the others more striking. They are also better dressed; for, though they retain the slouched woollen hat, they have caps; and towards the borders of Switzerland their appearance becomes picturesque. Here they frequently wear a blue petticoat with a cherry-coloured boddice, full white sleeves fastened above the elbow, and a muslin handkerchief thrown gracefully round the neck in a sort of roll; the hair sometimes platted round the head, and held on the crown with a large bodkin. On holidays,

the

the girls have often a flat ftraw hat, with bows of ribband hanging behind. Higher up, the women wear their long black hair platted, but falling in a queue down the back.

The cottages are alfo fomewhat better, and the fides entirely covered with vines, on which, in the beginning of July, were grapes bigger than capers, and in immenfe quantities. Sometimes Turkey corn is put to dry under the projections of the firft floor, and the gardens are ornamented with a fhort alley of hops. Meat is however bad and fcarce; the appearance fo difgufting before it is dreffed, that thofe, who can accommodate their palates to the cooking, muft endeavour to forget what they have feen. Butter is ftill more fcarce, and the little cheefe that appears, is only a new white curd, made up in rolls, fcarcely bigger than an egg. A fort of beer is here made for fervants, the tafte of which affords no fymptom of either malt or hops; it is often nearly white, and appears to have been brewed but a few hours; what is fomewhat browner is bottled, and fold at about three-pence a quart.

Our road, this day, was feldom more than two leagues diftant from the Rhine, and we expected to have heard the fire, which the Auftrian and French pofts, who have their batteries on the two banks of the river, frequently exchange with each other. The tranquillity was, however, as found as in any other country, and nothing but the continuance of patroles and convoys reminded us of our nearnefs to the war. The peafants were as leifurely cutting their harveft, and all the other bufinefs of rural life was proceeding as uninterruptedly, as if there was no poffibility of an attack.

Yet

Yet we afterwards learned, that the French had, very early on the morning of this day, ineffectually attempted the paſſage of the Rhine, about fifteen miles higher up ; and the firing had been diſtinctly heard at a little village where we dined.

One road, as ſhort as this, lies immediately upon the margin of the river ; and, as we were aſſured that none but military parties were fired at, we wiſhed to paſs it, for the purpoſe of obſerving the ingenious methods, by which a country ſo circumſtanced is defended; but our poſtillion, who dreaded, that he might be preſſed by the Auſtrians, for the intruſion, refuſed to venture upon it, and, inſtead of proceeding to Kehl, which is directly oppoſite to Straſbourg, we took the road for Offenburg, about three leagues from the Rhine.

The country through which our route now lay, better as it is than more northern parts, has ſuffered ſome poſitive injuries by the war. Before this, all the little towns, from Carlſruhe downwards, maintained ſome commerce with France, on their own account, and ſupplied carriage for that of others. In return for proviſions and coarſe commodities for manufacture, carried to Straſbourg, they received the ſilks and woollens of France, to be diſperſed at Franckfort, or Manheim. The intercourſe between the two countries was ſo frequent, that nearly all the tradeſmen, and many of the labouring perſons in this part of Germany ſpeak a little French. The landlord of the houſe, where we dined, aſſured us that, though his village was ſo ſmall, he had ſufficient buſineſs before the war ; now he was upon the

point

point of removing to Offenburg, being unable to
pay his rent, during the interruption of travelling.

A little before fun-fet, we came to Appenweyer,
one of thefe towns, from the entrance of which
the fpires of Strafbourg were fo plainly vifible
that we could fee the fame glittering againft the
light, and even the forms of the fortifications near
the water could be traced. In the midft of the
ftraggling town of Appenweyer the loud founds
of martial mufic and then the appearance of
troops, entering at the oppofite end, furprifed us.
This was the advanced guard of feveral Auftrian
regiments, on their march to re-inforce the allied
army in the Low Countries. Our poftillion had
drawn up, to furrender as much of the road as
poffible to them, but their march was fo irregular, that they frequently thronged round the carriage; affording us fufficient opportunity to obferve how far their air correfponded with what has
been fo often faid of the Auftrian foldiery.

Except as to their drefs and arms, their appearance is not military, according to any notion,
which an Englifhman is likely to have formed;
that is, there is nothing of activity, nothing of
fpirit, of cheerfulnefs, of the correctnefs of difcipline, or of the eagernefs of the youthful in it.
There is much of ferocity, much of timid cruelty,
of fullennefs, indolence and awkwardnefs. They
drefs up their faces with muftachios, and feem
extremely defirous to imprefs terror. How far
this may be effectual againft other troops we cannot know; but they certainly are, by their ferocious manners, and by the traits, which a nearer
view

view of them difclofes, very terrible to the peaceful traveller. Though now immediately under
the eyes of their officers they could fcarcely re-
frain from petty infults, and from wifhfully laying
their hands upon our baggage.

About a thoufand men paffed in two divifions,
which had commenced their march a few hours
before, for the purpofe of avoiding the heat of
the day. As we proceeded, the trodden corn in
the fields fhewed where they had refted.

It was night before we reached Offenburg, where
we were compelled to lodge at a wretched inn
called the Poft-houfe, the mafter of the other
having that day removed to admit a new tenant;
but the condition of the lodging was of little importance, for, all night, the heavy trampling of
feet along the road below prevented fleep, and
with the firft dawn the found of martial mufic
drew us to the windows. It feemed like a dream,
when the Auftrian bands played ça ira, with double drums, and cymbals thrown almoft up to our
cafements, louder than any we had ever heard
before. This was the main body of the army,
of which we had met the advanced party. Each
regiment was followed by a long train of baggage
carriages, of various and curious defcriptions,
fome of the cabriolets having a woman nearly in
man's apparel in the front, and behind, a large
bafket higher than the carriage, filled with hay.
This " tide of human exiftence" continued to
pafs for feveral hours. But the whole army did
not confift of more than three regiments of infan-
try, among which were thofe of D'Arcy, and
Pellegrini, and one of horfe; for each of the
Auftrian regiments of foot contains, when complete,

plete, two thousand three hundred men. They
had with them a small train of artillery, and were
to proceed to the Low Countries as quick as they
could march.; but, so uniform are the expedients
of the councils of Vienna, that the opportunity of
carrying these troops down the Rhine in barges
from Phillipsburg, where it was practicable, was
not adopted, though this method would have saved two weeks out of three, and have landed the
army unfatigued at its post.

All their regimentals were white, faced either
with light blue, or pompadour, and seemed un-
suitably delicate for figures so large and heavy.
The cavalry were loaded with many articles of
baggage, but their horses appeared to be of the
strongest and most serviceable kind. This was a
grand military show, which it was impossible to
see without many reflections on human nature and
human misery.

Offenburg is a small town, in the Margraviate
of Baden Baden, pleasantly seated at the feet of
the Bergstraffe, which the road again approaches
so near as to be somewhat obstructed by its ac-
clivities. Our way lay along the base of these
steeps, during the whole day; and as we drew
nearer to Switzerland, their height became still
more stupendous, and the mountains of Alsace
seemed advancing to meet them in the long perspective; the plains between, through which the
Rhine gleamed in long sweeps, appeared to be
entirely covered with corn, and in the nearer
scene joyous groups were loading the waggons
with the harvest. An harvest of another kind
was ripening among the lower rocks of the Bergstraffe, where the light green of the vines enlivened

ed every cliff, and fometimes overfpread the ruinous walls of what had once been fortreffes.

We paffed many villages, fhaded with noble
trees, which had more appearance of comfort
than any we had feen, and which were enviable for
the pleafantnefs of their fituation; their fpacious
ftreet generally opening to the grandeur of the
mountain vifta, that extended to the fouth. In
thefe landfcapes the peafant girl, in the fimple
drefs of the country, and balancing on her large
ftraw hat an harveft keg, was a very picturefque
figure.

It was evening when we came within view of
Friburg, the laft city of Germany on the borders
of Switzerland, and found ourfelves among mountains, which partook of the immenfity and fublimity of thofe of that enchanting country. But
what was our emotion, when, from an eminence,
we difcovered the pointed fummits of what we
believed to be the Swifs mountains themfelves, a
multitudinous affemblage rolled in the far-diftant
profpect! This glimpfe of a country of all
others in Europe the moft aftonifhing and
grand, awakened a thoufand interefting recollections and delightful expectations; while
we watched with regret even this partial vifion vanifhing from our eyes as we defcended
towards Friburg. The mountains, that encompafs this city, have fo much the character of the
great, that we immediately recollect the line of
feparation between Germany and Switzerland to
be merely artificial, not marked even by a river.
Yet while we yield to the awful pleafure which
this eternal vaftnefs infpires, we feel the infignificance

ficance of our temporary nature, and, feeming more than ever confcious by what a flender fyftem our exiftence is upheld, fomewbat of dejecti-on and anxiety mingle with our admiration.

FRIBURG

IS an ancient Imperial city and the capital of the Brifgau. Its name alludes to the privileges granted to fuch cities ; but its prefent condition, like that of many others, is a proof of the virtual difcontinuance of the rights, by which the Sovereign intended to invite to one part of his dominions the advantages of commerce. Its appearance is that, which we have fo often defcribed; better than Cologne, and worfe than Mentz; its fize is about a third part of the latter city. On defcending to it, the firft diftinct object is the fpire of the great church, a remarkable ftructure, the ftones of which are laid with open interftices, fo that the light appears through its tapering fides. Of this fort of ftone fillagree work there are faid to be other fpecimens in Germany. The city was once ftrongly fortified, and has endured fome celebrated fieges. In 1677, 1713, and 1745 it was taken by the French, who, in the latter year, deftroyed all the fortifications, which had rendered it formidable, and left nothing but the prefent walls.

Being, however, a frontier place towards Switzerland, it is provided with a fmall Auftrian garrifon;

rifon; and the bufinefs of permitting, or preventing the paffage of travellers into that country is entrufted to its officers. The malignity, or ignorance of one of thefe, called the Lieutenant de Place, prevented us from reaching it, after a journey of more than fix hundred miles; a difappointment, which no perfon could bear without fevere regret, but which was alloyed to us by the reports we daily heard of fome approaching change in Switzerland unfavourable to England, and by a confcioufnefs of the deduction which, in fpite of all endeavours at abftraction, encroachments upon phyfical comfort and upon the affurance of peacefulnefs make from the difpofition to enquiry, or fancy.

We had delivered at the gate the German paffport, recommended to us by M. de Schwartzkoff, and which had been figned by the Commandant at Mentz; the man, who took it, promifing to bring it properly attefted to our inn. He returned without the paffport, and, as we afterwards found, carried our voiturier to be examined by an officer. We endeavoured in vain to obtain an explanation, as to this delay and appearance of fufpicion, till, at fupper, the Lieutenant de Place announced himfelf, and prefently fhewed, that he was not come to offer apologies. This man, an illiterate Piedmontefe in the Auftrian fervice, either believed, or affected to do fo, that our name was not Radcliffe, but fomething like it, with a German termination, and that we were not Englifh, but Germans. Neither my Lord Grenville's, or M. de Sckwartzkoff's paffports, our letters from London to families in Switzerland, nor one of credit from the Meffrs. Hopes of Amfterdam to the Banking-houfe of Porta at Laufanne, all of which

which he pretended to examine, could remove
this difcerning fufpicion as to our country. While
we were confidering, as much as vexation would
permit, what circumftance could have afforded a
pretext for any part of this intrufion, it came out
incidentally, that the confirmation given to our
paffport at Mentz, which we had never examined,
expreffed "returning to England," though the
pafs itfelf was for Bafil, to which place we were
upon our route.

Such a contradiction might certainly have juf-
tified fome delay, if we had not been enabled to
prove it accidental to the fatisfaction of any perfon
defirous of being right. The paffport had been
produced at Mentz, together with thofe of two
Englifh artifts, then on their return from Rome,
whom we had the pleafure to fee at Franckfort.
The Secretary infcribed all the paffports alike for
England, and M. de Lucadou, the Commandant,
haftily figned ours, without obferving the miftake,
though he fo well knew us to be upon the road to
Switzerland, that he politely endeavoured to render us fome fervice there. Our friends in Mentz
being known to him, he defired us to accept an
addrefs from himfelf to M. de Wilde, Intendant
of falt mines near Bec. We produced to Mr.
Lieutenant this addrefs, as a proof, that the Commandant both knew us, and where we were going; but it foon appeared, that, though the former might have honeftly fallen into his fufpicions
at firft, he had a malignant obftinacy in refufing
to abandon them. He left us, with notice that
we could not quit the town without receiving the
Commandant's permiffion by his means; and it
was with fome terror, that we perceived ourfelves
to be fo much in his power, in a place where there
was

was a pretext for military authority, and where the leaft expreffion of juft indignation feemed to provoke a difpofition for further injuftice.

The only relief, which could be hinted to us, was to write to the Commandant at Mentz, who might re-teftify his knowledge of our deftination; yet, as an anfwer could not be received in lefs than eight days, and, as imagination fuggefted not only all the poffible horrors of oppreffion, during that period, but all the contrivances, by which the malignant difpofition we had already experienced, might even then be prevented from difappointment, we looked upon this refource as little better than the worft, and refolved in the morning to demand leave for an immediate return to Mentz.

There being then fome witneffes to the application, the Lieutenant conducted himfelf with more propriety, and even propofed an introduction to the Commandant, to whom we could not before hear of any direct means of accefs; there being a poffibility, he faid, that a paffage into Switzerland might be permitted. But the difguft of Auftrian authority was now fo complete, that we were not difpofed to rifk the mockery of an appeal. The Lieutenant expreffed his readinefs to allow our paffage, if we fhould choofe to return from Mentz with another paffport; but we had no intention to be ever again in his power, and, affuring him that we fhould not return, left Friburg without the hope of penetrating through the experienced, and prefent difficulties of Germany, into the far-feen delights of Switzerland.

As thofe, who leave one home for another, think,

think, in the firft part of their journey, of the friends they have left, and, in the laft, of thofe, to whom they are going; fo we, in quitting the borders of Switzerland, thought only of that country; and, when we regained the eminence from whence the tops of its mountains had bee'n fo lately viewed with enthufiaftic hope, and th . delightful expectation occurred again to the mi d only to torture it with the certainty of our lofs; but, as the diftance from Switzerland increafed, the attractions of home gathered ftrength, and the inconveniences of Germany, which had been fo readily felt before, could fcarcely be noticed when we knew them to lie in the road to England.

We paffed Offenburg, on the firft day of our return, and, travelling till midnight, as is cuftomary in Germany during the fummer, traverfed the unufual fpace of fifty miles in fourteen hours. Soon after paffing Appenweyer we overtook the rear-guard of the army, the advanced party of which we had met at that place three nights before. The troops were then quartered in the villages near the road, and their narrow waggons were fometimes drawn up on both fides of it. They had probably but lately feparated, for there were parties of French ladies and gentlemen, who feemed to have taken the benefit of moonlight to be fpectators, and fome of the glow-worms, that had been numerous on the banks, now glittered very prettily in the hair of the former.

At Biel, a fmall town, which we reached about midnight, the ftreet was rendered nearly impaffable by military carriages, and we were furprifed to find, that every room in the inn was not occupied by troops; but one muft have been very faftidious

tidious to have complained of any part of our reception here. As to lodging, though the apartment was as bare as is ufual in Germany, there was the infcription of "Chambre de Monfieur" over the door, and on another near it "Chambre de Condé le Grand;" perfonages, who, it appeared, had once been accommodated there, for the honour of which the landlord chofe to retain their infcriptions. Their meeting here was probably in 1791, foon after the departure of the former from France.

The fecond day's journey brought us again to Schwezingen, from whence we hoped to have reached Manheim, that night; but the poft horfes were all out, and none others could be hired, the village being obliged to furnifh a certain number for the carriage of ftores to the Auftrian army. Eighteen of thefe we had met, an hour before, drawing flowly in one waggon, laden with cannon balls. We ftayed the following day at Manheim, and, on the next, reached Mentz, where our ftatement of the obftruction at Friburg excited lefs furprife than indignation, the want of agreement between the Auftrian and Pruffian officers being fuch, that the former, who are frequently perfons of the loweft education, are faid to neglect no opportunity of preying upon accidental miftakes in paffports, or other bufinefs committed by the Pruffians. Before our departure we were, however, affured, that a proper reprefentation of the affair had been fent by the firft eftaffette to the Commandant at Friburg.

Further intelligence of the courfe of affairs in Flanders was now made known in Germany; and our regrets, relative to Switzerland, were leffened ed by the apparent probability, that a return homeward might in a few months be rendered difficult by some still more unfortunate events to the allies. Several effects of the late reverses and symptoms of the general alarm were indeed already apparent at Mentz. Our inn was filled with refugees not only from Flanders, but from Liege, which the French had not then threatened. Some of the emigrants of the latter nation, in quitting the places where they had temporarily settled, abandoned their only means of livelihood, and several parties arrived in a state almost too distressful to be repeated. Ladies and children, who had passed the night in fields, came with so little property, and so little appearance of any, that they were refused admittance at many inns; for some others, it seemed, after resting a day or two, could offer only tears and lamentations, instead of payment. Our good landlord, Philip Bolz, relieved several, and others had a little charity from individuals; but, as far as we saw and heard, the Germans very seldom afforded them even the consolations of compassion and tender manners.

Mentz is the usual place of embarkment for a voyage down the Rhine, the celebrated scenery of whose banks we determined to view, as some compensation for the loss of Switzerland. We were also glad to escape a repetition of the fatigues of travel by land, now that these were to be attended with the uncertainties occasioned by any unusual influx of travellers upon the roads.

The business of supplying post-horses is here not the private undertaking of the innkeepers; so that the emulation and civility, which might be excited by their views of profit, are entirely wanting.

ing. The Prince de la Tour Taxis is the Hereditary Grand Poft-mafter of the Empire, an office, which has raifed his family from the ftation of private Counts, to a feat in the College of Princes. He has a monopoly of the profits arifing from this concern, for which he is obliged to forward all the Imperial packets gratis. A fettled number of horfes and a poft-mafter are kept at every ftage; where the arms of the prince, and fome line entreating a blefling upon the poft, diftinguifh the door of his office. The poft-mafter determines, according to the number of travellers and the quantity of baggage, how many horfes muft be hired; three perfons cannot be allowed to proceed with lefs than three horfes, and he will generally endeavour to fend out as many horfes as there are perfons.

The price for each horfe was eftablifhed at one florin, or twenty pence per poft, but, on account of the war, a florin and an half is now paid; half a florin is alfo due for the carriage; and the poftillion is entitled to a trinkgeld, or drink-money, of another half florin; but, unlefs he is promifed more than this at the beginning of the ftage, he will proceed only at the regulated pace of four hours for each poft, which may be reckoned at ten or twelve Englifh miles. We foon learned the way of quickening him, and, in the Palatinate and the Brifgau, where the roads are good, could proceed nearly as faft as we wifhed, amounting to about five miles an hour.

If the poft-mafter fupplies a carriage, he demands half a florin per ftage for it; but the whole expence of a chaife and two horfes, including the tolls and the *trinkgeld*, which word the poftillions

T accommodate

accommodate to Englifh ears by pronouncing it
drinkhealth, does not exceed eight pence per mile.
We are, however, to caution all perfons againft
fuppofing, as we did, that the chaifes of the poft
muft be proper ones, and that the neceffity of
buying a carriage, which may be urged to them,
is merely that of fhew; thefe chaifes are more inconvenient and filthy, than any travelling carriage,
feen in England, can give an idea of, and a ftranger fhould not enter Germany, before he has
purchafed a carriage, which will probably coft
twenty pounds in Holland and fell for fifteen, at
his return. Having neglected this, we efcaped
from the chaifes de pofte as often as poffible, by
hiring thofe of voituriers, whofe price is about
half as much again as that of the poft.

The regular drivers wear a fort of uniform,
confifting of a yellow coat, with black cuffs and
cape, a fmall bugle horn, flung over the fhoul-
ders, and a yellow fafh. At the entrance of towns
and narrow paffes, they fometimes found the horn,
playing upon it a perfect and not unpleafant tune,
the mufic of their order. All other carriages
give way to theirs, and perfons travelling with
them are confidered to be under the protection of
the Empire; fo that, if they were robbed, information would be forwarded from one poft-houfe
to another throughout all Germany, and it would
become a common caufe to detect the aggreffors.
On this account, and becaufe there can be no
concealment in a country fo little populous, high-
way robberies are almoft unknown in it, and the
fear of them is never mentioned. The Germans,
who, in fummer, travel chiefly by night, are feldom armed, and are fo far from thinking even
watchfulnefs neceffary, that moft of their carriages,

riages, though open in front, during the day-time, are contrived with curtains and benches, in order to promote reft. The poft-mafters alfo affure you, that, if there were robbers, they would content themfelves with attacking private voituriers, without violating the facrednefs of the poft ; and the fecurity of the poftillions is fo ftrictly attended to, that no man dare ftrike them, while they have the yellow coat on. In difputes with their paffengers they have, therefore, fometimes been known to put off this coat, in order to fhew, that they do not claim the extraordinary protection of the laws.

These poftillions acknowledge no obligation to travellers, who ufually give double what can be demanded, and feem to confider them only as fo many bales of goods, which they are under a contract with the poft-mafter to deliver at a certain place and within a certain time. Knowing, that their flownefs, if there is no addition to their *trinkgeld*, is of itfelf fufficient to compel fome gratuity, they do not depart from the German luxury of incivility, and frequently return no anfwer, when they are queftioned, as to diftance, or defired to call the fervant of an inn, or to quit the worft part of a road. When you tell them, that they fhall have a good *drinkhealth* for fpeed, they reply, " Yaw, yaw ;" and, after that, think it unneceffary to reply to any enquiry till they afk you for the money at the end of a ftage. They are all provided with tobacco boxes and combuftible bark, on which they ftop to ftrike with a flint and fteel, immediately after leaving their town ; in the hotteft day and on the moft dufty road, they will begin to fmoke, though every whiff flies into the faces of the paffengers behind ; and it muft be fome

T 2

very

very pofitive interference, that prevents them from continuing it.

As long as there are horfes not engaged at any poft-houfe, the people are bound to fupply travellers, within half an hour after their arrival; but all the German Princes and many of their Minifters are permitted to engage the whole ftock on the road they intend to pafs; and it frequently happens, that individuals may be detained a day, or even two, by fuch an order, if there fhould be no voiturier to furnifh them with others. At Cologne and Bonn, when we were firft there, all the horfes were ordered for the Emperor, who paffed through, however, with only one carriage, accompanied by an Aide-de-camp and followed by two fervants, on horfeback. It happens alfo frequently, that a fudden throng of private travellers has employed the whole ftock of the poft-mafters; and the prefent emigrations from Liege and Juliers, we were affured, had filled the roads fo much, that we might be frequently detained in fmall towns, and fhould find even the beft overwhelmed with crowds of fugitives.

During a ftay of five days at Mentz, we often wandered amidft the ruins of the late fiege, efpecially on the fite of the Favorita, from whence the majeftic Rhine is feen rolling from one chain of mountains to another. Near this fpot, and not lefs fortunately fituated, ftood a Carthufian convents, known in Englifh hiftory for having been the head-quarters of George the Second, in the year 1743, foon after the battle of Dettingen. The apartments, ufed by this monarch, were preferved in the ftate, in which he left them, till a fhort time before the late fiege, when the whole building
ing

ing was demolished, so that scarcely a trace of it
now remains.

By our enquiries for a passage vessel we discovered the unpleasant truth, that the dread of another invasion began now to be felt at Mentz,
where, a fortnight before, not a symptom of it
was discernible. Several of the inhabitants had
hired boats to be in readiness for transporting
their effects to Franckfort, if the French should
approach much nearer to the Rhine; and our
friends, when we mentioned the circumstance,
confessed, that they were preparing for a removal
to Saxony. The state of the arsenal had been
lately enquired into, and a deficiency, which was
whispered to have been discovered in the gunpowder, was imputed to the want of cordiality
between the Austrians and Prussians, of whom
the latter, being uncertain that they should stay in
the place, had refused to replenish the stores, at
their own expence, and the former would not
spare their ammunition, till the departure of the
Prussians should leave it to be guarded by themselves. The communication with the other shore
of the Rhine, by the bridge and the fortifications
of Caffel, secured, however, to a German garrison the opportunity of receiving supplies, even if
the French should occupy all the western bank of
the river.

VOYAGE DOWN THE RHINE.

THE boats, to be hired at Mentz, are awkward imitations of the Dutch trechtfchuyts, or, what, upon the Thames, would be called Houfeboats; but, for the fake of being allowed to difpofe of one as the varieties of the voyage fhould feem to tempt, we gave four louis for the ufe of a cabin, between Mentz and Cologne; the boatmen being permitted to take paffengers in the other part of the veffel. In this we embarked at fix o'clock, on a delightful morning in the latter end of July, and, as we left the fhore, had leifure to obferve the city in a new point of view, the moft picturefque we had feen. Its principal features were the high quays called the Rheinftraffe, the caftellated palace, with its gothic turrets, of pale red ftone, the arfenal, the lofty ramparts, far extended along the river, and the northern gate; the long bridge of boats completed the fore-ground, and fome foreft hills the picture.

We foon paffed the wooded ifland, called *Peters-au*, of fo much confequence, during the fiege, for its command of the bridge; and, approaching the mountains of the Rheingau to the morth, the moft fublime in this horizon, faw their fummits veiled in clouds, while the fun foon melted the mifts, that dimmed their lower fides, and brought out their various colouring of wood, corn and foils. It was, however, nearly two hours before the windings of the Rhine permitted

mitted us to reach any of their bafes. Meanwhile
the river flowed through highly cultivated plains,
chiefly of corn, with villages thickly fcattered on
its banks, in which are the country houfes of the
richer inhabitants of Mentz, among pleafant orchards and vineyards. Thofe on the right bank
are in the dominions of the Prince of Naffau
Ufingen, who has a large chateau in the midft of
them, once tenanted, for a night, by George the
Second, and the Duke of Cumberland.

The Rhine is here, and for feveral leagues
downward, of a very noble breadth, perhaps
wider than in any other part of its German
courfe; and its furface is animated by many iflands
covered with poplars and low wood. The weftern fhore, often fringed with pine and elms, is
flat; but the eaftern begins to fwell into hillocks
near Wallauf, the laft village of Naffau Ufingen,
and once fomewhat fortified.

Here the *Rheingau*, or the country of the vines,
commences, and we approached the northern
mountains, which rife on the right in fine fweeping undulations. Thefe increafed in dignity as
we advanced, and their fummits then appeared to
be darkened with heath and woods, which form
part of the extenfive foreft of *Landefwald*, or
Woodland. Hitherto the fcenery had been open
and pleafant only, but now the eaftern fhore began to be romantic, ftarting into heights, fo abrupt, that the vineyards almoft overhung the
river, and opening to foreft glens, among the
mountains. Still, however, towns and villages
perpetually occurred, and the banks of the river
were populous, though not a veffel befides our
own appeared upon it.

On

On the eastern margin are two small towns, Oder and Niederingelheim, which, in the midst of the dominions of Mentz, belong to the Elector Palatine. On this shore also is made one of the celebrated wines of the Rhine, called Markerbrunner, which ranks next to those of Johannesberg and Hockheim. At no great distance on the same shore, but beneath a bank somewhat more abrupt, is the former of these places, alienated in the sixteenth century from the dominions of Mentz, to those of the Abbot, now Prince Bishop of Fulde.

The wine of the neighbouring steeps is the highest priced of all the numerous sorts of Rhenish; a bottle selling upon the spot, where it is least likely to be pure, for three, four, or five shillings, according to the vintages, the merits and distinctions of which are in the memory of almost every German. That of 1786 was the most celebrated since 1779; but we continually heard that the heat of 1794 would render this year equal in fame to any of the others.

Behind the village is the large and well-built abbey of Johannesberg, rich with all this produce, for the security of which there are immense cellars, cut in the rock below, said to be capable of containing several thousand tons of wine. The abbey was founded in 1105; and there is a long history of changes pertaining to it, till it came into the possession of the Abbot of Fulde, who rebuilt it in its present state. This part of the Rheingau is, indeed, thickly set with similar edifices, having, in a short space, the nunnery of Marienthal, and the monasteries of Nothgottes, Aulenhausen, and Eibingen.

Further on is the large modern chateau of Count Ostein, a nobleman of great wealth, and, as it appears, of not less taste. Having

disposed

difpofed all his nearer grounds in a ftyle for the moft part Englifh, he has had recourfe to the ridge of precipices, that rife over the river, for fublimity and grandeur of profpect. On the brink of thefe woody heights, feveral pavilions have been erected, from the moft confpicuous of which Coblentz, it is faid, may be diftinguifhed, at the diftance of forty miles. The view muft be aftonifhingly grand, for to the fouth-eaft the eye overlooks all the fine country of the Rheingau to Mentz; to the weft, the courfe of the Mofelle towards France; and, to the north, the chaos of wild mountains, that fcreen the Rhine in its progrefs to Coblentz.

So general was the alarm of invafion, that Count Oftein had already withdrawn into the interior of Germany, and was endeavouring to difpofe of this charming refidence, partly protected as it is by the river, at the very difadvantageous price now paid for eftates on the weftern frontier of the Empire.

The vineyards, that fucceed, are proofs of the induftry and fkill to which the Germans are accuftomed in this part of their labours, the fcanty foil being prevented from falling down the almoft perpendicular rocks, by walls that frequently require fome new toil from the careful farmer. Every addition, made to the mould, muft be carried in bafkets up the fteep paths, or rather ftaircafes, cut in the folid rock. At the time of the vintage, when thefe precipices are thronged with people, and the founds of merriment are echoed along them, the fpectacle muft here be as ftriking and gay as can be painted by fancy.

BINGEN.

BINGEN.

ABOUT eleven o'clock, we reached Bingen,
a town of which the antiquity is so clear, that one
of its gates is still called Drusithor, or, the gate
of Drusus. Its appearance, however, is neither
rendered venerable by age, or neat by novelty.
The present buildings were all raised in the distress
and confusion produced in 1689, after Louis the
Fourteenth had blown up the fortifications, that
endured a tedious siege in the beginning of the
century, and had destroyed the city, in which
Drusus is said to have died.

It has now the appearance, which we have
often mentioned is characteristic of most German
towns, nearly every house being covered with
symptoms of decay and neglect, and the streets
abandoned to a few idle passengers. Yet Bingen
has the advantage of standing at the conflux of two
rivers, the Nahe making there its junction with
the Rhine; and an antient German book mentions it as the central place of an hundred villages,
or chateaux, the inhabitants of which might come
to its market and return between sun-rise and
sun-set.

Since the revolution in France, it has occasionally been much the residence of emigrants;
and, in a plain behind the town, which was
pointed out to us, the King of Prussia reviewed
their army before the entrance into France in
1792. A part of his speech was repeated to us

by

by a gentleman who bore a high commiffion in it; " Gentlemen, be tranquil and happy; in a little time I fhall conduct you to your homes and your property."

Our companion, as he remembered the hopes excited by this fpeech, was deeply affected; an emigrant officer, of whom, as well as of an Ex-Nobleman of the fame nation, with the latter of whom we parted here, we muft paufe to fay, that had the old fyftem in France, oppreffive as it was, and injurious as Englifhmen were once juftly taught to believe it, been univerfally adminiftered by men of their mildnefs, integrity and benevolence, it could not have been entirely overthrown by all the theories, or all the eloquence in the world.

Soon after this review, the march commenced; the general effect of which it is unneceffary to repeat. When the retreat was ordered, the emigrant army, comprifing feventy fquadrons of cavalry, was declared by the King of Pruffia to be difbanded, and not any perfon was allowed to retain an horfe, or arms. No other purchafers were prefent but the Pruffians, and, in confequence of this order, the fineft horfes, many of which had coft forty louis each, were now fold for four or five, fome even for one! It refulted accidentally, no doubt, from this meafure, that the Pruffian army was thus reprovided with horfes almoft as cheaply as if they had feized them from Dumourier.

Bingen was taken by the French in the latter end of the campaign of 1792, and was then nearly the northermoft of their pofts on the Rhine.

It

It was regained by the Pruffians in their advances to Mentz, at the commencement of the next campaign, and has fince occafionally ferved them as a depôt of ftores.

This town, feated on the low weftern margin, furrounded with its old walls, and overtopped by its ruined caftle, harmonizes well with the gloomy grandeur near it; and here the afpect of the country changes to a character awfully wild. The Rhine, after expanding to a great breadth, at its conflux with the Nahe, fuddenly contracts itfelf, and winds with an abrupt and rapid fweep among the dark and tremendous rocks, that clofe the perfpective. Then, difappearing beyond them, it leaves the imagination to paint the dangers of its courfe. Near the entrance of this clofe pafs, ftands the town of Bingen, immediately oppofite to which appear the ruins of the caftle of Ehrenfels, on a cliff highly elevated above the water, broken, craggy and impending, but with vines crawling in narrow crevices, and other rocks ftill afpiring above it. On an ifland between thefe fhores is a third ruined caftle, very antient, and of which little more than one tower remains. This is called Maufthurm, or, The Tower of the Rats, from a marvellous tradition, that, in the tenth century, an Archbifhop Statto was devoured there by thefe animals, after many cruelties to the poor, whom he called Rats, that eat the bread of the rich.

EHRENFELS.

EHRENFELS.

EHRENFELS is fynonymous to Majeftic, or Noble Rock; and Fels, which is the prefent term for rock in all the northern counties of England, as well as in Germany, is among feveral inftances of exact fimilarity, as there are many of refemblance, between the prefent Britifh and German languages. A German of the fouthern diftricts, meaning to enquire what you would have, fays, " *Was woll zu haben?*" and in the north there is a fort of Patois, called *Plat Deutfche*, which brings the words much nearer to our own. In both parts the accent, or rather tone, is that, which prevails in Scotland and the adjoining counties of England. To exprefs a temperate approbation of what they hear, the Germans fay, " So—fo;" pronouncing the words flowly and long; exactly as our brethren of Scotland would. In a printed narrative of the fiege of Mentz there is this paffage, " *Funfzehn bundert menfchen, meiftens weiber und kinder - - - - - - wanderten mit dem bundel under dem arm uber die brucke;*"—Fifteen hundred perfons, moftly wives and children, wandered, with their bundles under their arms, upon the bridge. So permanent has been the influence over our language, which the Saxons acquired by their eftablifhment of more than five centuries amongft us; exiling the antient Britifh tongue to the mountains of Scotland and Wales; and afterwards, when incorporated with this, refifting

the

the perfecution of the Normans; rather improving than yielding under their endeavours to extirpate it. The injuries of the Bifhop of Winchefter, who, in Henry the Second's time, was deprived of his fee for being " *an Englifh ideot, that could not fpeak French*," one would fondly imagine had the effeét due to all perfecutions, that of ftrength-ening, not fubduing their objeéts.

After parting with fome of the friends, who had accompanied us from Mentz, and taking in provifion for the voyage, our oars were again plyed, and we approached Bingerloch, the com-mencement of that tremendous pafs of rocky mountains, which enclofe the Rhine nearly as far as Coblentz. Bingerloch is one of the moft dan-gerous parts of the river; that, being here at once impelled by the waters of the Nahe, compreffed by the projeétion of its boundaries, and irritated by hidden rocks in its current, makes an abrupt de-fcent, frequently rendered further dangerous by whirlpools. Several German authors affert, that a part of the Rhine here takes a channel beneath its general bed, from which it does not iffue, till it reaches St. Goar, a diftance of probably twenty miles. The force and rapidity of the ftream, the afpeét of the dark disjointed cliffs, under which we paffed, and the ftrength of the wind; oppofing our entrance among their chafms; and uniting with the founding force of the waters to baffle the dexterity of the boatmen, who ftruggled hard to prevent the veffel from being whirled round, were circumftances of the true fublime, in-fpiring terror in fome and admiration in a high degree.

Reviewing

Reviewing this now, in the leisure of recollection, these nervous lines of Thomson appear to describe much of the scene:

> The rous'd up river pours along;
> Resistless, roaring, dreadful, down it comes
> From the rude mountain, and the mossy wild,
> Tumbling through rocks abrupt, and founding far;
> - - - - - - - - - - - - - - again conftrain'd
> Between two meeting hills, it bursts away,
> Where rocks and woods o'erhang the turbid stream;
> There gathering triple force, rapid, and deep,
> It boils, and wheels, and foams, and thunders through.

Having doubled the sharp promontory, that alters the course of the river, we saw in perspective, sometimes perpendicular rocks, and then mountains dark with dwarf-woods, shooting their precipices over the margin of the water; a boundary which, for many leagues, was not broken, on either margin, except where, by some slight receding, the rocks embosomed villages, lying on the edge of the river, and once guarded them by the antient castles on their points. A stormy day, with frequent showers, obscured the scenery, making it appear dreary, without increasing its gloomy grandeur; but we had leisure to observe every venerable ruin, that seemed to tell the religious, or military history of the country. The first of these beyond Bingen, is the old castle of Bauzberg, and, next, the church of St. Clement, built in a place once greatly infested by robbers.
There

There are then the modern caftle of Konigftein, in which the French were befieged in 1793, and the remains of the old one, deferted for more than two hundred years. Oppofite to thefe is the village of Affmans, or Hafemanfhaufen, cele- brated for the flavour of its wines; and near them was formerly a warm bath, fupplied by a fpring, now loft from its fource to the Rhine, notwithftanding many expenfive fearches to re- gain it. About a mile farther, is the antient caftle of Falkenburg, and below it the village of Drechfen; then the ruins of an extenfive chateau, called Sonneck, beneath which the Rhine ex- pands, and encircles two fmall iflands, that con- clude the diftrict of the Rheingau.

After paffing the fmall town of Lorrich, on the eaftern bank, the Rhine is again ftraightened by rocky precipices, and rolls haftily paft the an- tient caftle of Furftenberg, which gives its name to one of the deareft wines of the Rhine.

We now reached Bacharach, a town on the left bank of the river, forming part of the widely fcattered dominions of the Elector Palatine, who has attended to its profperity by permitting the Calvinifts and Lutherans to eftablifh their forms of worfhip there, under equal privileges with the Roman Catholics.

It has a confiderable commerce in Rhenifh wine; and its toll-houfe, near which all veffels are compelled to ftop, adds confiderably to the revenues of the Palatinate. For the purpofe of enforcing thefe, the antient caftle called Stahleck, founded in 1190, was probably built; for Bacha- rach is the oldeft town of the Palatinate, and has
                                                    fcarcely

scarcely any history between the period when it was annexed to that dominion and the departure of the Romans, who are supposed to have given it the name of *Bacchi ara*, and to have performed some ceremonies to that deity upon a stone, said to be still concealed in the Rhine. In the year 1654, 1695, 1719, and 1750, when the river was remarkably low, this stone is recorded to have been seen near the opposite island of Worth, and the country people have given it the name of the *Aelterstein*. As this extreme lowness of the waters never happens but in the hottest years, the sight of the Aelterstein is earnestly desired, as the symptom of a prosperous vintage. The river was unusually low when we passed the island, but we looked in vain for this stone, which is said to be so large, that five-and-twenty persons may stand upon its surface.

Bacharach is in the list of places, ruined by Louis the Fourteenth in 1689. The whole town was then so carefully and methodically plundered that the French commander, during the last night of his stay, had nothing to sleep on but straw; and, the next day, this bedding was employed in assisting to set fire to the town, which was presently reduced to ashes.

U   PFALZ.

PFALTZ.

ABOUT a mile lower is the island of Pfaltz, or Pfalzgrafenſtein, a place of ſuch antient importance in the hiſtory of the Palatinate, that it has given its name to the whole territory in Germany called Pfaltz. It was probably the firſt reſidence of the Counts, the peaceable poſſeſſion of which was one means of atteſting the right to the Palatinate; for, as a ſign of ſuch poſſeſſion, it was antiently neceſſary, that the heir apparent ſhould be born in a caſtle, which ſtill ſubſiſts in a repaired ſtate upon it. This melancholy fortreſs is now provided with a garriſon of invalids, who are chiefly employed in guarding ſtate priſoners, and in giving notice to the neighbouring toll-houſe of Kaub, of the approach of veſſels on the Rhine. Being much ſmaller than is ſuitable to the value placed upon it, it is ſecured from ſurprife by having no entrance, except by a ladder, which is drawn up at night.

KAUB.

KAUB.

KAUB, a Palatine town on the right bank of the river, is alfo fortified, and claims a toll upon the Rhine, notwithftanding its neighbourhood to Bacharach; an oppreffion, of which the expence is almoft the leaft inconvenience, for the toll-gatherers do not come to the boats, but demand, that each fhould ftop, while one at leaft of the crew goes on fhore, and tells the number of his paffengers, who are alfo fometimes required to appear. The officers do not even think it necef-fary to wait at home for this information, and our boatmen had frequently to fearch for them throughout the towns. So familiar, however, is this injuftice, that it never appeared to excite furprife, or anger. The boatman dares not pro-ceed till he has found and fatisfied the officers; nor has he any means of compelling them to be punctual. Ours was aftonifhed when we enquired, whether the merchants, to whom fuch delays might be important, could not have redrefs for them.

The ftay we made at Kaub enabled us, howe-ver, to perceive that fine flate made a confiderable part of its traffic.

The Rhine, at Bacharach and Kaub, is of great breadth; and the dark mountains, that afcend from its margin, form a grand vifta, with antient chateaux ftill appearing on the heights, and fre-

U 2 quent

quent villages edging the ftream, or ftudded among the cliffs.

Though the diftrict of the Rheingau, the vines of which are the moft celebrated, terminated fome miles paft, the vineyards are fcarcely lefs abundant here, covering the lower rocks of the mountains, and creeping along the fractures of their upper crags. Thefe, however, fometimes exhibit huge projecting maffes and walls of granite, fo entire and perpendicular, that not an handful of foil can lodge for the nourifhment of any plant. They lie in vaft oblique ftrata; and, as in the valley of Andernach, the angles of the promontories on one fhore of the river frequently correfpond with the receffes on the other.

OBERWESEL

Is another town, fupported by the manufacture and trade of wines, which are, however, here fhared by too many places to beftow much wealth fingly upon any. Wine is alfo fo important a production, that all the Germans have fome degree of connoiffeurfhip in it, and can diftinguifh its quantities and value fo readily, that the advantage of dealing in it cannot be great, except to thofe, who fupply foreign countries. The merits of the different vineyards form a frequent topic of converfation, and almoft every perfon has his own fcale of their rank; running over with familiar fluency the uncouth names of Johannefberg, Ammanfhaufen, Hauptberg, Fuldifche Schoffberg, Rudefheim.

Rudesheim, Hockheim, Rodtland, Hinterhaufer, Markerbrunner, Grafenberg, Laubenheim, Bifcheim, Nierstein, Harfcheim and Kapellgarren; all celebrated vineyards in the Rheingau. The growth and manufacture of thefe wines are treated of in many books, from one of which we tranflate an account, that feems to be the moft comprehenfive and fimple.

OF THE RHENISH VINEYARDS AND WINES.

THE ftrongeft and, as they are termed, fulleftbodied wines, thofe of courfe, which are beft for keeping, are produced upon mountains of a cold and ftrong foil; the moft brifk and fpirited on a warm and gravelly fituation. Thofe produced near the middle of an afcent are efteemed the moft wholefome, the foil being there fufficiently watered, without becoming too moift; and on this account, the vineyards of Hockheim are more efteemed than fome, whofe produce is better flavoured; on the contrary, thofe at the feet of hills are thought fo unwholefome, on account of their extreme humidity, that the wine is directed to be kept for feveral years, before it is brought to table. The fineft flavour is communicated by foils either argillaceous, or marly. Of this fort is a mountain near Bacharach, the wines of which are faid to have a Mufcadine flavour and to be fo highly valued, that an Emperor, in the fourteenth century, demanded four large barrels of them, inftead

inftead of 10,000 florins, which the city of Nu-
remberg would have paid for its privileges.

A vineyard, newly manured, produces a ftrong,
fpirited and well-flavoured, but ufually an unwholefome wine; becaufe the manure contains a
corrofive falt and a fat fulphur, which, being
diffolved, paffes with the juices of the earth into
the vines. A manure, confifting of ftreet mud,
old earth, the ruins of houfes well broken, and
whatever has been much expofed to the elements,
is, however, laid on, once in five or fix years,
between the vintage and winter.

The forts of vines, cultivated in the *Rheingau*,
are the low ones, called the *Reiftinge*, which are
the moft common and ripen the firft; thofe of
Klebroth, or red Burgundy, the wine of which is
nearly purple; of Orleans and of Lambert; and
laftly the tall vine, raifed againft houfes, or fupported by bowers in gardens. The wines of the
two firft claffes are wholefome; thofe of the latter
are reputed dangerous, or, at leaft, unfit to be
preferved.

The vintagers do not pluck the branches by
hand, but carefully cut them, that the grapes
may not fall off; in the Rheingau and about
Worms the cultivators afterwards bruife them
with clubs, but thofe of Franckfort with their
feet; after which the grapes are carried to the
prefs, and the wine flows from them by wooden
pipes into barrels in the cellar. That, which
flows upon the firft preffure, is the moft delicately
flavoured, but the weakeft; the next is ftrongeft
and moft brifk; the third is four; but the
mixture of all forms a good wine. The fkins
are fometimes preffed a fourth time, and a

bad

bad brandy is obtained from the fermented juice; laftly, in the fcarcity of pafturage in this part of Germany, they are given for food to oxen, but not to cows, their heat being deftructive of milk.

To thefe particulars it may be ufeful to add, that one of the fureft proofs of the purity of Rhe-nifh is the quick rifing and difappearance of the froth, on pouring it into a glafs : when the beads are formed flowly and remain long, the wine is mixed and factitious.

OBERWESEL,

THE account of which has been interrupted by this digreffion, is the firft town of the Electo-rate of Treves, on this fide, to which it has be-longed fince 1312, when its freedom as an impe-rial city, granted by the Emperor, Frederic the Second, was perfidioufly feized by Henry the Seventh, and the town given to him by his bro-ther Baldwin, the then Elector. The new So-vereign enriched it with a fine collegiate church, which ftill dignifies the fhore of the river. If he ufed any other endeavours to make the profperity of the place furvive its liberties, they appear to have failed; for Oberwefel now refembles the other towns of the Electorate, except that the great number of towers and fteeples tell what it was before its declenfion into that territory. The Town-houfe, rendered unneceffary by the power of Baldwin, does not exift to infult the inhabi-tants with the memory of its former ufe; but is in ruins, and thus ferves for an emblem of the effects, produced by the change.

Between

Between Oberwesel and St. Goar, the river is of extraordinary breadth, and the majestic mountains are covered with forests, which leave space for little more than a road between their feet and the water. A group of peasants, with baskets on their heads, appeared now and then along the winding path, and their diminutive figures, as they passed under the cliffs, seemed to make the heights shew more tremendous. When they disappeared for a moment in the copses, their voices, echoing with several repetitions among the rocks, were heard at intervals, and with good effect, as our oars were suspended.

Soon after passing the island of Sand, we had a perspective view of St. Goar, of the strong fortress of Rhinfels, on the rocks beyond, and of the small fortified town of Goarhausen, on the opposite bank. The mountains now become still more stupendous, and many rivulets, or *becks*, which latter is a German, as well as an English term, descend from them into the river, on either hand, some of which, in a season less dry than the present, roar with angry torrents. But the extreme violence, with which the Rhine passes in this district, left us less leisure than in others to observe its scenery,

ST. GOAR.

ST. GOAR.

WE foon reached St. Goar, lying at the feet of rocks on the weftern fhore, with its ramparts and fortifications fpreading far along the water, and mounting in feveral lines among the furround-ing cliffs, fo as to have a very ftriking and ro-mantic appearance. The Rhine no where, per-haps, prefents grander objects either of nature, or of art, than in the northern perfpective from St. Goar. There, expanding with a bold fweep, the river exhibits, at one coup d'œil, on its moun-tainous fhores, fix fortreffes or towns, many of them placed in the moft wild and tremendous fituations; their antient and gloomy ftructures giving ideas of the fullen tyranny of former times. The height and fantaftic fhapes of the rocks, upon which they are perched, or by which they are overhung, and the width and rapidity of the ri-ver, that, unchanged by the viciffitudes of ages and the contentions on its fhores, has rolled at their feet, while generations, that made its moun-tains roar, have paffed away into the filence of eternity,—thefe were objects, which, combined, formed one of the fublimeft fcenes we had viewed.

The chief of the fortreffes is that of Rhinfels, impending over St. Goar, on the weft fhore, its high round tower rifing above maffy buildings, that crown two rocks, of fuch enormous bulk and threatening power, that, as we glided under them, it was neceffary to remember their fixed founda-tions, to foften the awe they infpired. Other fortifications extend down the precipices, and margin

margin the river, at their bafe. Further on in the perfpective, and where the eaft bank of the Rhine makes its boldeft fweep, is the very ftriking and fingular caftle of Platz, a clufter of towers, overtopped by one of immenfe height, that, perched upon the fummit of a pyramidal rock, feems ready to precipitate itfelf into the water below. Wherever the cliffs beneath will admit of a footing, the fharp angles of fortifications appear.

On another rock, ftill further in the perfpective, is the caftle of Thumberg, and, at its foot, on the edge of the water, the walled tower of Wel-mick. Here the Rhine winds from the eye among heights, that clofe the fcene.

Nearly oppofite to St. Goar, is Goarfhauffen, behind which the rocks rife fo fuddenly, as fcarcely to leave fpace for the town to lie between them and the river. A flying bridge maintains a communication between the two places, which, as well as the fortrefs of Rhinfels, are under the dominion of the Prince of Heffe Caffel.

The number of fortreffes here, over which Rhinfels is in every refpect paramount, feem to be the lefs neceffary, becaufe the river itfelf, fuddenly fwoln by many ftreams and vexed by hidden rocks, is a fort of natural fortification to both fhores, a very little refiftance from either of which muft render it impaffable. Whether the water has a fubterraneous paffage from Bingen hither or not, there are occafionally agitations in this part, which confound the fkill of naturalifts; and the river is univerfally allowed to have a fall. Near St. Goar, a fudden guft of wind, affifted by the current, rendered our boat fo unmanageable, that, in fpite of its heavinefs and of all the efforts of the watermen,

watermen, it was whirled round, and nearly forced upon the oppofite bank to that, on which they would have directed it.

St. Goar is a place of great antiquity. A difpute about the etymology of its name is remarkable for the ludicrous contrariety of the two opinions. One author maintains, that it is derived from an hermit named Goar, who, in the fixth century, built a fmall chapel here. Another fuppofes that Gewerb, the name of a neighbouring fall in the Rhine, has been corrupted to Gewer, and thence to Goar ; after which, confidering that there is an ifland called *Sand* in the river, and that a great quantity of that material is hereabouts thrown up, he finds the two words combine very fatisfactorily into a likenefs of the prefent denomination. The former opinion is, however, promoted by this circumftance, which the advocates of the latter may complain of as a partiality, that a ftatue of St. Goar is actually to be feen in the great church, founded in 1440; and that, notwithftanding the robberies and violences committed in the church by a Spanifh army, the following infcription is ftill entire :

S. GOAR
MONACHUS GALLUS
OBIIT 611.

St. Goar is one of the largeft places we had yet paffed, and has a confiderable fhare of the commerce carried on by the Rhine. Having in time of war a numerous garrifon, and being a little reforted to on account of its romantic fituation, it has an air of fomewhat more animation than

might

might be expected, mingling with the gloom of its walls, and the appearance of decay, which it has in common with other German towns. We were here required to pay the fifth toll from Mentz, and were visited by a Hessian serjeant, who demanded, that our names and condition should be written in his book. These being given, not in the Saxon, but the Roman character, he returned to require another edition of them in German; so that his officer was probably unable to read any other language, or characters. This being complied with, it seemed, that the noble garrison of St. Goar had no further fears concerning us, and we were not troubled by more of the precautions used,

" Left foul invasion in disguise approach."

The fortress of Rhinfels, which commands St. Goar, is frequently mentioned in the histories of German wars. In the year 1255 it endured forty assaults of an army, combined from sixty towns on the Rhine. In 1692, the French General Tallard besieged it in vain, retreating with the loss of four thousand men, and nearly two hundred officers; but, in 1758, the Marquis de Castries surprised it with so much ingenuity and vigour, that not a life was lost, and it remained in possession of the French till 1763, when it was restored by the treaty of peace.

BOPPART.

BOPPART.

WE next reached the difmal old town of Boppart, once an imperial city, ftill furrounded with venerable walls, and dignified by the fine Benedictine nunnery and abbey of Marienberg, perched upon a mountain above; an inftitution founded in the eleventh century, for the benefit of noble families only, and enriched by the donations of feveral Emperors and Electors. Boppart, like many other towns, is built on the margin of the Rhine, whence it fpreads up the rocks, that almoft impend over the water, on which the cluftered houfes are fcarcely diftinguifhable from the cliffs themfelves. Befides the Benedictine abbey, here is a convent of Carmelites, and another of Francifcans; and the fpot is fuch as fuited well the fuperftition of former times, for

> —" O'er the twilight groves, and dufky caves,
> Long-founding aifles, and intermingled graves,
> Black Melancholy fits, and round her throws
> A death-like filence, and a dread repofe;
> Her gloomy prefence faddens all the fcene,
> Shades every flower, and darkens every green,
> Deepens the murmur of the falling floods,
> And breathes a browner horror o'er the woods."

The

The river, expanding into a vaſt bay, ſeems nearly ſurrounded by mountains, that aſſume all ſhapes, as they aſpire above each other ; ſhooting into cliffs of naked rock, which impend over the water, or, covered with foreſts, retiring in multiplied ſteeps into regions whither fancy only can follow. At their baſe, a few miſerable cabins, and half-famiſhed vine-yards, are all, that diverſify the ſavageneſs of the ſcene. Here two Capuchins, belonging probably to the convent above, as they walked along the ſhore, beneath the dark cliffs of Boppart, wrapt in the long black drapery of their order, and their heads ſhrowded in cowls, that half concealed their faces, were intereſting figures in a picture, always gloomily ſublime.

PLACE OF ANTIENT ELECTIONS.

PASSING the town of Braubach and the majeſtic caſtle of Markſberg, which we had long obſerved, above the windings of the ſtream, on a ſteep mountain, we came to Renſe, a ſmall town, remarkable only for its neighbourhood to a ſpot, on which the elections of kings of the Romans, or, at leaſt, the meetings preliminary to them, are believed to have antiently taken place. This is diſtinguiſhed at preſent by the remains of a low octagonal building, open at top, and acceſſible beneath by eight arches, in one of which is a flight of ſteps. Within, is a ſtone bench, ſuppoſed to be formed for the Electors, who might aſcend to it by theſe ſteps. In the centre of the
pavement

pavement below is a thick pillar, the use of which, whether as a tribune for the new king, or as a table for receiving the attestations of the electors, is not exactly known. That the building itself, now called Koningstuhl, or King's Throne, was used for some purposes of election, appears from several German historians, who mention meetings there in the fourteenth and fifteenth centuries, and impute them to antient customs.

INTERMIXTURE OF GERMAN TERRITORIES.

NEARLY opposite to *Rense* is the small town of *Oberlahnstein*, which belongs to the Elector of Mentz, though separated from his other dominions by those of several Princes. To such intersections of one territory with another the individual weakness of the German Princes is partly owing; while their collected body has not only necessarily the infirmities of each of its members, but is enfeebled by the counteraction arising from an arrangement, which brings persons together to decide a question, according to a common interest, who are always likely to have an individual one of more importance to each than his share in the general concern.

The banks of the Rhine afford many instances of this disjunction of territory. The Elector of Cologn has a town to the southward of nearly all the dominions of Treves; the Elector Palatine, whose possessions on the east bank of the Rhine are intersected by those of five or six other Princes,

crosses

croffes the river to occupy fome towns between
the Electorates of Mentz and Treves; the Landgrave of Heffe Caffel does the fame to his fortrefs
of Rhinfels ; and the Elector of Mentz, in return,
has a ftrip of land and his chief country refidence,
between the dominions of the two houfes of Heffe.

That this intermixture of territory exifts, without producing domeftic violences, is, however,
obvioufly a proof, that the prefent ftate of the
Germanic body, weak as it may be, with refpect
to foreign interefts, is well formed for the prefervation of interior peace. The aggrandizement of
the Houfes of Auftria and Pruffia, which has been
fuppofed dangerous to the conftitution of the Empire, tends confiderably to fecure its domeftic
tranquillity, though it diminifhes the independence of the leffer Sovereigns; for the interefts of
the latter are known to be ranged on one, or the
other fide ; and, as the Houfe, to which each is
attached, is likely to interfere, upon any aggref-
fion againft them, the weaker Princes are with-
held from contefts among themfelves, which
would be accompanied by wars, fo very extenfive
and fo difproportionate to their caufes.

Nor is the Chamber of Wetzlaar, or the Court
for deciding the caufes of Princes, as well as all
queftions relative to the conftitution, to be confidered as a nullity. The appointment of the judges
by the free but fecret votes of all Princes, fubject to their decrees, is alone wanting to make its
purity equal to its power. In minute queſti-
ons, the chief Princes readily receive its decifion,
inftead of that of arms, which, without it,
might fometimes be adopted; and the other Sovereigns

reigns may be compelled to obey it, the Chamber being authorifed to command any Prince to enforce its decrees by his army, and to take payment of the expences out of the dominions of his refractory neighbour. An inftance of fuch a command, and of its being virtually effectual, notwithftanding the ridicule, with which it was treated, occurred, during the reign of the late Frederic of Pruffia; the ftory is varioufly told, but the following account was confirmed to us by an Advocate of the Chamber of Wetzlaar.

The Landgrave of Heffe Caffel had difobeyed feveral injunctions of the Chamber, relative to a queftion which had been conftitutionally fubmitted to them. At length, the Judges had recourfe to their power of calling out what is called the *Armée Exécutrice de l'Empire*, confifting of fo many troops of any Prince, not a party in the caufe, as may be fufficient for enforcing fubmiffion. The Sovereign of Heffe Caffel was not to be conquered by any of his immediate neighbours, and they were induced to direct their order to the King of Pruffia, notwithftanding the probability, that fo unjuft a monarch would fhew fome refentment of their controul.

Frederic confented to the propriety of fupporting the Chamber, but did not choofe to involve himfelf with the Landgrave, on their account. He, therefore, fent him a copy of their order, accompanied by a letter, which, in his own ftyle of courteous pleafantry, yet with a fufficient fhew of fome further intentions, admonifhed him to obey them. The Landgrave affured him of his readinefs to conform, and the two Princes had privately fettled the matter, when the King of

X

Pruffia

Pruffia refolved to obey and to ridicule the Chamber of Wetzlaar. He fent, by a public diligence, a ferjeant of foot, who, at the firft Heffian garrifon, delivered a paper to the captain of the guard, declaring himfelf to be the commander of the *Armée Exécutrice*, fet on foot by order of the Chamber; and the army confifted of two corporals, who waited at the door! The Judges of Wetzlaar did not fhew, that they knew the difrefpect, and were contented that the King of Pruffia had reduced the Landgrave of Heffe Caffel to obedience.

To this Court fubjects may make appeals from the orders of their immediate fovereigns, when the queftion can be fhewn to have any general, or conftitutional tendency. Such a caufe we heard of in Germany, and it feemed likely to place the Chamber in fomewhat a delicate fituation. The Elector of Treves had banifhed a magiftrate, for having addreffed himfelf to Cuftine, during the invafion of the French, in 1792, and requefted to know whether he might remain on a part of his property, near their pofts, and perform the duties of his office, as ufual. The magiftrate appealed to Wetzlaar; admitted the facts charged; and fet forth, that, in this part of his conduct, he had exactly followed the example of the Chamber itfelf, who, though at a greater diftance, had made a fimilar application.

Soon after leaving Oberlahnftein, we paffed the mouth of the Lahn, a fmall river, which defcends from

from the mountains of Wetteravia on the right, and washes silver and lead mines in its course. It issues from one of those narrow and gloomy forest-glens, which had continually occurred on the eastern bank since we left Boppart, and which were once terrible for more than their aspect, having been the haunt of robbers, of whose crimes some testimonies still remain in the tombs of murdered travellers near the shore. In the ruins of castles and abandoned fortresses within the recesses of these wild mountains, such banditti took up their abode; and these are not fancied personages, for, in the year 1273, an Elector of Mentz destroyed the deserted fortress of Rheinberg, because it had been a rendezvous for them.

Towards sun-set, the rain, which had fallen at intervals during the day, ceased; a fiery flush from the west was reflected on the water, and partially coloured the rocks. Sometimes, an oblique gleam glanced among these glens, touching their upper cliffs, but leaving their depths, with the rivulets, that roared there, in darkness. As the boat glided by, we could now and then discover on the heights a convent or a chateau, lighted up by the rays, and which, like the pictures in a magic lanthorn, appeared and vanished in a moment, as we passed on the current.

But the shores soon begin to wear a milder aspect; the mountains of the western bank soften into gradual heights; and vineyards, which had disappeared near Boppart, again climb along them. The eastern shore is more abrupt, still bearing on its points some antient buildings, till, opposite to Coblentz, it shoots up into that enormous mass, which sustains the fortress of Ehrenbreitstein.

Having

Having paſſed a Benedictine convent, ſeated on the iſland of Oberworth, we reached Coblentz as the moon began to tint the rugged Ehrenbreitſtein, whoſe towers and pointed angles caught the light. Part of the rock below, ſhaded by projecting cliffs, was dark and awful, but the Rhine, expanding at its feet, trembled with radiance. There the flying-bridge, and its ſweeping line of boats, were juſt diſcernible. On the left, the quay of Coblentz extended, high and broad, crowned with handſome buildings; with tall veſſels lying along its baſe.

EHRENBREITSTEIN.

WE were now ſomewhat more pleaſantly lodged than before, at an inn near the Rhine, almoſt oppoſite to the fortreſs, the importance of which had, in the mean time, greatly increaſed by the approach of the French armies. The ſtrength of it was ſomewhat a popular topic. Being conſidered as one of the keys of Germany towards France, the Governor takes the oaths not only to the Elector of Treves, but to the Emperor and the Empire. As it can be attacked but on one ſide, and that is not towards the Rhine, a blockade is more expected than a ſiege; and there are ſtorehouſes in the rock for preſerving a great quantity of proviſions. The ſupply of water has been provided for ſo long ſince as the fifteenth century, when three years were paſſed in digging, with incredible labour, a well through the ſolid rock. An inſcription on a part of the caſtle mentions

mentions this work, and that the rock was hewn to the depth of two hundred and eighty feet. The poffeffion of the fortrefs was confirmed to the Elector of Treves by the treaty of Weftphalia in 1650.

In the morning, our boatmen croffed the river from Coblentz, to pafs under the walls of Ehrenbreitftein, perhaps an eftablifhed fymptom of fubmiffion. The river is ftill of noble breadth, and, after the junction with the Mofelle, which immediately fronts the old palace, flows with great, but even rapidity. Its fhores are now lefs romantic, and more open; fpreading on the left into the plains of Coblentz, and fwelling on the right into retiring mountains.

CONVERSATION RELATIVE TO FRANCE.

BUT our attention was withdrawn from the view, and our party in the cabin this day increafed, by a circumftance, that occurred to our emigrant friend. Having found a large fabre, which he thought was of French manufacture, he was enquiring for the owner, when it was claimed by a gentleman, whom he recognifed to be an old friend, but with whofe efcape from France he was unacquainted; fo that he had fuppofed, from his rank, he muft have fallen there. The meeting, on both fides, was very affecting, and they fhed fome tears, and embraced again and again, with all the ardour of Frenchmen, before the ftranger was introduced to us, after which we had the pleafure of his company as far as Cologne.

This

This gentleman, a Lieutenant-Colonel before the Revolution, had made his escape from France so lately as May last, and his conversation of course turned upon his late condition. There were in most towns many persons who, like himself, were obnoxious for their principles, yet, being unsuspected of active designs, and unreached by the private malice of Roberspierre's agent, were suffered to exist out of prison. They generally endeavoured to lodge in the houses of persons favourable to the Revolution ; went to no public places ; never visited each other ; and, when they met in the street, passed with an hasty or concealed salutation. Their apartments were frequently searched ; and those, who had houses, took care to have their cellars frequently dug for saltpetre.

With respect to the prospect of any political change, they had little hopes, and still less of being able, by remaining in France, to give assistance to the Combined Powers. They expected nothing but some chance of escape, which in general they would not attempt, without many probabilities in their favour, knowing the sure consequences of being discovered. It was impossible for them to pass by the common roads, being exposed to examination at every town, and by every patrol ; but, in the day-time, they might venture upon tracts through forests, and, at night, upon cultivated ground ; a sort of journey, to which they were tempted by the successes of others in it, but which could not be performed, without experienced guides. It will be heard with astonishment, that, notwithstanding the many difficulties and dangers of such an employment, there were persons, who obtained a living by

conducting

conducting others to the frontiers, without paffing any town, village, or military poft; who,
having delivered one perfon, returned, with his
recommendation, to another, and an offer to efcort
him for a certain fum. Our companion had waited feveral months for a guide, the perfon, whom
he chofe to truft, being under prior engagements,
in all of which he was fuccefsful. They fet out,
each laden with his fhare of provifions, in the
drefs of peafants; and, without any other accident
than that of being once fo near the patrols as to
hear their converfation, arrived in the Electorate
of Treves, from whence this gentleman had been
to Raftadt, for the purpofe of prefenting himfelf
to M. de Condé.

It was remarkable, that fome of thefe guides
did not fhare the principles of thofe, whom they
conducted; yet they were faithful to their engagements, and feemed to gratify their humanity,
as much as they ferved their interefts. Confidering the many contrivances, which are behind
almoft every political tranfaction, it feems not im-
probable, that thefe men were fecretly encouraged
by fome of the rulers, who wifhed to be difen-
cumbered from their enemies, without the guilt
of a maffacre, or the unpopularity of appearing
to affift them.

The attachment to the new principles feemed
to be increafed, when any circumftances either of
fignal difadvantage, or fuccefs, occurred in the
courfe of a campaign. The difafters of an army,
it was faid, attracted fympathy; their victories
aroufed pride. Such a change of manners and of
the courfe of education had taken place, that the
rifing generation were all *enragées* in favour of
the

the Revolution; of which the following was a remarkable inftance: Two young ladies, the daughters of a baron, who had remained paffively in the country, without promoting, or refifting the Revolution, were then engaged in a law-fuit with their father, by which they demanded a maintenance, feparate from him, " he being either an Ariftocrat, or a Neutralift, with whom they did not choofe to refide." They did not pretend to any other complaint, and, it was pofitively believed, had no other motive. Yet thefe ladies had been previoufly educated with the niceft care, by the moft accomplifhed inftructors, and, in fact, with more expence than was fuitable to their father's income, having been intended for places at the Court. The children of the poorer claffes were equally changed by education, and thofe of both fexes were proficients in all the Revolutionary fongs and catechifms.

This converfation paffed while we were floating through the vale of Ehrenbreitftein, where the river, bending round the plains of Coblentz, flows through open and richly cultivated banks, till it enters the valley of Andernach, where it is again enclofed among romantic rocks. The places, wafhed by it in its paffage thither, are the villages of Neuralf, Warfchheim, Nerenberg, Malter, the old caftle of Malterberg, the village of Engus, the fine electoral palace of Schonbornuft, the neat town and palace of Neuwied, and the chateau of Friedrichftein,
called

called by the country people the Devil's Caſtle, from that love of the wonderful, which has taught them to people it with apparitions.

NEUWIED

WAS now the head-quarters of a legion raiſed by the Prince of Salm, for the pay of Great Britain; and a ſcarlet uniform, ſomewhat reſembling the Engliſh, was frequent on the quay. We heard of ſeveral ſuch *corps* in Germany, and of the facility with which they are raiſed, the Engliſh pay being as eight-pence to two-pence better than thoſe of Auſtria and Pruſſia. Recruits receive from one to two crowns bounty: whether it is equally true, that the officers are, notwithſtanding, allowed ten pounds for each, we cannot poſitively aſſert; but this was ſaid within the hearing of ſeveral at Cologne, and was not contradicted. *La ſolde d' Angleterre* is extremely popular in Germany; and the great wealth of the Engliſh nation begins to be very familiarly known.

ANDERNACH

ANDERNACH

WAS occupied by Imperial troops; and, as we entered the gorge of its rocky pafs, it was curious to obferve the appearances of modern mixed with thofe of ancient warfare; the foldiers of Francis the Second lying at the foot of the tower of Drufus; their artillery and baggage waggons lining the fhore along the whole extent of the walls.

In this neighbourhood are three celebrated mineral fprings, of which one rifes in the domain of the Carmelite monaftery of Jonniieftein; the fecond, called Ponterbrunnen, is fo brifk and fpirited, that the labourers in the neighbouring fields declare it a remedy for fatigue as well as thirft; and a third, called Heilbrunnen, has fo much fixed air, as to effervefce flightly when mixed with wine.

The interefting valley of Andernach has been already defcribed. Its fcenery, viewed now from the water, was neither fo beautiful, or fo ftriking, as from the road, by which we had before paffed. The elevation of the latter, though not great, enabled the eye to take a wider range, and to fee mountains, now fcreened by the nearer rocks of the fhore, which added greatly to the grandeur of the fcene. The river itfelf was then alfo a noble object, either expanding below, or winding in the diftance; but, now that we were upon its level, its appearance loft much both in dignity and extent, and even the rocks on its

margin

margin feemed lefs tremendous, when viewed from below. Something, however, fhould be allowed in this laft refpect to our having juft quitted wilder landfcapes; for, though the banks of the Rhine, in its courfe from Bingen to Coblentz, are lefs various and beautiful, than in its paffage between Andernach and Bonn, they are more grand and fublime.

But the merits of the different fituations for the view of river-fcenery have been noticed and contended for by the three perfons moft authorifed by their tafte to decide upon them; of whom GRAY has left all his enthufiafm, and nearly all his fublimity, to his two furviving friends; fo that this opinion is to be underftood only with refpect to the fcenery of the Rhine, and does not prefume to mingle with the general queftion between them. The Rhine now paffes by the village and caftle of Hammerftein, which, with thofe of Rheineck, were nearly laid wafte by Louis the Fourteenth, the caftle of Argendorff and the towns of Lintz and Rheinmagen, all exhibiting fymptoms of decay, though Lintz is called a commercial town.

ROLAND's Caftle appears foon after, and, almoft beneath it, the ifland, that bears Adelaide's convent, called Rolands Werth, or the Worth of Roland.

We were now again at the bafe of the Seven Mountains, whofe fummits had long afpired in the diftance, and, as we paffed under the cliffs of Drakenfels, hailed the delightful plain of Goodefberg, though much of it was concealed by the high fedgy bank of the Rhine on the left. The fpreading fkirts of thefe favourite mountains accompanied

companied us nearly to Bonn, and difplayed all their various charms of form and colouring in this our farewell view of them.

The town and palace of Bonn extend with much dignity along the weftern bank, where the Rhine makes a very bold fweep ; one wing of the former overlooking the fhore, and the want of uniformity in the front, which is feen obliquely, being concealed by the garden groves ; the many tall fpires of the great church rife over the roof of the palace, and appear to belong to the building.

After leaving Bonn, the fhores have little that is interefting, unlefs in the retrofpect of the Seven Mountains, with rich woodlands undulating at their feet ; and when thefe, at length, difappear, the Rhine lofes for the reft of its courfe the wild and fublime character, which diftinguifhes it between Bingen and Bonn. The rich plain, which it waters between the latter place and Cologne, is ftudded, at every gentle afcent, that bounds it, with abbeys and convents, moft of them appropriated to the maintenance of noble Chapters.

Of thefe, the firft is the Ladies Chapter of Vilich, founded in the year 1190, by Megiegor, a Count and Prince of Guelderland, who endowed it richly, and made his own daughter the firft abbefs ; a lady; who had fuch excellent notions of difcipline, that, when any nuns neglected to fing in the choir, fhe thought a heavy blow on the cheek the beft means of reftoring their voices. This Chapter is one of the richeft in Germany, and is peculiarly valuable to the nobility of this Electorate from its neighbourhood to Bonn, where many of the ladies pafs great part of the year with their

their families. On the other fide of the river is the Benedictine abbey of Siegberg, appropriated alfo to nobles, and lying in the midft of its own domains, of which a fmall town, at the foot of its vineyards, is part. Admiffion into this fociety is an affair of the moft ftrict and ceremonious proof, as to the fixteen quarterings in the arms of the candidate, each of which muft be unblemifhed by any plebeian fymptoms. Accompanied by his genealogy, thefe quarterings are expofed to view for fix weeks and three days, before the election; and, as there is an ample income to be contended for, the candidates do not hefitate to impeach each others' claims by every means in their power. The prelate of this abbey writes himfelf Count of Guls, Strahlen and Neiderpleis, and has fix provoftfhips within his jurifdiction.

Befides this, and fimilar buildings, the Rhine paffes not lefs than twenty villages in its courfe from Bonn to Cologne, a diftance of probably five-and-twenty Englifh miles.

COLOGNE

COLOGNE

NOW began to experience the inconveniences of its neighbourhood to the feat of war, some of which had appeared at Bonn from the arrival of families, who could not be lodged in the former place. We were no fooner within the gates, than the throng of people and carriages in a city, which only a few weeks before was almost as filent as gloomy, convinced us we should not find a very eafy welcome. The fentinels, when they made the ufual enquiry as to our inn, affured us, that there had been no lodgings at the Hotel de Prague for feveral days, and one of them followed us, to fee what others we fhould find. Through many obftructions by military and other carriages, we, however, reached this inn, and were foon convinced that there could be no room, the landlord fhewing us the chaifes in which fome of his guefts flept, and his billiard table already loaden with beds for others. There was fo much confufion meanwhile in the adjoining fquare, that, upon a flight affurance, we could have believed the French to be within a few miles of the city, and have taken refuge on the oppofite bank of the Rhine.

At length, our hoft toft us, that what he believed to be the worft room in the place was ftill vacant, but might not be fo half an hour longer. We followed his man to it, in a diftant part of the city, and faw enough in our way of parties taking refrefhment in carriages, and gentlemen

carrying

carrying their own baggage, to make us contented with a viler cabin than any perfon can have an idea of, who has not been out of England. The next morning we heard from the miftrefs of it how fortunately we had been fituated, two or three families having paffed the night in the open market-place, and great numbers in their carriages.

The occafion of this exceffive preffure upon Cologue was the entry of the French into Bruffels, their advances towards Liege, and the immediate profpect of the fiege of Maeftricht, all which had difpeopled an immenfe tract of territory of its wealthier inhabitants, and driven them, together with the French emigrants, upon the confines of Holland and Germany. The Auftrian hofpitals having been removed from Maeftricht, five hundred waggons, laden with fick and wounded, had paffed through Cologne the day before. The carriages on the roads from Maeftricht and Liege were almoft as clofe as in a proceffion, and at *Aix la Chapelle*, where thefe roads meet, there was an obftruction for fome hours. While we were at Cologne, another detachment of hofpital waggons arrived, fome hundreds of which we had the misfortune to fee, for they paffed before our window. They were all uncovered, fo that the emaciated figures and ghaftly countenances of the foldiers, laid out upon ftraw in each, were expofed to the rays of a burning fun, as well as to the fruitlefs pity of paffengers ; and, as the carriages had no fprings, it feemed as if thefe half-facrificed victims to war would expire before they could be drawn over the rugged pavement of Cologne. Any perfon, who had once witneffed fuch a fight, would know how to eftimate the glories of war, even though there fhould be a

mercenary

mercenary at every corner to infult his unavoida-
ble feelings and the eternal facrednefs of peace,
with the flander of difaffection to his country.

We had fome thoughts of refuming our courfe
by land from this place, but were now convinced,
that it was impracticable, feeing the number of
poft-horfes, which were engaged, and judging of
the crowds of travellers, that muft fill the inns on
the road. Our watermen from Mentz were, however, not allowed to proceed lower, fo that we
had to comply with the extortions of others,
and to give nine louis for a boat from Cologne to
Nimeguen. Having, not without fome difficulty,
obtained this, and ftored it with provifions, we
again embarked on the Rhine, rejoicing that we
were not, for a fecond night, to make part of the
crowd on fhore.

Cologne, viewed from the river, appears with
more of antient majefty than from any other
point. Its quays, extending far along the bank,
its lofty ramparts, fhaded with old chefnuts, and
crowned by many maffy towers, black with age;
the old gateways opening to the Rhine, and the
crowd of fteeples, overtopping all, give it a venerable and picturefque character. But, however
thronged the city now was, the fhore without was
filent and almoft deferted; the fentinels, watching at the gates and looking out from the ramparts, or a few women gliding beneath, wrapt in
the nun-like fcarf, fo melancholy in its appearance and fo generally worn at Cologne, were nearly the only perfons feen.

The

The shores, though here flat, when compared with those to the southward, are high enough to obstruct the view of the distant mountains, that rise in the east; in the south, the wild summits of those near Bonn were yet visible, but, after this faint glimpse, we saw them no more.

About two miles below Cologne, the west bank of the Rhine was covered with hospital waggons and with troops, removed from them, for the purpose of crossing the river, to a mansion converted by the Elector into an hospital. About a mile lower, but on the oppofite bank, is Muhleim, a small town in the dominions of the Elector Palatine, which, in the beginning of the present century, was likely to become a rival of Cologne. A persecution of the Protestant merchants of the latter place drove them to Muhleim, where they erected a staple, and began to trade with many advantages over the mother city; but the pufillanimity of the Elector Palatine permitted them to sink under the jealousy of the Colonefe merchants; their engines for removing heavy goods from vessels to the shore were ordered to be demolished; and the commerce of the place has since confisted chiefly in the exportation of grain.

The shores are now less enlivened by villages than in the *Rheingau* and other districts to the southward, where the cultivation and produce of the vineyards afford, at least, so much employment, that fix or feven little towns, each clustered round its church, are frequently visible at once. The course of the river being also wider and less rapid, the succession of objects is flower, and the eye is often wearied with the uniform lowness of the nearer country, where the antient castle and the perched abbey, so frequent in the Rheingau, seldom appear. Corn lands, with a slight intermixture of wood, border the river from hence to Dusseldorff, and the stream flows, with an even force, through long reaches, scarcely distinguished from each other by any variety of the country, or intervention of towns. Those, which do occur, are called Stammel, Niel, Flietert, Merkenich, Westdorff, Langelt, and Woringen; in which last place, the burgesses of Cologne, at the latter end of the thirteenth century, stood a siege against their Archbishop, and, by a successful resistance, obtained the enjoyment of some commercial rights, here so rare as to be called privileges. After Dormagen, a small town very slightly provided with the means of benefiting itself by the river, we came opposite to Zons, the fortifications of which are so far preserved, as that the boatmen on the Rhine are required to stop before them and give an account of their cargoes.

We were listening to an old French song, and had almost forgotten the chance of interruption from any abuses of power, when the steersman called to us in a low, but eager voice, and enquired whether we would permit him to attempt passing the castle, where, if we landed, we might probably be detained an hour, or, if the officer was at supper, for the whole night. By the help of twilight and our silence, he thought it possible to glide unnoticed under the opposite bank, or that we should be in very little danger, if the sentinels should obey their order for firing upon all vessels that might attempt to pass. The insolent tediousness of a German custom-house, and the probable

probable wretchednefs of inns at fuch a place as this, determined us in favour of the man's propo- fal ; we were filent for a quarter of an hour ; the men with-held their oars ; and the watchful garri- fon of Zons faw us not, or did not think a boat of two tons burthen could be laden with an army for the conqueft of Germany.

The evening was not fo dark as entirely to deny the view of either fhore, while we continued to float between both, and to trace the features of three or four fmall towns upon them. Neufs, being at fome little diftance from the river, was concealed ; but we had an accurate remembrance of its hideoufnefs, and, recognizing it for the mo- del of many towns fince feen, were pleafed with a mode of travelling, which rendered us in- dependent of them. The fame mode, how- ever, prevented us from vifiting Duffeldorff, which we did not reach, till after the fhut- ting of the gates ; fo that, had we ftayed, we muft have paffed the night in our boat on the outfide, a facrifice of too much time to be made, while an army was advancing to the oppofite fhore. Being compelled to remain in the boat, we thought it defirable to be, at the fame time, proceeding with the ftream, and fuffered the fteerfman to attempt paffing another garrifon, by whom, as he faid, we fhould otherwife be inevita- bly detained for the night. He did not effect this, without being noticed by the fentinels, who called and threatened to fire ; but, as the boatmen affur- ed us this would fcarcely be done, without leave from an officer, who might not be immediately at hand, we yielded to their method of preffing for- ward as haftily as poffible, and were prefently out of fight of Duffeldorff, of which we had feen only the walls and the extenfive palace, rifing imme-

diately

diately above the water. In the next reach, the boatmen stopped to take breath, and then confessed, that, though we had escaped being detained, as they had said, they had saved some florins due for tolls here and at Zons; which saving was their motive for running the risk. Though we would not have encouraged such a purpose, had we been aware of it, since the neglect of an unjust payment might produce an habitual omission of a just one, it did not seem necessary to say much, in behalf of a toll on the Rhine, for which there is no other pretence and no other authority than the power to enforce it.

The loss of Dusseldorff, we were assured, was the less, because the pictures of the celebrated gallery had been carried off to meet those of Manheim, at Munich.

It was now dark for two or three hours, but we did not hear of any town or view worth waiting to observe. The first object in the dawn was the island of Kaiferwerth, on which there is a small town, twice besieged in the wars of Louis the Fourteenth, and now in the condition, to which military glory has reduced so many others. One of the mines in the last siege blew so large a part of the walls over the island into the Rhine, that the navigation of the river was, for some time, obstructed by them. The dominion of this island, for which the Elector of Cologne and the Elector Palatine contended, was decided so lately as 1768 by the authority of the Chamber of Wetzlaar, who summoned the King of Prussia to assist them with his troops, as the *Armée exécutrice de l'Empire*, and the Elector Palatine was put in possession of it, notwithstanding the remonstrances of his rival.

As

As the morning advanced, we reached the villages of Kreuzberg, Rheinam and Einingen; and, at five, stopped at Urdingen, a town on the west bank of the Rhine, at which the Elector of Cologne takes his northernmost toll, and a place of more commerce than we had expected to fee short of Holland.   Great part of this is in timber, which it adds to the floats annually fent to that country; a fort of expedition fo curious and useful, that we should make no apology for introducing the following account of it.

TIMBER FLOATS ON THE RHINE.

THESE are formed chiefly at Andernach, but confist of the fellings of almost every German forest, which, by streams, or short land carriage, can be brought to the Rhine.   Having passed the rocks of Bingen and the rapids of St. Goar in small detachments, the several rafts are compacted at some town not higher than Andernach, into one immense body, of which an idea may be formed from this list of dimensions.

The length is from 700 to 1000 feet; the breadth from 50 to 90; the depth, when manned with the whole crew, usually seven feet. The trees in the principal rafts are not lefs than 70 feet long, of which ten compofe a raft.

On this fort of floating island, five hundred labourers of different classes are employed, maintained and lodged, during the whole voyage; and
a little

a little ftreet of deal huts is built upon it for their reception. The captain's dwelling and the kitchen are diftinguifhed from the other apartments by being fomewhat better built.

The firft rafts, laid down in this ftructure, are called the foundation, and are always either of oak, or fir-trees, bound together at their tops, and ftrengthened with firs, faftened upon them croffways by iron fpikes. When this foundation has been carefully compacted, the other rafts are laid upon it, the trees of each being bound together in the fame manner, and each *ftratum* faftened to that beneath it. The furface is rendered even; ftorehoufes and other apartments are raifed: and the whole is again ftrength-ened by large mafts of oak.

Before the main body proceed feveral thin and narrow rafts, compofed only of one floor of timbers, which, being held at a certain diftance from the float by mafts of oak, are ufed to give it direction and force, according to the efforts of the labourers upon them.

Behind it, are a great number of fmall boats, of which fifteen or fixteen, guided by feven men each, are laden with anchors and cables, others contain articles of light rigging, and fome are ufed for meffages from this populous and important fleet to the towns, which it paffes. There are twelve forts of cordage, each having a name ufed cnly by the float-mafters; among the largeft are cables of four hundred yards long and eleven inches diameter. Iron chains are alfo ufed in feveral parts of the ftructure,

The

The confumption of provifions on board fuch a float is eftimated for each voyage at fifteen or twenty thoufand pounds of frefh meat, between forty and fifty thoufand pounds of bread, ten or fifteen thoufand pounds of cheefe, one thoufand or fifteen hundred pounds of butter, eight hundred or one thoufand pounds of dried meat, and five or fix hundred tons of beer.

The apartments on the deck are, firft, that of the pilot, which is near one of the magazines, and, oppofite to it, that of the perfons called maf-ters of the float: another clafs, called mafters of the valets, have alfo their apartment; near it is that of the valets, and then that of the fub-valets; after this are the cabins of the *tyrolois*, or laft clafs of perfons, employed in the float, of whom eigh-ty or an hundred fleep upon ftraw in each, to the number of more than four hundred in all. There is, laftly, one large eating-room, in which the greater part of this crew dine at the fame time.

The pilot, who conducts the fleet from Ander-nach to Duffeldorff, quits it there, and another is engaged at the fame falary, that is, five hundred florins, or 42l.; each has his fub-pilot, at nearly the fame price. About twenty tolls are paid in the courfe of the voyage, the amount of which varies with the fize of the fleet and the eftimation of its value, in which latter refpect the proprietors are fo much fubject to the caprice of cuftom-houfe officers, that the firft fignal of their intention to depart is to collect all thefe gentlemen from the neighbourhood, and to give them a grand dinner on board. After this, the float is founded and meafured, and their demands upon the owners fettled.

On

On the morning of departure, every labourer takes his poſt, the rowers on their benches, the guides of the leading rafts on theirs, and each boat's crew in its own veſſel. The eldeſt of the valet-maſters then makes the tour of the whole float, examines the labourers, paſſes them in review, and diſmiſſes thoſe, who are unfit. He afterwards addreſſes them in a ſhort ſpeech; recommends regularity and alertneſs; and repeats the terms of their engagement, that each ſhall have five crowns and a half, beſides proviſions, for the ordinary voyage; that, in caſe of delay by accident, they ſhall work three days, gratis; but that, after that time, each ſhall be paid at the rate of twelve creitzers, about four pence, per day.

After this, the labourers have a repaſt, and then, each being at his poſt; the pilot, who ſtands on high near the rudder, takes off his hat and calls out, "Let us all pray." In an inſtant there is the happy ſpectacle of all theſe numbers on their knees, imploring a bleſſing on their undertaking.

The anchors, which were faſtened on the ſhores, are now brought on board, the pilot gives a ſignal, and the rowers put the whole float in motion, while the crews of the ſeveral boats ply round it to facilitate the departure.

Dort in Holland is the deſtination of all theſe floats, the ſale of one of which occupies ſeveral months; and frequently produces 350,000 florins, or more than 30,000l.

URDINGEN

URDINGEN

HAS a neat market-place and some symptoms of greater comfort than are usual in the towns of the Electorate of Cologne; but it is subject to violent floods, so much so, that at the inn, which is, at least, an hundred and fifty yards from the shore, a brass plate, nailed upon the door of the parlour, relates, that the river had risen to that height; above five feet from the ground.

After resting here, five hours, we returned to our little bark, with the spirits inspired by favourable weather, and were soon borne away on the ample current of the Rhine.

Large Dutch vessels, bound to Cologne, now frequently appeared, and refreshed us once again with the shew of neatness, industry and prosperity. The boatmen learned, that several of these were from Rotterdam, laden with the effects of Flemish refugees, brought thither from Ostend; and others were carrying military stores for the use, as they said, of the Emperor. The ordinary trade of the Dutch with Germany, in tea, coffee, English cloths and English hardware, which we had heard at Mentz was slackened by the expected approach of armies, now seemed to be exchanged for the conveyance of property from scenes of actual distress to those not likely to be long exempted from it.

A little beyond Urdingen, the town of Bodberg marks the northern extremity of the long and

and narrow dominions of Cologne, once fo far connected with Holland, as that the Archbifhop had jurifdiction over the bifhop of Holland, and the Chapter of Utrecht. But Philip the Second, before the States had refifted his plundering, obtained of the Pope, that they fhould not be fubject to any foreign fee; and the Bifhop had a refidence affigned to him at Haerlem.

The Rhine is now bounded on the left by the country of Meurs; and, having, after a few miles, part of the Duchy of Cleves on the right, it becomes thus enclofed by the territories of the King of Pruffia, under whofe dominion it rolls, till the States of Guelderland repofe upon one bank, and, foon after, thofe of Utrecht, on the other. We were here, of courfe, in the country of tolls; and our waterman could not promife how far we fhould proceed in the day, fince it was impoffible to eftimate the delays of the collectors. Meurs has no place, except fmall villages, near the river; but, at the commencement of the Duchy of Cleves, the influx of the Ruhr into the Rhine makes a fmall port, at which all veffels are obliged to ftop, and pay for a Pruffian pafs. Some Dutch barks, of probably one hundred and twenty tons burthen, we were affured would not be difmiffed for lefs than fifty ducats, or twenty guineas each. The town is called the Ruhort, and we had abundance of time to view it, for the Collector would not come to the boat, but ordered that we fhould walk up, and make our appearance before him,

It is a fmall place, rendered bufy by a dockyard for building veffels to be employed on the Rhine, and has fomewhat of the frefh appearance, exhibited

exhibited by fuch towns as feem to be built for prefent ufe, rather than to fubfift becaufe they have once been erected. In the dock, which opens to the Ruhr, two veffels of about fixty tons each were nearly finifhed, and with more capital, many might no doubt be built for the Dutch, timber and labour being here much cheaper than in Holland.

After the boatman had fatisfied the Collector, we refumed our voyage, very well contented to have been detained only an hour. The woody heights of Cleves now broke the flat monotony of the eaftern fhore, the antiquity of whofe forefts is commemorated by Tacitus in the name of *Saltus Teutoburgenfis*, fuppofed to have been bounded here by the town now called Duifbourg :

- - - - - "*haud procul Teutoburgenfi faltu, in quo reliquiæ Vari legionumque infepultæ dicebantur*"—

"Unburied remain,
Inglorious on the plain."

Thefe forefts were alfo celebrated for their herds of wild horfes; and the town of Duifbourg, having been rendered an Univerfity in 1655, is thus panegyrized by a German poet :

Dis ift die Deutfche Burg, vor langft gar hochgeehrt
Von vielen König und auch Kaiferlichen Kronen :
Der fchöne Mufenthron, wo kluge Leute wohnen ;
Und wo die Kaufmannufchaft fo manchen Bürger nährt.

This

This is the German town, that's fam'd so long
By throned Kings, and gentle Mufes' fong ;
Where learned folks live well on princely pay,
And commerce makes so many Burghers gay.

Of the commerce there weree ftill fome figns
in half a dozen veffels, collected on the beach.
Whether the Univerfity alfo fubfifts, or is any
thing more than a free fchool, which is frequently
called an Univerfity in Germany, we did not
learn.

WESEL.

AFTER five or fix fmall towns, or villages,
more, the Rhine reaches the well known fortified
town and ftate prifon of Wefel; a place, not
always unfavourable to freedom, for here RAPIN,
driven from the diftrict now called La Vendée in
France, by Louis the Fourteenth's perfecution of
Proteftants, retired to write his Hiftory; recol-
lecting, perhaps, that it had before fheltered refugees from the tyranny of the Duke of Alva, and
our fanguinary Mary.

The towers and citadel of Wefel give it the
appearance of a military place, and it is frequently
fo mentioned ; but the truth is, that the late King
of Pruffia, with the fame fear of his fubjects, which
was felt by Jofeph the Second in Flanders, demolifhed all the effectual works, except thofe of the
citadel;

citadel; a policy not very injurious to the Monarch in this inftance, but which, in Flanders, has fubmitted the country to be twice over-run in three years, and has in fact been the moft decifive of paffed events in their influence upon prefent circumftances.

The reformed worfhip is exercifed in the two principal churches; but the Catholics have two or three monafteries, and there is a Chapter of Noble Ladies, of whom two thirds are Proteftants, and one third Catholic; an arrangement which probably accounts for their having no fettled and common refidence.

Oppofite to Wefel is Burick; the fortifications of which remain, and are probably intended to ferve inftead of the demolifhed works of the former place; being connected with it by a flying-bridge over the Rhine. A little lower are the remains of the old chateau of Furftemberg, on a hill where the ladies of the noble Ciftercian nunnery of Furftemberg had once a delightful feat, now deferted for the fociety of Xanten.

Xanten, the firft place at which we had ftopped in Germany, and the laft, for a long tract, which we had feen with pleafure, Xanten, now diftinguifhable, at a fmall diftance from the river, by its fpires, reminded us of the gay hopes we had formed ou leaving it; with a new world fpread out before us, for curiofity, and, as we thought, for admiration; yet did not render the remembrance of difappointment, as to the laft refpect, painful, for even the little information we had gained feemed to be worth the labour of acquiring it.

The

The exchange of indefinite for exact ideas is for ever defirable. Without this journey of eleven or twelve hundred miles we fhould have confidered Germany, as its pofition in maps and defcription in books reprefent it, to be important, powerful and profperous; or, even if it had been called wretched, the idea would have been indiftinct, and the affertion, perhaps, not wholly credited. The greateft and, as it is reafonable to believe, the beft part of Germany we have now feen, and, in whatever train of reafoning it is noticed, have an opinion how it fhould be valued. Thofe, who cannot guefs at caufes, may be fure of effects; and having feen, that there is little individual profperity in Germany, little diffufion of intelligence, manners, or even of the means for comfort, few fources of independence, or honourable wealth, and no examples of the poverty, in which there may be pride, it was not lefs perceptible, that there can be no general importance, no weight in the balance of ufeful, that is, peaceful power, and no place, but that of an inftrument, even in the defperate exercifes of politics.

A refpect for the perfons of learning, or thought, who live, as the impertinence of high and the ignorance of low fociety forces them to live, in a ftrict and faftidious retirement, cannot alter the general eftimation of the country, in any refpect here confidered; their converfation with each other has no influence upon the community; their works cannot have a prefent, though they will have a general and a permanent effect. The humbler claffes, from whom profperity fhould refult in peace, and ftrength in war, give little of
either

either to Germany; and man is very seldom negatively stationed; when not useful to his fellow-creatures, he is generally somewhat injurious. The substantial debasement of the German peasantry, that is, their want of ordinary intelligence, re-acts upon the means that produced it, and, continuing their inferiority, continues many injurious effects upon the rest of Europe.

That Germany should be thus essentially humble, perhaps, none would have ventured to foresee. The materialist could not have found it in the climate. The politician might hastily expect it from the arbitrary character of the governments, but must hesitate, when he recollects how France advanced in science and manufactures, under the dominion of Louis the Fourteenth, greatly more despotic than the usual administrations in Germany. Perhaps, the only solution for this difference of effects from apparently similar causes is, that the greater extent of his territory, as well as the better opportunities of his subjects for commerce, enabled Louis to gratify his taste for splendour, at the same time that they shewed his ambition a means of indulgence, by increasing the means of his people. Germany, frittered into several score of sovereignties, has no opulent power; no considerable income, remaining after the payment of its armies; few wealthy individuals. The Emperror, with fifty-six titles, does not gain a florin by his chief dignity; or Granvelle, the Minister of Charles the Fifth, would have been contradicted when he said so in the Chamber of Princes. The Elector Palatine is almost the only Prince, whose revenue is not absorbed by political, military

military and houſehold eſtabliſhments; and though, in an advanced ſtate of ſociety, or in opulent nations, what is called patronage is ſeldom neceſſary; and muſt, perhaps, be as injurious to the happineſs as it is to the dignity of thoſe who receive it, nothing is more certain than that there have been periods in the hiſtory of all countries, when the liberality of the Prince, or the more independent protection of beneficed inſtitutions, was neceſſary to the exiſtence of curioſity and knowledge. At ſuch times, a large expenditure, if directed by taſte, or even by vanity, afforded a ſlow recompenſe for the aggreſſions, that might ſupport it, by ſpreading a deſire of diſtinction for ſome intellectual accompliſhment, as the claim to notice from the court; and the improvement of mind circulated, by more general encouragement, till every town and village had its men of ſcience. Thus it was that the deſpotiſm of Louis the Fourteenth had a different effect from that of his contemporary German Princes, who, by no oppreſſions, could raiſe a ſufficient income, to make their own expenditure the involuntary means of improving the intellectual condition of their people.

From the neighbourhood of Xanten, in which we were induced thus to eſtimate what had been gained, ſince we ſaw it laſt, and from a ſhore that gradually riſes into the many woody heights around Calcar and Cleves, the Rhine ſpeedily reaches Rees, a town on the right bank, built advantageouſly at an angle, made by a flexure of the river to the left.

We

We landed to view this place, and were soon perfuaded by the Dutch-like cleanlinefs and civility of the people at the inn, to remain there for the night, rather than to attempt reaching Emmerick.

Rees is near enough to Holland to have fome of its advantages; and, whatever contempt it may be natural for Englifh travellers, at the commencement of their tour, to feel for Dutch dullnefs and covetoufnefs, nothing but fome experience of Germany is neceffary to make them rejoice in a return to the neatnefs, the civility, the comforts, quietnefs, and even the good humour and intelligence to be eafily found in Holland. Such, at leaft, was the change, produced in our minds by a journey from Nimeguen to Friburg. The lower claffes of the Dutch, and it is the conduct of fuch claffes, that every where has the chief influence upon the comforts of others, are not only without the malignant fullennefs of the Germans, and, therefore, ready to return you fervices for money, but are alfo fuperior to them in intelligence and docility. Frequent opportunities of gain, and the habit of comparing them, fharpen intellects, which might otherwife never be exercifed. In a commercial country, the humbleft perfons have opportunities of profiting by their qualifications; they are, therefore, in fome degree prepared for better conditions, and do not feel that angry envy of others, which arifes from the confcioufnefs of fome irremediable diftinction.

The inhabitants of Rees fpeak both Dutch and German; and it was pleafing to hear at the inn the fulky *yaw* of the latter exchanged for the civil *Yaw well, Mynheer,* of the Dutch. The town is

A a

built

built chiefly of brick, like thofe of Holland; the
ftreets light; the market-place fpacious, and the
houfes well preferved. It is of no great extent,
but the fpace within the walls is filled, though
this muft have been fometimes partly cleared by
the fieges, to which Rees was fubject in the war of
Philip the Second upon the Dutch. A few emigrants
from Bruffels and Maeftricht were now fheltered
in it; but there was no garrifon and no other
fymptom of its neighbourhood to the fcene of
hoftilities, than the arrival of a Pruffian commiffary to collect hay and corn. We were cheered
by the re-appearance of profperity in a country,
where it is fo feldom to be feen, and paffed a better evening in this little town, than in any other
between Friburg and Holland.

In the morning, having no difguft to impel us,
we were fomewhat tardy in embarking; and the
boatman, who had found out the way of reviving
our impatience, talked of the great diftance of
Holland, till they had us on board. Five or fix
well-looking villages prefently appear after leaving Rees, the next port to which is Emmerick,
once an Hanfeatic town, and ftill a place of fome
dignity, for fpires and towers, but certainly not
of much commerce, for we could not fee more
than two veffels on the beach.

This is the town, at which a Governor and
General, appointed by Philip the Second, with
probably half a dozen titles, afferting his excel-
lence, ferenity and honour, gave an inftance of
bafenefs, fcarcely ever exceeded even by Philip
himfelf. Approaching the place, which was then
neutral, the inhabitants went out to him with an
entreaty, that he would not fend troops into it,
and,

and, probably by something more than entreaty, obtained his promise, that they should be spared. In spite of this promise, of the remonstrances of the inhabitants, and of the representations of a clergyman, that the Spanish assurances of having engaged in the war chiefly for the interests of the Catholic religion could not be credited, if acts, contrary to the precepts of all religion, were daily perpetrated; in spite of these, Mendoza, the Spanish commander, sent in four hundred troops, but with another promise, that their number should not be increased, and with this confolation for the burgesses, that the Spanish Colonel of the detachment was directed to swear in their presence, to admit no more, even if they should be offered to him.

Mendoza had estimated this man's heart by his own, and considered his oath only as a convenient delusion for preventing the resistance of the inhabitants. He accordingly sent other troops to him, under the command of a foreign hireling, and with a peremptory order for their admission; but the honest Spaniard gave him this reply, " Though the General has set the example, I will not violate my faith."

Passing Emmerick with much pleasure, we speedily came to the point at which the Rhine, dividing itself into two streams, loses its name immediately in the one, and presently after in the other. Some writer has compared this merging to the voluntary surrender of exertions and views, by which affectionate parents lose themselves in their children. The stream, which bends to the west, takes the name of the Waal; that, which flows in the general direction of the river, retains its name, for a few miles, when another stream issues to the northward, and takes that of the Yssel. The old river is still recognized, after this separation, and the town of Rhenen takes its name from it; but, about a mile lower, it yields to the denomination of the Leck, which, like that of the Waal, does not long enjoy its usurped distinction. The Waal, or Wahl, being joined by the Maas, as the Dutch, or the Meuse, as the French call it, near Bommel, takes the name of that river, and, soon after, the Leck merges in their united stream, which carries the title of the Maas by Rotterdam, Schiedam and Flaarding, into the German ocean.

We did not yield to this artificial distinction so far as to think ourselves taking leave of the Rhine, or losing the stream, that had presented to us, at first, features of the boldest grandeur, mingled with others of the sweetest beauty, and then borne us safely past a shore, pressed by the hasty steps of distress, as well as threatened by those of ravage from a flying and a pursuing army. Nor does the river change the character it has lately assumed; but still passes with an even, wide and forceful current between cultivated or pastoral levels, bounded, at some distance, by gradual, woody ascents.

Among these heights and woods, Cleves is visible to the left, and those, who see it only at this distance, may repeat the dictionary descriptions of its grandeur and consequence as a capital. Soon after, Schenckenkanze, a small fort, built on the point of the long island, round which the Rhine and the Waal flow, occurs; and then

the

the southern extremity of the province of Utrecht. We were glad to see this commencement of the dominions of the United States, though the shore opposite to them was still Prussian; and, telling the boatmen, if they had occasion to stop at any town, to touch only upon the free bank, they humoured us so far as to row out of the current for the sake of approaching it; in short, we stepped no more upon German land; and, within a few miles, were enveloped, on both sides, by the prospering, abounding plains of the Dutch provinces. *Italiam! Italiam!*

Early in the afternoon, the lofty tower of the Belvidere, or prospect-house at Nimeguen, came in sight; then the bright pinnacles of the public buildings, and the high, turf coloured angles of the fortifications. The town was thronged with fugitives from Flanders, but we found sufficient accommodation, as before, at the inn in the market-place, and were not in a tone of spirits to be fastidious about any thing, heightened as the appearance of prosperity was to us by contrast, and happy as even the refugees appeared to be at finding peace and safety. The mall before the Prince of Orange's house was filled with parties of them, as gay as if they had left their homes in Flanders but for an holiday excursion.

We were at the Belvidere till evening, lingering over the rich prospect of probably forty miles diameter, from Arnheim and Duisbourg in the

north

north to Cleves and Guelders in the south, with an eastern view over half the forests of Guelderland to those of Westphalia. Such an extent of green landscape, richly varied with towns, villages and woods, spreading and gradually ascending to the horizon, was now almost as novel to us, as it was placidly beautiful. On the east, the blue mountainous lines of Germany broke in upon the reposing character of the scene.

In the Waal below, two or three vessels bore the Emperor's flag, and were laden, as it was said, with some of his *regalia* from Flanders. Near them, several bilanders, the decks of which were covered with awnings, had attracted spectators to the opposite bank, for to that side only they were open; and the company in all were objects of curiosity to the Dutch, being no less than the sisterhood of several Flemish convents, in their proper dresses, and under the care of their respective abbesses. These ladies had been thus situated, for several days and nights, which they had passed on board their vessels. They were attended by their usual servants, and remained together, without going on shore, being in expectation, as we were told, of invitations to suitable residences in Germany; but it was then reported at Nimeguen, that Prince Cobourg was re-advancing to Brussels, and these societies had probably their misfortunes increased by the artifices of a political rumour. We could not learn, as we wished, that they had brought away many effects. Their plate it was needless to enquire about; the contributions of the preceding spring had no doubt swallowed up that.

Having

Having difmiffed our Cologne watermen, we embarked upon the Waal, the next day, in a public boat for Rotterdam; a neat fchuyt, well equipped and navigated, in which, for a few floiins, you have the ufe of the cabin. Our voyage, from the want of wind, was flow enough to fhew as much as could be feen of the Waal; which, at Nimeguen, runs almoft conftantly downward, but is foon met by the tide, and overcome, or, at leaft, refifted by it. The breadth, which varies but little above Bommel, is, to our recollection, not lefs than that of the Thames, at Fulham; the depth, during the beginning of the fame fpace, is probably confiderable in the ftream, for, even upon the fhore, our dextrous old fteerfman found water enough to fweep the rufhy bank at almoft every tack, with a boat, drawing about five feet. The figns of activity in commerce are aftonifh-ing. A fmall hamlet, one cannot call any place in Holland contemptible, or miferable, a hamlet of a dozen houfes has two or three veffels, of twenty tons each; a village has a herring boat for almoft every houfe, and a trading veffel for Rotterdam two or three times a week. Heavy, high-rigged veffels, fcarcely breafting the ftream, and fit only for river voyages, we frequently met; many of them carrying coals for the nearer part of Germany, fuch as we faw on the banks between Rees and Nimeguen, and, with much pleafure, recognized for fymptoms of neighbourhood to England.

The firft town from Nimeguen, on the right bank of the Waal, is Thiel, which we had only time to fee enclofed by modern fortifications, and was not inferior in neatnefs to other Dutch towns, at leaft not fo in one good ftreet, which we were

able

able to traverfe. A fand bank before the port has much leffened the trade of the place, which, in the tenth century, was confiderable enough to be acknowledged by the Emperor Otto, in the grant of feveral privileges.

About a league lower, on the oppofite fide of the Waal, or rather on the fmall ifland of Voorn, ftood formerly a fort, called Naffau, which the French, in 1672, utterly deftroyed. Near its fite, at the northern extremity of the ifland of Bommel, which lies between the Maas and the Waal, a fort, built by Cardinal Andrew of Auftria, ftill fubfifts, under the name of *Fort St. André.* The founder, who built it upon the model of the citadel of Antwerp, had no other view than to command by it the town of Bommel; but, in the year 1600, Prince Maurice of Naffau reduced the garrifon, after a fiege of five weeks, and it has fince contributed to protect what it was raifed to deftroy, the independence of the Dutch commonwealth.

In the evening, we came oppofite to the town of Bommel, where we were put on fhore to pafs the night and the next day, being Sunday; the boat proceeded on the voyage for Rotterdam, but could not reach it before the next morning.

Bommel is a fmall town on the edge of the river, furrounded by wood enough to make it remarkable in Holland; light, neat and pretty. The two principal ftreets crofs each other at right angles, and are without canals. Being at fome diftance from the general roads, it is ill provided with inns; but one of them has a delightful profpect, and there is no dirt, or other fymptom of negligence

negligence within. The inhabitants are advanced enough in profperity and intelligent curiofity to have two *Sociétés,* where they meet to read new publications; a luxury, which may be found in almoft every Dutch town. At the ends of the two principal ftreets are gates; that towards the water between very old walls; thofe on the land fide modern and ftronger, with draw-bridges over a wide foffé, that nearly furrounds the town.

On the other fide of this ditch are high and broad embankments, well planted with trees, and fo fuitable to be ufed as public walks, that we fuppofed them to have been raifed partly for that purpofe, and partly as defences to the country againft water. They are, however, greater curiofities, having been thrown up by Prince Maurice in 1599, chiefly becaufe his garrifon of four thoufand foot and two thoufand horfe were too numerous for the old works; and between thefe intrenchments was made what is thought to have been the firft attempt at a covered way, fince improved into a regular part of fortifications. This was during the ineffectual fiege of three weeks, in which Mendoza loft two thoufand men, Maurice having then a conftant communication with the oppofite bank of the Waal by means of two bridges of boats, one above, the other below the town.

Bommel was otherwife extremely important in the ftruggle of the Dutch againft Philip. It was once planned to have been delivered by treachery, but, that being difcovered, the Earl of Mansfeldt, Philip's commander, raifed the fiege. It adhered to the affembly at Dort, though the Earl of March, the commander of the firft armed

force

force of the Flemings, had committed such violences in the town, that the Prince of Orange found it necessary to send him to prison. In the campaign of 1606, when Prince Maurice adopted defensive operations, this was one of the extreme points of his line, which extended from hence to Schenck.

The natural honesty of mankind is on the side of the defensive party, and it is, therefore, that in reading accounts of sieges one is always on the side of the besieged. The Dutch, except when subject to some extraordinary influence, have been always defensive in their wars; from their first astonishing resistance to Philip, to that against the petty attack, which Charles the Second incited the Bishop of Munster to make, who had the coolness to tell Sir WILLIAM TEMPLE, that he had thought over the probabilities of his enterprise, and, if it failed, he should not care, for he could go into Italy and buy a Cardinal's cap; but that he had first a mind to make some figure in the world. The territory of the United Provinces is so small, that, in these wars, the whole Dutch Nation has been in little better condition, than that of a people, besieged in one great town ; and Louis the Fourteenth, in the attempt, which Charles the Second's wicked sister concerted between the two Monarchs, sent, for the first time, to a whole people a threat, similar to those sometimes used against a single town. His declaration of the 24th of June, 1672, after boasting how his " just designs" and undertakings had prospered, since his arrival in the army, and how he would treat the Dutch, if, by submission, they would " deserve his great goodness," thus proceeds:

" On

" On the contrary, all of whatever quality and condition, who shall refuse to comply with these offers, and shall resist his Majesty's forces, either by the inundation of their dyke, or otherwise, shall be punished with the utmost rigour. At present, all hostilities shall be used against those, who oppose his Majesty's designs; and, when the ice shall open a passage on all sides, his Majesty will not give any quarter to the inhabitants of such cities, but give order, that their goods be plundered and their houses burnt."

It is pleasant, in every country, to cherish the recollections, which make it a spectacle for the mind as well as the eye, and no country is enriched by so many as Holland, not even the West of England, where patriotism and gratitude hover in remembrance over the places, endeared by the steps of our glorious WILLIAM.

Bommel is built on a broad projection of the island of the same name into the Waal, which thus flows nearly on two sides of its walls, and must be effectually commanded by them. But, though it is therefore important in a military view, and that the French were now so near to Breda, as to induce families to fly from thence, whom we saw at Bommel, yet the latter place was in no readiness for defence. There was not a cannon upon the walls, or upon the antient outworks, which we mistook for terraces, and not ten soldiers in the place; a negligence, which was, however, immediately after remedied.

The

The Dutch tardiness of exertion has been often blamed, and, in such instances, deservedly; but, as to the influence of this sparingness in their general system of politics and in former periods, a great deal more wit than truth has been circulated by politicians. The chief value of power is in the known possession of it. Those who are believed to have exerted it much, will be attacked, because the exertion may be supposed to have exhausted the power. The nation, or the individual, that attempts to rectify every error and punish every trivial offence of others, may soon lose, in worthless contests, the strength, that should be preserved for resisting the most positive and unequivocal attacks.

Ministers have appeared in Holland, who could plan unnecessary contests, and meditate the baseness, falsely called ambition, of putting the whole valour and wealth of a nation into exercise, for the purpose of enforcing whatever they may have once designed, or said; and, as there is, perhaps, no country in Europe, which cannot justly allege some injury against another, they have exaggerated the importance of such injuries, for the purpose of impelling their own country, by aggravated anger, or fear, into precipitate hostilities. But the Dutch, accustoming themselves to as much vigilance, as confidence, have withheld encouragement from such artifices, and hence that general tardiness in beginning wars, which every politician, capable of an inflammatory declamation, thinks it wisdom to ridicule.

We left Bommel at seven in the morning, in a stout, decked sea-boat, well rigged, and, as appeared, very dextrously navigated. The wind
was

was directly contrary, and there are sometimes islands, sometimes shoals in the Waal, which narrowed the channel to four or five times the length of the vessel; yet there was not any failure in tacking, and the boom was frequently assisted to traverse by the reeds of the bank, which it swept. The company in the cabin were not very numerous, but there was amongst them at least one lamentable group; the minister of a Protestant church at Maestricht, an aged and decrepid gentleman, flying with his wife and two daughters from the approaching siege of that place; himself laid on pillows upon the floor of the cabin; his daughters attending him; all neglected, all victims to the glories of war.

The boat soon passed Louvenstein, on the left bank of the Maese, a brick castellated building, apparently about two centuries old, surrounded by some modern works, which render it one of the defences of the river. Count Byland, the late commander of Breda, was then imprisoned in this fortress, which has been long used for state purposes. Here those friends of Barneveldt were confined, who derived from it, and left to their posterity the name of the Louvenstein party; and hence Grotius, who was of the number, made his escape, concealed in a trunk, which the sentinels had so often seen filled with Arminian books, that his wife persuaded them they carried nothing more than their usual cargo.

From Louvenstein, near which the Waal unites with the Maese, and assumes the name of that river, we soon reached Gorcum, where the short stay of the boat permitted us only to observe the neatness of the town, and that the fortifications had

had the appearance of being ftrong, though fmall, and feemed to be in moft exaƈt repair. This, indeed, is one of the forts chiefly relied upon by the province of Holland; for, in 1787, their States made Gorcum and Naarden the extreme points of their line of defence, and ordered a dyke to be thrown acrofs the Linge, which flows into the Maefe at the former place, for the purpofe of overflowing the furrounding country.

The next town in the voyage is Dort, formerly one of the moft confiderable in Holland, and ftill eminent for its wealth, though the trade is diminifhed by that of Rotterdam. This is the town, which Dumourier ftrove to reach, in the invafion of 1792, and forty thoufand ftand of arms were found to have been colleƈted there for him. Our boat paffed before one quarter, in which the houfes rife immediately over a broad bay of the Maefe, with an air of uncommon gaiety and lightnefs; but the evennefs of the town prevented us from feeing more than the part directly neareft.

In the bay was one of thofe huge timber floats, the conftruƈtion of which has been before defcribed. It was crowded with vifitors from the town; and the wooden huts upon it, being ornamented with flags, had the appearance of booths at a fair. Large as this was, it had been confiderably diminifhed, fince its arrival at Dort, and feveral hundreds of the workmen had departed.

A little further on, and within fight of this joyous company, was the melancholy reverfe of nearly an hundred ladies, driven from fome convent in Flanders, now refiding, like thofe near Nimeguen,

Nimeguen, in bilanders moored to the bank.
Their veffels being open on the fide towards the
water, we caught as full a view of them as could
be had, without difrefpect; and faw that they
ftill wore their conventual dreffes, and were feated, apparently according to their ages, at fome
fort of needle-work. It might have been cen-
fured, a few years fince, that miftakes, or decep-
tions, as to religious duties, fhould have driven
them from the world; but it was certainly now
only to be lamented, that any thing fhort of the
gradual and peaceful progrefs of reafon fhould
have expelled them from their retirement.

We reached Rotterdam, in the evening. and
ftayed there the next day, to obferve whether the
confidence of the Dutch in their dykes and fortreffes, was fufficient to preferve their tranquillity
in a place almoft within hearing of the war, the
French being then befieging Sluys. There was
no perceptible fymptom of agitation, or any diminution of the ordinary means for increafing
wealth. The perfons, with whom we converfed,
and they were not a few, fpoke of the tranfactions of the campaign with almoft as much calmnefs and curiofity, as if thefe had been paffing
in India. They could not fuppofe it poffible,
that the French might reach the city; or, if they
did, feemed to rely upon the facility, with which
their property could be removed by the canals
through Leyden and Haerlem, to the fhore of the
Zuyder Zee, then acrofs it by failing barges, and
then again by the canals as far as Groningen,
whither the French would certainly not pene-
trate. So valuable was water thought in Holland, not only as a means of opulence in peace,
but of defence, or prefervative flight in war. An
.exceffive

exceffive felfifhnefs, which is the vice of the Dutch, appeared fometimes to prevent thofe, who could fly, from thinking of their remaining countrymen.

An intention of difpenfing with the cuftomary fair, was the only circumftance, which diftinguifhed this feafon from others at Rotterdam, and that was imputed to the prudence of preventing any very numerous meetings of the populace.

About three weeks fooner than was neceffary, for it was fo long before a convenient paffage occurred, we went from hence to Helvoetfluys, and there remained, a fortnight, watching an inflexible north-wefterly wind, and liftening to accounts but too truly certified of French frigates and privateers, almoft unoppofed in thofe latitudes. Lloyd's Lift brought the names of five, or feven, French fhips, then known to be cruifing in the north; and one packet was delayed in its voyage by the fight of feveral Dutch veffels, fet on fire within a few leagues of *Goree*. The Dutch lamented, that the want of feamen crippled the operations of their Admiralty Board: an Englifhman, who was proud to deny, that any fuch want, or want in fuch a degree, exifted, as to his country, was reduced to filence and fhame, when it was enquired, Why, then, have thefe feas been, for twelve months, thus expofed to the dominion of the French?

At length, a convoy arrived for a noble family, and we endeavoured to take the benefit of it, by embarking in a packet, which failed at the fame time;

time; but the floop of war was unable to pafs
over what are called the Flats, and our captain
had refolved to proceed without it, notwithftanding the contrarieties of the wind, when, with
much joy, we difcerned a fmall boat, and knew
it to be Englifh by the fkilful impetuofity of the
rowers. Having induced the people of the packet to make a fignal, by paying them for the paffage to Harwich, we were fortunately taken on
board this boat, at the diftance of about three
leagues from Helvoetfluys, and foon re-landed at
that place; the packet proceeding on her voyage, which, fuppofing no interruption from the
French veffels, was not likely to be made in lefs
than three days. We rejoiced at the releafe from
fatigue and from fear, at leaft, if not from danger; and, feeing little probability of an immediate paffage, returned, the next day, to Rotterdam, with the hope of finding fome neutral veffel, bound to an Englifh port.

We were immediately gratified by the promife
of an American captain to meet us with his veffel at Helvoetfluys, and, the next day, had a
delightful voyage thither, in a hired yacht, partly
by the Maefe, and partly by channels inacceffible
to large veffels.

FLAARDING.

THE Maefe prefently brought us oppofite to this fmall port, the metropolis of the herring fifhers; rendered interefting by the patient induftry and ufeful courage of its inhabitants. We landed at it, but faw only what was immediately open for obfervation. Like moft of the Dutch towns, on the banks of rivers, it is protected from floods by ftanding at the diftance of three or four hundred yards from the fhore, and communicates with the ftream only by a narrow, but deep canal. The beft ftreet is built upon the quays of this channel, on which the herring boats depofit their cargoes before the doors of the owners. We did not fee more than fifty, a great number being then at fea. Except the bufinefs in this ftreet, and the fmell of herrings, which prevailed every where, there was nothing to fhew that we were in a place fupported folely by the induftry of fifhermen; no neglected houfes, no cottages, no dirty ftreets, no inferiority, in point of neatnefs and brightnefs, to the other towns of Holland.

The inhabitants are remarkable for adhering to the drefs, as well as the employments, of their anceftors; fo much fo, that their clothing is mentioned in other towns as the reprefentation of the antient national drefs, common through-

out

but all the provinces two centuries fince; and it is certain, that their appearance is exactly fuch as is delineated in pictures of that date.

Some miles further, we entered the old Maefe, a channel in feveral parts very narrow, and evidently preferved by art, but in others nobly expanfive, and filled almoft to the level of the luxuriant paftures and groves that border it. In one part, where the antient ftream takes a circuitous courfe, a canal has been cut, that fhortens the voyage, for light veffels, by feveral miles, and barks in one channel are fometimes vifible in the other, their fails fwelling over fields, in which, at a diftance, no water is difcernible. Neat and fubftantial farm-houfes, with meadows flanting from them to the river, frequently occurred; and there were more appearances of the careful labours, peculiar to the Dutch, than in the great Maefe itfelf, the banks being occafionally fupported, like their dykes, by a compact bafket-work of flags and faggots.

Paffing many fmall villages, or hamlets, we came, at fun-fet, to the large branch of the fea, which fpreads from Williamftadt to Helvoetfluys, and from thence to the German ocean. The former fortrefs was faintly vifible at a great diftance over the water; and, while we were ftraining our fight towards it, there was proof enough of a nearnefs to the prefent theatre of war, the founds of the fiege of Sluys coming loudly and diftinctly in the breeze. The characters of even-

ing

ing had fallen upon the fcene in mild and deep folemnity; but the glories of nature were unfelt, while a dreadful eftimation of the miferies, produced at each return of the fullen roar, preffed almoft exclufively upon the mind; confiderations, which were foon after prolonged by the melancholy view of feveral Englifh tranfports, filled with wounded foldiers, whofe blythe mufic, now at the firing of the evening gun, was rendered painful by its contraft to the truth of their conditions.

At Helvoetfluys, nothing was to be heard, but accounts, derived from many refpectable officers, on their way to England, of the unexampled difficulties borne, cheerfully borne, by the Britifh army, within the laft three months, and defervedly mentioned, not as complaints, but as proofs of their firmnefs. There were, however, mingled with thefe, many reports as to the contrary conduct even of thofe continental troops, which ftill kept the field with us; of their tardinefs, their irregularity, of the readinefs with which they permitted the Britifh to affume all the dangers of attacks, and of their little co-operation even in the means of general refift-ance. *Brave Anglois! Brave Anglois!* was the conftant fhout of thefe troops, when they had recourfe to the Britifh to regain the pofts themfelves had juft loft, or to make fome affault, which they had refufed, or had attempted with ineffectual formality. They would then follow our troops, and, when an advantage was gained, feemed to think they had fhare enough of the victory, if they were at hand to continue the flaughter of the retreating, and to engrofs all the plunder of the dead.

We

We were as glad to escape from such considerations, as from the crowded inns of Helvoetsluys, now little more convenient than ships; and, the next morning, embarked on board the American vessel, then arrived from Rotterdam. A fair wind soon wafted us out of fight of the low coast of Holland; but we were afterwards becalmed, and carried by tides so far towards the Flemish shore as to have the firing before Sluys not only audible, but terribly loud. For part of three days, we remained within hearing of this noise; but did not, therefore, think ourselves very distant from the English coast, knowing that the fire, at the preceding siege of Nieuport, had been heard as far as the Downs; Nieuport, the wretched scene of so many massacres, and of distress, which, in Holland, had been forcibly described to us by eye-witnesses.

So keenly, indeed, were the horrors of this place conceived by those, who personally escaped from them, that of the emigrants, rescued by the intrepidity of our seamen, many suppressed all joy at their own deliverance by lamentations for the fate of their brethren. One gentleman was no sooner on board a ship, then exposed to the batteries on shore, than he climbed the shrouds and remained aloft, notwithstanding all entreaties, till a severe wound obliged him to descend. Another, who had been saved from the beach by a young sailor, was unable to swim so far as the ship; and the honest lad, having taken him upon his back, struggled hard amidst a shower of balls to save both their lives. At length, he, too, began to falter; and the weakness of his efforts, not his complaints, seemed to shew his companion, that one, or both of them, must
perish :

perifh: the latter nobly afked the lad, whether he could fave his own life, if left to himfelf; and receiving a reluctant reply, that probably he might do fo, but that he would ftrive for both, the emigrant inftantly plunged into the ocean, and was feen no more. The glorious failor reached his fhip, juft as he began again to fail, and was faved.

The calm continued during the day, and the fun fet with uncommon grandeur among clouds of purple, red and gold, that, mingling with the ferene azure of the upper fky, compofed a richnefs and harmony of colouring which we never faw furpaffed. It was moft interefting to watch the progrefs of evening and its effect on the waters; ftreaks of light fcattered among the dark weftern clouds, after the fun had fet, and gleaming in long reflection on the fea, while a grey obfcurity was drawing over the eaft, as the vapours rofe gradually from the ocean. The air was breathlefs; the tall fails of the veffel were without motion, and her courfe upon the deep fcarcely perceptible; while, above, the planet Jupiter burned with fteady dignity, and threw a tremulous line of light on the fea, whofe furface flowed in fmooth wavelefs expanfe. Then, other planets appeared, and countlefs ftars fpangled the dark waters. Twilight now pervaded air and ocean, but the weft was ftill luminous, where one folemn gleam of dufky red edged the horizon, from under heavy vapours.

It was now that we firft difcovered fome fymptoms of England; the lighthoufe on the South-Foreland appeared like a dawning ftar above the margin of the fea.

The

The veffel made little progrefs during the night. With the earlieft dawn of morning we were on deck, in the hope of feeing the Englifh coaft; but the mifts veiled it from our view. A fpectacle, however, the moft grand in nature, repaid us for our difappointment, and we found the circumftances of a fun-rife at fea, yet more interefting than thofe of a fun-fet. The moon, bright and nearly at her meridian, fhed a ftrong luftre on the ocean, and gleamed between the fails upon the deck; but the dawn, beginning to glimmer, contended with her light, and, foon touching the waters with a cold grey tint, difcovered them fpreading all round to the vaft horizon. Not a found broke upon the filence, except the lulling one occafioned by the courfe of the veffel through the waves, and now and then the drowfy fong of the pilot, as he leaned on the helm; his fhadowy figure juft difcerned, and that of a failor pacing near the head of the fhip with croffed arms and a rolling ftep. The captain, wrapt in a fea-coat, lay afleep on the deck, wearied with the early watch. As the dawn ftrengthened, it difcovered white fails ftealing along the diftance, and the flight of fome fea-fowls, as they uttered their flender cry, and then, dropping upon the waves, fat floating on the furface. Meanwhile, the light tints in the eaft began to change, and the fkirts of a line of clouds below to affume a hue of tawny red, which gradually became rich orange and purple. We could now perceive a long tract of the coaft of France, like a dark ftreak of vapour hovering in the fouth, and were fomewhat alarmed on finding ourfelves within view of the French fhore, while that of England was ftill invifible.

The

The moon-light faded fast from the waters, and soon the long beams of the sun shot their lines upwards through the clouds and into the clear blue sky above, and all the sea below glowed with fiery reflections, for a confiderable time, before his difk appeared. At length he rofe from the waves, looking from under clouds of purple and gold; and as he feemed to touch the water, a diftant veffel paffed over his difk, like a dark fpeck.

We were foon after cheered by the faintly feen coaft of England, but at the fame time difcovered, nearer to us on the fouth-weft, the high blue headlands of Calais; and, more eaftward, the town, with its large church and the fleeples of two others, feated on the edge of the fea. The woods, that fringe the fummits of hills rifing over it, were eafily diftinguifhed with glaffes, as well as the national flag on the fleeple of the great church. As we proceeded, Calais cliffs, at a confiderable diftance weftward of the town, loft their aërial blue, and fhewed an high front of chalky precipice, overtopped by dark downs. Beyond, far to the fouth-weft, and at the foot of a bold promontory, that fwelled above all the neighbouring heights, our glaffes gave us the towers and ramparts of Boulogne, floping upward

ward from the shore, with its tall lighthouse on a low point running out into the sea; the whole appearing with confiderable dignity and picturefque effect. The hills beyond were tamer, and funk gradually away in the horizon. At length, the breeze wafting us more to. the north, we difcriminated the bolder features of the Englifh coaft, and, about noon, found ourfelves nearly in the middle of the channel, having Picardy on our left and Kent on the right, its white cliffs afpiring with. great majefty over the flood. The fweeping bay of Dover, with all its chalky heights, foon after opened. The town appeared low on the fhore within, and the caftle, with round and maffy towers, crowned the vaft rock, which, advancing into the fea, formed the eaftern point of the crefcent, while Shakefpeare's cliff, bolder ftill and fublime as the eternal name it bears, was the weftern promontory of the bay. The height and grandeur of this cliff were particularly ftriking, when a fhip was feen failing at its bafe, diminifhed by comparifon to an inch. From hence the cliffs towards Folkftone, though ftill broken and majeftic, gradually decline. There are, perhaps, few profpects of fea and fhore more animated and magnificent than this. The vaft expanfe of water, the character of the cliffs, that guard the coaft, the fhips of war and various merchantmen moored in the Downs, the lighter veffels fkimming along the channel, and the now diftant fhore of France, with Calais glimmering faintly, and hinting of different modes of life and a new world, all thefe circumftances formed a fcene of pre-eminent combination, and led to interefting reflection.

Our

Our veſſel was bound to Deal, and, leaving Dover and its cliffs on the ſouth, we entered that noble bay, which the rich ſhores of Kent open for the ſea. Gentle hills, ſwelling all round from the water, green with woods, or cultivation, and ſpeckled with towns and villages, with now and then the towers of an old fortreſs, offered a landſcape particularly cheering to eyes accuſtomed to the monotonous flatneſs of Dutch views. And we landed in England under impreſſions of delight more varied and ſtrong than can be conceived, without referring to the joy of an eſcape from diſtricts where there was ſcarcely an home for the natives, and to the love of our own country, greatly enhanced by all that had been ſeen of others.

Between Deal and London, after being firſt ſtruck by the ſuperior appearance and manners of the people to thoſe of the countries we had been lately accuſtomed to, a contraſt too obvious as well as too often remarked to be again inſiſted upon, but which made all the ordinary circumſtances of the journey ſeem new and delightful, the difference between the landſcapes of England and Germany occurred forcibly to notice. The large ſcale, in which every diviſion of land appeared in Germany, the long corn grounds, the huge ſtretches of hills, the vaſt plains and the wide vallies could not but be beautifully oppoſed by the varieties and undulations of Engliſh ſurface, with gently ſwelling ſlopes, rich in verdure, thick incloſures, woods, bowery hop grounds, ſheltered manſions, announcing the wealth, and ſubſtantial farms, with neat villages, the comfort of the country. Engliſh landſcape may be be compared to cabinet pictures, delicately beautiful and highly finished; German scenery to paintings for a vestibule, of bold outline and often sublime, but coarse and to be viewed with advantage only from a distance.

Northward, beyond London, we may make one stop, after a country, not otherwise necessary to be noticed, to mention Hardwick, in Derbyshire, a seat of the Duke of Devonshire, once the residence of the Earl of Shrewsbury, to whom Elizabeth deputed the custody of the unfortunate Mary. It stands on an easy height, a few miles to the left of the road from Mansfield to Chesterfield, and is approached through shady lanes; which conceal the view of it, till you are on the confines of the park. Three towers of hoary grey then rise with great majesty among old woods, and their summits appear to be covered with the lightly shivered fragments of battlements, which, however, are soon discovered to be perfectly carved open work, in which the letters E. S. frequently occur under a coronet, the initials, and the memorials of the vanity, of Elizabeth, Countess of Shrewsbury, who built the present edifice. Its tall features, of a most picturesque tint, were finely disclosed between the luxuriant woods and over the lawns of the park, which, every now and then, let in a glimpse of the Derbyshire hills. The scenery reminded us of the exquisite descriptions of Harewood,

" The deep embowering shades, that veil Elfrida;"

and those of Hardwick once veiled a form as lovely as the ideal graces of the Poet, and conspired

ſpired to a fate more tragical than that, which Harewood witneſſed.

In front of the great gates of the caſtle court, the ground, adorned by old oaks, ſuddenly ſinks to a darkly ſhadowed glade, and the view opens over the vale of Scarſdale, bounded by the wild mountains of the Peak. Immediately to the left of the preſent reſidence, ſome ruined features of the antient one, enwreathed with the rich drapery of ivy, give an intereſt to the ſcene, which the later, but more hiſtorical ſtructure heightens and prolongs. We followed, not without emotion, the walk, which Mary had ſo often trodden, to the folding doors of the great hall, whoſe lofty grandeur, aided by ſilence and ſeen under the influence of a lowering ſky, ſuited the temper of the whole ſcene. The tall windows, which half ſubdue the light they admit, juſt allowed us to diſtinguiſh the large figures in the tapeſtry, above the oak wainſcoting, and ſhewed a colonnade of oak ſupporting a gallery along the bottom of the hall, with a pair of gigantic elk's horns flouriſh-ing between the windows oppoſite to the en-trance. The ſcene of Mary's arrival and her feelings upon entering this ſolemn ſhade came involuntarily to the mind; the noiſe of horſes' feet and many voices from the court; her proud yet gentle and melancholy look, as, led by my Lord Keeper, ſhe paſſed ſlowly up the hall; his ſomewhat obſequious, yet jealous and vigilant air, while, awed by her dignity and beauty, he remembers the terrors of his own Queen; the ſilence and anxiety of her maids, and the buſtle of the ſurrounding attendants.

From

From the hall a ftair-cafe afcends to the gallery of a fmall chapel, in which the chairs and cufhions, ufed by Mary, ftill remain, and proceeds to the firft ftory, where only one apartment bears memorials of her imprifonment, the bed, tapeftry and chairs having been worked by herfelf. This tapeftry is richly emboffed with emblematic figures, each with its title worked above it, and, having been fcrupuloufly preferved, is ftill entire and frefh.

Over the chimney of an adjoining dining-room, to which, as well as to other apartments on this floor, fome modern furniture has been added, is this motto carved in oak:

" There is only this: To fear God and keep his Com-
" mandments."

So much lefs valuable was timber than workmanfhip, when this manfion was conftructed, that, where the ftair-cafes are not of ftone, they are formed of folid oaken fteps, inftead of planks; fuch is that from the fecond, or ftate ftory to the roof, whence, on clear days, York and Lincoln Cathedrals are faid to be included in the extenfive profpect. This fecond floor is that, which gives its chief intereft to the edifice. Nearly all the apartments of it were allotted to Mary; fome of them for ftate purpofes; and the furniture is known by other proofs, than its appearance, to remain as fhe left it. The chief room, or that of audience, is of uncommon loftinefs, and ftrikes by its grandeur, before the veneration and tendernefs arife, which its antiquities, and the plainly told tale of the fufferings they witneffed, excite.

The

The walls, which are covered to a considerable height with tapeſtry, are painted above with hiſtorical groups. The chairs are of black velvet, nearly concealed by a raiſed needlework of gold, ſilver and colours, that mingle with ſurpriſing richneſs, and remain in freſh preſervation. The upper end of the room is diſtinguiſhed by a lofty canopy of the ſame materials, and by ſteps which ſupport two chairs; ſo that the Earl and Counteſs of Shrewſbury probably enjoyed their own ſtatelineſs here; as well as aſſiſted in the ceremonies practiſed before Mary. A carpeted table, in front of the canopy, was, perhaps, the deſk of Commiſſioners, or Secretaries, who here recorded ſome of the proceedings concerning her; below which, the room breaks into a ſpacious receſs, where a few articles of furniture are depoſited, not originally placed in it; a bed of ſtate, uſed by Mary, the curtains of gold tiſſue, but in ſo tattered a condition, that its original texture can ſcarcely be perceived. This and the chairs, which accompany it, are ſuppoſed to have been much earlier than Mary's time.

A ſhort paſſage leads from the ſtate apartment to her own chamber, a ſmall room, overlooked from the paſſage by a window, which enabled her attendants to know, that ſhe was contriving no means of eſcape through the others into the court. The bed and chairs of this room are of black velvet, embroidered by herſelf; the toilet of gold tiſſue; all more decayed than worn, and probably uſed only towards the concluſion of her impriſonment here, when ſhe was removed from ſome better apartment, in which the antient bed, now in the ſtate-room, had been placed. The date 1599 is once or twice inſcribed in this chamber;

chamber; for no reason, that could relate to Mary, who was removed hence in 1585; and fell, by the often-blooded hands of Elizabeth, in 1587.

These are the apartments, diftinguifhed by having been the refidence of fo unhappy a perfonage. On the other fide of the manfion, a grand gallery occupies the length of the whole front, which is 165 feet, and contains many portraits, now placed carelefsly on chairs, or the floor; amongft them a head of Sir Thomas More, apparently very fine; heads of Henries the Fourth, Seventh and Eighth; a portrait of Lady Jane Gray, meek and fair, before a harpfichord, on which a pfalm-book is opened; at the bottom of the gallery, Elizabeth, flyly proud and meanly violent; and at the top, Mary, in black, taken a fhort time before her death, her countenance much faded, deeply marked by indignation and grief, and reduced as if to the fpectre of herfelf, frowning with fufpicion upon all who approached it; the black eyes looking out from their corners, thin lips, fomewhat aquiline nofe and beautiful chin.

What remains of the more antient building is a ruin, which, ftanding nearly on the brink of the glade, is a fine object from this. A few apartments, though approached with difficulty through the fragments of others, are ftill almoft entire, and the dimenfions of that called the Giant's Chamber are remarkable for the beauty of their proportion.

From Hardwick to within a few miles of Middleton, the beauty of the country declines, while the fublimity is not perfected; but, from the north-

north-west brow of Brampton Moor, the vast hills of Derbyshire appear in wild and ghastly succession. Middleton, hewn out of the grey rocks, that impend over it, and scarcely distinguishable from them, is worth notice for its very small and neat octagon church, built partly by brief and partly by a donation from the Duke of Devonshire. The valley, or rather chasm, at the entrance of which it stands, is called Middleton Dale, and runs, for two miles, between perpendicular walls of rock, which have more the appearance of having been torn asunder by some convulsive rent of the earth, than any we have elsewhere seen. The strata are horizontal, and the edges of each are often distinct and rounded; one of the characteristics of granite. Three grey rocks, resembling castles, project from these solid walls, and, now and then, a lime-kiln, round like a bastion, half involves in smoke a figure, who, standing on the summit, looks the Witch of the Dale, on an edge of her cauldron, watching the workings of incantation.

The chasm opened, at length, to a hill, whence wild moorish mountains were seen on all sides, some entirely covered with the dull purple of heath, others green, but without enclosures, except sometimes a stone wall, and the dark sides of others marked only by the blue smoke of weeds, driven in circles near the ground.

Towards sun-set, from a hill in Cheshire, we had a vast view over part of that county and nearly all Lancashire, a scene of fertile plains and gentle heights, till some broad and towering mountains, at an immense distance, were but uncertainly

uncertainly diftinguifhed from the clouds. Soon after, the cheerful populoufnefs of the rich towns and villages in Lancafhire fupplied objects for attention of a different character; Stockport firft, crowded with buildings and people, as much fo as fome of the bufieft quarters in London, with large blazing fires in every houfe, by the light of which women were frequently fpinning, and manufacturers iffuing from their workfhops and filling the fteep ftreets, which the chaife rolled down with dangerous rapidity; then an almoft continued ftreet of villages to Man: chefter, fome miles before which the road was bufy with paffengers and carriages, as well as bordered by handfome country houfes ; and, finally for this day, Manchefter itfelf; a fecond London; enormous to thofe, who have not feen the firft, almoft tumultuous with bufinefs, and yet well proved to afford the neceffary peacefulnefs to fcience, letters and tafte. And not only for itfelf may Manchefter be an object of admiration, but for the contraft of its ufeful profits to the wealth of a neighbouring place, immerfed in the dreadful guilt of the Slave Trade, with the continuance of which to believe national profperity compatible, is to hope, that the actions of nations pafs unfeen before the Almighty, or to fuppofe extenuation of crimes by increafe of criminality, and that the eternal laws of right and truth, which fmite the wickednefs of individuals, are too weak to ftruggle with the accumulated and comprehenfive guilt of a national participation in robbery, cruelty and murder.

From Manchefter to Lancafter the road leads through a pleafant and populous country, which rifes gradually as it approaches the huge

C e hills.

hills we had noticed in the diſtance from the brow of Cheſhire, and whoſe attitudes now reſembled thoſe of the Rheingau as ſeen from Mentz. From ſome moors on this ſide of Lancaſter the proſpects open very extenſively over a rich tract fading into blue ridges; while, on the left, long lines of diſtant ſea appear, every now and then, over the dark woods of the ſhore, with veſſels ſailing as if on their ſummits. But the view from a hill deſcending to Lancaſter is preeminent for grandeur, and comprehends an extent of ſea and land, and a union of the ſublime in both, which we have never ſeen equalled. In the green vale of the Lune below lies the town, ſpreading up the ſide of a round hill overtopped by the old towers of the caſtle and the church. Beyond, over a ridge of gentle heights, which bind the weſt ſide of the vale, the noble inlet of the ſea, that flows upon the Ulverſton and Lancaſter ſands, is ſeen at the feet of an amphitheatre formed by nearly all the mountains of the Lakes; an exhibition of alpine grandeur, both in form and colouring, which, with the extent of water below, compoſe a ſcenery perhaps faintly rivalling that of the Lake of Geneva. To the ſouth and weſt, the Iriſh Channel finiſhes the view.

The antient town and caſtle of Lancaſter have been ſo often and ſo well deſcribed, that little remains to be ſaid of them. To the latter conſiderable additions are building in the Gothic ſtyle, which, when time ſhall have ſhaded the ſtone, will harmonize well with the venerable towers and gate-houſe of the old ſtructure. From a turret riſing over the leads of the caſtle, called John o'Gaunt's Chair, the proſpect is ſtill finer

than

than from the terrace of the church-yard below. Overlooking the Lune and its green slopes, the eye ranges to the bay of the sea beyond, and to the Cumberland and Lancashire mountains. On an island near the extremity of the peninsula of Low Furness, the double point of Peel Castle starts up from the sea, but is so distant that it resembles a forked rock. This peninsula, which separates the bay of Ulverston from the Irish Channel, swells gradually into a pointed mountain called Blackcomb, thirty miles from Lancaster, the first in the amphitheatre, that binds the bay. Hence a range of lower, but more broken and forked summits, extends northward to the fells of High Furness, rolled behind each other, huge, towering, and dark; then, higher still, Langdale Pikes; with a confusion of other fells, that crown the head of Windermere and retire towards Keswick, whose gigantic mountains, Helvelyn and Saddleback, are, however, funk in distance below the horizon of the nearer ones. The top of Skiddaw may be discerned when the air is clear, but it is too far off to appear with dignity. From Windermere-Fells the heights soften towards the Vale of Lonsdale, on the east side of which Ingleborough, a mountain in Craven, rears his rugged front, the loftiest and most majestic in the scene. The nearer country, from this point of the landscape, is intersected with cultivated hills, between which the Lune winds its bright but shallow stream, falling over a weir and passing under a very handsome stone bridge at the entrance of the town, in its progress towards the sea. A ridge of rocky eminences shelters Lancaster on the east, whence they decline into the low and uninteresting country, that stretches to the Channel.

The

The appearance of the northern Fells is ever changing with the weather and shifting lights. Sometimes they resemble those evening clouds on the horizon, that catch the last gleams of the sun; at others, wrapt in dark mist, they are only faintly traced, and seem like stormy vapours rising from the sea. But in a bright day their appearance is beautiful; then, their grand outlines are distinctly drawn upon the sky, a vision of Alps; the rugged sides are faintly marked with light and shadow, with wood and rock, and here and there a cluster of white cottages, or farms and hamlets, gleam at their feet along the water's edge. Over the whole landscape is then drawn a softening azure, or sometimes a purple hue, exquisitely lovely, while the sea below reflects a brighter tint of blue.

FROM LANCASTER TO KENDAL.

LEAVING Lancaster, we wound along the southern brow of the vale of the Lune, which there serpentizes among meadows, and is soon after shut up between steep shrubby banks. From the heights we had some fine retrospects of Lancaster and the distant sea; but, about three miles from the town, the hills open forward to a view as much distinguished by the notice of Mr. GRAY, as by its own charms. We here looked down over a woody and finely broken fore-ground upon the Lune and the vale of Lonsdale, undulating in richly cultivated slopes, with Ingleborough, for the back ground, bearing its bold promontory on high, the very crown and paragon of the landscape. To the west, the vale winds from sight among smoother hills; and the gracefully failing line of a mountain, on the left, forms, with the wooded heights, on the right, a kind of frame for the distant picture.

The road now turned into the sweetly retired vale of Caton, and by the village church-yard, in which there is not a single grave-stone, to Hornby, a small straggling town, delightfully seated near the entrance of the vale of Lonsdale. Its thin toppling castle is seen among wood, at a considerable distance, with a dark hill rising over it. What remains of the old edifice is a square grey building, with a slender watch-tower, rising in one corner, like a feather in a hat, which

joins

joins the modern manfion of white ftone, and gives it a fingular appearance, by feeming to ftart from the centre of its roof.

In front, a fteep lawn defcends between avenues of old wood, and the park extends along the fkirts of the craggy hill, that towers above. At its foot, is a good ftone bridge over the Wenning, now fhrunk in its pebbly bed, and, further on, near the caftle, the church, fhewing a handfome octagonal tower, crowned with battlements. The road then becomes extremely interefting, and, at Melling, a village on a brow fome miles further, the view opens over the whole vale of Lonfdale. The eye now paffes, beneath the arching foliage of fome trees in the foreground, to the fweeping valley, where meadows of the moft vivid green and dark woods, with white cottages and villages peeping from among them, mingle with furprifing richnefs, and undulate from either bank of the Lune to the feet of hills. Ingleborough, rifing from elegantly fwelling ground, overlooked this enchanting vale, on the right, clouds rolling along its broken top, like fmoke from a cauldron, and its hoary tint forming a boundary to the foft verdure and rich woodlands of the flopes, at its feet. The perfpective was terminated by the tall peeping heads of the Weftmoreland fells, the nearer ones tinged with fainteft purple, the more diftant with light azure; and this is the general boundary to a fcene, in the midft of which, enclofed between nearer and lower hills, lies the vale of Lonfdale, of a character mild, delicate and repofing, like the countenance of a Madona.

Defcending Melling brow, and winding among the perpetually-changing fcenery of the valley, we

we approached Ingleborough; and it was interefting to obferve the lines of its bolder features
gradually ftrengthening, and the fhadowy mark-
ings of its minuter ones becoming more diftinct,
as we advanced. Rock and grey crags looked
out from the heath, on every fide; but its form
on each was very different. Towards Lonfdale,
the mountain is bold and majeftic, rifing in abrupt
and broken precipices, and often impending, till,
at the fummit, it fuddenly becomes flat, and is
level for nearly a mile, whence it defcends, in a
long gradual ridge, to Craven in Yorkfhire. In
fummer, fome feftivities are annually celebrated
on this top, and the country people, as they
" drink the frefhnefs of the mountain breeze *,"
look over the wild moorlands of Yorkfhire, the
rich vales of Lancafhire, and to the fublime
mountains of Weftmoreland.

Croffing a fmall bridge, we turned from Ingleborough, and paffed very near the antient walls
of Thirlham Caftle, little of which is now remaining. The ruin is on a green broken knoll,
one fide of which is darkened with brufh-wood
and dwarf-oak. Cattle were repofing in the fhade,
on the bank of a rivulet, that rippled through
what was formerly the caftle ditch. A few old
trees waved over what was once a tower, now
covered with ivy.

Some miles further, we croffed the Leck, a
fhrunk and defolate ftream, nearly choked with
pebbles, winding in a deep rocky glen, where
trees and fhrubs marked the winter boundary of
the waters. Our road, mounting a green eminence of the oppofite bank, on which ftands

* Mrs. Barbauld.

Overborough,

Overborough, the handfome modern manfion of
Mr. Fenwick, wound between plantations and
meadows, painted with yellow and purple flowers, like thofe of fpring. As we paffed through
their gentle flopes, we had, now and then, fweet
views between the foliage, on the left, into the
vale of Lonfdale, now contracting in its courfe,
and winding into ruder fcenery, Among thefe
catches, the beft picture was, perhaps, where the
white town of Kirby Lonfdale fhelves along the
oppofite bank, having rough heathy hills immediately above it, and, below, a venerable Gothic
bridge over the Lune, rifing in tall arches, like
an antient aqueduct; its grey tint agreeing well
with the filvery lightnefs of the water and the
green fhades, that flourifhed from the fteep margin over the abutments.

The view from this bridge, too, was beautiful.
The river, foaming below among maffes of dark
rock, variegated with light tints of grey, as if
touched by the painter's pencil, withdrew towards the fouth in a ftraight channel, with the
woods of Overborough on the left. The vale,
dilating, opened a long perfpective to Ingleborough and many blue mountains more diftant,
with all the little villages we had paffed, glittering on the intervening eminences. The colouring of fome low hills, on the right, was particularly beautiful, long fhades of wood being overtopped with brown heath, while, below, meadows of foft verdure fell gently towards the river
bank.

Kirby Lonfdale, a neat little town, commanding the whole vale, is on the weftern fteep. We
ftaid two hours at it, gratified by witneffing, at
the firft inn we reached, the abundance of the
country

country and the goodwill of the people. In times, when the prices of neceſſary articles are increaſing with the, taſte for all unneceſſary diſplay, inſtances of cheapneſs may be to perſons of ſmall incomes ſomething more than mere phyſical treaſures; they have a moral value in contributing to independence of mind.

Here we had an early and, as it afterwards appeared, a very exaggerated ſpecimen of the dialect of the country. A woman talked, for five minutes, againſt our window, of whoſe converſation we could underſtand ſcarcely a word. Soon after, a boy replied to a queſtion, " *I do na ken*," and " *gang*" was preſently the common word for *go*; ſymptoms of nearneſs to a country, which we did not approach, without delighting to enumerate the inſtances of genius and worth, that adorn it.

Leaving Kirby-Lonſdale by the Kendal road, we mounted a ſteep hill, and, looking back from its ſummit upon the whole vale of Lonſdale, perceived ourſelves to be in the mid-way between beauty and deſolation, ſo enchanting was the retroſpect and ſo wild and dreary the proſpect. From the neighbourhood of Caton to Kirby the ride was ſuperior, for elegant beauty, to any we had paſſed; this from Kirby to Kendal is of a character diſtinctly oppoſite. After loſing ſight of the vale, the road lies, for nearly the whole diſtance, over moors and perpetually ſucceeding hills, thinly covered with dark purple heath flowers, of which the moſt diſtant ſeemed black. The drearineſs of the ſcene was increaſed by a heavy rain and by the ſlowneſs of our progreſs, joſtling amongſt coal carts, for ten miles of rugged ground.

ground. The views over the Weftmoreland mountains wére, however, not entirely ob-fcured; their vaft ridges were vifible in the horizon to the north and weft, line over line, frequently in five or fix ranges. Sometimes the interfecting mountains opened to others beyond, that fell in deep and abrupt precipices, their profiles drawing towards a point below, and feeming to fink in a bottomlefs abyfs.

On our way over thefe wilds, parts of which are called Endmoor and Cowbrows, we over-took only long trains of coal carts, and, after ten miles of bleak mountain road, began to de-fire a temporary home, fomewhat fooner than we perceived Kendal, white-fmoking in the dark vale. As we approached, the outlines of its ruinous caftle were juft diftinguifhable through the gloom, fcattered in maffes over the top of a fmall round hill, on the right. At the entrance of the town, the river Kent dafhed in foam down a weir; beyond it, on a green flope, the gothic tower of the church was half hid by a clufter of dark trees; gray fells glimmered in the dif-tance.

We were lodged at another excellent inn, and, the next morning, walked over the town, which has an air of trade mingled with that of antiquity. Its hiftory has been given in other places, and we are not able to difcufs the doubt, whether it was the Roman *Brocanonacio*, or not. The ma-nufacture of cloth, which our ftatute books teftify to have exifted as early as the reign, in which *Falftaff* is made to allude to it, appears to be ftill in vigour, for the town is furrounded, towards the river, with dying grounds. We faw, how-ever,

ever, no shades of " Kendal green," or, indeed, any but bright scarlet.

The church is remarkable for three chapels, memorials of the antient dignity of three neighbouring families, the Bellinghams, Stricklands and Parrs. Thefe are inclofures, on each fide of the altar, differing from pews chiefly in being large enough to contain tombs. Mr. Gray noticed them minutely in the year 1769. They were then probably entire; but the wainfcot or railing, which divided the chapel of the Parrs from the aifle, is now gone. Of two ftone tombs in it one is inclofed with modern railing, and there are many remnants of painted arms on the adjoining windows. The chapel of the Stricklands, which is between this and the altar, is feparated from the church aifle by a folid wainfcot, to the height of four feet, and after that by a wooden railing with broken fillagree ornaments. That of the Bellinghams contains an antient tomb, of which the brafs plates, that bore infcriptions and arms, are now gone, but fome traces of the latter remain in plaiftered ftone at the fide. Over it, are the fragments of an helmet, and, in the roof, thofe of armorial bearings, carved in wood. On a pillar, near this, is an infcription, almoft obliterated, in which the following words may yet be traced:

" Dame Thomafin Thornburgh
Wiffe of Sir William Thornburgh Knyght
Daughter of Sir Robert Bellingham
Gentle Knyght: the ellventhe of Auguft
On thoufand fyue hundreth eightie too."

The Saxon has been fo ftrongly engrafted on our language, that, in reading old infcriptions, efpecially especially those, which are likely to have been spelt, according to the pronunciation, one is frequently reminded by antient English words of the modern German synonyms. A German of the present day would say for eleven, eilf, pronounced long like eilve, and for five, funf, pronounced like fuynf.

Over the chief seat in the old pew of the Bellinghams is a brass plate, engraved with the figure of a man in armour, and, on each side of it, a brass escutcheon, of which that on the right has a motto thus spelled *Ains. y L'est.* Under the figure is the following inscription, also cut in brass:

Heer lyeth the bodye of Alan Bellingham esquier who maryed Cathetyan daughter of Anthonye Ducket esquier by whom he had no children after whose deceafe he maryed Dorothie daughter of Thomas Sanford esquier of whom he had —— sonnes and eight daughters, of which five sonnes & 7 daughters with the said Dorothie ar yeat lyving, he was threescore and one yares of age & dyed y[e] 7 of Maye A° dni 1577.

The correctness of inserting the unpronounced consonants in the words Eight and Daughters, notwithstanding the varieties of the other orthography in this inscription, is a proof of the universality of the Saxon mode of spelling, with great abundance and even waste of letters; a mode, which is so incorporated with our language, that those, who are for dispensing with it in some instances, as in the final k in " publick". and other words, should confider
what

what a general change they have to effect, or what partial incongruities they muft fubmit to.

Kendal is built on the lower fteeps of a hill, that towers over the principal ftreet, and bears on one of its brows a teftimony to the independence of the inhabitants, an obelifk dedicated to liberty and to the memory of the Revolution in 1688. At a time, when the memory of that revolution is reviled, and the praifes of liberty itfelf endeavoured to be fuppreffed by the artifice of imputing to it the crimes of anarchy, it was impoffible to omit any act of veneration to the bleffings of this event. Being thus led to afcend the hill, we had a view of the country, over which it prefides; a fcene fimple, great and free as the fpirit revered amidft it:

FROM KENDAL TO BAMPTON AND HAWKS WATER.

Of two roads from Kendal to Bampton one is through Long Sleddale, the other over Shapfell, the king of the Weftmoreland mountains; of which routes the laft is the moft interefting for fimple fublimity, leading through the heart of the wildeft tracts and opening to fuch vaft highland fcenery as even Derbyfhire cannot fhew. We left Kendal by this road, and from a very old, ruinous bridge had a full view of the caftle, ftretching its dark walls and broken towers round the head of a green hill, to the fouthward of the town. Thefe reliques are, however, too far feparated by the decay of large maffes of the original edifice, and contain little that is individually picturefque.

The road now lay through fhady lanes and over undulating, but gradually afcending ground, from whence were pleafant views of the valley, with now and then a break in the hills, on the left, opening to a glimpfe of the diftant fells towards Windermere, gray and of more pointed form than any we had yet feen; for hitherto the mountains, though of huge outline, were not fo broken, or alpine in their fummits as to ftrike the fancy with furprize. After about three miles, a very fteep hill fhuts up the vale to the North, and from a gray rock, near the fummit, called Stonecragg, the profpect opens over the vale of Kendal

with

with great dignity and beauty. Its form from hence seems nearly circular; the hills spread round it, and sweep with easy lines into the bottom, green nearly to their summits, where no fantastic points bend over it, though rock frequently mingles with the heath. The castle, or its low green hill, looked well, nearly in the centre of the landscape, with Kendal and its mountain, on the right. Far to the south, were the groves of Leven's park, almost the only wood in the scene, and, over the heights beyond, blue hills bounded the horizon. On the west, an opening in the near steeps discovered clusters of huge and broken fells, while other breaks, on the east, shewed long ridges stretching towards the south. Nearer us and to the northward, the hills rose dark and awful, crowding over and interfecting each other in long and abrupt lines, heath and crag their only furniture.

The rough knolls around us and the dark mountain above gave force to the verdant beauty and tranquillity of the vale below, and seemed especially to shelter from the storms of the north some white farms and cottages, scattered among enclosures in the hollows. Soon after reaching the summit of the mountain itself

" A vale appear'd below, a deep retir'd abode,"

and we looked down on the left into Long Sleddale, a little scene of exquisite beauty, surrounded with images of greatness. This narrow vale, or glen, shewed a level of the brightest verdure, with a few cottages scattered among groves, enclosed by dark fells, that rose steeply, yet gracefully,

fully, and, at their fummits, bent forward in maffes of fhattered rock. An hugely pointed mountain, called Keintmoor-head, fhuts up this fweet fcene to the north, rifing in a fudden precipice from the vale, and heightening, by barren and gloomy fteps, the miniature beauty, that glowed at its feet. Two mountains, called Whitefide and Potter's-fell, fcreen the perfpective; Stonecrag is at the fouthern end, fronting Keintmoorhead. The vale, feen beyond the broken ground we were upon, formed a landfcape of, perhaps, unexampled variety and grace of colouring; the tender green of the lowland, the darker verdure of the woods afcending the mountains, the brown rough heath above them, and the impending crags over all, exhibit their numerous fhades, within a fpace not more than two miles long, or half a mile in breadth.

From the right of our road another valley extended, whofe character is that of fimple fublimity, unmixed with any tint of beauty. The vaft, yet narrow perfpective fweeps in ridges of mountains, huge, barren and brown, point beyond point, the higheft of which, Howgill-fell, gives its name to the whole diftrict, in which not a wood, a village, or a farm appeared to cheer the long vifta. A fhepherd boy told us the names of almoft all the heights within the horizon, and we are forry not to have written them, for the names of mountains are feldom compounded of modern, or trivial denominations, and frequently are fomewhat defcriptive of their prototypes. He alfo informed us, that we fhould go over eight miles of Shap-fell, without feeing a houfe; and foon after, at Haw's-foot, we took
leave

leave of the laft on the road, entering then a clofe valley, furrounded by ftupendous mountains of heath and rock, more towering and abrupt than thofe, that had appeared in moorlands on the other fide of Kendal. A ftream, rolling in its rocky channel, and croffing the road under a rude bridge, was all that broke the folitary filence, or gave animation to the view, except the flocks, that hung upon the precipices, and which, at that height, were fcarcely diftinguifhable from the grey round ftones, thickly ftarting out from the heathy fteeps. The Highlands of Scotland could fcarcely have offered to Ossian more images of fimple greatnefs, or more circumftances for melancholy infpiration. Dark glens and fells, the moffy ftone, the lonely blaft, defcending on the valley, the roar of diftant torrents every where occurred; and to the bard the " fong of fpirits" would have fwelled with thefe founds, and their fleeting forms have appeared in' the clouds, that frequently floated along the mountain tops.

The road, now afcending Shap-fell, alternately climbed the fteeps and funk among the hollows of this fovereign mountain, which gives its name to all the furrounding hills ; and, during an afcent of four miles, we watched every form and attitude of the features, which compofed this vaft fcenery. Sometimes we looked from a precipice into deep vallies, varied only with fhades of heath, with the rude fummer hut of the fhepherd, or by ftreams accumulating into torrents; and, at others, caught long profpects over high lands as huge and wild as the nearer ones, which partially intercepted them.

The flocks in this high region are fo feldom difturbed by the footfteps of man, that they have not learned to fear him; they continued to graze within a few feet of the carriage, or looked quietly at it, feeming to confider thefe mountains as their own.

Near the fummit of the road, though not of the hill, a retrofpective glance gave us a long view over the fells, and of a rich diftance towards Lancafter, rifing into blue hills, which admitted glimpfes of fparkling fea in the bay beyond. This gay perfpective, lighted up by a gleam of funfhine, and viewed between the brown lines of the nearer mountains, fhewed like the miniature painting of a landfcape, illuminated beyond a darkened foreground.

At the point of every fteep, as we afcended, the air feemed to become thinner, and, at the northern fummit of Shap-fell, which we reached after nearly two hours' toil, the wind blew with piercing intenfenefs, making it difficult to remain as long as was due to our admiration of the profpect. The fcene of mountains, which burft upon us, can be compared only to the multitudinous waves of the fea. On the northern, weftern and eaftern fcope of the horizon rofe vaft ridges of heights, their broken lines fometimes appearing in feven or eight fucceffive ranges, though fhewing nothing either fantaftic or peaked in their forms. The autumnal lights, gleaming on their fides, or fhadows fweeping in dark lines along them, produced a very fublime effect; while fummits more remote were often mifty with the ftreaming fhower, and others glittered in the partial rays, or were coloured with the mild azure of diftance. The greater tract of the intervening hills and Shap-fell itfelf were, at this time, darkened with clouds, while

while Fancy, awed by the gloom, imaged the genius of Weftmoreland brooding over it and directing the fcowling ftorm.

A defcent of nearly four miles brought us to Shap, a ftraggling village, lying on the fide of a bleak hill, feebly fheltered by clumps of trees. Here, leaving the moorlands, we were glad to find ourfelves again where " bells have knolled to church," and in the midft of civilized, though fimple life. After a fhort reft at a cleanly, little inn, we proceeded towards Bampton, a village five miles further in a vale, to which it gives its name, and one mile from Hawfwater, the lake, that invited us to it. As the road advanced, the fells of this lake fronted it, and, clofing over the fouthern end of Bampton vale, were the moft interefting objects in the view. They were of a character very different from any yet feen; tall, rocky, and of more broken and pointed form. Among them was the high blue peak, called Kidftowpike; the broader ridge of Wallow-crag; a round and ftill loftier mountain—Ikolm-moor, beyond, and, further yet, other ranges of peaked fummits, that overlook Ullfwater.

In a hollow on the left of the road, called the Vale of Magdalene, are the ruins of Shap-abbey, built in the reign of John, of which little now appears except a tower with pointed windows. The fituation is deeply fecluded, and the gloom of the furrounding mountains may have accorded well with monaftic melancholy.

Proceeding towards Bampton we had a momentary peep into Hawfwater, funk deep among black and haggard rocks, and over-topped by the

towering

towering fells before named, whofe fummits were involved in tempeft, till the fun, fuddenly breaking out from under clouds, threw a watery gleam aflant the broken top of Kidftowpike ; and his rays, ftruggling with the fhower, produced a fine effect of light, oppofed to the gloom, that wrapt Ickolm-moor and other huge mountains.

We foon after looked down from the heights of Bampton upon its open vale, checkered with corn and meadows, among which the flender Lowther wound its way from Hawfwater to the vale of Eden, croffing that of Bampton to the north. The hills, enriched here and there with hanging woods and feats, were cultivated nearly to their fummits, except where in the fouth the rude heights of Hawfwater almoft excluded the lake and fhut up the valley. Immediately below us Bampton-grange lay along the fkirt of the hill, and croffed the Lowther, a grey, rambling and antient village, to which we defcended among rough common, darkened by plantations of fir, and between corn enclofures.

The interruption, which inclofed waters and pathlefs mountains give to the intercourfe and bufinefs of ordinary life, renders the diftrict, that contains the lakes of Lancafhire, Weftmoreland and Cumberland, more thinly inhabited than is due to the healthinefs of the climate and, perhaps, to the richnefs of the vallies. The roads are always difficult from their fteepnefs, and in winter are greatly obftructed by fnow. That over Shap-fell to Kendal was, fome years fince, entirely impaffable, till the inhabitants of a few fcattered towns fubfcribed thirty pounds, and a way was cut wide enough for one horfe, but fo deep, that the snow was, on each side, above the rider's head. It is not in this age of communication and intelligence, that any person will be credulously eager to suppose the inhabitants of one part of the island considerably or generally distinguished in their characters from those of another; yet, perhaps, none can immerge themselves in this country of the lakes, without being struck by the superior simplicity and modesty of the people. Secluded from great towns and from examples of selfish splendour, their minds seem to act freely in the sphere of their own affairs, without interruption from envy or triumph, as to those of others. They are obliging, without servility, and plain but not rude, so that, when, in accosting you, they omit the customary appellations, you perceive it to be the familiarity of kindness, not of disrespect; and they do not bend with meanness, or hypocrify, but shew an independent well meaning, without obtrusiveness and without the hope of more than ordinary gain.

Their views of profit from strangers are, indeed, more limited than we could have believed, before witnessing it. The servants at the little inns confess themselves by their manner of receiving what you give, to be almost as much surprised as pleased. A boy, who had opened four or five gates for us between Shap and Bampton, blushed when we called to him to have some halfpence; and it frequently happened, that persons, who had looked at the harness, or rendered some little services of that sort on the road, passed on, before any thing could be offered them. The confusion of others, on being paid, induced us to suppose, at first, that enough had not been given; but we were soon informed, that nothing was expected.

The

The inns, as here at Bampton, are frequently humble; and thofe, who are difpofed to clamour for luxuries, as if there was a crime in not being able to fupply them, may confound a fimple people, and be themfelves greatly difcontented, before they go. But thofe, who will be fatisfied with comforts, and think the experience of integrity, carefulnefs and goodwill is itfelf a luxury, will be glad to have ftopped at Bampton and at feveral other little villages, where there is fome fort of preparation for travellers.

Nor is this fecluded fpot without provifion for the mind. A beneficed grammar fchool receives the children of the inhabitants, and fends, we believe, fome to an Univerfity. Bifhop GIBSON received his education at it. Bifhop LAW, who was born at Bampton, went daily acrofs one, or two of the rudeft fells on the lake to another fchool, at Martindale; an exercife of no trifling fatigue, or refolution; for among the things to be gained by feeing the lakes is a conception of the extreme wildnefs of their boundaries. You arrive with a notion, that you can and dare rove any where amongft the mountains; and have only to fee three to have the utmoft terror of lofing your way.

The danger of wandering in thefe regions without a guide is increafed by an uncertainty, as to the titles of heights; for the people of each village have a name for the part of a mountain neareft to themfelves, and they fometimes call the whole by that name. The circumference of fuch heights is alfo too vaft, and the flexures too numerous

merous to admit of great accuracy. Skiddaw, Saddleback and Helvellyn, may however, be certainly diftinguifhed. There are others, a paffage over which would fave, perhaps, eight or ten miles out of twenty, but which are fo little known, except to the fhepherds, that they are very rarely croffed by travellers. We could not truft to any perfon's knowledge of Harter-fell, beyond the head of Hawfwater.

HAWSWATER.

THIS is a lake, of which little has been mentioned, perhaps becaufe it is inferiour in fize to the others, but which is diftinguifhed by the folemn grandeur of its rocks and mountains, that rife in very bold and awful charaĉters. The water, about three miles long, and at the wideft only half a mile over, nearly defcribes the figure 8, being narrowed in the centre by the projeĉting fhores ; and, at this fpot, it is· faid to be fifty fathom deep.

Croffing the meadows of Bampton vale and afcending the oppofite heights, we approached the fells of Hawfwater, and, having proceeded for a mile along the fide of hills, the views over the vale and of the foutheru mountains changing with almoft every ftep, the lake began to open between a very lofty ridge, covered with foreft, and abrupt fells of heath, or naked rock. Soon after, we looked upon the firft expanfe of the lake. Its

eaftern

eastern shore, rising in a tremendous ridge of
rocks, darkened with wood to the summit, appears to terminate in Wallow-crag, a promontory
of towering height, beyond which the lake winds
from view. The finely broken mountains on the
west are covered with heath, and the tops impend
in crags and precipices; but their ascent from the
water is less sudden than that of the opposite rocks,
and they are skirted by a narrow margin of vivid
green, where cattle were feeding, and tufted
shrubs and little groves overhung the lake and
were reflected on its dark surface. Above, a very
few white cottages among wood broke in upon
the solitude; higher still, the mountain-flocks
were browsing, and above all, the narrow perspective was closed by dark and monstrous summits.

As we wound along the bank, the rocks unfolded and disclosed the second expanse, with scenery yet more towering and sublime than the first.
This perspective seemed to be terminated by the
huge mountain called Castle-street; but, as we
advanced, Harter-fell reared his awful front, impending over the water, and shut in the scene,
where, amidst rocks, and at the entrance of a
glen almost choked by fragments from the heights,
stands the chapel of Martindale, spoken by the
country people Mardale. Among the fells of
this dark prospect are Lathale, Wilter-crag,
Castle-crag and Riggindale, their bold lines
appearing beyond each other as they fell into
the upper part of the lake, and some of
them shewing only masses of shattered rock.
Kidstow-pike is pre-eminent among the crowding
summits

fummits beyond the eaftern fhore, and the clouds frequently fpread their gloom over its point, or fall in fhowers into the cup within; on the weft High-ftreet, which overlooks the head of Ullf-water, is the moft dignified of the mountains.

Leaving the green margin of the lake, we af-cended to the Parfonage, a low, white building on a knoll, fheltered by the mountain and a grove of fycamores, with a fmall garden in front, falling towards the water. From the door we had a view of 'the whole lake and the furrounding fells, which the eminence we were upon was juft raifed enough to fhew to advantage. Nearly oppofite to it the bold promontory of Wallow-crag pufhed its bafe into the lake, where a peninfula advanced to meet it, fpread with bright verdure, on which the hamlet of Martindale lay half concealed among a grove of oak, beech and fycamore, whofe tints contrafted with the darker one of the fpiry fpruce, or more clumped Englifh fir, and accorded fweetly with the paftoral green beneath. The ridge of precipices, that fwept from Wallow-crag fouth-ward, and formed a bay for the upper part of the lake, was defpoiled of its foreft; but that, which curved northward, was dark with dwarf-wood to the water's brim, and, opening diftantly to Bampton vale, let in a gay miniature landfcape, bright in funfhine. Below, the lake reflected the gloom of the woods, and was fometimes marked with long white lines, which, we were told, in-dicated bad weather; but, except when a fudden guft fwept the furface, it gave back every image on the fhore, as in a dark mirror.

The

The interior of the Parfonage was as comfortable as the fituation was interefting. A neat parlour opened from the paffage, but it was newly painted, and we were fhewn into the family room, having a large old fafhioned chimney corner, with benches to receive a focial party, and forming a moft enviable retreat from the ftorms of the mountains. Here, in the winter evening, a family circle, gathering round a blazing pile of wood on the hearth, might defy the weather and the world. It was delightful to picture fuch a party, happy in their home, in the fweet affections of kindred and in honeft independence, converfing, working and reading occafionally, while the blaft was ftruggling againft the cafement and the fnow pelting on the roof.

The feat of a long window, overlooking the lake, offered the delights of other feafons; hence the luxuriance of fummer and the colouring of autumn fucceffively fpread their enchantments over the oppofite woods, and the meadows that margined the water below; and a little garden of fweets fent up its fragrance to that of the honeyfuckles, that twined round the window. Here, too, lay a ftore of books, and, to inftance that an inhabitant of this remote nook could not exclude an intereft concerning the diftant world, among them was a hiftory of paffing events. Alas! to what fcenes, to what difplay of human paffions and human fuffering did it open! How oppofite to the fimplicity, the innocence and the peace of thefe!

The venerable father of the manfion was engaged in his duty at his chapel of Martindale, but we were hofpitably received within, and heard
the

the next day how gladly he would have rendered any civilities to ftrangers.

On leaving this enviable little refidence, we purfued the fteeps of the mountain behind it, and were foon amidft the flocks and the crags, whence the look down upon the lake and among the fells was folemn and furprifing. About a quarter of a mile from the Parfonage, a torrent of fome dignity rufhed paft us, foaming down a rocky chafm in its way to the lake. Every where, little ftreams of chryftal clearnefs wandered filently among the mofs and turf, which half concealed their progrefs, or dafhed over the rocks; and, acrofs the largeft, fheep-bridges of flat ftone were thrown, to prevent the flocks from being carried away in attempting to pafs them in winter. The grey ftones, that grew among the heath, were fpotted with moffes of fo fine a texture, that it was difficult to afcertain whether they were vegetable; their tints were a delicate pea-green and primrofe, with a variety of colours, which it was not neceffary to be a botanift to admire.

An hour, paffed in afcending, brought us to the brow of Bampton-vale, which floped gently downward to the north, where it opened to lines of diftant mountains, that extended far into the eaft. The woods of Lowther-park capped two remote hills, and fpread luxuriantly down their fides into the valley; and nearer, Bampton-grange lay at the bafe of a mountain, crowned with fir plantations, over which, in a diftant vale, we difcovered the village of Shap and long ridges of the highland, paffed on the preceding day.

One

One of the fells we had juft croffed is called Blanarafa, at the fummit of which two grey ftones, each about four feet high, and placed upright, at the diftance of nine feet from each other, remain of four, which are remembered to have been formerly there. The place is ftill called Four Stones; but tradition does not relate the defign of the monument; whether to limit adjoining diftricts, or to commemorate a battle, or a hero.

We defcended gradually into the vale, among thickets of rough oaks, on the bank of a rivulet, which foamed in a deep channel beneath their foliage, and came to a glade fo fequeftered and gloomily overfhadowed, that one almoft expected to fee the venerable arch of a ruin, peeping between the branches. It was the very fpot, which the founder of a monaftery might have chofen for his retirement, where the chantings of a choir might have mingled with the foothing murmur of the ftream, and monks have glided beneath the folemn trees in garments fcarcely diftinguifhable from the fhades themfelves.

This glade, floping from the eye, opened under fpreading oaks to a remote glimpfe of the vale, with blue hills in the diftance; and on the graffy hillocks of the fore-ground cattle were every where repofing.

We returned, about funfet, to Bampton, after a walk of a little more than four miles, which had exhibited a great variety of fcenery, beautiful, romantic and fublime. At the entrance of the village, the Lowther and a namelefs rivulet, that runs from Hawfwater, join their waters; both ftreams were now funk in their beds; but in

winter

winter they.fometimes contend for the conqueft and ravage of the neighbouring plains. The waters have then rifen to the height of five or fix feet in a meadow forty yards' from their fummer channels. In an inclofure of this vale was fought the laft battle, or fkirmifh, with the Scots in Weftmoreland; and it is within the telling of the fons of great-grandfathers, that the conteft continued, till the Scots were difcovered to fire only pebbles; the villagers had then the folly to clofe with them and the fuccefs to drive them away; but fuch was the fimplicity of the times, that it was called a victory to have made one prifoner. Stories of this fort are not yet entirely forgotten in the deeply inclofed vales of Weft-moreland and Cumberland, where the greater part of the prefent inhabitants can refer to an anceftry of feveral centuries, on the fame fpot.

We thought Bampton, though a very ill-built village, an enviable fpot; having a clergyman, as we heard, of exemplary manners, and, as one of us witneffed, of a moft faithful earneftnefs in addreffing his congregation in the church; being but flightly removed from one of the lakes; that accumulates in. a fmall fpace many of the varieties and attractions of the others; and having the adjoining lands diftributed, for the moft part, into fmall farms, fo that, as it is not thought low to be without wealth, the poor do not acquire the offenfive and difreputable habits, by which they are too often tempted to revenge, or refift the oftentation of the rich.

.ULLS-

ULLS-WATER.

THE ride from Bampton to Ullf-water is very various and delightful. It winds for about three miles along the weftern heights of this green and open vale, among embowered lanes, that alternately admit and exclude the paftoral fcenes below, and the fine landfcapes on the oppofite hills, formed by the plantations and antient woods of Lowther-park. Thefe fpread over a long tract, and mingle in fweet variety with the lively verdure of lawns and meadows, that flope into the valley, and fometimes appear in gleams among the dark thickets. The houfe, of white ftone with red window-cafes, embofomed among the woods, has nothing in its appearance anfwerable to the furrounding grounds. Its fituation and that of the park are exquifitely happy, juft where the vale of Bampton opens to that of Eden, and the long mountainous ridge and peak of Crofs-fell, afpiring above them all, ftretch before the eye; with the town of Penrith fhelving along the fide of a diftant mountain, and its beacon on the fummit; the ruins of its caftle appearing diftinctly at the fame time, crowning a low round hill. The horizon to the north and the eaft is bounded by lines of mountains, range above range, not romantic and furprifing, but multitudinous and vaft. Of thefe, Crofs-fell, faid to be the higheft mountain in Cumberland, gives its name to the whole northern ridge, which in its full extent, from

the

the neigbourhood of Gillfland to that of Kirkby-
Steven, is near fifty miles. This perfpective of
the extenfive valé of Eden has grandeur and magnificence in as high a degree as that of Bampton
has paftoral beauty, clofing in the gloomy folitudes
of Hawfwater. The vale is finely wooded, and
variegated with manfions, parks, meadow-land,
corn, towns, villages, and all that make a diftant
landfcape rich. Among the peculiarities of it,
are little mountains of alpine fhape, that ftart up
like pyramids in the middle of the vale, fome
covered with wood, others barren and rocky.
The fcene perhaps only wants a river like the
Rhine, or the Thames, to make it the very fineft
in England for union 'of grandeur, beauty and
extent.

Oppofite Lowther-hall, we gave a farewell
look to the pleafant vale of Bampton and its
fouthern fells, as the road, winding more to the
weft, led us over the high lands, that feparate it from
the vale of Emont. Then, afcending through
fhady lanes and among fields where the oat harveft
was gathering, we had enchanting retrofpects of
the vale of Eden, fpreading to the eaft, with all
its chain of mountains chequered by the autumnal
fhadows.

Soon after the road brought us to the brows of
Emont, a narrow well-wooded vale, the river
from which it takes its name, meandering through
it from Ullf-water among paftures and pleafure-
grounds, to meet the Lowther near Brougham
Caftle. Penrith and its caftle and beacon look
up the vale from the north, and the aftonifhing
fells of Ullf-water clofe upon 'it in the fouth;
while Delemain, the houfe and beautiful grounds

of

of Mr. Haffel, Hutton St. John, a venerable old manfion, and the fingle tower called Dacre-caftle adorn the valley. But who can paufe to admire the elegancies of art, when furrounded by the wonders of nature? The approach to this fublime lake along the heights of Emont is exquifitely interefting; for the road, being fhrouded by woods, allows the eye only partial glimpfes of the gigantic fhapes, that are affembled in the diftance, and awakening high expectation, leaves the imagination, thus elevated, to paint the " forms of things unfeen." Thus it was, when we caught a firft view of the dark broken tops of the fells, that rife round Ullf-water, of fize and fhape moft huge, bold, and awful; overfpread with a blue myfterious tint, that feemed almoft fupernatural, though according in gloom and fublimity with the fevere features it involved.

Further on, the mountains began to unfold themfelves; their outlines, broken, abrupt and interfecting each other in innumerable directions, feemed, now and then, to fall back like a multitude at fome fupreme command, and permitted an oblique glimpfe into the deep vales. A clofe lane then defcended towards Pooly-bridge, where, at length, the lake itfelf appeared beyond the fpreading branches, and, foon after, the firft reach expanded before us, with all its mountains tumbled round it; rocky, ruinous and vaft, impending, yet rifing in wild confufion and multiplied points behind each other.

This view of the firft reach from the foot of Dunmallet, a pointed woody hill, near Poolybridge, is one of the fineft on the lake, which here fpreads in a noble fheet, near three miles long,

long, and almoſt two miles broad, to the baſe of Thwaithill-nab, winding round which it diſappears, and the whole is then believed to be ſeen. The character of this view is nearly that of ſimple grandeur; the mountains, that impend over the ſhore in front, are peculiarly awful in their forms and attitudes; on the left, the fells ſoften; woodlands, and their paſtures, colour their lower declivities, and the water is margined with the tendereſt verdure, oppoſed to the dark woods and crags above. On the right, a green conical hill ſlopes to the ſhore, where cattle were repoſing on the graſs, or ſipping the clear wave; further, riſe the bolder rocks of Thwaithill-nab, where the lake diſappears, and, beyond, the dark precipices and ſummits of fells, that crown the ſecond reach.

Winding the foot of Dunmallet, the almoſt pyramidal hill, that ſhuts up this end of Ullſwater, and ſeparates it from the vale of Emont, we croſſed Barton bridge, where this little river, clear as cryſtal, iſſues from the lake, and through a cloſe paſs hurries over a rocky channel to the vale. Its woody ſteeps, the tufted iſland, that interrupts its ſtream, and the valley beyond, form altogether a picture in fine contraſt with the majeſty of Ullſwater, expanding on the other ſide of the bridge.

We followed the ſkirts of a ſmooth green hill, the lake, on the other hand, flowing ſoftly againſt the road and ſhewing every pebble on the beach beneath, and proceeded towards the ſecond bend; but ſoon mounted from the ſhore among the broken knolls of Dacre-common, whence we had various views of the firſt reach,

its

its fcenery appearing in darkened majefty as the autumnal fhadows fwept over it. Sometimes, however, the rays, falling in gleams upon the water, gave it the fineft filvery tone imaginable, fober though fplendid. Dunmallet at the foot of the lake was a formal unpleafing object, not large enough to be grand, or wild enough to be romantic.

The ground of the common is finely broken, and is fcattered fparingly with white cottages, each picturefquely fhadowed by its dark grove; above, rife plantations and gray crags which lead the eye forward to the alpine forms, that crown the fecond reach, changing their attitudes every inftant as they are approached.

Ullfwater in all its windings, which give it the form of the letter S, is nearly nine miles long; the width is various, fometimes nearly two miles and feldom lefs than one; but Skelling-nab, a vaft rock in the fecond reach, projects fo as to reduce it to lefs than a quarter of a mile. Thefe are chiefly the reputed meafurements, but the eye lofes its power of judging even of the breadth, confounded by the boldnefs of the fhores and the grandeur of the fells, that rife beyond; the proportions however are grand, for the water retains its dignity, notwithftanding the vaftnefs of its accompaniments; a circumftance, which Derwent-water can fcarcely boaft.

The fecond bend, affuming the form of a river, is very long, but generally broad, and brought ftrongly to remembrance fome of the paffes of the Rhine beyond Coblentz: though, here, the rocks, that rife over the water, are little wooded;

and,

and, there, their skirts are never margined by pasture, or open to such fairy summer scenes of vivid green mingling with shades of wood and gleams of corn, as sometimes appear within the recesses of these wintry mountains. These cliffs, however, do not shew the variety of hue, or marbled veins, that frequently surprise and delight on the Rhine, being generally dark and gray, and the varieties in their complexion, when there are any, purely aerial; but they are vast and broken; rise immediately from the stream, and often shoot their masses over it; while the expanse of water below accords with the dignity of that river in many of its reaches. Once too, there were other points of resemblance, in the ruins of monasteries and convents, which, though reason rejoices that they no longer exist, the eye may be allowed to regret. Of these, all which now remains on record is, that a society of Benedictine monks was founded on the summit of Dunmallet, and a nunnery of the same order on a point behind Sowlby-fell; traces of these ruins, it is said, may still be seen.

Thus grandeur and immensity are the characteristics of the left shore of the second reach; the right exhibits romantic wildness in the rough ground of Dacre-common and the craggy heights above, and, further on, the sweetest forms of reposing beauty, in the grassy hillocks and undulating copses of Gowbarrow-park, fringing the water, sometimes over little rocky eminences, that project into the stream, and, at others, in shelving bays, where the lake, transparent as crystal, breaks upon the pebbly bank, and laves the road, that winds there. Above these pastoral and sylvan landscapes, rise broken precipices, less tre-

E e 2   mendous

mendous than thofe of the oppofite fhore, with paftures purfuing the crags to a confiderable height, fpeckled with cattle, which are exqui-fitely picturefque, as they graze upon the knolls and among the old trees, that adorn this finely declining park.

Leaving the hamlet of Watermillock at fome diftance on the left, and paffing the feat of Mr. Robinfon, fequeftered in the gloom of beech and fycamores, there are fine views over the fe-cond reach, as the road defcends the common towards Gowbarrow. Among the boldeft fells, that breaft the lake on the left fhore, are Holling-fell and Swarth-fell, now no longer boafting any part of the foreft of Martindale, but fhewing huge walls of naked rock, and fcars, which many torrents have inflicted. One channel only in this dry feafon retained its fhining ftream; the chafm was dreadful, parting the mountain from the fummit to the bafe; and its waters in winter, leaping in foam from precipice to precipice, muft be infinitely fublime; not, however, even then from their mafs, but from the length and preci-pitancy of their defcent.

The perfpective as the road defcends into Gowbarrow-park is perhaps the very fineft on the lake. The fcenery of the firft reach is almoft tame when compared with this, and it is difficult to fay where it can be equalled for Alpine fubli-mity, and for effecting wonder and awful eleva-tion. The lake, after expanding at a diftance to great breadth, once more lofes itfelf beyond the enormous pile of rock called Place-fell, oppofite to which the fhore, feeming to clofe upon all fur-ther progrefs, is bounded by two promontories
covered

covered with woods, that shoot their luxuriant foliage to the water's edge. The shattered mass of gray rock, called Yew-crag, rises immediately over these, and, beyond, a glen opens to a chaos of mountains more solemn in their aspect, and singular in their shapes, than any which have appeared, point crowding over point in lofty succession. Among these is Stone-crofs-pike and huge Helvellyn, scowling over all; but, though this retains its pre-eminence, its dignity is lost in the mass of alps around and below it. A fearful gloom involved them; the shadows of a stormy sky upon mountains of dark rock and heath. All this is seen over the woody foreground of the park, which, soon shrouding us in its bowery lanes, allowed the eye and the fancy to repose, while venturing towards new forms and assemblages of sublimity.

Meantime, the green shade, under which we passed, where the sultry low of cattle, and the sound of streams hurrying from the heights through the copses of Gowbarrow to the lake below, were all that broke the stillness; these, with gleamings of the water, close on the left, between the foliage, and which was ever changing its hue, sometimes assuming the soft purple of a pigeon's neck, at others the silvery tint of sunshine—these circumstances of imagery were in soothing and beautiful variety with the gigantic visions we had lost.

The road still pursuing this border of the lake, the copses opened to partial views of the bold rocks, that form the opposite shore, and many a wild recess and solemn glen appeared and vanished among them, some shewing only broken

fells,

fells, the fides of others shaggy with forests, and nearly all lined, at their bases, with narrow pastures of the most exquisite verdure. Thus descending upon a succession of sweeping bays, where the shades parted, and admitted the lake, that flowed even with us, and again retreating from it over gentle eminences, where it glittered only between the leaves; crossing the rude bridges of several becks, rapid, clear and foaming among dark stones, and receiving a green tint from the closely shadowing trees, but neither precipitous enough in their descent, nor ample enough in their course, to increase the dignity of the scene, we came, after passing nearly three miles through the park, to Lyulph's Tower. This mansion, a square, gray edifice, with turreted corners, battlements and windows in the Gothic style, has been built by the present Duke of Norfolk in one of the finest situations of a park, abounding with views of the grand and the sublime. It stands on a green eminence, a little removed from the water, backed with wood and with pastures rising abruptly beyond, to the cliffs and crags that crown them. In front, the ground falls finely to the lake's edge, broken, yet gentle, and scattered over with old trees, and darkened with copses, which mingle in fine variety of tints with the light verdure of the turf beneath. Herds of deer, wandering over the knolls, and cattle, reposing in the shade, completed this sweet landscape.

The lake is hence seen to make one of its boldest expanses, as it sweeps round Place-fell, and flows into the third and last bend of this wonderful vale. Lyulph's Tower looks up this reach to the south, and to the east traces all the fells and curving banks of Gowbarrow, that bind the
second;

fecond ; while, to the weft, a dark glen opens to
a glimpfe of the folemn alps round Helvellyn ;
and all thefe objects are feen over the mild beauty
of the park.

Paffing the fweeps of the fhore and over bold
headlands, we came oppofite to the vaft promontory, called Place-fell, that pufhes its craggy
foot into the lake, like a lion's claw, round
which the waters make a fudden turn, and enter
Patterdale, their third and final expanfe. In this
reach, they lofe the form of a river, and refume
that of a lake, being clofed, at three miles diftance, by the ruinous rocks, that guard the gorge
of Patterdale, backed by a multitude of fells.
The water, in this fcope, is of oval form, bounded on one fide by the precipices of Place-fell,
Martindale-fell, and feveral others equally rude
and awful that rife from its edge, and fhew no
lines of verdure, or maffes of wood, but retire
in rocky bays, or project in vaft promontories
athwart it. The oppofite fhore is lefs fevere and
more romantic; the rocks are lower and richly
wooded, and, often receding from the water,
leave room for a tract of pafture, meadow land
and corn, to margin their ruggednefs. At the
upper end, the village of Patterdale, and one or
two white farms, peep out from among trees
beneath the fcowling mountains, that clofe the
fcene; pitched in a rocky nook, with corn and
meadow land, floping gently in front to the lake,
and, here and there, a fcattered grove. But this
fcene is viewed to more advantage from one of
the two woody eminences, that overhang the
lake, juft at the point where it forms its laft angle, and, like an opened compafs, fpreads its two
arms before the eye. Thefe heights are extremely
beautiful,

beautiful, viewed from the oppofite fhore, and had long charmed us at a diftance. Approaching them, we croffed another torrent, Glencoynbeck, or Airey-force, which here divides not only the eftates of the Duke of Norfolk and Mr. Hodgkinfon, but the counties of Weftmoreland and Cumberland; and all the fells beyond, that enclofe the laft bend of Ullfwater, are in Patterdale. Here, on the right, at the feet of awful rocks, was fpread a gay autumnal fcene, in which the peafants were finging merrily as they gathered the oats into fheafs; woods, turfy hillocks, and, above all, tremendous crags, abruptly clofing round the yellow harveft. The figures, together with the whole landfcape, refembled one of thofe beautifully fantaftic fcenes, which fable calls up before the wand of the magician.

Entering Glencoyn woods and fweeping the boldeft bay of the lake, while the water dafhed with a ftrong furge upon the fhore, we at length mounted a road frightful from its fteepnefs and its crags, and gained one of the wooded fummits fo long admired. From hence the view of Ullfwater is the moft extenfive and various, that its fhores exhibit, comprehending its two principal reaches, and though not the moft picturefque, it is certainly the moft grand. To the eaft, extends the middle fweep in long and equal perfpective, walled with barren fells on the right, and margined on the left with the paftoral receffes and bowery projections of Gowbarrow park. The rude mountains above almoft feemed to have fallen back from the fhore to admit this landfcape within their hollow bofom, and then, bending abruptly, appear like Milton's Adam viewing the fleeping Eve, to hang over it enamoured.

Lyulph's

Lyulph's Tower is the only object of art, except the hamlet of Watermillock, seen in the distant perspective, that appears in the second bend of Ullswater; and this loses much of its effect from the square uniformity of the structure, and the glaring green of its painted window-cases. This is the longest reach of the lake.

Place-fell, which divides the two last bends, and was immediately opposite to the point we were on, is of the boldest form. It projects into the water, an enormous mass of grey crag, scarred with dark hues; thence retiring a little it again bends forward in huge cliffs, and finally starts up into a vast perpendicular face of rock. As a single object, it is wonderfully grand; and, connected with the scene, its effect is sublime. The lower rocks, are called Silver-rays, and not inaptly; for, when the sun shines upon them, their variegated sides somewhat resemble in brightness the rays streaming beneath a cloud.

The least reach of Ullswater, which is on the right of this point, expands into an oval, and its majestic surface is spotted with little rocky islets, that would adorn a less sacred scene; here they are prettinesses, that can scarcely be tolerated by the grandeur of its character. The tremendous mountains, which scowl over the gorge of Patterdale; the cliffs, massy, broken and over-looked by a multitude of dark summits, with the grey walls of Swarth and Martindale fells, that upheave themselves on the eastern shore, form altogether one of the most grand and awful pictures on the lake; yet, admirable and impressive as it is, as to solemnity and astonishment, its effect with us was not equal to that of the
more

more alpine sketch, caught in distant perspective from the descent into Gowbarrow-park.

In these views of Ullswater, sublimity and greatness are the predominating characters, though beauty often glows upon the western bank. The mountains are all bold, gloomy and severe. When we saw them, the sky accorded well with the scene, being frequently darkened by autumnal clouds; and the equinoctial gale swept the surface of the lake, marking its blackness with long white lines, and beating its waves over the rocks to the foliage of the thickets above. The trees, that shade these eminences, give greater force to the scenes, which they either partially exclude, or wholly admit, and become themselves fine objects, enriched as they are with the darkest moss.

From hence the ride to the village of Patterdale, at the lake's head, is, for the first part, over precipices covered with wood, whence you look down, on the left, upon the water, or upon pastures stretching to it; on the right, the rocks rise abruptly, and often impend their masses over the road; or open to narrow dells, green, rocky and overlooked by endless mountains.

About half way to the village of Patterdale, a peninsula spreads from this shore into the lake, where a white house, peeping from a grove and surrounded with green enclosures, is beautifully placed. This is an inn, and, perhaps, the principal one, as to accommodation; but, though its situation, on a spot which on each side commands the lake, is very fine, it is not comparable, in point of wildness and sublimity, to that
of

of the cottage, called the King's Arms, at Patterdale. In the way thither, are enchanting catches of the lake, between the trees on the left, and peeps into the glens, that wind among the alps towards Helvellyn, on the right. These multiply near the head of Ullfwater, where they start off as from one point, like radii, and conclude in trackless solitudes.

It is difficult to spread varied pictures of such scenes before the imagination. A repetition of the same images of rock, wood and water, and the same epithets of grand, vast and sublime, which necessarily occur, must appear tautologous, on paper, though their archetypes in nature, ever varying in outline, or arrangement, exhibit new visions to the eye, and produce new shades of effect on the mind. It is difficult also, where these delightful differences have been experienced, to forbear dwelling on the remembrance, and attempting to sketch the peculiarities, which occasioned them. The scenery at the head of Ullfwater is especially productive of such difficulties, where a wish to present the picture, and a consciousness of the impossibility of doing so, except by the pencil, meet and oppose each other.

Patterdale itself is a name somewhat familiar to recollection, from the circumstance of the chief estate in it having given to its possessors, for several centuries, the title of Kings of Patterdale. The last person so distinguished was richer than his ancestors, having increased his income, by the most ludicrous parsimony, to a thousand pounds a year. His son and successor is an industrious country gentleman, who has improved the

the fort of farming manfion, annexed to the
eftate, and, not affecting to depart much from
the fimple manners of the other inhabitants, is
refpectable enough to be generally called by his
own name of Mounfey, inftead of the title,
which was probably feldom given to his anceftors,
but in fome fort of mockery.

The village is very humble, as to the conditions and views of the inhabitants; and very refpectable, as to their integrity and fimplicity, and
to the contentment, which is proved by the infrequency of emigrations to other diftricts. It
ftraggles at the feet of fells, fomewhat removed
from the lake and near the entrance of the wild
vale of Glenridding. Its white church is feen
nearly from the commencement of the laft reach,
rifing among trees, and in the church-yard are
the ruins of an antient yew, of remarkable fize
and venerable beauty; its trunk, hollowed and
filvered by age, refembles twifted roots; yet, the
branches that remain above, are not of melancholy black, but flourifh in rich verdure and
flaky foliage.

The inn is beyond the village, fecurely fheltered under high crags, while enormous fells,
clofe on the right, open to the gorge of Patterdale; and Coldrill-beck, iffuing from it, defcends
among the corn and meadows, to join the lake
at a little diftance. We had a happy evening
at this cleanly cottage, where there was no want,
without its recompenfe, from the civil offices of
the people. Among the rocks, that rofe over it,
is a ftation, which has been more frequently fe-
lected than any other on the lake by the painter
and the lover of the *beau idée*, as the French and
Sir

Sir Joshua Reynolds expreffively term what Mr. Burke explains in his definition of the word *fine.* Below the point, on which we ftood, a tract of corn and meadow land fell gently to the lake, which expanded in great majefty beyond, bounded on the right by the precipices of many fells, and, on the left, by rocks finely wooded, and of more broken and fpiry outline. The undulating paftures and copfes of Gowbarrow clofed the perfpective. Round the whole of thefe fhores, but particularly on the left, rofe clufters of dark and pointed fummits, affuming great variety of fhape, amongft which Helvellyn was ftill preeminent. Immediately around us, all was vaft and gloomy; the fells mount fwiftly and to enormous heights, leaving at their bafes only crags and hillock, tufted with thickets of dwarf-oak and holly, where the beautiful cattle, that adorned them, and a few fheep, were picking a fcanty fupper among the heath.

From this fpot glens open on either hand, that lead the eye only to a chaos of mountains. The profile of one near the fore-ground on the right is remarkably grand, fhelving from the fummit in one vaft fweep of rock, with only fome interruption of craggy points near its bafe, into the water. On one fide, it unites with the fells in the gorge of Patterdale, and, on the other, winds into a bold bay for the lake. Among the highlands, feen over the left fhore, is Common-fell, a large heathy mountain, which appeared to face us. Somewhat nearer, is a lower one, called Glenridding, and above it the Nab. Graffdale has Glenridding and the Nab on one fide towards the water, and Birk's-fell and St. Sunday's-crag over that, on the other. The points, that rife
above

above the Nab, are Stridon-edge, then Cove's head, and, over all, the precipices of dark Helvellyn, now appearing only at intervals among the clouds.

Not only every fell of this wild region has a name, but almost every crag of every fell, so that shepherds sitting at the fire-side can direct each other to the exact spot among the mountains, where a stray sheep has been seen.

Among the rocks on the right shore, is Martindale-fell, once shaded with a forest, from which it received its name, and which spreading to a vast extent over the hills and vallies beyond, even as far as Hawswater, darkened the front of Swarth-fell and several others, that impend over the first and second reach of Ullswater. Of the mountains, which tower above the glen of Patterdale, the highest are Harter's-fell, Kidstow-pike, and the ridge, called the High-street; a name, which reminded us of the German denomination, *Bergstrasse.*

The effect of a stormy evening upon the scenery was solemn. Clouds smoked along the fells, veiling them for a moment, and passing on to other summits; or sometimes they involved the lower steeps, leaving the tops unobscured and resembling islands in a distant ocean. The lake was dark and tempestuous, dashing the rocks with a strong foam. It was a scene worthy of the sublimity of Ossian, and brought to recollection some touches of his gloomy pencil. "When the storms of the mountains come, when the north lifts the waves on high, I sit by the sounding shore, &c."

A large

A large hawk, failing proudly in the air, and wheeling among the ftormy clouds, fuperior to the fhock of the guft, was the only animated object in the upward profpect. We were told, that the eagles had forfaken their aeries in this neighbourhood and in Borrowdale, and are fled to the ifle of Man; but one had been feen in Patterdale, the day before, which, not being at its full growth, could not have arrived from a great diftance.

We returned to our low-roofed habitation, where, as the wind fwept in hollow gufts along the mountains and ftrove againft our cafements, the crackling blaze of a wood fire lighted up the cheerfulnefs, which, fo long fince as Juvenal's time, has been allowed to arife from the contraft of eafe againft difficulty. *Suave mari magno, turbantibus æquora ventis;* and, however we might exclaim,

> —————" be my retreat
> Between the groaning foreft and the fhore,
> Beat by the boundlefs multitude of waves!"

it was pleafant to add,

> " Where ruddy fire and beaming tapers join
> To cheer the gloom."

BROUGHAM

BROUGHAM CASTLE.

THE next morning, we proceeded from Ullf-water along the vale of Emont, fo fweetly adorned by the woods and lawns of Dalemain, the feat of Mr. Haffel, whofe manfion is feen in the bottom. One of the moft magnificent profpects in the country is when this vale opens to that of Eden. The mountainous range of Crofs-fell fronted us, and its appearance, this day, was very ftriking, for the effect of autumnal light and fhade. The upper range, bright in funfhine, appeared to rife, like light clouds above the lower, which was involved in dark fhadow, fo that it was a confiderable time before the eye could detect the illufion. The effect of this was inexpreffibly interefting.

Within view of Emont bridge, which divides the counties of Cumberland and Weftmoreland, is that memorial of antient times, fo often defcribed under the name of Arthur's Round Table; a green circular fpot of forty paces diameter, inclofed by a dry ditch, and, beyond this, by a bank; each in fufficient prefervation to fhew exactly what has been its form. In the midft of the larger circle is another of only feven paces diameter. We have no means of adding to, or even of corroborating any of the well known conjectures, concerning the ufe of this rude and certainly very antient monument. Thofe not qualified to propofe decifions in this refpect may,

may, however, suffer themselves to believe, that the bank without the ditch and the enclosure within it were places for different classes of persons, interested as parties, or spectators, in some transactions, passing within the inner circle ; and that these, whether religious, civil, or military ceremonies, were rendered distinct and conspicuous, for the purpose of impressing them upon the memory of the spectators, at a time when memory and tradition were the only preservatives of history.

Passing a bridge, under which the Lowther, from winding and romantic banks, enters the vale of Eden, we ascended between the groves of Bird's Nest, or, as it is now called, Brougham Hall ; a white mansion, with battlements and gothic windows, having formerly a bird painted on the front. It is perched among woods, on the brow of a steep, but not lofty hill, and commands enchanting prospects over the vale. The winding Emont ; the ruins of Brougham Castle on a green knoll of Whinfield park, surrounded with old groves ; far beyond this, the highlands of Crofs-fell ; to the north, Carleton-hall, the handsome modern mansion of Mr. Wallace, amidst lawns of incomparable verdure and luxuriant woods falling from the heights ; further still, the mountain, town and beacon of Penrith ; these are the principal features of the rich landscape, spread before the eye from the summit of the hill, at Bird's Nest.

As we descended to Brougham Castle, about a mile further, its ruined masses of pale red stone, tufted with shrubs and plants, appeared between groves of fir, beach, oak and ash, amidst the

F f   broken

broken ground of Whinfield park, a quarter of a mile through which brought us to the ruin itself. It was guarded by a sturdy maftiff, worthy the office of porter to such a place, and a good effigy of the Sir Porter of a former age. Brougham Caftle, venerable for its well-certified antiquity and for the hoary maffes it now exhibits, is rendered more interefting by having been occafionally the refidence of the humane and generous Sir Philip Sydney; who had only to look from the windows of this once noble edifice to fee his own "Arcadia" fpreading on every fide. The landfcape probably awakened his imagination, for it was during a vifit here, that the greateft part of the work was written.

This edifice, once amongft the ftrongeft and moft important of the border fortreffes, is fuppofed to have been founded by the Romans; but the firft hiftorical record concerning it is dated in the time of William the Conqueror, who granted it to his nephew, Hugh de Albinois. His fucceffors held it, till 1170, when Hugh de Morville, one of the murderers of Thomas a Becket, forfeited it by his crime. Brougham was afterwards granted by King John to a grandfon of Hugh, Robert de Vipont, whofe grandfon again forfeited the eftate, which was, however, reftored to his daughters, one of whom marrying a De Clifford, it remained in this family, till a daughter of the celebrated Countefs of Pembroke gave it by marriage to that of the Tuftons, Earls of Thanet, in which it now remains.

This caftle has been thrice nearly demolifhed; firft by neglect, during the minority of Roger de Vipont, after which it was fufficiently reftored to
receive

receive James the Firſt, on his return from Scotland, in 1617; ſecondly, in the civil wars of Charles
the Firſt's time; and thirdly, in 1728, when great
part of the edifice was deliberately taken down,
and the materials ſold for one hundred pounds.
Some of the walls ſtill remaining are twelve feet
thick, and the places are viſible, in which the
maſſy gates were held to them by hinges and bolts
of uncommon ſize. A fuller proof of the many
ſacrifices of comfort and convenience, by which
the higheſt claſſes in former ages were glad to pur-
chaſe ſecurity, is very ſeldom afforded, than by
the three detached parts ſtill left of this edifice;
but they ſhew nothing of the magnificence and
gracefulneſs, which ſo often charm the eye in gothic ruins. Inſtead of theſe, they exhibit ſymptoms of the cruelties, by which their firſt lords
revenged upon others the wretchedneſs of the continual ſuſpicion felt by themſelves. Dungeons,
ſecret paſſages and heavy iron rings remain to hint
of unhappy wretches, who were, perhaps, reſcu-
ed only by death from theſe horrible engines of a
tyrant's will. The bones probably of ſuch victims
are laid beneath the damp earth of theſe vaults.

A young woman from a neighbouring farm-
houſe conducted us over broken banks, waſhed by
the Emont, to what had been the grand entrance
of the caſtle; a venerable gothic gateway, dark
and of great depth, paſſing under a ſquare tower,
finely ſhadowed by old elms. Above, are a croſs-
loop and two tier of ſmall pointed windows; no
battlements appear at the top; but four rows of
corbells, which probably once ſupported them,
now prop ſome tufts of antient thorn, that have
roots in their fractures.

As

As we paſſed under this long gateway, we looked into what is ſtill called the Keep, a ſmall vaulted room, receiving light only from loops in the outward wall. Near a large fire-place, yet entire, is a trap door leading to the dungeon below; and, in an oppoſite corner, a door-caſe to narrow ſtairs, that wind up the turret, where too, as well as in the vault, priſoners were probably ſecured. One almoſt ſaw the ſurly keeper deſcending through this door-caſe, and heard him rattle the keys of the chambers above, liſtening with indifference to the clank of chains and to the echo of that groan below, which ſeemed to rend the heart it burſt from.

This gloomy gateway, which had once ſounded with the trumpets and horſes of James the Firſt, when he viſited the Earl of Cumberland, this gateway, now ſerving only to ſhelter cattle from the ſtorm, opens, at length, to a graſſy knoll, with bold maſſes of the ruin ſcattered round it and a few old aſh trees, waving in the area. Through a fractured arch in the rampart ſome features in the ſcenery without appear to advantage; the Emont falling over a weir at ſome diſtance, with fulling-mills on the bank above; beyond, the paſtured ſlopes and woodlands of Carleton park, and Croſs-fell ſweeping the back-ground.

Of the three ruinous parts, that now remain of the edifice, one large ſquare maſs, near the tower and gateway, appears to have contained the principal apartments; the walls are of great height, and, though roofleſs, nearly entire. We entered what ſeemed to have been the great hall, now choaked with rubbiſh and weeds. It was intereſting to look upwards through the void, and trace by the many window-caſes, that appeared at diffe-

rent

rent heights in the walls, fomewhat of the plan of apartments, whofe floors and ceilings had long fince vanifhed; majeftic reliques, which fhewed, that here, as well as at Hardwick, the chief rooms had been in the fecond ftory. Door-cafes, that had opened to rooms without this building, with remains of paffages within the walls, were frequently feen, and, here and there, in a corner at a vaft height, fragments of a winding ftaircafe, appearing beyond the arch of a flender door-way.

We were tempted to enter a ruinous paffage below, formed in the great thicknefs of the walls; but it was foon loft in darknefs, and we were told that no perfon had ventured to explore the end of this, or of many fimilar paffages among the ruins, now the dens of ferpents and other venomous reptiles. It was probably a fecret way to the great dungeon, which may ftill be feen, underneath the hall; for the roof remains, though what was called the Sweating Pillar, from the dew, that was owing to its damp fituation and its feclufion from outward air, no longer fupports it. Large iron rings, faftened to the carved heads of animals, are ftill fhewn in the walls of this dungeon. Not a fingle loop-hole was left by the contriver of this hideous vault for the refrefhment of prifoners; yet were they infulted by fome difplay of gothic elegance, for the pillar already mentioned, fupporting the centre of the roof, fpread from thence into eight branches, which defcended the walls, and terminated at the floor in the heads, holding the iron rings.

The fecond mafs of the ruin, which, though at a confiderable diftance from the main building,
was

was formerly connected with it, shews the walls of many small chambers, with reliques of the passages and stairs, that led to them. But, perhaps, the only picturefque feature of the castle is the third detachment; a small tower finely shattered, having near its top a flourishing ash, growing from the solid walls, and overlooking what was once the moat. We mounted a perilous stair-case, of which many steps were gone, and others trembled to the preffure; then gained a turret, of which two sides were also fallen, and, at length, ascended to the whole magnificence and sublimity of the profpect.

To the east, spread nearly all the rich vale of Eden, terminated by the Stainmore hills and other highlands of Yorkfhire; to the north-east, the mountains of Crofs-fell bounded the long landfcape. The nearer grounds were Whinfield-park, broken, towards the Emont, into fhrubby steeps, where the deep red of the soil mingled with the verdure of foliage; part of Sir Michael le Fleming's woods rounding a hill on the oppofite bank, and, beyond, a wide extent of low land. To the south, fwelled the upland boundaries of Bamptonvale, with Lowther-woods, fhading the paftures and diftantly crowned by the fells of Hawfwater; more to the weft, Bird's Neft, " bofomed high in tufted trees;" at its foot, Lowther-bridge, and, a little further, the neat hamlet and bridge of Emont. In the low lands, ftill nearer, the Lowther and Emont united, the latter flowing in fhining circles among the woods and deep-green meadows of Carleton-park. Beyond, at a vaft diftance to the weft and north, rofe all the alps of all the lakes! an horizon fcarcely

to

to be equalled in England. Among thefe broken mountains, the fhaggy ridge of Saddleback was proudly pre-eminent; but one forked top of its rival Skiddaw peeped over its declining fide. Helvellyn, huge and mif-fhapen, towered above the fells of Ullfwater. The fun's rays, ftreaming from beneath a line of dark clouds, that overhung the weft, gave a tint of filvery light to all thefe alps, and reminded us of the firft exquifite appearance of the mountains, at Goodefberg, which, however, in grandeur and elegance of outline, united with picturefque richnefs, we have never feen equalled.

Of the walls around us every ledge, marking their many ftories, was emboffed with luxuriant vegetation. Tufts of the hawthorn feemed to grow from the folid ftone, and flender faplings of afh waved over the deferted door-cafes, where, at the transforming hour of twilight, the fuperftitious eye might miftake them for fpectres of fome early poffeffor of the caftle, reftlefs from guilt, or of fome fufferer perfevering from vengeance.

THE TOWN AND BEACON OF PENRITH.

HAVING purfued the road one mile further, for the purpofe of vifiting the tender memorial of pious affection, fo often defcribed under the name of Countefs' Pillar, we returned to Emont-bridge, and from thence reached Penrith, pronounced Peyrith, the moft fouthern town of Cumberland. So far off as the head of Ullfwater, fourteen miles, this is talked of as an important place, and looked to as the ftorehoufe of whatever is wanted more than the fields and lakes fupply. Thofe, who have lived chiefly in large towns, have to learn from the wants and dependencies of a people thinly fcattered, like the inhabitants of all mountainous regions, the great value of any places of mutual refort, however little diftinguifhed in the general view of a country. Penrith is fo often mentioned in the neighbourhood, that the firft appearance of it fomewhat difappointed us, becaufe we had not confidered how many ferious reafons thofe, who talked of it, might have for their eftimation, which fhould yet not at all relate to the qualities, that render places interefting to a traveller.

The town, confifting chiefly of old houfes, ftraggles along two fides of the high north road, and is built upon the fide of a mountain, that towers to great height above it, in fteep and heathy knolls, unfhaded by a fingle tree. Eminent, on the fummit of this mountain, ftands the old, folitary

litary beacon, vifible from almoft every part of
Penrith, which, notwithftanding its many fymptoms of antiquity, is not deficient of neatnefs.
The houfes are chiefly white, with door and window cafes of the red ftone found in the neighbourhood. Some of the fmaller have over their doors
dates of the latter end of the fixteenth century.
There are feveral inns, of which that called Old
Buchanan's was recommended to us, firft, by the
recollection, that Mr. Gray had mentioned it,
and afterwards by the comfort and civility we
found there.

Some traces of the Scottifh dialect and pronunciation appear as far fouth as Lancafhire; in Weftmoreland, they become ftronger; and, at Penrith, are extremely diftinct and general, ferving
for one among many peaceful indications of an
approach, once notified chiefly by preparations
for hoftility, or defence. Penrith is the moft
fouthern town in England at which the guinea
notes of the Scotch bank are in circulation. The
beacon, a fort of fquare tower, with a peaked
roof and openings at the fides, is a more perfect
inftance of the direful neceffities of paft ages, than
would be expected to remain in this. The circumftances are well known, which made fuch
watchfulnefs efpecially proper, at Penrith; and
the other traces of warlike habits and precautions,
whether appearing in records, or buildings, are
too numerous to be noticed in a fketch, which rather pretends to defcribe what the author has feen,
than to enumerate what has been difcovered by the
refearches of others. Dr. Burn's Hiftory contains
many curious particulars; and there are otherwife abundant and fatisfactory memorials, as to
the ftate of the debateable ground, the regulations

for

for fecuring paffes or fords, and even to the public maintenance of flough dogs, which were to
purfue aggreffors with hot-trod, as the inhabitants
were to follow them by horn and voice. Thefe
are all teftimonies, that among the many evils, inflicted upon countries by war, that, which is not
commonly thought of, is not the leaft; the public encouragement of a difpofition to violence, under the names of gallantry, or valour, which will
not ceafe exactly when it is publicly prohibited;
and the education of numerous bodies to habits of
fupplying their wants, not by conftant and ufeful
labour, but by fudden and deftructive exertions
of force. The miftake, by which courage is re-
leafed from all moral eftimation of the purpofes,
for which it is exerted, and is confidered to be
neceffarily and univerfally a good in itfelf, rather
than a means of good, or of evil, according to its
application, is among the fevereft misfortunes of
mankind. Tacitus has an admirable reproof of
it—

" Ubi manu agitur, modeftia et probitas nomina fupe-
rioris funt."

Though the fituation of Penrith, looking up
the vales of Eden and Emont, is remarkably
pleafant, that of the beacon above is infinitely
finer, commanding an horizon of at leaft an hundred miles diameter, filled with an endlefs variety
of beauty, greatnefs and fublimity. The view extends over Cumberland, parts of Weftmoreland,
Lancafhire, Yorkfhire, and a corner of Northumberland and Durham. On a clear day,
the

the Scottish high lands, beyond Solway Firth, may be diftinguished, like faint clouds, on the horizon and the fteeples of Carlifle are plainly vifible. All the intervening country, fpeckled with towns and villages, is fpread beneath the eye, and, nearly eighty miles to the eaftward, part of the Cheviot hills are traced, a dark line, binding the diftance and marking the feparation between earth and fky. On the plains towards Carlifle, the nearer ridges of Crofs-fell are feen to commence, and thence ftretch their barren fteeps thirty miles towards the eaft, where they difappear among the Stainmore-hills and the huge moorlands of York-fhire, that clofe up the long landfcape of the vale of Eden. Among thefe, the broken lines of Ingleborough ftart above all the broader ones of the moors, and that mountain ftill proclaims itfelf fovereign of the Yorkfhire heights.

Southward, rife the wonders of Weftmoreland, Shapfells, ridge over ridge, the nearer pikes of Hawfwater, and then the mountains of Ullfwater, Helvellyn pre-eminent amongft them, diftinguifhed by the grandeur-and boldnefs of their outline, as well as the variety of their fhapes; fome hugely fwelling, fome afpiring in clufters of alpine points, and fome broken into fhaggy ridges. The fky, weft-ward from hence and far to the north, difplays a vifion of Alps, Saddleback fpreading towards Kefwick its long fhattered ridge, and one top of Skiddaw peering beyond it; but the others of this diftrict are inferior in grandeur to the fells of Ullfwater, more broken into points, and with lefs of contraft in their forms. Behind Saddle-back, the fkirts of Skiddaw fpread themfelves, and thence low hills fhelve into the plains of

Cumberland,

Cumberland, that extend to Whitehaven; the only level line in the scope of this vast horizon. The scenery nearer to the eye exhibited cultivation in its richest state, varied with pastoral and sylvan beauty; landscapes embellished by the elegancies of art, and rendered venerable by the ruins of time. In the vale of Eden, Carleton-hall, flourishing under the hand of careful attention, and Bird's Nest, luxuriant in its spiry woods, opposed their cheerful beauties to the neglected walls of Brougham Castle, once the terror, and, even in ruins, the pride of the scene, now half-shrouded in its melancholy grove. These objects were lighted up by partial gleams of sunshine, which, as they fled along the valley, gave magical effect to all they touched.

The other vales in the home prospect were those of Bampton and Emont; the first open and gentle, shaded by the gradual woods of Lowther-park; the last closer and more romantic, withdrawing in many a lingering bend towards Ullf-water, where it is closed by the pyramidal Dun-mallard, but not before a gleam of the lake is suffered to appear beyond the dark base of the hill. At the nearer end of the vale, and immediately under the eye, the venerable ruins of Penrith Castle crest a round green hill. These are of pale-red stone, and stand in detached masses; but have little that is picturesque in their appearance, time having spared neither tower, or gateway, and not a single tree giving shade, or force, to the shattered walls. The ground about the castle is broken into grassy knolls, and only cattle wander over the desolated tract. Time has also obscured the name of the founder; but it is
known,

known, that the main building was repaired, and some addition made to it by Richard the Third, when Duke of Gloucefter, who lived here, for five years, in his office of fheriff of Cumberland, promoting the York intereft by artful hofpitalities, and endeavouring to ftrike terror into the Lancaftrians. Among the ruins is a fubterraneous paffage, leading to a houfe in Penrith, above three hundred yards diftant, called Dockwray Caftle. The town lies between the fortrefs and the Beaconhill, fpreading prettily along the fkirts of the mountain, with its many roofs of blue flate, among which the church rifes near a dark grove.

Penrith, from the latter end of the laft century, till lately, when it was purchafed by the Duke of Devonfhire, belonged to the family of Portland, to whom it was given by William the Third; probably inftead of the manors in Wales, which it was one of William's few faulty defigns to have given to his favourite companion, had not Parliament remonftrated, and informed him, that the Crown could not alienate the territories of the Principality. The church, a building of red ftone, unufually well difpofed in the interior, is a vicarage of fmall endowment; but the value of money in this part of the kingdom is fo high, that the merit of independence, a merit and a happinefs which fhould always belong to clergymen, is attainable by the poffeffors of very moderate incomes. What is called the Giant's Grave in the church-yard is a narrow fpot, inclofed, to the length of fourteen or fifteen feet, by rows of low ftones, at the fides, and, at the ends, by two pillars, now flender, but apparently worn by the weather from a greater thicknefs.

The

The height of thefe is eleven or twelve feet; and all the ftones, whether in the borders, at the fides, or in thefe pillars, bear traces of rude carving, which fhew, at leaft, that the monument muft have been thought very important by thofe that raifed it, 'fince the fingularity of its fize was not held a fufficient diftinction. We pored intently over thefe traces, though certainly without the hope of difcovering any thing not known to the eminent antiquarians, who have confeffed their ignorance concerning the origin of them.

FROM PENRITH TO KESWICK.

THE Grayftock road, which we took for the fir five or fix miles, is uninterefting, and offers nothing worthy of attention, before the approach to the caftle, the feat of the Duke of Norfolk. The appearance of this from the road is good; a gray building, with gothic towers, feated in a valley among lawns and woods, that ftretch, with great pomp of fhade, to gently-rifing hills. Behind thefe, Saddleback, huge, gray and barren, rifes with all its ridgy lines; a grand and fimple background, giving exquifite effect to the dark woods below. Such is the height of the mountain, that, though eight or ten miles off, it appeared, as we approached the caftle, almoft to impend over it. Southward from Saddleback, a multitude of pointed fummits crowd the horizon; and it is moft
interefting,

interefting, after leaving Grayftock, to obferve their changing attitudes, as you advance, and the gradual difclofure of their larger features. Perhaps a fudden difplay of the fublimeft fcenery, however full, imparts lefs emotion, than a gradually increafing view of it; when expectation takes the higheft tone, and imagination finifhes the fketch.

About two miles beyond Grayftock, the moorlands commence, and, as far as fimple greatnefs conftitutes fublimity, this was, indeed, a fublime profpect; lefs fo only than that from Shapfell itfelf, where the mountains are not fo varied in their forms and are plainer in their grandeur. We were on a vaft plain, if plain that may be called, which fwells into long undulations, furrounded by an amphitheatre of heathy mountains, that feem to have been fhook by fome grand convulfion of the earth, and tumbled around in all fhapes. Not a tree, a hedge, and feldom even a ftone wall, broke the grandeur of their lines; what was not heath was only rock and gray crags; and a fhepherd's hut, or his flocks, browfing on the fteep fides of the fells, or in the narrow vallies, that opened diftantly, was all that diverfified the vaft fcene. Saddleback fpread his fkirts weftward along the plain, and then reared himfelf in terrible and lonely majefty. In the long perfpective beyond, were the crowding points of the fells round Kefwick, Borrowdale, and the vales of St. John and Leyberthwaite, ftretching awa to thofe near Grafmere. The weather was in folemn harmony with the fcenery; long fhadows fwept over the hills, followed by gleaming lights. Tempeftuous gufts alone broke the filence. Now and then, the fun's rays had a fingular appearance; pouring,

pouring, from under clouds, between the tops of fells into some deep vale at a distance, as into a focus.

This is the very region, which the wild fancy of a poet, like Shakespeare, would people with witches, and shew them at their incantations, calling spirits from the clouds and spectres from the earth.

On the now lonely plains of this vast amphitheatre, the Romans had two camps, and their Eagle spread its wings over a scene worthy of its own soarings. The lines of these encampments may still be traced on that part of the plain, called Hutton Moor, to the north of the high road; and over its whole extent towards Kefwick a Roman way has been discovered. Funereal urns have also been dug up here, and an altar of Roman form, but with the inscription obliterated.

Nearer Saddleback, we perceived crags and heath mingled on its precipices, and its base broken into a little world of mountains, green with cultivation. White farms, each with its grove to shelter it from the descending gusts, corn and pastures of the brightest verdure enlivened the skirts of the mountain all round, climbing towards the dark heath and crags, or spreading downwards into the vale of Threlkeld, where the slender Lowther shews his shining stream.

Leaving Hutton Moor, the road soon began to ascend the skirts of Saddleback, and passed between green hillocks, where cattle appeared most elegantly in the mountain scene, under the crags, or sipping at the clear stream, that gushed from the rocks, and wound to the
vale

vale below. Such cryſtal rivulets croſſed our way continually, as we roſe upon the ſide of Saddleback, which towers abruptly on the right, and, on the left, ſinks as ſuddenly into the vale of Threlkeld, with precipices ſometimes little leſs than tremendous. This mountain is the northern boundary of the vale in its whole length to Keſwick, the points of whoſe fells cloſe the perſpective. Rocky heights guard it to the ſouth. The valley between is green, without wood, and, with much that is grand, has little beautiful, till near its concluſion; where, more fertile and ſtill more wild, it divides into three narrower vallies, two of which diſcloſe ſcenes of ſuch ſublime ſeverity as even our long view of Saddleback had not prepared us to expect.

The firſt of theſe is the vale of St. John, a narrow, cultivated ſpot, lying in the boſom of tremendous rocks, that impend over it in maſſes of gray crag, and often reſemble the ruins of caſtles. Theſe rocks are overlooked by ſtill more awful mountains, that fall in abrupt lines, and cloſe up the viſta, except where they alſo are commanded by the vaſt top of Helvellyn. On every ſide, are images of deſolation and ſtupendous greatneſs, cloſing upon a narrow line of paſtoral richneſs; a picture of verdant beauty, ſeen through a frame of rock work. It is between the cliffs of Threlkeld-fell and the purple ridge of Nadale-fell, that this vale ſeems to repoſe in its moſt ſilent and perfect peace. No village and ſcarcely a cottage diſturbs its retirement. The flocks, that feed at the feet of the cliffs, and the ſteps of a ſhepherd, " in this office of his mountain watch," are all, that haunt the " dark ſequeſtered nook."

G g   The

The vale of Nadale runs parallel with that of St. John, from which it is feparated by the ridge of Nadale-fell, and has the fame ftyle of character, exeept that it is terminated by a well wooded mountain. Beyond this, the perfpective is over looked by the fells, that terminate · the vale of St. John.

The third valley, opening from the head of Threlkeld, winds along the feet of Saddleback and Skiddaw to Kefwick, the approach to which, with all its world of rocky fummits, the lake being ftill funk below the light, is fublime beyond the power of defcription. Within three miles of Kefwick, Skiddaw unfolds itfelf, clofe behind Saddleback; their fkirts unite, but the former is lefs huge and of very different form from the laft; being more pointed and feldomer broken into precipices, it darts upward with a vaft fweep into three fpiry fummits, two of which only are feen from this road, and fhews fides dark with heath and little varied with rock. Such is its afpect from the Penrith road; from other ftations its attitude, fhape and colouring are very different, though its alpine terminations are always vifible.

Threlkeld itfelf is a fmall village, about thirteen miles from Penrith, with a very humble inn, at which thofe, who have paffed the bleak fides of Saddleback, and thofe, who are entering upon them, may rejoice to reft. We had been blown about, for fome hours, in an open chaife, and hoped for more refrefhment than . could be obtained; but had the fatisfaction, which was, indeed, general in thefe regions, of obferving the good intentions, amounting almoft to kindnefs,

nefs, of the cottagers towards their guefts. They have nearly always fome fare, which lefs civility than theirs might render acceptable; and the hearth blazes in their clean fanded parlours, within two minutes after you enter them. Some fort of preferved fruit is conftantly ferved after the repaft, with cream, an innocent luxury, for which no animal has died.

It is not only from thofe, who are to gain by ftrangers, but from almoft every perfon, accidentally accofted by a queftion, that this favourable opinion will be formed, as to the kind and frank manners of the people. We were continually remarking, between Lancafter and Kefwick, that fevere as the winter might be in thefe diftrics, from the early fymptoms of it then apparent, the conduct of the people would render it fcarcely unpleafant to take the fame journey in the depths of December.

In thefe countries, the farms are, for the moft part, fmall, and the farmers and their children work in the fame fields with their fervants. Their families have thus no opportunities of temporary infight into the fociety, and luxuries of the great, and have none of thofe miferies, which dejected vanity and multiplied wifhes inflict upon the purfuers of the higher ranks. They are alfo without the bafenefs, which fuch purfuers ufually have, of becoming abject before perfons of one clafs, that by the authority of an apparent connection with them, they may be infolent to thofe of another; and are free from the effential humiliation of fhewing, by a general and undiftinguifhing admiration of all perfons richer than themfelves, that the original diftinctions between virtue and vice

have

have been erafed from their minds by the habit of comparing the high and the low.

The true confcionfnefs of independence, which labour and an ignorance of the vain appendages, falfely called luxuries, give to the inhabitants of thefe diftricts, is probably the caufe of the fupe-riority, perceived by ftrangers in their tempers and manners, over thofe of perfons, apparently better circumftanced. They have no remem-brance of flights, to be revenged by infults; no hopes from fervility, nor irritation from the defire of unattainable diftinctions. Where, on the con-trary, the encouragement of artificial wants has produced dependence, and mingled with the fic-titious appearance of wealth many of the moft real evils of poverty, the benevolence of the temper flies with the fimplicity of the mind. There is, perhaps, not a more odious profpect of human fociety, than where an oftentatious, ma-nœuvring and corrupted peafantry, taking thofe, who induced them to crimes, for the models of their morality, mimic the vices, to which they were not born, and attempt the coarfe covering of cunning and infolence for practices, which it is a fcience and frequently an object of education to conceal by flagitious elegancies. Such perfons form in the country a bad copy of the worft London fociety; the vices, without the intelli-gence, and without the affuaging virtues.

DRUIDICAL

DRUIDICAL MONUMENT.

AFTER paffing the very fmall, but neatly furnifhed church of Threlkeld, the condition of which may be one teftimony to the worthinefs of the neighbourhood, and rifing beyond the vales before defcribed, we came to the brow of a hill, called Caftle Rigg, on which, to the left of the road, are the remains of one of thofe circular monuments, which, by general confent, are called Druids' Temples. This is formed of thirty-feven ftones, placed in a circle of about twenty-eight yards diameter, the largeft being not lefs than feven feet and a half high, which is double the height of the others. At the eaftern part of this circle, and within it, fmaller ftones are arranged in an oblong of about feven yards long, and, at the greateft breadth, four yards wide. Many of thofe round the circle appear to have fallen and now remain at unequal diftances, of which the greateft is towards the north.

Whether our judgment was influenced by the authority of a Druid's choice, or that the place itfelf commanded the opinion, we thought this fituation the moft feverely grand of any hitherto paffed. There is, perhaps, not a fingle object in the fcene, that interrupts the folemn tone of feeling, impreffed by its general characters of profound folitude, greatnefs and awful wildnefs. Caftle Rigg is the central point of three vallies, that dart immediately under it from the eye, and whofe mountains form part of an amphitheatre,
which

which is completed by thofe of Derwentwater, in the weft, and by the precipices of Skiddaw and Saddleback, clofe on the north. The hue, which pervades all thefe mountains, is that of dark heath, or rock; they are thrown into every form and direction, that Fancy would fuggeft, and are at that diftance, which allows all their grandeur to prevail; nearer than the high lands, that furround Hutton-Moor, and further removed than the fells in the fcenery of Ullfwater.

To the fouth open the rocks, that difclofe the vale of St. John, whofe verdant beauty bears no proportion to its fublimity; to the weft, are piled the fhattered and fantaftic points of Derwentwater; to the north, Skiddaw, with its double top, refembling a volcano, the cloudy vapours afcending from its higheft point, like fmoke, and fometimes rolling in wreaths down its fides; and to the eaft, the vale of Threlkeld, fpreading green round the bafe of Saddleback, its vaft fide-fkreen, opened to the moorlands, beyond which the ridge of Crofs-fell appeared; its dignity now diminifhed by diftance. This point then is furrounded by the three grand rivals of Cumberland; huge Helvellyn, fpreading Saddleback and fpiry Skiddaw.

Such feclufion and fublimity were, indeed, well fuited to the deep and wild myfteries of the Druids. Here, at moon-light, every Druid, fummoned by that terrible horn, never awakened but upon high occafions, and defcending from his mountain, or fecret cave, might affemble without intrution from one facrilegious footftep, and celebrate a midnight feftival by a favage facrifice—

" rites

- - - - - " rites of fuch ftrange potency
As, done in open day, would dim the fun,
Tho' thron'd in noontide brightnefs."

CARACTACUS.

Here, too, the Bards,

" Rob'd in their flowing vefts of innocent white,
Defcend, with harps, that glitter to the moon,
Hymning immortal ftrains. The fpirits of air,
Of earth, of water, nay of heav'n itfelf,
Do liften to their lay ; and oft, 'tis faid,
In vifible fhapes, dance they a magic round
To the high minftrelfy."

As we defcended the fteep mountain to Kefwick, the romantic fells round the lake opened
finely, but the lake itfelf was concealed, deep
in its rocky cauldron. We faw them under the
laft glow of fun-fet, the upper rays producing a
mifty purple glory between the dark tops of
Cawfey-pikes and the bending peaks of Thornthwaite fells. Soon after, the fun having fet to
the vale of Kefwick, there appeared, beyond
breaks in its weftern mountains, the rocks of
other vallies, ftill lighted up by a purple gleam,
and receiving ftrong rays on fhaggy points, to
which their receffes gave foft and fhadowy contraft. But the magical effect of thefe funfhine
rocks, oppofed to the darknefs of the nearer valley, can fcarcely be imagined.

Still as we defcended, the lake of Derwentwater was fcreened from our view ; but the rich
level of three miles wide, that fpreads between
it and Baffenthwaite-water in the fame vale, lay,
like a map, beneath us, chequered with groves

and

and cottages, with enclofures of corn and meadows, and adorned by the pretty village of Crofthwaite, its neat white church confpicuous among trees. The fantaftic fells of Derwentwater bordered this repofing landfcape, on the weft, and the mighty Skiddaw rofe over it, on the eaft, concealing the lake of Baffenthwaite.

The hollow dafhings of the Greta, in its rocky channel, at the foot of Skiddaw, and in one of the moft wizard little glens that nature ever fancied, were heard long before we looked down its fteep woody bank, and faw it winding away, from clofe inacceffible chafms, to the vale of Kefwick, corn and meadows fpread at the top of the left bank, and the crags of Skiddaw fcowling over it, on the right.

At length, we had a glimpfe of the north end of Derwentwater, and foon after entered Kefwick, a fmall place of ftone houfes, lying at the foot of Caftle Rigg, near Skiddaw, and about a quarter of a mile from the lake, which, however, is not feen from the town.

We were impatient to view this celebrated lake, and immediately walked down to Crowpark, a green eminence at its northern end, whence it is generally allowed to appear to great advantage. Expectation had been raifed too high: Shall we own our difappointment? Prepared for fomething more than we had already feen, by what has been fo eloquently faid of it, by the view of its vaft neighbourhood and the grandeur of its approach, the lake itfelf looked infignificant ; and, however rude, or awful, its nearer rocks might have appeared, if feen unexpectedly,

pectedly, they were not in general fo vaft, or fo boldly outlined, as to retain a character of fublimity from comparifon. Oppofed to the fimple majefty of Ullfwater, the lake of Derwent was fcarcely interefting. Something muft, indeed, be attributed to the force of firft impreffions; but, with all allowance for this, Ullfwater muft ftill retain an high pre-eminence for grandeur and fublimity.

Derwentwater, however, when more minutely viewed, has peculiar charms both for beauty and wildnefs, and as the emotions, excited by difappointed expectation, began to fubfide, we became fenfible of them. It feems to be nearly of a round form, and the whole is feen at one glance, expanding within an amphitheatre of mountains, rocky, but not vaft, broken into many fantaftic fhapes, peaked, fplintered, impending, fometimes pyramidal, opening by narrow vallies to the view of rocks, that rife immediately beyond and are again overlooked by others. The precipices feldom overfhoot the water, but are arranged at fome diftance, and the fhores fwell with woody eminences, or fink into green, paftoral margins. Maffes of wood alfo frequently appear among the cliffs, feathering them to their fummits, and a white cottage fometimes peeps from out their fkirts, feated on the fmooth knoll of a pafture, projecting to the lake, and looks fo exquifitely picturefque, as to feem placed there purpofely to adorn it. The lake in return faithfully reflects the whole picture, and fo even and brilliantly tranflucent is its furface, that it rather heightens, than obfcures the colouring. Its mild bofom is fpotted by four fmall iflands, of which thofe called Lords' and St. Herbert's are well wooded;

and

and adorn the fcene, but another is deformed by buildings, ftuck over it, like figures upon a twelfth-cake.

Beyond the head of the lake, and at a direct diftance of three or four miles from Crow-park, the pafs of Borrowdale opens, guarded by two piles of rock, the boldeft in the fcene, overlooked by many rocky points, and, beyond all, by rude mountain tops which come partially and in glimpfes to the view. Among the moft ftriking features of the eaftern fhore are the woody cliffs of Lowdore; then, nearer to the eye, Wallow-crags, a title ufed here as well as at Hawfwater, of dark brown rock, loofely impending; nearer ftill, Caftle-nill, pyramidal and richly wooded to its point, the moft luxuriant feature of the land-fcape. Cawfey-pike, one of the moft remarkable rocks of the weftern fhore, has its ridge fcolloped into points as if with a row of corbells.

The cultivated vale of Newland flopes upward from the lake between thefe and Thornthwaite fells. Northward, beyond Crow-park, rifes Skid-daw; at its bafe commences the beautiful level, that fpreads to Baffenthwaite-water, where the rocks in the weft fide of the perfpective foon begin to foiten, and the vale becomes open and cheerful.

Such is the outline of Derwentwater, which has a much greater proportion of beauty, than Ullfwater, but neither its dignity, nor grandeur. Its fells, broken into fmaller maffes, do not fwell, or ftart, into fuch bold lines as thofe of Ullfwa-ter; nor does the fize of the lake accord with the general importance of the rocky vale; in which

which it lies. The water is too fmall for its accompaniments; and its form, being round and
feen entirely at once, leaves nothing for expectation to purfue, beyond the ftretching promontory,
or fancy to transform within the gloom and obfcurity of the receding fell; and thus it lofes an
ample fource of the fublime. The greateft breadth
from eaft to weft is not more than three miles.
It is not large enough to occupy the eye, and it
is not fo hidden as to have the affiftance of the
imagination in making it appear large. The
beauty of its banks alfo, contending with the
wildnefs of its rocks, gives oppofite impreffions
to the mind, and the force of each is, perhaps,
deftroyed by the admiffion of the other. Sublimity can fcarcely exift, without fimplicity; and
even grandeur lofes much of its elevating effect,
when united with a confiderable portion of
beauty; then defcending to become magnificence. The effect of fimplicity in affifting that
high tone of mind, produced by the fublime, is
demonftrated by the fcenery of Ullfwater, where
very feldom a difcordant object obtrudes over
the courfe of thought, and jars upon the feelings.

But it is much pleafanter to admire than to
examine, and in Derwentwater is abundant fubject for admiration, though not of fo high a character as that, which attends Ullfwater. The
foft undulations of its fhores, the mingled wood
and pafture, that paint them, the brilliant purity
of the water, that gives back every landfcape on
its bank, and frequently with heightened colouring, the fantaftic wildnefs of the rocks and the
magnificence of the amphitheatre they form;
thefe are circumftances, the view of which excites

emotions

emotions of fweet, though tranquil admiration, foftening the mind to tendernefs, rather than elevating it to fublimity. We firſt faw the whole beneath fuch ſober hues as prevailed when

> " the gray hooded Even,
> Like a fad votariſt, in Palmer's weed,
> Rofe from the hindmoſt wheels of Phœbus' wain."

The wildnefs, feclufion, and magical beauty of this vale, feem, indeed, to render it the very abode for Milton's Comus, " deep ſkilled in all his mother's witcheries;" and, while we furvey its fantaſtic features, we are almoſt tempted to fuppofe, that he has hurled his

> " dazzling ſpells into the air,
> Of power to cheat the eye with blear illufion
> And give it falfe prefentments."

Nay more, to believe

> " All the fage poets, taught by th' heavenly mufe,
> Storied of old, in high immortal verfe,
> Of dire chimæras and enchanted iſles;

and to fancy we hear from among the woody cliffs, near the ſhore,

> " the found
> Of riot and ill manag'd merriment,"

fucceeded

fucceeded by fuch ftrains as oft

" in pleafing flumbers lull the fenfe,
And, in fweet madnefs, rob it of itfelf."

SKIDDAW.

ON the following morning, having engaged a guide, and with horfes accuftomed to the labour, we began to afcend this tremendous mountain by a way, which makes the fummit five miles from Kefwick. Paffing through bowery lanes, luxuriant with mountain afh, holly, and a variety of beautiful fhrubs, to a broad, open common, a road led us to the foot of Latrigg, or, as it is called by the country people, Skiddaw's Cub, a large round hill, covered with heath, turf, and browfing fheep. A narrow path now wound along fteep green precipices, the beauty of which prevented what danger there was from being perceived. Derwentwater was concealed by others that rofe above them, but that part of the vale of Kefwick, which feparates the two lakes, and fpreads a rich level of three miles, was immediately below; Croffthwaite church, nearly in the centre,

centre, with the white vicarage, rifing among trees. More under fhelter of Skiddaw, where the vale fpreads into a fweet retired nook, lay the houfe and grounds of Dr. Brownrigg.

Beyond the level, opened a glimpfe of Baffenthwaite water; a lake, which may be called elegant, bounded, on one fide, by well-wooded rocks, and, on the other, by Skiddaw.

Soon after, we rofe above the fteeps, which had concealed Derwentwater, and it appeared, with all its enamelled banks, funk deep amidft a chaos of mountains, and furrounded by ranges of fells, not vifible from below. On the other hand, the more cheerful lake of Baffenthwaite expanded at its entire length. Having gazed a while on this magnificent fcene, we purfued the path, and foon after reached the brink of a chafm, on the oppofite fide of which wound our future track; for the afcent is here in an acutely zig-zag direction. The horfes carefully picked their fteps along the narrow precipice, and turned the angle, that led them to the oppofite fide.

At length, as we afcended, Derwentwater dwindled on the eye to the fmallnefs of a pond, while the grandeur of its amphitheatre was increafed by new ranges of dark mountains, no longer individually great, but fo from accumulation; a fcenery to give ideas of the breaking up of a world. Other precipices foon hid it again, but Baffenthwaite continued to fpread immediately below us, till we turned into the heart of Skiddaw, and were enclofed by its fteeps. We had

had now loft all track even of the flocks, that were fcattered over thefe tremendous wilds. The guide conducted us by many curvings among the heathy hills and hollows of the mountain; but the afcents were fuch, that the horfes panted in the floweft walk, and it was neceffary to let them reft every fix or feven minutes. An opening to the fouth, at length, fhewed the whole plan of the narrow vales of St. John and of Nadale, feparated by the dark ridge of rock, called St. John's-rigg, with each its fmall line of verdure at the bottom, and bounded by enormous gray fells, which we were, however, now high enough to overlook.

A white fpeck, on the top of St. John's rigg, was pointed out by the guide to be a chapel of eafe to Kefwick, which has no lefs than five fuch, fcattered among the fells. From this chapel, dedicated to St. John, the rock and the vale have received their name, and our guide told us, that Nadale was frequently known by the fame title.

Leaving this view, the mountain foon again fhut out all profpect, but of its own vallies and precipices, covered with various fhades of turf and mofs, and with heath, of which a dull purple was the prevailing hue. Not a tree, or bufh appeared on Skiddaw, nor even a ftone wall any where broke the fimple greatnefs of its lines. Sometimes, we looked into tremendous chafms, where the torrent, heard roaring long before it was feen, had worked itfelf a deep channel, and fell from ledge to ledge, foaming and fhining amidft the dark rock. Thefe ftreams are fublime from the length and precipitancy of their courfe, which, hurrying the fight with them into

the

the abyfs, act, as it were, in fympathy upon the
nerves, and, to fave ourfelves from following,
we recoil from the view with involuntary horror.
Of fuch, however, we faw only two, and thofe
by fome departure from the ufual courfe up the
mountain; but every where met gufhing fprings,
till we were within two miles of the fummit,
when our guide added to the rum in his bottle
what he faid was the laft water we fhould find in
our afcent.

The air now became very thin, and the fteeps
ftill more difficult of afcent; but it was often delightful to look down into the green hollows of
the mountain, among paftoral fcenes, that wanted
only fome mixture of wood to render them enchanting.

About a mile from the fummit, the way was,
indeed, dreadfully fublime, laying, for nearly
half a mile, along the ledge of a precipice, that
paffed, with a fwift defcent, for probably near a
mile, into a glen within the heart of Skiddaw;
and not a bufh, or a hillock interrupted its vaft
length, or, by offering a midway check in the
defcent, diminifhed the fear it infpired. The
ridgy fteeps of Saddleback formed the oppofite
boundary of the glen, and, though really at a
confiderable diftance, had, from the height of
the two mountains, fuch an appearance of nearnefs, that it almoft feemed as if we could fpring
to its fide. How much too did fimplicity increafe the fublime of this fcenery, in which nothing but mountain, heath and fky appeared.

But our fituation was too critical, or too unufual, to permit the juft impreffions of fuch
sublimity.

fublimity. The hill rofe fo clofely above the precipice as fcarcely to allow a ledge wide enough for a fingle horfe. We followed the guide in filence, and, till we regained the more open wild, had no leifure for exclamation. After this, the afcent appeared eafy and fecure, and we were bold enough to wonder, that the fteeps near the beginning of the mountain had excited any anxiety.

At length, paffing the fkirts of the two points of Skiddaw, which are neareft to Derwentwater, we approached the third and loftieft, and then perceived, that their fteep fides, together with the ridges, which connect them, were entirely covered near the fummits with a whitifh fhivered flate, which threatens to flide down them with every guft of wind. The broken ftate of this flate makes the prefent fummits feem like the ruins of others; a circumftance as extraordinary in appearance as difficult to be accounted for.

The ridge, on which we paffed from the neighbourhood of the fecond fummit to the third, was narrow, and the eye reached, on each fide, down the whole extent of the mountain, following, on the left, the rocky precipices, that impend over the lake of Baffenthwaite, and looking, on the right, into the glens of Saddleback, far, far below. But the profpects, that burft upon us from every part of the vaft horizon, when we had gained the fummit, were fuch as we had fcarcely dared to hope for, and muft now rather venture to enumerate, than to defcribe.

We ftood on a pinnacle, commanding the whole dome of the fky. The profpects below,

each

each of which had been before considered separately as a great scene, were now miniature parts of the immense landscape. To the north, lay, like a map, the vast tract of low country, which extends between Baffenthwaite and the Irish Channel, marked with the silver circles of the river Derwent, in its progress from the lake. Whitehaven and its white coast were distinctly seen, and Cockermouth seemed almost under the eye. A long blackish line, more to the west, resembling a faintly formed cloud, was said by the guide to be the Isle of Man, who, however, had the honesty to confess, that the mountains of Down in Ireland, which have been sometimes thought visible, had never been seen by him in the clearest weather.

Bounding the low country to the north, the wide Solway Firth, with its indented shores, looked like a gray horizon, and the double range of Scottish mountains, seen dimly through mist beyond, like lines of dark clouds above it. The Solway appeared surprisingly near us, though at fifty miles distance, and the guide said, that, on a bright day, its shipping could plainly be discerned. Nearly in the north, the heights seemed to soften into plains, for no object was there visible through the obscurity, that had begun to draw over the furthest distance; but, towards the east, they appeared to swell again, and what we were told were the Cheviot hills dawned feebly beyond Northumberland. We now spanned the narrowest part of England, looking from the Irish Channel, on one side, to the German Ocean, on the other, which latter was, however, so far off as to be discernible only like a mist.

Nearer

Nearer than the county of Durham, ſtretched
the ridge of Croſs-fell, and an indiſtinét multitude
of the Weſtmoreland and Yorkſhire highlands,
whoſe lines diſappeared behind Saddleback, now
evidently pre-eminent over Skiddaw, ſo much ſo
as to exclude many a height beyond it. Paſſing
this mountain in our courſe to the ſouth, we ſaw,
immediately below, the fells round Derwentwater, the lake itſelf remaining ſtill concealed in their
deep rocky boſom. Southward and weſtward, the
whole proſpeét was a " turbulent chaos of dark
mountains." All individual dignity was now loſt
in the immenſity of the whole, and every variety
of charaéter was overpowered by that of aſtoniſhing and gloomy grandeur.

Over the fells of Borrowdale, and far to the
ſouth, the northern end of Windermere appeared,
like a wreath of gray ſmoke, that ſpreads along
the mountain's ſide. More ſouthward ſtill, and
beyond all the fells of the lakes, Lancaſter ſands
extended to the faintly ſeen waters of the ſea.
Then to the weſt, Duddon ſands gleamed in a
long line among the fells of High Furneſs. Immediately under the eye, lay Baſſenthwaite, ſurrounded by many ranges of mountains, inviſible
from below, We overlooked all theſe dark mountains, and ſaw green cultivated vales over the tops
of lofty rocks, and other mountains over theſe
vales in many ridges, whilſt innumerable narrow
glens were traced in all their windings and ſeen
uniting behind the hills with others, that alſo
ſloped upwards from the lake.

The air on this ſummit was boiſterous, intenſe-
ly cold and difficult to be inſpired, though the
day was below warm and ſerene. It was dreadful
to look down from nearly the brink of the point,
on which we ſtood, upon the lake of Baſſenth-

waite and over a fharp and feparated ridge of rocks,
that from below appeared of tremendous height,
but now feemed not to reach half way up Skiddaw; it was almoft as if

> " the precipitation might down ftretch
> Below the beam of fight."

Under the lee of an heaped up pile of flates,
formed by the cuftomary contribution of one from
every vifitor, we found an old man fheltered, whom
we took to be a fhepherd, but afterwards learned
was a farmer and, as the people in this neighbourhood fay, a ' ftatefman;' that is, had land of his
own. He was a native and ftill an inhabitant of
an adjoining vale; but, fo laborious is the enterprife reckoned, that, though he had paffed his life
within view of the mountain, this was his firft afcent. He defcended with us, for part of our way,
and then wound off towards his own valley, ftalking amidft the wild fcenery, his large figure
wrapt in a dark cloak and his fteps occafionally
affifted by a long iron pronged pike, with which
he had pointed out diftant objects.

In the defcent, it was interefting to obferve each
mountain below gradually re-affuming its dignity,
the two lakes expanding into fpacious furfaces, the
many little vallies, that floped upwards from their
margins, recovering their variegated tints of cultivation, the cattle again appearing in the meadows, and the woody promontories changing
from fmooth patches of fhade into richly tufted
fummits. At about a mile from the top, a great
difference was perceptible in the climate, which
became

became comparatively warm, and the summer hum of bees was again heard among the purple heath.

We reached Keswick, about four o'clock, after five hours passed in this excursion, in which the care of our guide greatly lessened the notion of danger. Why should we think it trivial to attempt some service towards this poor man? We have reason to think, that whoever employs, at Keswick, a guide of the name of Doncaster, will assist him in supporting an aged parent.

BASSENTHWAITE WATER.

IN a gray autumnal morning, we rode out along the western bank of Bassenthwaite to Ouse Bridge, under which the river Derwent, after passing through the lake, takes its course towards the Sea. The road on this side, being impassable by carriages, is seldom visited, but it is interesting for being opposed to Skiddaw, which rises in new attitudes over the opposite bank. Beyond the land, that separates the two lakes, the road runs high along the sides of hills and sometimes at the feet of tremendous fells, one of which rises almost spirally over it, shewing a surface of slates, shivered from top to bottom. Further on, the heights gradually soften from horror into mild and graceful beauty, opening distantly to the cheerful country, that spreads towards Whitehaven; but the road soon immerges among woods, which allow only partial views of the opposite shore, ini-

mitably

mitably beautiful with copfes, green lawns and pastures, with gently fweeping promontories and bays, that receive the lake to their full brims.

From the houfe at Oufe Bridge the profpect is exquifite up the lake, which now lofing the air of a wide river, re-affumes its true character, and even appears to flow into the chafm of rocks, that really inclofe Derwentwater. Skiddaw, with all the mountains round Borrowdale, from a magnificent amphitheatrical perfpective for this noble fheet of water; the vallies of the two lakes extending to one view, which is, therefore, fuperior to any exhibited from Derwentwater alone. The profpect terminates in the dark fells of Borrowdale, which by their fublimity enhance the beauty and elegance, united to a furprifing degree in the nearer landfcape.

Beyond Oufe Bridge, but ftill at the bottom of the lake, the road paffes before Armithwaite-houfe, whofe copfy lawns flope to the margin of the water from a manfion more finely fituated than any we had feen. It then recedes fomewhat from the bank, and afcends the fkirt of Skiddaw, which it fcarcely leaves on this fide of Kefwick. On the oppofite fhore, the moft elegant features are the fwelling hills, called Wythop-brows, flourifhing with wood from the water's edge; and, below the meadows of the eaftern bank, by which we were returning, two peninfulæ, the one paftoral, yet well wooded and embellifhed by a white hamlet, the other narrow and bearing only a line of trees, iffuing far into the lake. But the fhores of Baffenthwaite, though elegant and often beautiful, are too little varied to be long dwelt upon; and attention is fometimes unpleafantly engaged by a precipice,

precipice, from which the road is not fufficiently
fecured ; fo that the effect of the whole upon the
imagination is much lefs than might be expected
from its fituation at the foot of Skiddaw, and its
fhape, which is more extended than that of Derwentwater.

BORROWDALE.

A SERENE day, with gleams of funfhine, gave
magical effect to the fcenery of Derwentwater, as
we wound along its eaftern fhore to Borrowdale,
under cliffs, parts of which, already fallen near
the road, increafed the opinion of danger from
the reft ; fometimes near the edge of precipices,
that bend over the water, and, at others, among
pleafure-grounds and copfes, which admit partial
views over the lake. Thefe, with every woody
promontory and mountain, were perfectly reflected
on its furface. Not a path-way, not a crag, or
fcar, that fculptured their bold fronts, but was
copied and diftinctly feen even from the oppofite
fhore in the dark purple mirror below. Now and
then, a pleafure-boat glided by, leaving long filver lines, drawn to a point on the fmooth water,
which, as it gave back the painted fides and
gleaming fail, difplayed a moving picture.

The colouring of the mountains was, this day,
furprifingly various and changeful, furpaffing
every thing of the fame nature, that we had feen.
The effect of the atmofphere on mountainous regions is fometimes fo fublime, at others fo en-
chantingly

chantingly beautiful, that the mention of it ought not to be confidered as trivial, when their afpect is to be defcribed. As the fun-beams fell on different kinds of rock, and diftance coloured the air, fome parts were touched with lilac, others with light blue, dark purple, or reddifh brown, which were often feen, at the fame moment, contrafting with the mellow green of the woods and the brightnefs of funfhine; then flowly and almoft imperceptibly changing into other tints. Skiddaw itfelf exhibited much of this variety, during our ride. As we left Kefwick, its points were overfpread with pale azure; on our return, a tint of dark blue foftened its features, which were, however, foon after involved in deepeft purple.

Winding under the woods of Barrowfide, we approached Lowdore, and heard the thunder of his cataract, joined by the founds of others, defcending within the gloom of the nearer rocks and thickets. The retrofpective views over the lake from Barrowfide are the fineft in the ride; and, when the road emerges from the woods, a range of rocks rifes over it, where many fhrubs, and even oaks, afh, yew, grow in a furprifing manner among the broken flates, that cover their fides. Beyond, at fome diftance from the fhore, appear the awful rocks, that rife over the fall of Lowdore; that on the right fhooting up, a vaft pyramid of naked cliff, above finely wooded fteeps; while, on the oppofite fide of the chafm, that receives the waters, impends Gowdar-crag, whofe trees and fhrubs give only fhagginefs to its terrible maffes, with fragments of which the meadows below are ftrewn. There was now little water at Lowdore; but the breadth of its channel and the height of the perpendicular rock, from which it leaps, told how tremendous it could be; yet even then

then its fublimity is probably derived chiefly from
the cliff and mountain, that tower clofely over it.

Here Borrowdale begins, its rocks fpreading in
a vaft fweep round the head of the lake, at the
diftance, perhaps, of half a mile from the fhore,
which bears meadow land to the water's brink.
The afpeft of thefe rocks, with the fragments,
that have rolled from their fummits, and lie on
each fide of the road, prepared us for the fcene of
tremendous ruin we were approaching in the gorge,
or pafs of Borrowdale, which opens from the
centre of the amphitheatre, that binds the head
of Derwentwater. Dark rocks yawn at its entrance, terrific as the wildnefs of a maniac; and
difclofe a narrow pafs, running up between mountains of granite, that are fhook into almoft every
poffible form of horror. All above refembles the
accumulations of an earthquake; fplintered, fhivered, piled, amaffed. Huge cliffs have rolled
down into the glen below, where, however, is
ftill a miniature of the fweeteft paftoral beauty, on
the banks of the river Derwent; but defcription
cannot paint either the wildnefs of the mountains,
or the paftoral and fylvan peace and foftnefs, that
wind at their bafe.

Among the moft ftriking of the fells are Gla-
ramara, fhewing rock on rock; and Eagle-crag,
where, till lately, that bird built its neft; but
the depredations, annually committed on its
young, have driven it from the place. Hence we
purfued the pafs for a mile, over a frightful road,
that climbs among the crags of a precipice above
the river, having frequently glimpfes into glens
and chafms, where all paffage feemed to be obftructed by the fallen fhivers of rock, and at length
reached

reached the gigantic ftone of Bowther, that appears to have been pitched into the ground from the fummit of a neighbouring fell, and is fhaped, like the roof of a houfe reverfed.

This is one of the fpectacles of the country. Its fize makes it impoffible to have been ever moved by human means; and, if it fell from the neareft of the rocks, it muft have rolled upon the ground much further than can be readily conceived of the motion of fuch a mafs. The fide towards the road projects about twelve feet over the bafe, and ferves to fhelter cattle in a penn, of which it is made to form one boundary. A fmall oak plant and a floe have found foil enough to flourifh in at the top; and the bafe is pitched on a cliff over the river, whence a long perfpective of the gorge is feen, with a little level of bright verdure, fpreading among more diftant fells and winding away into tracklefs regions, where the mountains lift their ruffian heads in undifputed authority. Below, the fhrunk Derwent ferpentized along a wide bed of pebbles, that marked its wintry courfe, and left a wooded ifland, flourifhing amidft the wafte. The ftillnefs around us was only feebly broken by the remote founds of many unfeen cataracts, and fometimes by the voices of mountaineer children, fhouting afar off, and pleafing themfelves with roufing the echoes of the rocks.

In returning, the view opened, with great magnificence, from the jaws of this pafs over the lake to Skiddaw, then feen from its bafe, with the upper fteeps of Saddleback obliquely beyond, and rearing itfelf far above all the heights of the eaftern fhore. At the entrance of the gorge, the
village

village or hamlet of Grange lies picturefquely on the bank of the Derwent among wood and meadows, and fheltered under the ruinous fell, called Caftlecrag, that takes its name from the caftle, or fortrefs, which from its crown once guarded this important pafs.

Borrowdale abounds in valuable mines, among which fome are known to fupply the fineft wadd, or black lead, to be found in England. Iron, flate, and free ftone of variops kinds, are alfo the treafures of thefe mountains.

THE road from Kefwick to Amblefide commences by the afcent of Caftle-rigg, the mountain, which the Penrith road defcends, and which,
on that fide, is crowned by a Druid's temple.
The rife is now very laborious, but the views it
affords over the vale of Kefwick are not dearly
purchafed by the fatigue. All Baffenthwaite, its
mountains foftening away in the perfpective, and
terminating, on the weft, in the fifter woods of
Wythorp-brows, extends from the eye; and, immediately beneath, the northern end of Derwentwater, with Cawfey-pike, Thornthwaite-fell, the
rich upland vale of Newland peeping from between
their bafes, and the fpiry woods of Foepark jut-
ting into the lake below. But the fineft profpect
is from a gate about half way up the hill, whence
you look down upon the head of Derwentwater,
with all the alps of Borrowdale, opening darkly.

After defcending Caftle-rigg and croffing the
top of St. John's vale, we feemed as if going into
banifhment from fociety, the road then leading over
a plain, clofely furrounded by mountains fo wild,
that neither a cottage, or a wood foften their rudenefs, and fo fteep and barren, that not even fheep
appear upon their fides. From this plain the road
enters Legberthwaite, a narrow valley, running at
the

the back of Borrowdale, green at the bottom, and
varied with a few farms, but without wood, and
with fells of gray precipices, rising to great
height and nearly perpendicular on either hand,
whose fronts are marked only by the torrents, that
tumble from their utmost summits, and perpetually occur. We often stopped to listen to their
hollow sounds amidst the solitary greatness of the
scene and to watch their headlong fall down the
rocky chasms, their white foam and silver line
contrasting with the dark hue of the clefts. In
sublimity of descent these were frequently much
superior to that of Lowdore, but as much inferior
to it in mass of water and picturesque beauty.

As the road ascended towards Helvellyn, we
looked back through this vast rocky vista to the
sweet vale of St. John, lengthening the perspective, and saw, as through a telescope, the broad
broken steeps of Saddleback and the points of
Skiddaw, darkly blue, closing it to the north.
The grand rivals of Cumberland were now seen
together; and the road, soon winding high over
the skirts of Helvellyn, brought us to Leathes-
water, to which the mountain forms a vast side-
skreen, during its whole length. This is a long,
but narrow and unadorned lake, having little else
than walls of rocky fells, starting from its margin.
Continuing on the precipice, at some height from
the shore, the road brought us, after three
miles, to the poor village of Wythburn, and soon
after to the foot of Dunmail Rays, which, though
a considerable ascent, forms the dip of two lofty
mountains, Steel-fell and Seat Sandle, that rise
with finely-sweeping lines, 'on each side, and shut
up the vale.

Beyond

Beyond Dunmail Rays, one of the grand paffes from Cumberland into Weftmoreland, Helm-crag rears its creft, a ftrange fantaftic fummit, round, yet jagged and fplintered, like the wheel of a water-mill, overlooking Grafmere, which, foon after, opened below. A green fpreading circle of mountains embofoms this fmall lake, and, beyond, a wider range rifes in amphitheatre, whofe rocky tops are rounded and fcolloped, yet are great, wild, irregular, and were then over-fpread with a tint of faint purple. The fofteft verdure margins the water, and mingles with corn enclofures and woods, that wave up the hills; but fcarcely a cottage any where appears, except at the northern end of the lake, where the village of Grafmere and its very neat white church ftand among trees, near the fhore, with Helm-crag and a multitude of fells, rifing over it and beyond each other in the perfpective.

The lake was clear as glafs, reflecting the headlong mountains, with every feature of every image on its tranquil banks; and one green ifland varies, but fcarcely adorns its furface, bearing only a rude and now fhadelefs hut. At a confide-rable height above the water, the road undulates for a mile, till, near the fouthern end of Graf-mere, it mounts the crags of a fell, and feemed carrying us again into fuch fcenes of ruin and privation as we had quitted with Legberthwaite and Leathes-water. But, defcending the other fide of the mountain, we were foon cheered by the view of plantations, enriching the banks of Rydal-water, and by thick woods, mingling among cliffs above the narrow lake, which winds through a clofe valley, for about a mile. This lake

lake is remarkable for the beauty of its small
round iſlands, luxuriant with elegant, trees and
ſhrubs, and whoſe banks are green to the water's
edge. Rydal-hall ſtands finely on an eminence,
ſomewhat withdrawn from the eaſt end, in a cloſe
romantic nook, among old woods, that feather
the fells, which riſe over their ſummits, and
ſpread widely along the neighbouring eminences. This antient white manſion looks over
a rough graſſy deſcent, ſcreened by groves of oak
and majeſtic planes, towards the head of Windermere, about two miles diſtant, a ſmall glimpſe of
which is caught beyond the wooded ſteeps of a
narrow valley. In the woods and in the diſpoſi-
tion of the ground round Rydal-hall there is a
charming wildneſs, that ſuits the character of the
general ſcene; and, wherever art appears, it is
with graceful plainneſs and meek ſubjection to
nature.

The taſte, by which a caſcade in the pleaſure-
grounds, pouring under the arch of a rude bridge,
amidſt the green tint of woods, is ſhewn through
a darkened garden-houſe, and, therefore, with all
the effect, which the oppoſition of light and ſhade
can give, is even not too artificial; ſo admirably
is the intent accompliſhed of making all the light,
that is admitted, fall upon the objects, which are
chiefly meant to be obſerved.

The road to Ambleſide runs through the valley
in front of Rydal-hall, and for ſome diſtance
among the grounds that belong to it, where again
the taſte of the owner is conſpicuous in the diſ-
poſition of plantations among paſtures of extraordinary richneſs, and where pure rivulets are
ſuffered

suffered to wind without reftraint over their dark rocky channels. Woods mantle up the cliffs on either fide of this fweet valley, and, higher ftill, the craggy fummits of the fells crowd over the fcene. Two miles among its pleafant fhades, near the banks of the murmuring Rotha, brought us to Amblefide, a black and very antient little town, hanging on the lower fteeps of a mountain, where the vale opens to the head of

WINDERMERE,

Which appeared at fome diftance below, in gentle yet ftately beauty; but its boundaries fhewed nothing of the fublimity and little of the romantic wildnefs, that charms, or elevates in the fcenery of the other lakes. The fhores, and the hills, which gradually afcend from them, are in general richly cultivated, or wooded, and correctly elegant; and when we defcended upon the bank the road feemed leading through the artificial fhades of pleafure-grounds. It undulates for two miles over low promontories and along fpacious bays, full to their fringed margin with the abundance of this expanfive lake; then, quitting the bank, it afcends gradual eminences, that look upon the vaft plain of water, and rife amidft the richeft landfcapes of its fhores. The manners of the people would have fufficiently informed us that Windermere is the lake moft frequented;

and

and with the great fublimity of the more fequeftered fcenes, we had to regret the interefting
fimplicity of their inhabitants, a fimplicity which
accorded fo beautifully with the dignified character
of the country. The next day, we vifited feveral
of the neighbouring heights, whence the lake is
feen to great advantage; and, on the following,
fkirted the eaftern fhore for fix miles to the
Ferry.

Windermere, above twelve miles long and generally above a mile broad, but fometimes two,
fweeps like a majeftic river with an eafy bend
between low points of land and eminences that,
fhaded with wood and often embellifhed with
villas, fwell into hills cultivated to their fummits;
except that, for about fix miles along the middle
of the weftern fhore, a range of rocky fells rife
over the water. But thefe have nothing either
picturefque or fantaftic in their fhape; they are
heavy, not broken into parts, and their rudenefs
foftens into infignificance, when they are feen
over the wide channel of the lake; they are
neither large enough to be grand, or wooded
enough to be beautiful. To the north, or head
of Windermere, however, the tamenefs of its
general character difappears, and the fcene foars
into grandeur. Here, over a ridge of rough brown
hills above a woody fhore, rife, at the diftance of a
mile and half, or two miles, a multitude of finely
alpine mountains, retiring obliquely in the perfpective, among which Langdale-pikes, Hardknot
and Wry-nofe, bearing their bold, pointed promontories aloft, are pre-eminent. The colouring
of thefe mountains, which are fome of the grandeft
of Cumberland and Weftmoreland, was this day

remarkably

remarkably fine. The weather was showery, with gleams of sunshine; sometimes their tops were entirely concealed in gray vapours, which, drawing upwards, would seem to ascend in volumes of smoke from their summits; at others, a few scattered clouds wandered along their sides, leaving their heads unveiled and effulgent with light. These clouds disappearing before the strength of the sun, a fine downy hue of light blue overspread the peeping points of the most distant fells, while the nearer ones were tinged with deep purple, which was opposed to the brown heath and crag of the lower hills, the olive green of two wooded slopes that, just tinted by autumn, seemed to descend to the margin, and the silver transparency of the expanding water at their feet. This view of Windermere appears with great majesty from a height above Culgarth, a seat of the Bishop of Landaff; while, to the south, the lake after sweeping about four miles gradually narrows and disappears behind the great island, which stretches across the perspective.

At the distance of two or three miles beyond Culgarth, from a hill advancing towards the water, the whole of Windermere is seen; to the right, is the white mansion at Culgarth, among wood, on a gentle eminence of the shore, with the lake spreading wide beyond, crowned by the fells half obscured in clouds. To the south, the hills of the eastern shore, sloping gradually, run out in elegant and often well wooded points into the water, and are spotted with villas and varied above with enclosures. The opposite shore is for about a mile southward a continuation of the line of rock before noticed, from which Rawlinson's-

nab

nab pushes a bold headland over the lake; the perspective then sinks away in low hills, and is crossed by a remote ridge, that closes the scene.

The villages of Rayrig and Bowness, which are passed in the way to the Ferry, both stand delightfully; one on an eminence commanding the whole lake, and the other within a recess of the shore, nearly opposite the large island. The winding banks of Windermere continually open new landscapes as you move along them, and the mountains, which crown its head, are as frequently changing their attitudes; but Langdale-pikes, the boldest features in the scene, are soon lost to the eye behind the nearer fells of the western shore.

The ferry is considerably below Christian's island, and at the narrowest span of the lake, where two points of the shore extend to meet each other. This island, said to contain thirty acres, intermingled with wood, lawn and shrubberies, embellishes, without decreasing the dignity of the scene; it is surrounded by attendant islets, some rocky, but others, beautifully covered with wood, seem to coronet the flood.

In crossing the water the illusions of vision give force to the northern mountains, which viewed from hence appear to ascend from its margin and to spread round it in a magnificent amphitheatre. This was to us the most interesting view on Windermere.

On our approaching the western shore, the range of rocks that form it, discovered their cliffs, and gradually assumed a consequence, which the

breadth

breadth of the channel had denied them; and their darkness was well opposed by the bright verdure and variegated autumnal tints of the isles at their base. On the bank, under shelter of these rocks, a white house was seen beyond the tall boles of a most luxuriant grove of plane-trees, which threw their shadows over it, and on the margin of the silver lake spreading in front. From hence the road ascends the steep and craggy side of Furness-fell, on the brow of which we had a last view of Windermere, in its whole course; to the south, its tame but elegant landscapes gliding away into low and long perspective, and the lake gradually narrowing; to the north, its more impressive scenery; but the finest features of it were now concealed by a continuation of the rocks we were upon.

Windermere is distinguished from all the other lakes of this country by its superior length and breadth, by the gentle hills, cultivated and enclosed nearly to their summits, that generally bind its shores, by the gradual distance and fine disposition of the northern mountains, by the bold sweeps of its numerous bays, by the villas that speckle and rich plantations that wind them, and by one large island, surrounded by many islets, which adds dignity to its bosom. On the other lakes the islands are prettinesses, that do not accord with the character of the scene; they break also the surface of the water where vast continuity is required; and the mind cannot endure to descend suddenly from the gigantic sublimity of nature to her fairy sports. Yet, on the whole, Windermere was to us the least impressive of all the lakes. Except to the north, where the retiring mountains

mountains are difpofed with uncommon grandeur
of outline and magnificence of colouring, its fcenery is tame, having little of the wild and nothing
of the aftonifhing energy that appears on the
features of the more fequeftered diftricts. The
characters of the three great lakes may, perhaps,
be thus diftinguifhed:

Windermere: Diffufivenefs, ftately beauty, and,
at the upper end, magnificence.

Ullf-water: Severe grandeur and fublimity; all
that may give ideas of vaft power and aftonifhing
majefty. The effect of Ullf-water is, that, awful
as its fcenery appears, it awakens the mind to
expectation ftill more awful, and, touching all
the powers of imagination, infpires that " fine
phrenfy" defcriptive of the poet's eye, which not
only bodies forth unreal forms, but imparts to
fubftantial objects a character higher than their
own.

Derwentwater: Fantaftic wildnefs and romantic beauty, but inferior to Ullf-water in greatnefs;
both of water and rocks; for, though it charms
and elevates, it does not difplay fuch features and
circumftances of the fublime, or call up fuch expectation of unimaged and uncertain wonder. A
principal defect, if we may venture to call it fo,
of Derwentwater is, that the water is too fmall in
proportion for the amphitheatre of the valley in
which it lies, and therefore lofes much of the
dignity, that in other circumftances it would exhibit. The fault of Windermere is, perhaps, exactly the reverfe: where the fhores, not generally
grand, are rendered tamer by the ample expanfe
of the lake. The proportions of Ullf-water are
more

more juft, and, though its winding form gives it in fome parts the air of a river, the abrupt and tremendous height of its rocks, the dark and crowding fummits of the fells above, the manner in which they enclofe it, together with the dignity of its breadth, empower it conftantly to affect the mind with emotions of aftonifhment and lofty expectation.

FROM WINDERMERE TO HAWKSHEAD, THURSTON LAKE AND ULVERSTON.

AFTER afcending the laborious crags and precipices of Furnefs-fell, enlivened, however, by frequent views of the fouthern end of Winder-mere, the road immediately defcends the oppofite fide of the mountain, which fhuts out the beautiful fcenery of the lake; but the profpect foon after opens to other mountains of Furnefs, in the diftance, which revive the expectation of fuch fublimity as we had lately regretted, and to Efthwait-water in the valley below. This is a narrow, pleafant lake, about half a mile broad and two miles long, with gradual hills, green to their tops, rifing round the margin; with plantations and paftures alternately fpreading along the eafy fhores and white farms fcattered fparingly upon the flopes above. The water feems to glide through the quiet privacy of pleafure-grounds; fo fine is the turf on its banks, fo elegant its copfes, and fuch an air of peace and
retirement

retirement prevails over it. : A neat white village lies at the feet of the hills near the head of the lake; beyond it is the gray town of Hawkſhead, with its church and parſonage on an eminence commanding the whole valley. Steep hills riſe over them, and, more diſtant, the tall heads of the Coniſton-fells, dark and awful, with a confuſion of other mountains.

Hawkſhead, thus delightfully placed, is an antient, but ſmall town, with a few good houſes, and a neat town-houſe, lately built by ſubſcriptions, of which the chief part was gratefully ſupplied by London merchants, who had been educated at the free ſchool here; and this ſchool itſelf is a memorial of gratitude, having been founded by Archbiſhop Sandys for the advantage of the town, which gave him birth. Near Hawkſhead are the remains of the houſe, where the Abbot of Furneſs " kept reſidence by one or more monks, who performed divine ſervice and other parochial duties in the neighbourhood." There is ſtill a court-room over the gateway, " where the bailiff of Hawkſhead held court, and diſtributed juſtice, in the name of the abbot."

From the tremendous ſteeps of the long fell, which towers over Hawkſhead, aſtoniſhing views open to the diſtant vales and mountains of Cumberland; overlooking all the groteſque ſummits in the neighbourhood of Graſmere, the fells of Borrowdale in the furtheſt diſtance, Langdale-pikes, and ſeveral ſmall lakes, ſeen gleaming in the boſom of the mountains. Before us, roſe the whole multitude of Coniſton-fells, of immenſe height and threatening forms, their tops thinly darkened with thunder miſts, and, on the left, Furneſs-

Furnefs-fells finking towards the bay, which Ulverfton fands form for the fea.

, As we advanced, Coniftop-fells feemed to multiply, and became ftill more impreffiye, till, having
reached at length the fummit of the mountain, we
looked down upon Thurfton-lake immediately
below, and faw them rifing abruptly round its
northern end in fomewhat of the fublime attitudes
and dark majefty of Ullf-water.   A range of lower
rocks, nearer to the eye, exhibited a very peculiar
and grotefque appearance,   coloured fcars and
deep channels marking their purple fides, as if
they had been rifted by an earthquake.

, The road defcends the flinty fteeps towards the
eaftern bank of the lake, that fpreads a furface
of fix miles in length and generally three quarters
of a mile in breadth, not winding in its courfe,
yet much indented with bays, and prefenting
nearly its whole extent at once to the eye.   The
grandeft features are the fells, that crown its
northern end, not diftantly and gradually, like
thofe of Windermere, nor varied like them with
magnificent colouring, but rifing in haughty ab-
ruptnefs, dark, rugged and ftupendous, within
a quarter of a mile of the margin, and fhutting
out all profpect of other mountain-fummits   At
their feet, paftures fpread a bright green to the
brim of the lake.   Nearly in the centre of thefe
fells, which open in a femicircle to receive the lake,
a cataract defcends, but its fhining line is not of a
breadth proportioned to the vaftnefs of its perpendicular fall. The village of Conifton is fweetly feated under fhelter of the rocks; and, at a diftance beyond, on the edge of the water, the antient hall,
                                                    or

or priory, shews its turret and ivyed ruins among
old woods. The whole picture is reflected in the
liquid mirror below. The gay, convivial chorus,
or solemn vesper, that once swelled along the lake
from these consecrated walls, and awakened, perhaps, the enthusiasm of the voyager, while evening stole upon the scene, is now contrasted by de-
solation and profound repose, and, as he glides by,
he hears only the dashing of his oars, or the surge
beating on the shore.

This lake appeared to us one of the most charming we had seen. From the sublime mountains,
which bend round its head, the heights, on either
side, decline towards the south into waving hills,
that form its shores, and often stretch in long
sweeping points into the water, generally covered
with tufted wood, but sometimes with the tender
verdure of pasturage. The tops of these woods
were just embrowned with autumn, and contrasted
well with other slopes, rough and heathy, that
rose above, or fell beside them to the water's
brink, and added force to the colouring, which
the reddish tints of decaying fern, the purple
bloom of heath, and the bright golden gleams of
broom, spread over these elegant banks. Their
hues, the graceful undulations of the marginal
hills and bays, the richness of the woods, the solemnity of the northern fells and the deep repose,
that pervades the scene, where only now and then
a white cottage or a farm lurks among the trees,
are circumstances, which render Thurston-lake one
of the most interesting and, perhaps the most beautiful of any in the country.

The road undulates over copsy hills, and dips
into shallow vallies along the whole of the eastern
bank,

bank, feldom greatly elevated above the water, or defcending to a level with it, but frequently opening to extenfive views of its beauties, and again fhrouding itfelf in verdant gloom. The moft impreffive pictures were formed by the fells, that crowd over the upper end of the lake, and which, viewed from a low ftation, fometimes appeared nearly to enclofe that part of it. The effect was then aftonifhingly grand, particularly about fun-fet, when the clouds, drawing upwards, difcovered the utmoft fummits of thefe fells, and a tint of dufky blue began to prevail over them, which gradually deepened into night. A line of lower rocks, that extend from thefe, are, independently of the atmofphere, of a dull purple, and their fhaggy forms would appear gigantic in almoft any other fituation. Even here, they preferve a wild dignity, and their attitudes fomewhat refemble thofe at the entrance of Borrowdale; but they are forgotten, when the eye is lifted to the folemn mountains immediately above. Thefe are rich in flate quarries, and have fome copper mines; but the latter were clofed, during the civil wars of the laft century, having been worked, as we are told in the defcriptive language of the miners, from *the day to the evening end*, forty fathom, and to the *morning end* feven fcore fathom; a figurative ftyle of diftinguifhing the weftern and eaftern directions of the mine. The lake, towards the lower end, narrows and is adorned by one fmall ifland; but here the hills of the eaftern fhore foar into fells, fome barren, craggy and nearly perpendicular, others entirely covered with coppice-wood. Two of thefe, rifing over the road, gave fine relief to each other: the one fhewing only precipices of fhelving rock, while its rival afpired with woods, that mantled from the bafe to the

summit,

fummit, confifting chiefly of oak, afh and holly. Not any lake, that we faw, is at prefent fo much embellifhed with wood as Thurfton. All the mountains of *High* and the vallies of *Low Furnefs* were, indeed, fome centuries ago, covered with forefts, part of which was called the Foreft of Lancafter; and thefe were of fuch entangled luxuriance as to be nearly impenetrable in many tracts. Here, wolves, wild boars, and a remarkably large breed of deer, called Leghs, the heads of which have frequently been found buried at a confiderable depth in the foil, abounded. So fecure an afylum did thefe animals find in the woods of High Furnefs, that, even after the low lands were cleared and cultivated, fhepherds were neceffary to guard the flocks from the ravages of the wolves. Towards the end of the thirteenth century, the upper forefts alfo were nearly deftroyed.

In winter, the fhepherds ufed to feed their flocks with the young fprouts of afh and holly, a cuftom faid to be ftill obferved; the fheep coming at the call of the fhepherd and affembling round the holly-tree to receive from his hand the young fhoots cropped for them *. Whenever the woods are felled, which is too frequently done, to fupply fuel for the neighbouring furnaces, the holly is ftill held facred to the flocks of thefe mountains.

Soon after paffing the ifland, the road enters the village of Nibthwaite, rich only in fituation; for the cottages are miferable. The people feemed to be as ignorant as poor; a young man knew not how far it was to Ulverfton, or as he called it Ulfon, though it was only five miles.

* Weft's "Antiquities of Furnefs."

On

On the point of a promontory of the oppofite fhore, embofomed in ancient woods, the chimnies and pointed roof of a gray manfion look out moft interestingly. The woods open partially to the north, and admit a view of the *Swifs* fcenery at the head of the lake, in its fineft pofition. On the other fides, the oaks fo embower the houfe and fpread down the rocks, as fcarcely to allow it a glimpfe of the water bickering between the dark foliage below.

At Nibthwaite, the lake becomes narrow and gradually decreafes, till it terminates at Lowick-bridge, where it glides away in the little river Crake, which defcends to Ulverfton fands. We ftopped upon the bridge to take a laft view of the fcene; the diftant fells were difappearing in twilight, but the gray lake gleamed at their bafe. From the fteeps of a lofty mountain, that rofe near us on the right, cattle were flowly defcending for the night, winding among the crags, fometimes ftopping to crop the heath, or broom, and then difappearing for a moment behind the darker verdure of yews, that grew in knots upon the cliffs.

It was night before we reached Ulverfton. The wind founded mournfully among the hills, and we perceived our approach to the fea only by the faint roaring of the tide, till from a brow, whence the hills open on either hand with a grand fweep, we could juft difcern the gray furface of the fea-bay, at a diftance below, and then, by lights that glimmered in the bottom, the town of Ulverfton, lying not far from the fhore and fcreened on the north by the heights, from which we were to defcend.

Ulverfton

Ulverſton is a neat but ancient town, the capital and chief port of Furneſs. The road from it to the majeſtic ruin of Furneſs Abbey lies through Low Furneſs, and loſes the general wildneſs and intereſt of the country, except where now and then the diſtant retroſpect of the mountains breaks over the tame hills and regular encloſures, that border it.

About a mile and a half on this ſide of the Abbey, the road paſſes through Dalton, a very antient little town, once the capital of Low Furneſs, and rendered ſo important by its neighbourhood to the Abbey, that Ulverſton, the preſent capital, could not then ſupport the weekly market, for which it had obtained a charter. Dalton, however, ſunk with the ſuppreſſion of its neighbouring patrons, and is now chiefly diſtinguiſhed by the pleaſantneſs of its ſituation, to which a church, built on a bold aſcent, and the remains of a caſtle, advantageouſly placed for the command of the adjoining valley, ſtill attach ſome degree of dignity. What now exiſts of the latter is one tower, in a chamber of which the Abbot of Furneſs held his ſecular Court; and the chamber was afterwards uſed as a gaol for debtors, till within theſe few years, when the dead ruin releaſed the living one. The preſent church-yard and the ſcite of this caſtle are ſuppoſed to have been included within the limits of a *caſtellum*, built by Agricola, of the foſſe of which there are ſtill ſome faint veſtiges.

Beneath the brow, on which the church and tower ſtand, a brook flows through a narrow valley, that winds about a mile and a half to the Abbey. In the way thither we paſſed the entrance of of one of the very rich iron mines, with which the neighbourhood abounds; and the deep red tint of the foil, that overfpreads almoft the whole country between Ulverfton and the monaftery, fufficiently indicates the nature of the treafures beneath.

In a clofe glen, branching from this valley, fhrouded by winding banks clumped with old groves of oak and chefnut, we found the magnificent remains of

FURNESS

FURNESS ABBEY.

THE deep retirement of its fituation, the venerable grandeur of its gothic arches and the luxuriant yet ancient trees, that fhadow this forfaken fpot, are circumftances of picturefque and, if the expreffion may be allowed, of fentimental beauty, which fill the mind with folemn yet delightful emotion. This glen is called the Vale of Nightfhade, or, more literally from its ancient title Bekangfgill, the "glen of deadly nightfhade," that plant being abundantly found in the neighbourhood. Its romantic gloom and fequeftered privacy particularly adapted it to the aufterities of monaftic life; and in the moft retired part of it King Stephen, while Earl of Mortaign and Bulloign, founded, in the year 1127, the magnificent monaftery of Furnefs, and endowed it with princely wealth and almoft princely authority, in which it was fecond only to Fontain's-abbey in Yorkfhire.

The windings of the glen conceal thefe venerable ruins, till they are clofely approached, and the bye road, that conducted us, is margined with a few ancient oaks, which ftretch their broad branches entirely acrofs it, and are finely preparatory objects to the fcene beyond. A fudden bend in this road brought us within view of the northern gate of the Abbey, a beautiful gothic arch, one fide of which is luxuriantly feftooned with nightfhade. A thick grove of plane-trees,
with

with fome oak and beech, overfhadow it on the right, and lead the eye onward to the ruins of the Abbey, feen through this dark arch in remote perfpective, over rough but verdant ground. The principal features are the great northern window and part of the eaftern choir, with glimpfes of fhattered arches and ftately walls beyond, caught between the gaping cafements. On the left, the bank of the glen is broken into knolls capped with oaks, which in fome places fpread downwards to a ftream that winds round the ruin, and darken it with their rich foliage. Through this gate is the entrance to the immediate precinēts of the Abbey, an area faid to contain fixty-five acres, now called the Deer-park. It is enclofed by a ftone wall, on which the remains of many fmall buildings and the faint veftiges of others, ftill appear ; fuch as the porter's lodge, mills, granaries, ovens and kilns that once fupplied the monaftery, fome of which, feen under the fhade of the fine old trees, that on every fide adorn the broken fteeps of this glen, have a very interefting effect.

Juft within the gate, a fmall manor houfe of modern date, with its ftables and other offices, breaks difcordantly upon the lonely grandeur of the fcene. Except this, the character of the deferted ruin is fcrupuloufly preferved in the furrounding area ; no fpade has dared to level the inequalities, which fallen fragments have occafioned in the ground, or fhears to clip the wild fern and underwood, that overfpread it ; but every circumftance confpires to heighten the folitary grace of the principal object and to prolong the luxurious melancholy, which the view of it infpires. We made our way among

the

the pathlefs fern and grafs to the north end of the church, now, like every other part of the Abbey, entirely rooflefs, but fhewing the lofty arch of the great window, where, inftead of the painted glafs that once enriched it, are now tufted plants and wreaths of nightfhade. Below is the principal door of the church, bending into a deep round arch, which, retiring circle within circle, is rich and beautiful ; the remains of a winding ftair-cafe are vifible within the wall on its left fide. Near this northern end of the edifice are feen one fide of the eaftern choir, with its two flender gothic window frames, and on the weft a remnant of the nave of the Abbey and fome lofty arches, which once belonged to the belfry, now detached from the main building.

To the fouth, but concealed from this point of view, are the chapter-houfe, fome years ago exhibiting a roof of beautiful gothic fretwork, and which was almoft the only part of the Abbey thus ornamented, its architecture having been characterifed by an air of grand fimplicity rather than by the elegance and richnefs of decoration, which in an after date diftinguifhed the gothic ftyle in England. Over the chapter-houfe were once the library and fcriptorium, and beyond it are ftill the remains of cloifters, of the refectory, the locutorium, or converfation-room, and the calefactory. Thefe, with the walls of fome chapels, of the veftry, a hall, and of what is believed to have been a fchool-houfe, are all the features of this noble edifice that can eafily be traced : winding ftair-cafes within the furprifing thicknefs of the walls, and door-cafes involved in darknefs and myftery, the place abounds with.

The abbey, which was formerly of such magnitude as nearly fill up the breadth of the glen, is built of a pale-red stone, dug from the neighbouring rocks, now changed by time and weather to a tint of dusky brown, which accords well with the hues of plants and shrubs that every where emboss the mouldering arches.

The finest view of the ruin is on the east side, where, beyond the vast, shattered frame that once contained a richly-painted window, is seen a perspective of the choir and of distant arches, remains of the nave of the abbey, closed by the woods. This perspective of the ruin is * said to be two hundred and eighty-seven feet in length; the choir part of it is in width only twenty-eight feet inside, but the nave is seventy: the walls, as they now stand, are fifty-four feet high and in thickness five. Southward from the choir extend the still beautiful, though broken, pillars and arcades of some chapels, now laid open to the day; the chapter-house, the cloisters, and beyond all, and detached from all, is the school-house, a large building, the only part of the monastery that still boasts a roof.

As, soothed by the venerable shades and the view of a more venerable ruin, we rested opposite to the eastern window of the choir, where once the high altar stood, and, with five other altars, assisted the religious pomp of the scene; the images and the manners of times, that were past, rose to reflection. The midnight procession of monks, clothed in white and bearing lighted tapers, appeared to the " mind's eye" issuing to the choir through the very door-case, by

* " Antiquities of Furness."

which

which such processions were wont to pass from the cloisters to perform the matin service, when, at the moment of their entering the church, the deep chanting of voices was heard, and the organ swelled a solemn peal. To fancy, the strain still echoed feebly along the arcades and died in the breeze among the woods, the rustling leaves mingling with the close. It was easy to image the abbot and the officiating priests seated beneath the richly-fretted canopy of the four stalls, that still remain entire in the southern wall, and high over which is now-perched a solitary yew-tree, a black funereal memento to the living of those who once sat below,

Of a quadrangular court on the west side of the church, three hundred and thirty-four feet long and one hundred and two feet wide, little vestige now appears, except the foundation of a range of cloisters, that formed its western boundary, and under the shade of which the monks on days of high solemnity passed in their customary procession round the court. What was the belfry is now a huge mass of detached ruin, picturesque from the loftiness of its shattered arches and the high inequalities of the ground within them, where the tower, that once crowned this building, having fallen, lies in vast fragments, now covered with earth and grass, and no longer distinguishable but by the hillock they form.

The school-house, a heavy structure attached to the boundary wall on the south, is nearly entire, and the walls, particularly of the portal, are of enormous thickness, but, here and there, a chasm disclofes the stair-cases, that wind within them to chambers above. The school-room below, shews

K k 2   only

only a ſtone bench, that extends round the walls, and a low ſtone pillar in the eaſtern corner, on which the teacher's pulpit was formerly fixed. The lofty vaulted roof is ſcarcely diſtinguiſhable by the duſky light admitted through one or two narrow windows placed high from the ground, perhaps for the purpoſe of confining the ſcholar's attention to his book.

Theſe are the principal features, that remain of this once magnificent abbey. It was dedicated to St. Mary, and received a colony of monks from the monaſtery of Savigny in Normandy, who were called Gray Monks, from their dreſs of that colour, till they became Ciſtercians, and, with the ſevere rules of St. Bernard, adopted a white habit, which they retained till the diſſolution of monaſtic orders in England. The original rules of St. Bernard partook in ſeveral inſtances of the auſterities of thoſe of La Trapp, and the ſociety did not very readily relinquiſh the milder laws of St. Benedict for the new rigours impoſed upon them by the parent monaſtery of Savigny. They were forbidden to taſte fleſh, except when ill, and even eggs, butter, cheeſe and milk, but on extraordinary occaſions; and denied even the uſe of linen and fur. The monks were divided into two claſſes, to which ſeparate departments belonged. Thoſe, who attended the choir, ſlept upon ſtraw in their uſual habits, from which, at midnight, they roſe and paſſed into the church, where they continued their holy hymns, during the ſhort remainder of the night. After this firſt maſs, having publicly confeſſed themſelves, they retired to their cells, and the day was employed in ſpiritual exerciſes

and

and in copying or illuminating manuscripts. An unbroken silence was observed, except when, after dinner, they withdrew into the locutorium, where for an hour, perhaps, they were permitted the common privilege of social beings. This class was confined to the boundary wall, except that, on some particular days, the members of it were allowed to walk in parties beyond it, for exercise and amusement; but they were very seldom permitted either to receive, or pay visits. Like the monks of La Trapp, however, they were distinguished for extensive charities and liberal hospitality; for travellers were so scrupulously entertained at the abbey, that it was not till the dissolution that an inn was thought necessary in this part of Furness, when one was opened for their accommodation, expressly because the monastery could no longer receive them.

To the second class were assigned the cultivation of the lands and the performance of domestic affairs in the monastery.

This was the second house in England, that received the Bernardine rules, the most rigorous of which were, however, dispensed with in 1485 by Sixtus the Fourth, when, among other indulgences, the whole order was allowed to taste meat on three days of the week. With the rules of St. Benedict, the monks had exchanged their gray habit for a white cassock with a white caul and scapulary. But their choir dress was either white or gray, with caul and scapulary of the same, and a girdle of black wool; over that a mozet, or hood,

and

and a rochet*. When they went abroad they wore a caul and full black hood.

"The privileges and immunities, granted to the Ciftercian order in general, were very abundant; and thofe to the Abbey of Furnefs were proportioned to its vaft endowments. The abbot, it has been mentioned, held his fecular court in the neighbouring caftle of Dalton, where he prefided with the power of adminiftering not only juftice but injuftice, fince the lives and property of the villain tenants of the lordfhip of Furnefs were configned by a grant of King Stephen to the difpofal of my lord abbot! The monks alfo could be arraigned for whatever crime, only by him. "The military eftablifhment of Furnefs likewife depended on the abbot. Every mefne lord and free homager, as well as the cuftomary tenants, took an oath of fealty to the abbot, to be true to him againft all men, excepting the king. Every mefne lord obeyed the fummons of the abbot, or his fteward, in raifing his quota of armed men, and every tenant of a whole tenement furnifhed a man and horfe of war for guarding the coaft, for the border-fervice, or any expedition againft the common enemy of the king and kingdom. The habiliments of war were a fteel coat, or coat of mail, a falce, or falchion, a jack, the bow, the bill, the crofs-bow and fpear. The Furnefs legion confifted of four divifions:—one of bowmen horfed and harneffed; bylmen horfed and harneffed; bowmen without horfe and harnefs; bylmen without horfe and harnefs †."

The deep forefts, that once furrounded the Abbey, and overfpread all Furnefs, contributed with

* "Antiquities of Furnefs." † Ibid.

its

its infulated fituation, on a neck of land running out into the fea, to fecure it from the depredations of the Scots, who were continually committing hoftilities on the borders. On a fummit over the Abbey are the remains of a beacon, or watch-tower, raifed by the fociety for their further fecurity. It commands extenfive views over Low Furnefs and the bay of the fea immediately beneath; looking forward to the town and caftle of Lancafter, appearing faintly on the oppofite coaft; on the fouth, to the ifles of Wanley, Foulney, and their numerous iflets, on one of which ftands Peel-caftle; and, on the north, to the mountains of High Furnefs and Conifton, rifing in grand amphitheatre round this inlet of the Irifh Channel. Defcription can fcarcely fuggeft the full magnificence of fuch a profpect, to which the monks, emerging from their concealed cells below, occafionally reforted to footh the afperities, which the fevere difcipline of fuperftition inflicted on the temper; or, freed from the obfervance of jealous eyes, to indulge, perhaps, the figh of regret, which a confideration of the world they had renounced, thus glorioufly given back to their fight, would fometimes awaken.

From Hawcoat, a few miles to the weft of Furnefs, the view is ftill more extenfive, whence, in a clear day, the whole length of the Ifle of Man may be feen, with part of Anglefey and the mountains of Caernarvon, Merionethfhire, Denbighfhire and Flintfhire, fhadowing the oppofite horizon of the channel.

The fum total of all rents belonging to the Abbey immediately before the diffolution was 946l. 2s. 10d. collected from Lancafhire, Cumberland, and

and even from the Ifle of Man; a fum, which confidering the value of money at that period; and the woods, meadows, paftures, and fifheries, retained by the fociety in their own hands; the quantity of provifions for domeftic ufe brought by the tenants inftead of rent, and the fhares of mines, mills, and faltworks, which belonged to the Abbey, fwells its former riches to an enormous amount.

Pyle, the laft abbot, furrendered with twenty-nine monks, to Henry the Eighth, April the 9th 1537, and in return was made Rector of Dalton, a fituation then valued at thirty-three .pounds fix fhillings and eight-pence a year.

FROM ULVERSTON TO LANCASTER.

FROM the abbey we returned to Ulverfton, and from thence croffed the fands to Lancafter, a ride fingularly interefting and fublime. From the Carter's houfe, which ftands on the edge of the Ulverfton fands, and at the point, whence paffengers enter them, to Lancafter, within the furtheft oppofite fhore, is fifteen miles. This noble bay is interrupted by the peninfula of Cartmel, extending a line of white rocky coaft, that divides the Leven and Ulverfton fands from thofe of Lancafter. The former are four miles over; the latter feven.

We took the early part of the tide, and entered thefe vaft and defolate plains before the fea had entirely left them, or the morning mifts were fufficiently

ficiently diffipated to allow a view of diftant objects; but the grand fweep of the coaft could be
faintly traced, on the left, and a vaft wafte of
fand ftretching far below it, with mingled ftreaks
of gray water, that heightened its dreary afpect.
The tide was ebbing faft from our wheels, and its
low murmur was interrupted, firft, only by the
fhrill fmall cry of fea-gulls, unfeen, whofe hovering flight could be traced by the found, near an
ifland that began to dawn through the mift; and
then, by the hoarfer croaking of fea-geefe, which
took a wider range, for their fhifting voices were
heard from various quarters of the furrounding
coaft. The body of the fea, on the right, was
ftill involved, and the diftant mountains on our
left, that crown the bay, were alfo viewlefs; but
it was fublimely interefting to watch the heavy
vapours beginning to move, then rolling in lengthening volumes over the fcene, and, as they gradually diffipated, difcovering through their veil
the various objects they had concealed—fifhermen
with carts and nets ftealing along the margin of
the tide, little boats putting off from the fhore,
and, the view ftill enlarging as the vapours expanded, the mean fea itfelf foftening into the horizon, with here and there a dim fail moving in
the hazy diftance. The wide defolation of the
fands, on the left, was animated only by fome
horfemen riding remotely in groups towards Lancafter, along the winging edge of the water, and
by a mufcle-fifher in his cart trying to ford the
channel we were approaching.

The coaft round the bay was now diftinctly,
though remotely, feen, rifing in woods, white
cliffs and cultivated flopes towards the mountains
of Furnefs, on whofe dark brows the vapours ho-
L l   vered.

vered. The shore falls into frequent recesses and juts out in promontories, where villages and country seats are thickly strewn. Among the latter, Holker-hall, deep among woods, stands in the north. The village and hall of Bardsea, once the site of a monastery, with a rocky back-ground and, in front, meadows falling towards the water; and Conishead priory, with its spiry woods, the paragon of beauty, lie along the western coast, where the hills, swelling gently from the isle of Walney, nearly the last point of land visible on that side the bay, and extending to the north, sweep upwards towards the fells of High Furness and the whole assemblage of Westmoreland mountains, that crown the grand boundary of this arm of the sea.

We set out rather earlier than was necessary, for the benefit of the guide over part of these trackless wastes, who was going to his station on a sand near the first ford, where he remains to conduct passengers across the united streams of the rivers Crake and Leven, till the returning tide washes him off. He is punctual to the spot as the tides themselves, where he shivers in the dark comfortless midnights of winter, and is scorched on the shadeless sands, under the noons of summer, for a stipend of ten pounds a year! and he said that he had fulfilled the office for thirty years. He has, however, perquisites occasionally from the passengers. In early times the prior of Conishead, who established the guide, paid him with three acres of land and an annuity of fifteen marks; at the dissolution, Henry the Eighth charged himself and his successors with the payment of the guide by patent.

Near

Near the firft ford is Chapel Ifle, on the right from Ulverfton, a barren fand, where are yet fome remains of a chapel, built by the monks of Furnefs, in which divine fervice was daily performed at a certain hour, for paffengers, who croffed the fands with the morning tide. The ford is not thought dangerous, though the fands frequently fhift, for the guide regularly tries for, and afcertains, the proper paffage. The ftream is broad and of formidable appearance, fpreading rapidly among the fands and, when you enter it, feeming to bear you away in its courfe to the fea. The fecond ford is beyond the peninfula of Cartmel, on the Lancafter fands, and is formed by the accumulated waters of the rivers, Ken and Winfter, where another guide waits to receive the traveller.

The fhores of the Lancafter fands fall back to greater diftance and are not fo bold, or the mountains beyond fo awful, as thofe of Ulverfton; but they are various, often beautiful, and Arnfide-fells have a higher character. The town and caftle of Lancafter, on an eminence, gleaming afar off over the level fands and backed by a dark ridge of rocky heights, look well as you approach them. Thither we returned and concluded a tour, which had afforded infinite delight in the grandeur of its landfcapes and a reconciling view of human nature in the fimplicity, integrity, and friendly difpofition of the inhabitants.

FINIS.

CPSIA information can be obtained at www.ICGtesting.com
Printed in the USA
BVOW04s1007070514

352841BV00012B/287/P